A Comparison of the European, Inter-American, African and Arab Human Rights Courts: Institutional Aspects

Ahmed Almutawa · Konstantinos D. Magliveras
Editors

A Comparison of the European, Inter-American, African and Arab Human Rights Courts: Institutional Aspects

ASSER PRESS

Springer

Editors
Ahmed Almutawa
Royal Academy of Police
Ministry of Interior
Jaw, Kingdom of Bahrain

Durham Law School
Durham University
Durham, UK

Konstantinos D. Magliveras
Department of Mediterranean Studies
University of the Aegean
Rhodes, Greece

ISBN 978-94-6265-694-9 ISBN 978-94-6265-695-6 (eBook)
https://doi.org/10.1007/978-94-6265-695-6

Published by T.M.C. ASSER PRESS, The Hague, The Netherlands www.asserpress.nl
Produced and distributed for T.M.C. ASSER PRESS by Springer-Verlag Berlin Heidelberg

This T.M.C. ASSER PRESS imprint is published by the registered company Springer-Verlag GmbH, DE, part of Springer Nature.
The registered company address is: Heidelberger Platz 3, 14197 Berlin, Germany

Foreword

Any visitor must surely be impressed by the European Court of Human Rights in Strasbourg. One encounters the visual spectacular in celebration of international human rights—the striking architecture of the Human Rights Building of 1995 (even adopted in the court's logo) and the symbolic location between the old foes of France and Germany. More fundamentally, there is the heartfelt message of respect for the humanity for all. That signal is reflected in the soaring aspiration of Winston Churchill,[1] calling in his speech of 19 September 1946 for a United States of Europe delivered in part by a Council of Europe. Equally, the Council of Europe and its European Court of Human Rights betoken a determination to deliver the practical protection of individual lives, reflected in the approach of UK Foreign Minister Ernest Bevin, a founding father of the Council of Europe, who is reputed to have said, 'Foreign policy isn't something that is great and big, it's common sense and humanity as it applies to my affairs and yours'.[2]

The European Court of Human Rights has since emerged as the prime example of a regional human rights court with its ability to move on from the usual exotic (and sometimes quixotic) diplomatic language of international institutions into hard decisions about the preoccupations and travails of human rights in Europe. Amongst its prime achievements, which often set standards for other regional courts, it has, albeit sometimes hesitantly and sometimes laggardly, provided stern messages in hard times. Cases such as *Ireland v UK*[3] narrowed the security options and prompted a rethink of strategies and legislation in the field of counter-terrorism.[4] The lesson had to be reinforced after the shock of 9/11, but, by 2004, that warning was understood by the UK courts without waiting for the pronouncement of the European

[1] University of Zurich, https://rm.coe.int/16806981f3. Accessed 10 April 2025.

[2] Cited in Beckett M, Foreign Secretary's address to Congress, TUC Congress, 13 September 2006, https://www.tuc.org.uk/speeches/foreign-secretarys-address-congress-2006. Accessed 10 April 2025.

[3] ECtHR, *Ireland v The United Kingdom*, App. no.5310/71, Judgment, 18 January 1978.

[4] Report of the Commission to Consider Legal Procedures to Deal with Terrorist Activities in Northern Ireland (Cmnd. 5185, December 1972).

Court of Human Rights in 2009.[5] The European Court of Human Rights eventually pronounced upon other aspects of the reverberations of 9/11, including secret renditions and torture[6] as well as deportation with assurances.[7]

Emergencies, conflicts, and political violence, not just in Ireland but also Cyprus, Turkey, Armenia, the Balkans, Chechnya, and now Ukraine, have been the most acute sites of disputation before the European Court of Human Rights, often pitching state against state.[8] But, in line with the vision of Ernest Bevin, the purview of the European Court of Human Rights extends into highways and byways of public and personal life, shaping debates and laws by its judgments affecting the plight of individuals and institutions. To illustrate the point, the jeopardy of life or death decisions about extradition has been ameliorated by reference to Article 3 since *Soering v UK*.[9] Criminal process safeguards have become substantially more fair through limits on police detention, access to lawyers during police questioning, disclosure of adverse evidence, and reason-giving by an independent tribunal.[10] Privacy rights have also been nurtured, especially in jurisdictions without any such juristic tradition and especially in regard to electronic communications.[11] In addition, a strong strand of cases express support for freedom of expression and information and depict the press as playing a 'watchdog' role in a democratic society.[12] Most recently, *Verein KlimaSeniorinnen Schweiz v Switzerland* demonstrates the ongoing confidence and relevance of the regional human rights courts system.[13] The ruling affirmed that climate change poses a direct and substantial threat to human rights, especially to private life under Article 8, as a result of which states are obliged to undertake effective action as

---

[5] House of Lords, *A (FC) and Others (FC) (Appellants) v Secretary of State for the Home Department (Respondent)*, Judgment, 16 December 2004, [2004] UKHL 56; ECtHR, *A and Others v The United Kingdom*, App. no. 3455/05, Judgment, 19 February 2009.

[6] European Court of Human Rights, 'Secret detention sites', Factsheet, March 2024. https://www.echr.coe.int/documents/d/echr/fs_secret_detention_eng. Accessed 10 April 2025.

[7] ECtHR, *Othman (Abu Qatada) v UK*, App. no.8139/09, Judgment, 17 January 2012.

[8] European Court of Human Rights, 'Armed conflicts', Factsheet, January 2023. https://www.echr.coe.int/documents/d/echr/fs_armed_conflicts_eng. Accessed 10 April 2025.

[9] ECtHR, App. no.14038/88, Judgment, 7 July 1989.

[10] ECtHR, *Brogan and Others v The United Kingdom*, App. nos. 11209/84, 11234/84, 11266/84 and 11386/85, Judgment, 29 November 1988; ECtHR, *Salduz v Turkey*, App. no. 36391/02, Judgment, 27 November 2008; ECtHR, *Rowe and Davis v The United Kingdom*, App. no. 28901/95, Judgment, 16 February 2000; ECtHR, *Findlay v UK*, App. no. 22107/93, Judgment, 25 February 1997; ECtHR, *Taxquet v Belgium*, App. no. 926/05, Judgment, 16 November 2010.

[11] See ECtHR, *Malone v The United Kingdom*, App. no.8691/79, Judgment, 2 August 1984; ECtHR, *Privacy International and Others v The United Kingdom*, App. no. 46259/16, Decision, 7 July 2020; ECtHR, *Big Brother Watch and Others v The United Kingdom*, App. nos. 58,170/13, 62,322/14 and 24,960/15, Judgment, 25 May 2021; ECtHR, *Centrum för rättvisa v Sweden*, App. no. 35252/08, Judgment [GC], 25 May 2021.

[12] ECtHR, *The Sunday Times v The United Kingdom (No. 2)*, App. no. 13166/87, Judgment, 26 November 1991.

[13] ECtHR, *Verein KlimaSeniorinnen Schweiz and Others v Switzerland*, App. no. 53600/20, Judgment [GC], 9 April 2024.

'one of the most pressing issues of our times'.[14] This intervention is not only boldly assertive but also considerably perilous at a time when courts are under swelling criticism for unwelcome and improper intrusions into the political sphere, a danger which is in turn recognized by the judicial refusal in that case to offer any concrete remedy.

The Eurocentricity of this brief survey must be indulged and forgiven. Of course, the European Court of Human Rights has no monopoly of wisdom and no certitude as to the correct blueprint for a regional court. Therefore, it must be fully recognized that other regional human rights mechanisms have made their mark in establishing further regional human rights courts. Thus, the Inter-American system of international protection of human rights was developed through the American Convention on Human Rights 1969,[15] the competent organs of which comprise the Inter-American Commission on Human Rights and the Inter-American Court of Human Rights. Since coming into operation in 1979, the latter has considered some of the worst excesses of member states during internal insurgencies, campaigns of political violence, and repressive regimes, such as torture, disappearances, excessive lethal force, and amnesties.[16] The court has also set new standards in protecting the rights of indigenous communities.[17]

For its part, the African Charter on Human and Peoples' Rights (the Banjul Charter) 1981 and the Protocol of 1998,[18] which establish the African Court on Human and Peoples' Rights, recognize most universal civil and political rights (not privacy and subject to a preamble which commits member states to the elimination of Zionism). More positive is the inclusion of some economic, social, and cultural rights, as well as some collective peoples' rights. However, only 7 out of 34 states that have ratified the Protocol (taking account of five withdrawals) have filed a Declaration under Article 34 of the Protocol by which they accept the competence of the

---

[14] Ibid. para. 410.

[15] 144 UNTS 123.

[16] IACtHR, *Velásquez-Rodríguez v Honduras*, Judgment (Merits), 29 July 1988, Series C No. 4; IACtHR, *Barrios Altos v Peru*, Judgment (Merits), 14 March 2001, Series C No. 87; IACtHR, *Plan de Sánchez Massacre v Guatemala*, Judgment (Merits), 29 April 2004, Series C No. 105; IACtHR, *Moiwana Community v Suriname*, Judgment (Preliminary Objections, Merits, Reparations and Costs), 15 June 2005, Series C No. 124; IACtHR, *"Mapiripán Massacre" v Colombia*, Judgment (Merits, Reparations and Costs), 15 September 2005, Series C No. 134; IACtHR, *Almonacid-Arellano et al v Chile*, Judgment (Preliminary Objections, Merits, Reparations and Costs), 26 September 2006, Series C No. 154; IACtHR, *La Cantuta v Peru*, Judgment (Merits, Reparations and Costs), 29 November 2006, Series C No. 162; IACtHR, *Gomes Lund* et al. *("Guerrilha do Araguaia") v Brazil*, Judgment (Preliminary Objections, Merits, Reparations and Costs), 24 November 2010, Series C No. 219.

[17] IACtHR, *Pueblos Rama y Kriol, Comunidad Negra Creole Indígena de Bluefields and others v Nicaragua*, Judgment (Merits, Reparations and Costs), 1 April 2024, Series C No. 522.

[18] 1520 UNTS 217; Protocol to the African Charter on Human And Peoples' Rights on the Establishment of an African Court on Human and Peoples' Rights 1998. See also Protocol on the Statute of the African Court of Justice and Human Rights of 1 July 2008.

court to consider applications filed by individuals and NGOs,[19] one reason for its modest impact to date.[20]

Next, the Statute of the Arab Court of Human Rights was adopted in 2014 but has yet to receive sufficient ratifications to enter into force. Nevertheless, the statute, alongside the Arab Charter on Human Rights (2004), forms another regional human rights system, a remarkable aspiration within a global region where autocracy is far more prevalent than democracy. Yet, those circumstances mean that work remains to be done. First, the Arab system of human rights currently lacks an operative court because the Statute of the Arab Court of Human Rights, adopted in 2014,[21] will only come into force when it has been ratified by seven member states. A second problem is the substance of the charter which reflects limits in protection more significant than those in other international human rights standards.

This short survey raises fundamental issues about whether the model of regional courts is worthwhile. In response, this book provides vital food for thought. For sure, the model of regional human rights courts seems valuable and attractive, given that it has spread to many corners of the world. But even a cursory survey suggests that the perceived prestige of foundation may be distinct from the commitment to its application.

Considering the darker side of the regional courts discourse, even in the hearts of the European founding fathers, there are now mounting doubts. To take the example of the UK, the European Convention on Human Rights Protocol No. 15 of 2013 (the Brighton Declaration)[22] was fostered as a way of inserting reassurance for the doubters through affirmation of the principle of subsidiarity and the doctrine of the margin of appreciation even though the UK has the lowest rate of applications and near to the lowest rate of adverse judgments per capita.[23] Yet, the perception remains that the Strasbourg Court stands in the way of UK sovereignty, especially concerning effective migration and deportation policies, to an extent that Robert Jenrick MP, one of the main contenders for the leadership of the Conservative Party, adopted the UK's withdrawal from the European Convention on Human Rights as a key part of his platform.[24] This antipathy is echoed by the political right in other jurisdictions.

---

[19] See African Court Coalition, 24 March 2025, https://africancourtcoalition.org/tunisia-withdraws-article-346-declaration-limiting-direct-access-for-individuals-ngos-to-the-african-court/. Accessed 10 April 2025.

[20] See Ssenyonjo M (2018), Responding to human rights violations in Africa: Assessing the role of the African Commission and Court on Human and Peoples' Rights (1987–2018), *International Human Rights Law Review* 7:1; Tufa GG (2024), The African Court on Human and Peoples' Rights: assessing its effectiveness, *African Human Rights Yearbook* 8:206.

[21] Resolution 7790/142 of the Council of the League of Arab States.

[22] CETS 213. See the UK government reaction: https://www.gov.uk/government/news/european-convention-on-human-rights-protocol-comes-into-force. Accessed 10 April 2025.

[23] UK Ministry of Justice, Responding to Human Rights Judgments: Report to the Joint Committee on Human Rights on the Government's response to human rights judgments 2023–2024 (CP 1192, November 2024) pp. 10, 11.

[24] See, Seddon P 2024, Tories must back ECHR exit to survive, says Jenrick, BBC News 30 September 2024, https://www.bbc.co.uk/news/articles/cy0lqzjwqx8o. Accessed 10 April 2025.

Beyond Europe, even more fundamental challenges face human rights advocacy and implementation, both at the regional and universal levels. The most powerful regimes in the world, China, Russia, and the United States, have all moved closer to the view that national self-interest must override the fundamental ethical pillars of the post-1945 world order, including universal human rights. First, China has disputed the universalism of human rights by fostering a state-indulgent reinterpretation.[25] The UN Vienna Declaration and Programme of Action in 1993[26] rebuffed the rival conception but did concede that regional organizations could complement the UN's efforts in promulgating universal human rights standards. A thorough assessment of this claim can be found in the chapters of this book.[27] The response of the Chinese government has been to continue to challenge Western concepts of universalism, including by the foundation in 2001 of the distinctly authoritarian club, the Shanghai Cooperation Organisation, which promotes the notions of state diversity and non-interference in internal sovereign affairs.[28] As for the Russian Federation, its renunciation of Council of Europe membership in 2022 (reciprocated by the Council's decision to exclude)[29] reacted to the animosity of fellow member states and the adverse findings of the European Court of Human Rights arising initially from crackdowns on free speech and dissent[30] and then arising from brutal armed action against separatists (especially in Chechnya) and against neighbouring states (such as Georgia and Ukraine) and probable crimes against humanity.[31] Third, the United States has demonstrated a long-standing antipathy to the notion of overriding international enforcement structures, evidenced by its refusal to ratify the Optional

[25] Qi Z (2005), Conflicts over human rights between China and the US, *Human Rights Quarterly* 27:105.

[26] Vienna Declaration and Programme of Action, UN Doc A/CONF.157/23 (12 July 1993).

[27] See also Weston B et al. (1987), Regional human rights regimes: a comparison and appraisal, *Vanderbilt Journal of Transnational Law* 20:585; Mugwanya G (1999), Realizing universal human rights norms through regional human rights mechanisms: Reinvigorating the African System, *Indiana International and Comparative Law Review* 10:35; Shelton D (2010), *Regional Protection of Human Rights*, Oxford University Press, Oxford.

[28] https://eng.sectsco.org/. Accessed 10 April 2025. See Kent A (2013), *China, the United Nations, and Human Rights: The Limits of Compliance*, University of Pennsylvania Press, Philadelphia; Ward D (2015), The Shanghai Cooperation Organization's bid to transform international law, *International Law & Management Review* 11:162; Marochkin S and Bezborodov Y (2022), *The Shanghai Cooperation Organization: Exploring New* Horizons, Routledge, London.

[29] The Ministry of Foreign Affairs of the Russian Federation 2022, Foreign Ministry statement on initiating the process of withdrawing from the Council of Europe, 15 March 2022, https://mid.ru/en/foreign_policy/news/1804379/. Accessed 10 April 2025; Council of Europe 2022, The Russian Federation is excluded from the Council of Europe, 16 March 2022, https://www.coe.int/en/web/portal/-/the-russian-federation-is-excluded-from-the-council-of-europe, Accessed 10 April 2025. See Magliveras KD (2023), Legal and procedural issues arising from the expulsion of the Russian Federation from the Council of Europe, *International and Comparative Law Review* 23:95.

[30] See European Court of Human Rights 2025, 'Russia', https://www.echr.coe.int/documents/d/echr/cp_russia_eng. Accessed 10 April 2025.

[31] See European Court of Human Rights 2023, 'Armed conflicts', https://www.echr.coe.int/documents/d/echr/fs_armed_conflicts_eng. Accessed 10 April 2025.

Protocol to the International Covenant on Civil and Political Rights 1966,[32] the American Convention on Human Rights, and the Rome Statute relating to the International Criminal Court.[33] Despite the shocking protestation by Vice President JD Vance in 2025 regarding lack of care for human rights on the part of European allies,[34] US claims to bear the beacon of Western freedoms have been undermined in the past year or so by the curtailment of rights, such as the removal of abortion as a federal constitutional right,[35] the sanctioning of ICC support activities,[36] and the summary removal of aliens.[37]

Given the disdain and hostility of the superpowers, it may not be easy to mark out the distinct necessity for regional human rights courts. Nevertheless, there is plenty of evidence in this book which offers support. A case may be mounted on several grounds.[38] External scrutiny can guard against what has sometimes been labelled as 'constitutional dictatorship' or 'elective dictatorship'—as represented in the UK by a parliament which is both unconstrained by a constitutional code while being dominated by the executive.[39] Second, as mentioned previously, the mechanism of external scrutiny can give pause for thought in the adoption of strategies and legislation. In the case of the UK, the European Convention on Human Rights has helped to rule out the option of government by emergency whether in colonies or Northern Ireland. Third, a rights agenda shared and understood by regional friends is more likely to give comfort and be capable of endorsement than more distant versions and judgments. Fourth, the faith reposed in human rights is repaid, reflecting a key theme of this book, by bolstering state legitimacy.

---

[32] 999 UNTS 171.

[33] See Bradley CA 2002, U.S. announces intent not to ratify International Criminal Court Treaty, *ASIL Insights* 7: https://www.asil.org/insights/volume/7/issue/7/us-announces-intent-not-ratify-international-criminal-court-treaty

[34] See Lu C 2025, The Speech That Stunned Europe, Foreign Policy 18 February 2025. https://foreignpolicy.com/2025/02/18/vance-speech-munich-full-text-read-transcript-europe/. Accessed 10 April 2025.

[35] US Supreme Court, *Dobbs v Jackson Women's Health Organization*, Decision, 24 June 2022, 597 U.S. 215 (2022).

[36] Executive Order 14203 of February 6, 2025: Imposing Sanctions on the International Criminal Court.

[37] US President Memorandum of 29 January 2025: Expanding Migrant Operations Center at Naval Station Guantanamo Bay to Full Capacity; Executive Order 14160 of January 20, 2025: Protecting the Meaning and Value of American Citizenship; Presidential Proclamation No. 10903, 90 FR 13033: Invocation of the Alien Enemies Act Regarding the Invasion of the United States by Tren de Aragua March 14, 2025 (see further, *Trump v JGG*, Decision, 7 April 2025, 604 US _, 2025).

[38] See Anderson D (2025), National security and human rights, *European Convention Human Rights Law Review*, Issue 2.

[39] Clinton L. Rossiter, *Constitutional Dictatorship; Crisis Government in the Modern Democracies* (Princeton University Press. 1948); Lord Hailsham, *'Elective Dictatorship': The Richard Dimbleby Lecture, 1976*

(British Broadcasting Corporation, 1976).

Despite the often adverse circumstances, and in the spirit of human rights as an essentially 'optimistic project' which assumes the potential best in others,[40] one cannot doubt the timeliness and value of a study of the legal and procedural aspects of the European, Inter-American, African, and Arab Human Rights Courts. These structures, which deliver fairness and humanity, deserve to be vaunted in contrast to the predations of those regimes which neither endorse the human rights movement nor appreciate its value in legitimizing the assertion of power.

May 2025

Clive Walker
Professor Emeritus of Criminal Justice Studies
University of Leeds
Leeds, UK

[40] See Brems E (2025), Sim Peter Baehr lecture 2024—The state of human rights: an attempt at optimism, *Netherlands Quarterly of Human Rights*, https://doi.org/10.1177/09240519251321890. Accessed 1 May 2025.

Contents

1 Introduction to the Regional Human Rights Systems and Their Courts 1
Ahmed Almutawa
1.1 Introduction 2
1.2 The European System 3
1.3 The Inter-American System 7
1.4 The African System 12
1.5 The Arab System 18
1.6 The Book's Structure 20
References 22

2 The Judges, The Bench, and The Rules of Court 25
Zoë Grossi and Jan Wouters
2.1 Introduction 26
2.2 Internal Functioning of the Courts 27
2.2.1 Composition of the Courts 27
2.2.2 The Working of the Courts 32
2.3 Appointment of Judges 33
2.3.1 Professional Qualifications 33
2.3.2 The Election Process 36
2.3.3 Vacancies 39
2.4 Conditions of Tenure 41
2.5 Incompatibilities 42
2.6 Privileges and Immunities 45
2.7 Concluding Remarks 46
References 46

3 The Jurisdiction of the Courts 51
Gino Naldi
3.1 Introduction 52
3.2 Compulsory Jurisdiction 52
3.2.1 Fourth Instance Doctrine 54

3.2.2 Inter-State Cases ... 55
3.2.3 Individual Complaints ... 56
3.2.4 Jurisdictional Requirements ... 61
3.3 Friendly Settlement ... 65
3.4 Withdrawal ... 66
3.5 Conclusions ... 70
References ... 71

4 Sources of Law ... 73
Lize R. Glas
4.1 Introduction ... 74
4.2 A Note on Legitimacy ... 75
4.3 The Principle of Effectiveness ... 76
4.4 The Principle of Subsidiarity ... 79
4.5 The Margin of Appreciation ... 81
4.6 Systemic Interpretation ... 83
4.7 Consensus ... 87
4.8 Evolutive Interpretation ... 88
4.9 Autonomous Interpretation ... 90
4.10 Conclusion ... 91
References ... 93

5 Admissibility Criteria and Access to Justice in Regional Human Rights Jurisdictions ... 99
Filippo Fontanelli and Kanstantsin Dzehtsiarou
5.1 Introduction ... 100
5.2 Admissibility of Claims in International Litigation ... 100
5.2.1 Inadmissibility at the ICJ ... 101
5.2.2 Customary Notions of Inadmissibility in Diplomatic Protection and State Responsibility ... 102
5.3 Individual Applications in Human Rights Courts/ Commissions: Access to Justice and Admissibility ... 103
5.4 Specific Courts and Commissions ... 105
5.4.1 The European Court of Human Rights ... 105
5.4.2 The System of the American Convention on Human Rights ... 112
5.4.3 The African Commission and the African Court on Human and Peoples' Rights ... 115
5.4.4 The Arab Court of Human Rights ... 119
5.5 Comparative Reflections ... 119
5.5.1 Common Traits ... 120
5.5.2 Differences ... 121
5.6 Conclusions ... 122
References ... 122

6 The Processes and the Procedures of Hearing a Case 125
Daniel M. Walyemera
6.1 Introduction 126
6.2 The Courts' Power to Determine Their Jurisdiction Under the Principle of *Kompetenz-Kompetenz* 127
6.2.1 Interpretation of International Instruments and the Jurisdiction of Human Rights Courts 128
6.2.2 Principle of *Kompetenz-Kompetenz* 129
6.2.3 Jurisdiction of Regional Human Rights Courts 130
6.3 The Commencement and Management of Proceedings 131
6.3.1 Institution of Court Proceedings and Admissibility of Applications 131
6.3.2 The Management of Court Proceedings 133
6.3.3 Effective Participation of the Parties 135
6.4 Representation of Litigants and Role of Amicus Curiae and Other Third-Party Interventions 136
6.4.1 Representation of Litigants 136
6.4.2 Third-Party Intervention Including *Amicus Curiae* 137
6.5 The Joinder of Court Proceedings and Preliminary Objections 138
6.5.1 The Joinder of Court Proceedings 138
6.5.2 Preliminary Objections 139
6.6 Management of Evidence at Regional Human Rights Courts 140
6.6.1 Rules of Adducing Evidence Before the Courts 140
6.6.2 Role of In-Situ Visits Undertaken by the Courts 141
6.7 The Ending of Proceedings 142
6.7.1 Dismissal of Applications 142
6.7.2 Non-Appearance of Parties and Default Judgments 143
6.8 Legal Costs, Legal and Financial Aid 144
6.9 Conclusion 146
References 146

7 Interim and Provisional Measures 149
Eleni Polymenopoulou
7.1 Introduction 150
7.2 Interim Measures in the Context of the European Human Rights System 151
7.2.1 The Power of the Court to Issue Interim Measures 151
7.2.2 Interim Measures Protecting a Variety of Rights 153
7.2.3 Compliance with Provisional Measures 154
7.3 Provisional Measures in the Context of the Inter-American Human Rights System 154
7.3.1 The Powers of the Inter-American Commission on Human Rights to Order Precautionary Measures (*Medidas Cautelares*) 155

7.3.2 The Powers of the Inter-American Court to Order Provisional Measures 157
7.4 Provisional Measures in the Context of the African Human Rights System 161
7.4.1 The Powers of the African Commission (ACommHPR) to Order Provisional Measures 161
7.4.2 The Powers of the ACtHPR to Order Provisional Measures 163
7.5 Provisional Measures in the Context of the Arab Human Rights System 165
7.6 Conclusion 165
References 167

8 Advisory Opinions 171
Elena Abrusci
8.1 Introduction: The Role of Advisory Opinions Before Regional Human Rights Courts 172
8.2 The Powers of the Regional Human Rights Courts to Issue Advisory Opinions 174
8.2.1 The African Court on Human and Peoples' Rights 174
8.2.2 The Arab Court of Human Rights 175
8.2.3 The European Court of Human Rights 175
8.2.4 The Inter-American Court of Human Rights 176
8.3 Who May Request an Advisory Opinion? Standing Before the Regional Human Rights Courts 177
8.3.1 The African Court of Human and Peoples' Rights 178
8.3.2 The European Court of Human Rights 179
8.3.3 The Inter-American Court of Human Rights 180
8.4 The Subject Matter of Advisory Opinions 181
8.4.1 The African Court of Human and Peoples' Rights 181
8.4.2 The European Court of Human Rights 182
8.4.3 The Inter-American Court of Human Rights 184
8.5 The Interpretative Value of Advisory Opinions and the Question of Legal Precedent 185
8.6 The Impact of Advisory Opinions on Contentious Cases and State Practice 187
8.6.1 The African Court of Human and Peoples' Rights 187
8.6.2 The European Court of Human Rights 188
8.6.3 The Inter-American Court of Human Rights 189
8.7 Conclusions 191
References 192

9 The Issuance of Judgments and Victims' Reparations 195
Konstantinos D. Magliveras and Ahmed Almutawa
9.1 The Different Purposes and Functions of Judgments 196
9.2 The Legal Validity of Judgments and the Question of Execution 197
9.3 The Temporal Element of Judgments 200
9.4 The Issuance of Judgments and Other Procedural Questions 202
9.5 Pilot Judgments 204
9.6 Errors, Reconsideration/Revision and Interpretation of Judgments 205
9.7 Reparation, Compensation and Just Satisfaction 207
9.8 Human Rights and Reparation 208
9.9 Provisions for Reparation 209
9.10 Prerequisites for Reparations 210
9.11 Reparation Awards 214
9.12 Conclusions 217
References 219

10 Execution of Judgments and Supervisory Mechanisms 223
Magnus Killander and Brian Kibirango
10.1 Introduction 224
10.2 Obligations Imposed on State Parties 226
10.2.1 Obligations: African Court on Human and Peoples' Rights 226
10.2.2 Obligations: European Court of Human Rights 227
10.2.3 Obligations: Inter-American Court of Human Rights 227
10.2.4 Obligations: Arab Court of Human Rights 228
10.3 Compliance Trends 228
10.3.1 Introduction 228
10.3.2 Compliance Trends: African Court on Human and Peoples' Rights 229
10.3.3 Compliance Trends: European Court of Human Rights 230
10.3.4 Compliance Trends: Inter-American Court of Human Rights 231
10.4 Mechanisms for Monitoring the Execution of Judgments 232
10.4.1 Introduction 232
10.4.2 Mechanisms: African Court on Human and Peoples' Rights 232
10.4.3 Mechanisms: European Court of Human Rights 234
10.4.4 Mechanisms: Inter-American Court of Human Rights 236
10.4.5 Mechanism: Arab Court of Human Rights 239
10.5 Efforts at Reform 240

10.5.1 Introduction 240
10.5.2 Reform: African Court on Human and Peoples' Rights 241
10.5.3 Reform: European Court of Human Rights 242
10.5.4 Reform: Inter-American Court of Human Rights 243
10.6 Conclusion 243
References 244

11 Regional Human Rights Justice: Past, Present and the Future 247
Konstantinos D. Magliveras
11.1 How It All Started and How It Developed 248
11.2 The Four Regional Human Rights Courts and Other Judicial Bodies of Regional Organisations, Which, Directly or Indirectly, Adjudicate Human Rights Issues 251
11.3 The Value of the Regional Human Rights Courts' Judgments as Evidence of Violation of Membership Obligations in the Respective International Organisation 256
11.4 The Regional Human Rights Courts, Criminal Jurisdiction, the International Criminal Court and the African Experiment in Combining Human Rights and International Crimes 258
11.5 Interactions: The Exchanges and Influences Between the Regional Human Rights Courts 259
11.6 The Case for a Global Human Rights Court of Justice 262
References 265

Table of Cases and Advisory Opinions 269

Abbreviations

ACHR	American Convention on Human Rights
ACHPR	African Charter on Human and Peoples' Rights
ACommHPR	African Commission on Human and Peoples' Rights
ACtHPR	African Court on Human and Peoples' Rights
ArabCHR	Arab Charter of Human Rights
ArabCtHR	Arab Court on Human Rights
Art.	Article
Arts	Articles
ASEAN	Association of Southeast Asian Nations
AU	African Union
CACJ	Central American Court of Justice
Cf.	Compare
CETS	Council of Europe Treaty Series
CIA	Central Information Agency
CIS	Commonwealth of Independent States
CJEU	Court of Justice of the European Union
Cmnd	Paper presented to the UK House of Commons by Royal Command, 1956–1986
CoE	Council of Europe
CoM	Committee of Ministers
COMESA	Common Market for Eastern and Southern Africa
CP	Command Paper
CRC	Convention on the Rights of the Child
Doc.	Document
EAC	East African Community
EACJ	East African Court of Justice
ed/ed.	Editor
edn.	edition
eds	Editors
ECHR	Convention for the Protection of Human Rights and Fundamental Freedoms

ECommHR	European Commission of Human Rights
ECOWAS	Economic Community of West African States
ECtHR	European Court of Human Rights
e.g.	exempli gratia
EFTA	European Free Trade Area
et al.	et alia
et seq.	et sequentes, et sequential (and the following)
ETS	European Treaty Series
EU	European Union
ff.	And the following
GC	Grand Chamber
HRC	UN Human Rights Committee
IACommHR	Inter-American Commission on Human Rights
IACtHR	Inter-American Court on Human Rights
ICCPR	International Covenant on Civil and Political Rights
ICESCR	International Covenant on Economic, Social and Cultural Rights
ICC	International Criminal Court
ICJ	International Court of Justice
ICL	International Criminal Law
i.e.	id est
IHL	International Humanitarian Law
IHRL	International Human Rights Law
ILC	International Law Commission
ILM	International Legal Materials
ITLOS	International Tribunal for the Law of the Sea
LAS	League of Arab States
LNTS	League of Nations Treaty Series
MERCOSUR	Mercado Común del Sur
MoA	Margin of Appreciation
MoU	Memorandum of Understanding
n.	Note/footnote
no.	Number
nos	Numbers
OAS	Organization of American States
OAU	Organization of African Unity
ODECA	Organization of Central American States
O.J.	Official Journal
p.	Page
PACE	Parliamentary Assembly of the Council of Europe
para.	Paragraph
paras	Paragraphs
PCA	Permanent Court of Arbitration
PCIJ	Permanent Court of International Justice
pp.	Pages
pt.	Part

REC	Regional Economic Community
REIO	Regional Economic Integration Organization
SADC	Southern Africa Development Community
SICA	Central American Integration System
TEU	Treaty on European Union
TFEU	Treaty on the Functioning of the European Union
VCLT	Vienna Convention on the Law of Treaties
vol.	Volume
UDHR	Universal Declaration of Human Rights
UK	United Kingdom
UKHL	United Kingdom House of Lords
UN	United Nations
UNTS	United Nations Treaty Series
USA	United States of America

1.1 Introduction

Regional human rights systems developed in an ad hoc way from the early aftermath of the Second World War onwards. Although the concept of human rights can be traced back at least to the Age of Enlightenment, the French Revolution (1789–1799) and the American Declaration of Independence (1776),[1] modern human rights law began in 1945 with the creation of the United Nations (UN).[2] Under Article 1(3) of its Charter, the UN seeks to 'achieve international co-operation … in promoting and encouraging respect for human rights'.[3] The international system of human rights evolved through the1948 Universal Declaration of Human Rights (UDHR), the 1966 International Covenants on Civil and Political Rights and on Economic, Social and Cultural Rights.[4] Currently with nine core human rights instruments, the international system of human rights continues to evolve.[5] Alongside the international system of human rights, regional human rights systems also emerged and evolved, albeit sporadically and independent of each other. Their significance lies largely in their mechanisms of enforcement, specifically their human rights Courts.

Although the focus of this book is on the human rights Courts, those Courts exist within the institutional framework of a regional system. To provide context for the subsequent comparative analyses of the institutional and procedural aspects of the Courts, this introduction considers the evolution of the European, Inter-American, African and Arab regional human rights systems. While the Arab system is the only one of these systems yet to establish a functioning Court, it is included because it has taken the first significant step of adopting a foundational statute, which allows some analysis of the proposed Court. The ASEAN, the Commonwealth of Independent States, and the Organisation of Islamic Cooperation human rights systems are not examined as they have not yet taken any steps to establish human rights courts.[6]

---

[1] See Hoffmann 2016.

[2] Ramcharan 2020, p 2.

[3] Charter of the United Nations, opened for signature 26 June 1945, XV UNCIO 335, amendments in 557 UNTS 143, 638 UNTS 308 and 892 UNTS 119 entered into force 24 October 1945, Article 1(3). See also Article 13(b).

[4] Whelan 2010, p 60. International Covenant on Civil and Political Rights, opened for signature 16 December 1966, 999 UNTS 171, entered into force 23 March 1976; International Covenant on Economic, Social and Cultural Rights, opened for signature 16 December 1966, 993 UNTS 3, entered into force 3 January 1976.

[5] UN Office of the High Commissioner for Human Rights (2025) The Core International Human Rights Instruments and their monitoring bodies. https://www.ohchr.org/en/core-international-human-rights-instruments-and-their-monitoring-bodies. Accessed 25 March 2025.

[6] See, further, Chap. 11.

1.2 The European System

On 19 September 1946, Winston Churchill's speech[7] calling for a United States of Europe built around a Council of Europe 'marked an important turning point', establishing the imperative of European unity on the 'agenda of high politics'.[8] The European system subsequently began, following a meeting of delegates from 18 European countries in the Hague in 1948,[9] with the establishment of the Council of Europe (CoE) in 1949 as a conservative, collective standard setting and monitoring body intended to secure and facilitate common 'ideals and principles' in the face of any threat from totalitarianism.[10] As an organisation founded on the ideal of European unity,[11] the CoE is grounded in 'the principles of democracy, respect for human rights and the rule of law'.[12]

The CoE was initially comprised of the ten states parties to the Statute,[13] but any European state able and willing to fulfil the obligations under article 3 may be invited to join.[14] Under article 3:

> Every member of the Council of Europe must accept the principles of the rule of law and of the enjoyment by all persons within its jurisdiction of human rights and fundamental freedoms, and collaborate sincerely and effectively in the realisation of the aim of the Council …

For the next 40 years, membership expanded but was confined to Western European states. Following the end of the Cold War most Eastern European states joined the CoE, which peaked at 47 member states in 2007.[15] Membership was subsequently reduced to 46 with the expulsion of the Russian Federation on 16 March 2022 following its invasion of Ukraine on 24 February 2022.[16]

The CoE has two main statutory organs supported by the Secretariat: the Committee of Ministers (CoM) and the Parliamentary Assembly (PA), which was originally known as the Consultative Assembly.[17] This binary structure resulted from a compromise between the Federalist and Unionist sub-groups of the European Movement, which was the driving force behind the establishment of the CoE.[18] Under article 13 of the Statute, the CoM is the decision-making body that acts on

---

[7] Churchill (1946) Speech delivered at the University of Zurich. https://rm.coe.int/16806981f3. Accessed 16 March 2025.

[8] Weiβ 2017, para 1.08.

[9] Wassenberg 2013, p 21.

[10] See Duranti 2017, pp. 4–5.

[11] Statute of the Council of Europe, opened for signature 5 May 1949, ETS No. 1, 87 UNTS 103, entered into force 3 August 1949, article 1.

[12] Polakiewicz 2019, paras 1–4.

[13] Weiβ 2017, para 1.31.

[14] CoE Statute, articles 2, 4.

[15] Weiβ 2017, paras 1.49–1.50. The exceptions are Kosovo and Belarus.

[16] Magliveras 2023.

[17] Statute of the Council of Europe (1949), article 10.

[18] Wassenberg 2013, pp. 20, 22.

behalf of the CoE. Comprised of a representative from each member state, the CoM is supported by its Bureau of Minister's Deputies, Rapporteur Groups, including one for human rights, Ad hoc Working Parties and Thematic Coordinators.[19] The PA is 'the deliberative organ' of the CoE, tasked to 'debate matters within [the aim and scope of the Council of Europe] ... and present its ... recommendations' to the CoM.[20]

Given that, by virtue of article 3 of the Statute (see above), 'human rights are part of the CoE's original DNA',[21] it is unsurprising that the European Convention on Human Rights (ECHR) was the CoE's first convention.[22] Indeed, the need for a human rights convention enforced by a European court formed one of the final resolutions of the 1948 Hague Congress (see above).[23] Discussion around human rights began at the first session of the Consultative Assembly (later the PA) on 19 August 1949, which established a Legal Affairs Committee to prepare a draft convention. The draft convention was approved by the Assembly and sent to the CoM as Recommendation 38. Unable to agree on the first draft, the CoM established a committee of legal experts to produce a second draft. After this committee was unable to agree on how to define the fundamental rights to be protected, a third committee of senior government officials was able to agree on a draft text in June 1950.[24] This draft provided for a European commission to examine complaints, a European court of human rights with optional jurisdiction and an optional right of individual petition.[25] After strengthening its supervisory role in the implementation of adverse Commission reports, the CoM accepted the draft, which was subsequently adopted as a treaty on 4 November 1950.[26]

Article 1 of the original Treaty established that the obligation to secure the rights and freedoms protected by the ECHR falls on states parties. Articles 2-14 provided for a wide range of civil and political rights.[27] To support these provisions, the ECHR also established an enforcement mechanism. Thus, article 19 of the original ECHR provided for the European Commission and the European Court of Human Rights (ECtHR). The primary enforcement role lay with Commission, which was established

---

[19] CoE (2025) About the Committee of Ministers. https://www.coe.int/en/web/cm/about-cm. Accessed 17 March 2025.

[20] Statute of the Council of Europe (1949) articles 22, 23.

[21] Dörr 2017, para 22.03.

[22] Convention for the Protection of Human Rights and Fundamental Freedoms, opened for signature 4 November 1950, ETS No. 5, 213 UNTS 221, entered into force 3 September 1953. For discussion of its drafting history, see Demir-Gürsel 2021.

[23] European Parliament 1999, 421.

[24] Dörr 2017, para 22.05–6.

[25] Wassenberg 2013, pp. 33–34.

[26] Dörr 2017, para 22.06.

[27] Economic and Social Rights are provided for by the European Social Charter, opened for signature 18 October 1961, ETS 35, entered into force 26 February 1965. The original Charter has been updated and extended by the European Social Charter (Revised), opened for signature 3 May 1996, ETS 163, entered into force 1 July 1999. Compliance is overseen by the European Committee of Social Rights under Articles 24 and 25 of the original Charter.

in 1954 and initially dealt just with interstate applications, becoming competent to accept individual petitions in 1955 when six states made declarations recognising the Commission's competence to receive them.[28] The ECtHR was established in 1959, when its jurisdiction had been accepted by eight contracting parties.[29] Initially, only the Commission and contracting parties could bring a case before the ECtHR.[30] With such procedural limitations, the Commission, with its significant, if optional, right of individual petition, was 'by far the most important organ established by the Convention'. Indeed, by 1973 the Commission had dealt with some 6000 applications compared to the 10 cases heard by the Court.[31] Nevertheless, even though most cases were declared inadmissible, the slow processing of cases resulted in an 'unacceptable' backlog of cases.[32]

Since its inception, the ECHR has been revised through protocols. There have been 16 Protocols to date,[33] several of which were replaced or repealed by Protocol No. 11.[34] These Protocols have, *inter alia*, added new rights such as the rights to property, education and free elections (Protocol No. 1), the right to freedom of movement (Protocol No. 4), and the right not to be tried or punished twice for the same crime (Protocol No. 7).[35] Others were used to abolish the death penalty (Protocols Nos. 6, 13) or to introduce reforms to improve the system's efficiency and efficacy and make the workload of the ECtHR and the CoM more manageable (Protocols Nos. 14, 15).[36] Protocol No. 15 also inserted additional text into the preamble, affirming the principle of subsidiarity and the doctrine of the margin of appreciation, while Protocol No. 16 allowed the highest court of a contracting party to request an advisory opinion from the ECtHR.[37] For the purposes of this book, however, Protocol No. 11 is the most significant. Intended to improve the efficiency and efficacy of the original ECHR supervisory mechanism, it replaced the three-tiered system with a single tier.

---

[28] ECHR (original text), Article 25. The countries were Belgium, Denmark Germany, Ireland and the Netherlands: Wassenberg 2013, p 35.

[29] Dörr 2017, para 22.07. See article 56 of the original text. Other states subsequently accepted jurisdiction of the court, e.g. the United Kingdom in 1966, Italy in 1973, France in 1974.

[30] ECHR (original text), Article 44.

[31] Boyle and Hannum 1974, p 441, relying on CoE (1973) Stock-Taking on the European Convention on Human Rights, DH(73)3, pp. 54, 57.

[32] Miller 1998, p 8.

[33] See ECtHR, Protocols to the Convention. https://www.echr.coe.int/documents/d/echr/Library_Collection_ProtocolsTable_ENG. Accessed 17 March 2025.

[34] Protocol No. 11, opened for signature 11 May 1994, ETS No. 155, entered into force 1 November 1998.

[35] Protocol No. 1, opened for signature 20 March 1952, ETS No. 9, entered into force 18 May 1954; Protocol No. 4, opened for signature 16 September 1963, ETS No. 46, entered into force 2 May 1968; Protocol No. 7, opened for signature 22 November 1984, ETS No. 117, entered into force 1 November 1988.

[36] Protocol No. 14, opened for signature 13 May 2005, CETS No. 194, entered into force 1 June 2010; Protocol No. 15, opened for signature 24 June 2013, CETS No. 213, entered into force 1 August 2021.

[37] Protocol No. 16, opened for signature 2 October 2013, CETS No. 214, entered into force 1 August 2018. See Chap. 8.

Under the original system, the Commission, the Court and the CoM all had decision making powers. Under the new system, the Commission and Court are replaced by a permanent ECtHR, coupled with a mandatory right of individual petition. The CoM also lost its decision-making powers,[38] but retained its role in supervising the execution of the ECtHR's decisions.[39]

Under the current system, the principle of subsidiarity means that the primary obligation for securing the rights protected by the ECHR lies with the contracting parties through their national parliaments.[40] The contracting parties are supported in their role by the Commissioner for Human Rights, 'an impartial non-judicial organ established in 1999 by the Council of Europe to promote awareness of and respect for human rights' through, inter alia, country visits and dialogue with states and civil society.[41] The ECtHR plays a supervisory role that allows it to set minimum standards for the protected rights by deciding cases arising from primarily individual applications, but also from interstate application.[42] The ECtHR also has an advisory jurisdiction for requests from the CM,[43] extended to the highest court of contracting parties by Protocol No. 16. Despite having to deal with the impact of an excessive workload of cases[44] and the political backlash from disgruntled states affected by an adverse judgment,[45] the ECtHR has adopted a two-pronged approach that aims to deliver both individual and constitutional justice.[46] However, the reforms to the Court introduced through the protocols and amendments to the Rules of Court have highlighted a tension between individual and constitutional justice.[47] Although retaining the aim of individual justice, the renewed emphasis on subsidiarity and the reforms, including the pilot judgment procedure[48] and Protocol 16, all emphasise the Court's role in delivering constitutional justice by 'concentrat[ing] on grave and essential issues'.[49] Through its quasi-constitutional role the ECtHR's interpretation of the ECHR has helped to establish a 'minimum standard for the legitimate exercise of public authority under the rule of law in Europe.[50]

---

38 ECHR (original text), article 32.

39 Wassenberg 2013, p 180. ECHR, article 46(2).

40 See Donald and Leach 2016, pp. 23ff.

41 CoE 2025, Commissioner for Human Rights: Mandate. https://www.coe.int/en/web/commissioner/the-commissioner/mandate. Accessed 25 March 2025. See CM, Resolution (99) 50 on the Council of Europe Commissioner for Human Rights, adopted 7 May 1999.

42 See Risini 2018.

43 ECHR, article 47. See Chap. 8.

44 Leach 2009.

45 Stiansen and Voeten 2020.

46 While the focus of individual justice is on remedying violations of the Convention for the benefit of the applicant/victim, constitutional justice is more concerned with the wider or systemic issues that serve to 'shape a European human rights order' and the legal relationship between state and citizen. See Greer and Williams 2009, p 466; Wildhaber 2014.

47 Madsen 2021, p 193.

48 See Chap. 9.

49 Wildhaber 2014, p 94.

50 Dörr 2017, para 22.72.

1.3 The Inter-American System

As with the European system, the origin of the Inter-American system of human rights lies in the development of a regional organisation to promote 'regional solidarity' by 'strengthening the regional political-legal system'.[51] While the European system originated in the aftermath of the Second World War, inter-American regionalism began earlier when the International Union of American Republics and the Commercial Bureau of the American Republics (Renamed the Pan-American Union in 1910) were established by the First International Conference of American States (1889–90).[52] Focused on 'institutional, collective security, and economic' issues, this USA-led system of 'norms, bodies and policies' lacked a foundational treaty, allowing the USA to exert excessive influence.[53] This changed with the end of the Second World War as the Americas sought to enhance and secure their place in the post-war world. Although the USA and Latin American countries prioritised different interests, the 1945 Chapultepec Conference adopted provisional instruments, including Resolutions (IX and XL) to reorganise, consolidate and strengthen the Inter-American System, formalised through a Charter, and for the Inter-American Juridical Committee to draft a Declaration on the 'International Rights and Duties of Man'.[54] These subsequently resulted in the creation of the Organisation of American States (OAS) and the adoption of the American Declaration of the Rights and Duties of Man (American Declaration) at the Bogotá Conference in 1948.[55]

The Charter of the OAS was adopted on 30 April 1948.[56] Established 'at the dawn of the Cold War', the OAS focused on non-intervention, stability and the peaceful settlement of inter-state disputes.[57] The OAS Charter, while emphasising 'American solidarity and good neighborliness', stated in the preamble that this could only be achieved 'within the framework of democratic institutions, a system of individual liberty and social justice based on a respect for the essential rights of man'. This was backed by two substantive articles. Article 5(j) of the Original Charter[58] proclaimed 'the fundamental rights of the individual' without discrimination and

---

[51] Quintana 2023, pp. 564–565.

[52] Spanish-American multilateralism began even earlier with Simón Bolívar's Spanish-American movement emerging in the 1820s: see Herz 2011, pp. 7–8.

[53] Quintana 2023, pp. 562–564.

[54] Caynes 1945, p 512; Kunz 1945, p 532.

[55] American Declaration of the Rights and Duties of Man, adopted on 2 May 1948 by the Ninth International Conference of American States as OAS Resolution XXX. https://www.oas.org/dil/access_to_information_human_right_American_Declaration_of_the_Rights_and_Duties_of_Man.pdf. Accessed 17 March 2025. For a history of the drafting of the American Declaration, see Romano 2021.

[56] Charter of the OAS, opened for signature 30 April 1948, 119 UNTS 3, entered into force 13 December 1951.

[57] Herz 2011, pp. 11–14.

[58] The OAS Charter has been amended four times by: Protocol of Amendment to the Charter of the Organization of American States (B-31) "Protocol of Buenos Aires" opened for signature 27 February 1967, OAS Treaty Series No. 1-A; 721 UNTS 324, entered into force 27 February

article 13 required state parties to 'respect the rights of the individual and the principles of universal morality'.[59] The Charter also provided for a right to work, a 'right to attain material well-being and spiritual growth under circumstances of liberty, dignity, equality of opportunity, and economic security', and a right to education.[60]

Those limited provisions, however, were supported by the American Declaration, which was 'originally conceived as a non-binding instrument', but has since become a 'pillar' of the Inter-American human rights system.[61] Indeed the Inter-American Commission on Human Rights (IACommHR) stated that, as a consequence of amendments to the OAS Charter made by the Protocol of Buenos Aires,[62] the American Declaration 'acquired binding force' applicable to OAS member states not parties to the American Convention on Human Rights 1969 (ACHR).[63] The Inter-American Court of Human Rights (IACtHR) stated that for member states, the American Declaration is 'a source of international obligations related to the Charter'.[64] Based on these statements and article 29 ACHR, it has been argued that the American Declaration has, 'ex post facto', acquired legally binding status, which 'crystallizes norms of customary international law generally accepted by the American States'.[65]

At the 1959 Consultation of Foreign Ministers in Santiago, a resolution on the protection of human rights was passed, part 1 of which tasked the Inter-American Council of Jurists with preparing draft conventions on human rights and the creation of an 'Inter-American Court for the protection of Human Rights'. Part 2 resolved to 'create an Inter-American Commission on Human Rights … charged with furthering respect for such rights'.[66] The first statute of the IACommHR was adopted on 25 May

---

1970; Protocol of Amendment to the Charter of the Organization of American States (A-50) "Protocol of Cartagena de Indias", opened for signature 5 December 1985, OAS Treaty Series No. 66, entered into force 16 November 1988; Protocol of Amendment to the Charter of the Organization of American States (A-58) "Protocol of Managua", opened for signature 6 October 1993, 1-F Rev. OEA Documentos Oficiales OEA/Ser.A/2 Add.4 (SEPF), entered into force 29 January 1996; and Protocol of Amendment to the Charter of the Organization of American States (A-56) "Protocol of Washington", opened for signature 14 December 1992, 1-E Rev. OEA Documentos Oficiales OEA/Ser.A/2 Add. 3 (SEPF), entered into force 25 September 1997.

[59] Articles 3(l) and 17 of the current text as amended.

[60] Articles 29 and 30 (original text); Articles 45 and 49 (current text as amended)

[61] Ghidirmic 2018, p 53.

[62] See n 58 above and text at n 69 below.

[63] Inter-American Commission on Human Rights 1981, Annual Report of the Inter-American Commission on Human Rights 1980-1981, Resolution 23/81, Case 2141 (United States) 6 March 1981 (*Baby Boy v United States*), OEA/Ser.L/V/II.54, Doc. 9 rev. 1, paras 15–17. https://www.cidh.org/annualrep/80.81eng/USA2141.htm. Accessed 17 March 2025. American Convention on Human Rights, opened for signature 22 November 1969, OAS Treaty Series No. 36, 1144 UNTS 123, entered into force 18 July 1978.

[64] IACtHR, Interpretation of the American Declaration of the Rights and Duties of Man within the Framework of Article 64 of the American Convention on Human Rights, Advisory Opinion OC-10/89, July 14, 1989, Series A, No. 10, para 45.

[65] Ghidirmic 2018, pp. 57–58.

[66] Fifth Meeting of Consultation of Ministers of Foreign Affairs, 12-18 August 1959, Final Act, p 11. https://www.oas.org/council/MEETINGS%20OF%20CONSULTATION/Actas/Acta%205.pdf. Accessed 17 March 2025.

1960 creating the Commission as an 'autonomous entity' with the role of promoting respect for the rights protected by the American Declaration.[67] The IACommHR elected its first members on 29 June 1960 and, in 1961, began to make country visits 'to observe the human rights situation in situ'. However, by 1962, it was recognised that the IACommHR lacked sufficient powers to fulfil its role, and its founding statute was amended in 1966.[68]

In 1967, with the aim of making the OAS more effective, the Protocol of Buenos Aires provided for the 'first significant change' of the OAS Charter.[69] Amongst other new bodies, the IACommHR was formalised as a principal OAS body by article 15 of the Protocol, which inserted article 112 into the amended Charter (article 106 of the current Charter). This states:

> There shall be an Inter-American Commission on Human Rights, whose principal function shall be to promote the observance and protection of human rights and to serve as a consultative organ of the Organization in these matters.
>
> An inter-American convention on human rights shall determine the structure, competence, and procedure of this Commission, as well as those of other organs responsible for these matters.

The ACHR, which 'considerably widen[ed] the scope and content' of the American Declaration,[70] was subsequently adopted in 1969 at a special Inter-American Conference on Human Rights in San José, Costa Rica. It entered into force in 1978 providing for a more effective IACommHR, which was implemented through the current IACommHR Statute adopted in 1979.[71] Like the ECHR, the ACHR provides for the enforceable protection of a range of civil and political rights with the death penalty being abolished by an additional Protocol.[72] Going beyond the scope of the ECHR, protection for economic, social and cultural rights, including rights to social security, health and a healthy environment, was added by the Protocol of

---

[67] Goldman 2009, p 862. Statute of the Inter-American Commission on Human Rights, adopted 25 May 1960, OAS Doc. OEA/Ser.L/V/I.1.

[68] IACommHR 2025, About the IACHR: Introduction. https://www.oas.org/en/IACHR/jsForm/?File=/en/iachr/mandate/basics/intro.asp#_ftn10. Accessed 17 March 2025.

[69] Herz 2011, p 15.

[70] Goldman 2009, p 866.

[71] IACommHR, Statute of the Inter-American Commission on Human Rights, approved through Resolution No. 447 and adopted in October 1979 by the OAS General Assembly, ninth period of sessions, La Paz, Bolivia. https://www.oas.org/en/IACHR/jsForm/?File=/en/iachr/mandate/basics/statuteiachr.asp. Accessed 17 March 2025.

[72] Protocol to the American Convention on Human Rights to Abolish the Death Penalty, opened for signature 8 June 1990, OAS Treaty Series No. 73, entered into force 28 August 1991. The Protocol has been ratified or acceded to by 12 states. IACommHR, A-53: Protocol to the American Convention on Human Rights to Abolish the Death Penalty. https://cidh.org/Basicos/English/Basic8.Death%20Penalty%20Ratif.htm. Accessed 17 March 2025.

San Salvador.[73] These developments must be understood in the context of the political and economic differences between Europe and Latin America where, at the time, the promotion and protection of human rights was made more difficult by 'non-democratic regimes and large-scale poverty'.[74]

Apart from a more effective IACommHR, the ACHR also provided for the establishment of the IACtHR.[75] Together, the IACommHR and IACtHR comprise the enforcement mechanism for the Inter-American regional human rights system. This two-tiered structure resembles the enforcement mechanism of the original ECHR, absent the role played by the CM. Although a much smaller body than the European Commission, having only 7 members, importantly, and in common with all the regional systems, members are elected in a personal capacity.[76] Along with its consultative role within the OAS,[77] the IACommHR's role is to 'promote respect for and defense of human rights'.[78] To fulfil its role, the IACommHR is empowered, *inter alia*, to recommend measures to member states, prepare reports, and to quasi-judicially 'take action on petitions and other communications'.[79] Under Article 44, there is an obligatory right of petition to the IACommHR for individuals, groups and nongovernmental organisations (NGOs). Inter-state complaints, however, are optional and may be lodged with the IACommHR only where both states have recognised the Commission's competence to examine and act on the communication.[80]

The Court came into existence in 1978, when the ACHR came into force. It is governed by three hierarchical instruments.[81] The ACHR sets out basic provisions for its organisation, its jurisdiction and function, and its procedure,.[82] These provisions are supplemented by the Statute of the Court,[83] which the ACtHR was empowered to

---

[73] Additional Protocol to the American Convention on Human Rights in the Area of Economic, Social, and Cultural Rights, opened for signature 17 November 1988, OAS Treaty Series No. 69, entered into force 16 November 1999. Ratified or acceded to by 18 states. OAS, Signatories and Ratifications. https://www.oas.org/juridico/english/sigs/a-52.html. Accessed 17 March 2025.

[74] Buergenthal 1980, p 156.

[75] ACHR, Article 33.

[76] ACHR, Articles 34, 36.

[77] Pinto 2013, p 34.

[78] This mandate extends beyond the ACHR and includes the American Declaration and other inter-American Human Rights instruments such as: Inter-American Convention to Prevent and Punish Torture, opened for signature 9 December 1985, OAS Treaty Series No. 67, entered into force 28 February 1987; Inter-American Convention on the Forced Disappearance of Persons, opened for signature 9 June 1994, entered into force 28 March 1996; Inter-American Convention on the Prevention, Punishment and Eradication of Violence against Women (Convention of Belem do Para), opened for signature 9 June 1994, entered into force 5 March 1995: Herz 2011, p 25.

[79] ACHR, Article 41.

[80] ACHR Article 45.

[81] Frost 1992, p 172.

[82] ACHR, Articles 52–69.

[83] Statute of the Inter-American Court of Human Rights, adopted October 1979 by the General Assembly of the OAS at its Ninth Regular Session, La Paz, Bolivia, Resolution No. 448.

draft.[84] Adopted by the OAS General Assembly in 1979, the Statute empowered the Court to draft Rules of Procedure.[85] The Rules 'provide the structure for the daily operation of the Court' and were adopted in 1980.[86] The IACtHR, like the ECtHR, has contentious and advisory jurisdiction, but the scope of its advisory jurisdiction is quite different from that of the ECtHR.[87] However, unlike the current European system, individuals have only an indirect right of access to the IACtHR through the IACommHR.[88] Furthermore, for the IACtHR to hear a case, the relevant state parties must have recognised its jurisdiction.[89]

With 21 original members and 14 countries subsequently joining the OAS, at its peak, membership included all 35 eligible American countries. Since Nicaragua denounced the OAS Charter and ceased to be a member state on 19 November 2023, there are currently 34 member states.[90] Of these 24 are state parties to the ACHR,[91] which may be distinguished from the European system where all CoE member states are parties to the ECHR. This is disadvantageous for the population of states that have not ratified the ACHR, although they may still be held to account by the IACommHR for violating their obligations under the American Declaration (see above). Of the 24 state parties to the ACHR, 20 states have recognised the contentious jurisdiction of the IACtHR.[92] Two other states, Trinidad and Tobago and Venezuela withdrew their recognition in 1998 and 2012 respectively when they denounced the ACHR.[93] Notably, neither Canada, nor the USA, have recognised the Court's jurisdiction, which means that the IACtHR is effectively the 'regional court for Latin America'.[94]

Like the European system, one of the major issues facing the Inter-American system has been the workload, which 'expanded dramatically in the 1990s',[95] and

[84] ACHR, Article 60.

[85] IACtHR Statute, Article 25.

[86] Frost 1992, p 172.

[87] ACHR, Articles 61-64. See Chap. 3.

[88] ACHR, Article 61. See Chap. 5.

[89] ACHR, Article 62. See Chap. 3.

[90] OAS (2025) Charter of the Organization of American States (A-41): Signatories and Ratifications. https://www.oas.org/en/sla/dil/inter_american_treaties_A-41_charter_OAS_signatories.asp. Accessed 17 March 2025.

[91] OAS (2021) American Convention on Human Rights "Pact of San Jose, Costa Rica" (B-32): Signatories and Ratifications. https://www.oas.org/dil/treaties_B-32_American_Convention_on_Human_Rights_sign.htm. Accessed 17 March 2025. Trinidad and Tobago denounced the ACHR in 1998.

[92] IACtHR (2025) What is the I/A Court H.R.? https://www.corteidh.or.cr/que_es_la_corte.cfm?lang=en#. Accessed 17 March 2025.

[93] Venezuela re-ratified the ACHR in 2019: OAS (2021) American Convention on Human Rights: Signatories and Ratifications. https://www.oas.org/dil/treaties_b-32_american_convention_on_human_rights_sign.htm. Accessed 17 March 2025.

[94] Sweet and Sandholtz 2024, p 77.

[95] Ibid., p 74.

continued rising,[96] This is compounded by the backdrop of underfunding from the OAS.[97] Also like the European system, the Inter-American system has faced its share of resistance and criticism from OAS member states.[98] Described as 'the apotheosis of a policy of descent into authoritarian hell', Nicaragua withdrew from the OAS,[99] while Trinidad and Tobago openly defied the IACommHR and the IACtHR and even went so far as to denounce the ACHR in 1998.[100] Furthermore, while compliance in the European system is supervised by the CM, the OAS lacks any similar mechanism.[101] Nevertheless, the Court has helped to support and 'consolidate' the 'wave of democratisation' from the mid-1970s to the early 1990s, become 'deeply embedded in the new constitutionalism in Latin America' and is 'the core of an authentically regional system' of human rights backed by a 'rich and innovative body of case law'.[102]

1.4 The African System[103]

Compared to the parent organisations of the European and Inter-American systems, the Organisation of African Unity (OAU) was born much later. The creation of the OAU was a culmination of the pan-African movement for African unity. This political movement evolved from the 'racial and cultural' ideology of Pan-Africanism, which 'had its roots in the slave trade and racial discrimination' and emerged in the late nineteenth century.[104] Between 1900 and 1945 there were six pan-African Congresses held outside Africa, with the sixth congress in Manchester, in October 1945, focusing on ending colonial rule and establishing independent African nations.[105] In 1958, the first Conference of Independent African States was held in Ghana and promoted a foreign policy grounded in 'loyalty to the UN Charter' and 'independence, sovereignty and territorial integrity'.[106] Further meetings followed,

---

[96] In 2006, the IACHR received 1325 petitions. This number increased over the year to a peak of 3034 in 2021 before stabilising at around 2500 per annum: IACHR (2023) Statistics. https://www.oas.org/en/iachr/multimedia/statistics/statistics.html. Accessed 25 March 2025.

[97] Goldman 2009, p 883; Sweet and Sandholtz 2024.

[98] Contesse 2016; Pinto 2013, p 36. For an analysis of the politics behind non-compliance and resistance, see: Parente 2025.

[99] Burgorgue-Larsen 2024, p 94.

[100] Goldman 2009, p 884.

[101] See Chap. 10.

[102] Sweet and Sandholtz 2024, pp. 74, 78, 80.

[103] The focus in this chapter is on the OAU/AU human rights system, not the subregional courts that have decided cases involving human rights (see Chap. 11).

[104] Bedjaoui 2012, p 10.

[105] Ibid., pp. 12–13.

[106] Johnson 1962, p 427.

with the 1963 Conference in Addis Ababa resulting in the adoption of the founding Charter and the creation of the OAU.[107]

Article 2 of Charter states the OAU's purposes as the promotion of African unity, solidarity and cooperation; the defence of sovereignty, territorial integrity and independence; the eradication of colonialism; and the promotion international co-operation 'having due regard to the Charter of the United Nations and the Universal Declaration of Human Rights'. This was the only reference to human rights within the Charter, with no mention of them in the Article 3 'principles', and no provision for any human rights body. At its inception, then, the focus of the OAU centred on sovereignty with barely a nod to human rights. Indeed, even grave human rights violations 'passed unnoticed, or at least [un]remarked upon, at the annual summits until the late 1970s'.[108] This changed in 1979 with the ousting of several African 'tyrants' with atrocious human rights records. Subsequently, the importance of human rights became more prominent within African politics and the OAU came under 'growing pressure from African and international human rights organisation stemming from unchecked rights abuses in the region'.[109] In response, the OAU convened a meeting of African legal experts to draft a human rights treaty, which took inspiration from the European and Inter-American Conventions but adapted to the unique context of post-colonial Africa.[110] Representing a 'drastic curtailment of the non-interference principle',[111] the African Charter on Human and Peoples' Rights (ACHPR; "Banjul Charter") was adopted at the 1981 summit.[112]

Like the ECHR and the ACHR, the ACHPR provided for non-discrimination and civil and political rights.[113] It also provided for a limited number of economic, social and cultural rights such as the rights to work and fair pay, to health and to education.[114] Based on a 'conceptualisation of human rights as shared responsibilities',[115] the Charter also '[broke] new ground' by protecting the rights of peoples and imposing duties on both states and individuals.[116] In 2003, the Charter was modified by the Maputo Protocol to include the rights of women, including sexual and reproductive rights.[117] The Maputo Protocol entered into force in 2005 and currently has 44 state

[107] Charter of the Organization of African Unity, opened for signature 25 May 1963, 479 UNTS 39, entered into force 13 September 1963.

[108] Welch 1991, p 536.

[109] Sanchez 2023, p 358.

[110] Ibid., p 358.

[111] Viljoen 2012, p 158.

[112] African Charter on Human and Peoples' Rights, opened for signature 27 June 1981, 1520 UNTS 217, entered into force 21 October 1986; Welch 1991, p 538.

[113] Articles 2, and 3–14

[114] Articles 15–18.

[115] Sanchez 2023, p 359.

[116] Welch 1991, pp. 538–539. ACHPR Articles 19–24 (rights) and 25–29 (duties).

[117] The Protocol to the African Charter on Human and Peoples' Rights on the Rights of Women in Africa, opened for signature 1 July 2003, 3268 UNTS, entered into force 25 November 2005.

parties.[118] Subsequently, the ACHPR has been modified by four further Protocols in 2016, 2018, 2022 and 2024 to provide for the rights of older people, the rights of persons with disabilities, rights to social security and rights to nationality.[119] None of these Protocols are yet in force.

While the original ECHR and ACHR provided for both a Commission and a Court, the ACHPR only established the African Commission on Human and People's Rights (ACommHPR).[120] The ACommHPR is comprised of 11 members sitting in a personal capacity.[121] Under Article 45 ACHPR, the ACommHPR has promotional, protective and advisory roles. Like the European and Inter-American systems, the ACommHPR is empowered to receive and consider both inter-state and 'other' communications, which may include individual, group or NGO petitions.[122] However, while the ACommHPR is authorised, in inter-state cases, to facilitate an amicable settlement or make recommendations, its protective role is constrained to submitting a report on its findings to the OAU Assembly of Heads of State (now, the AU Assembly).[123] Where a communication concerned 'a series of serious or massive violations of human and peoples' rights', the ACommHPR's role is to submit a Report to the Assembly.[124] These Reports remain confidential until the Assembly 'shall otherwise decide'.[125] Thus, the ACHPR 'hamstring[s] the Commission' and 'leaves to its major political arm any possible implementation of steps'.[126] Furthermore, beyond the 'state-centric, conservative nature of both the Banjul and OAU Charters', the early years of the ACommHPR were hampered by inadequate funding, 'limited support' and political will from the OAU, and 'the relative impotence of human Rights NGOs' in the region.[127]

The ACHPR lacked any provision detailing how the ACommHPR should deal with 'other' communications for individuals, groups or NGOs. However, a process has since been developed through its Rules of Procedure,[128] which were first adopted

---

[118] AU (2023) The Protocol to the African Charter on Human and Peoples' Rights on the Rights of Women in Africa. https://au.int/en/treaties/protocol-african-charter-human-and-peoples-rights-rights-women-africa. Accessed 17 March 2025.

[119] Protocol to the African Charter on Human and Peoples' Rights on the Rights of Older Persons, opened for signature 31 January 2016; Protocol to the African Charter on Human and Peoples' Rights on the Rights of Persons with disabilities in Africa, opened for signature 29 January 2018; Protocol to the African Charter on Human and Peoples' Rights on the Rights of Citizens to Social Protection and Social Security, opened for signature 16 February 2023; Protocol to the African Charter on Human and Peoples' Rights Relating to the Specific Aspects of the Right to a Nationality and the Eradication of Statelessness in Africa, opened for signature 18 February 2024.

[120] Article 30.

[121] Articles 31, 33.

[122] Articles 47–53, 55–58.

[123] Articles 52, 53; Welch 1991, p 540.

[124] Article 58.

[125] Article 59.

[126] Welch 1991, p 548. See also Hansungule 2012, p 451.

[127] Welch 1991, pp. 552–555.

[128] Hansungule 2012, p 443.

in 1988 and amended in 1995, 2010 and most recently in 2020.[129] The1988 Rules provided the ACommHPR with the power to communicate its views to a state party on the adoption of provisional measures while it considered the communication. They also provided for a 'Final Decision' and the communication of its observations to the Assembly.[130] In the 2010 version of the Rules, provisional measures could be 'request[ed]', the ACommHPR could facilitate an amicable settlement, and the 'final decision' became a 'decision on the merit', although remaining confidential until publication was authorised by the Assembly.[131] In the 2020 Rules, the ACommHPR's power to award costs and reparations was made explicit.[132]

Although the ACHPR did not provide for a human rights court, the possibility was discussed during the drafting process but considered 'untimely'.[133] This was most likely because of sovereignty-based concerns that meant the post-colonial states were not yet ready to submit to a supranational court.[134] Following a 'post-1989 wave of democratisation and increasing international attention to human rights concerns in the region',[135] the African Court on Human and Peoples' Rights (ACtHPR) was legally established in 1998 with the adoption of the ACtHPR Protocol.[136] However, the Protocol did not come into force until 2004, with the first nomination of judges in 2006. The ACtHPR became operational in 2006, holding its early sessions in temporary locations before moving to its seat in Tanzania in 2007.[137] Under the Protocol, the ACtHPR is intended to 'complement the protective mandate' of the ACommHPR.[138] To achieve this it is empowered to draw up its own Rules of Court[139] and has both advisory and contentious jurisdiction.[140] Under Article 5(1), the Court's jurisdiction is 'automatic upon ratification of the Protocol' for cases bought by the ACommHPR

---

[129] ACommHPR (2021) Rules of Procedure of the African Commission on Human and Peoples' Rights of 2020. https://achpr.au.int/en/rules-procedure. Accessed 17 March 2025.

[130] Rules of Procedure of the ACommHPR (1988) Rules 109, 118. https://caselaw.ihrda.org/api/files/1583154711821aoeag2cpwk.pdf. Accessed 17 March 2025.

[131] Rules of Procedure of the ACommHPR (2010) Rules 98, 109, 110. https://achpr.au.int/en/rules-procedure. Accessed 17 March 2025.

[132] Rule 121.

[133] OAU (1981) Report of the Secretary-General on the draft African Charter on Human and Peoples' Rights, CM/1149 (XXXVII), para 117. https://archives.au.int/handle/123456789/10172. Accessed 17 March 2025.

[134] Heyns 2004, p 686. Heyns alternatively suggests that it may be due to African traditions of resolving disputes through non-adversarial processes.

[135] Sanchez 2023, pp. 359–360.

[136] Protocol to the African Charter on Human and Peoples' Rights on the Establishment of an African Court on Human and Peoples' Rights, opened for signature 10 June 1998, entered into force 25 January 2004. https://au.int/en/treaties/protocol-african-charter-human-and-peoples-rights-establishment-african-court-human-and. Accessed 17 March 2025.

[137] De Silva 2018, pp. 97–102.

[138] Article 2.

[139] Article 33. The current Rules of Court were adopted on 25 September 2020. https://www.african-court.org/wpafc/wp-content/uploads/2021/03/RULES-OF-THE-COURT-25-September-2020.pdf. Accessed 17 March 2025.

[140] Articles 3,4.

or state parties.[141] For cases brought by individual's or NGO's, however, a declaration accepting the Court's competence must be made under Article 34(6). Thus, the African system sits between the Inter-American and the European systems. Like the European system, individuals can directly access the ACtHPR but, unlike the European system, access is optional and dependent on a state declaration. Like the Inter-American system, the African system operates both a Commission and a Court, with individuals also having access to the Court through the ACommHPR. Unfortunately, while 34 states have ratified the Protocol only seven have active declarations allowing individuals and NGOs to directly access the Court.[142]

In 2002, 2 years before the Protocol came into force, the OAU was dissolved and reformed as the African Union (AU). This followed a period of political change with the redrafting of constitutions and renewed democratisation.[143] Driven by a dissatisfaction with progress towards African unification, the AU Constitutive Act was adopted in 2000.[144] Unlike the OAU Charter, the AU Constitutive Act 'provides extensively for human rights in its Preamble, objectives and founding principles'.[145] Indeed, one of the stated objectives is to 'promote and protect human and peoples' rights' according to the ACHPR and 'other relevant human rights instruments'.[146] However, membership of the AU is not conditional on ratifying the ACHPR. Nevertheless, of the 55 AU member states,[147] 54 (all but Morocco) are state parties to the ACHPR.[148] This may be contrasted with the Inter-American system, where only 24 of 34 OAS member states are party to the ACHR.

Despite not being explicitly listed as AU organs under article 5(1) of the Constitutive Act, the main bodies responsible for the promotion and protection of human rights are the ACtHPR, the ACommHPR and African Children's Rights Committee, which was established by the African Charter on the Rights and Welfare of the Child.[149] Although it should be noted that the AU Assembly is responsible for 'adopting,

---

141 Naldi and Magliveras 1998, p 434.

142 Rwanda (2016); Tanzania (2019); Côte d'Ivoire (2020); Benin (2020); and Tunisia (2025) withdrew their declarations: ACtHPR (no date) Declarations. https://www.african-court.org/wpafc/declarations/. Accessed 7 April 2025. See Chaps. 3 and 5.

143 Viljoen 2012, p 162.

144 Constitutive Act of the African Union, opened for signature 11 July 2000, 2158 UNTS 3, entered into force 26 May 2001.

145 Viljoen 2012, p 164.

146 AU Constitutive Act, Article 3(h).

147 AU (no date) Member States. https://au.int/en/member_states/countryprofiles2. Accessed 17 March 2025.

148 ACommHPR (2025) State Parties to the African Charter. https://achpr.au.int/en/states. Accessed 17 March 2025.

149 See Yeshanew 2010. African Charter on the Rights and Welfare of the Child, opened for signature 1 July 1990, entered into force 29 November 1999. Note the Protocol on the Statute of the African Court of Justice and Human Rights, opened for signature 1 July 2008, not yet in force. When in force, the African Court of Justice and the ACtHPR would be merged into a single AU organ. https://au.int/en/treaties/protocol-statute-african-court-justice-and-human-rights. Accessed 17 March 2025.

amending and monitoring implementation of human rights standards'.[150] Furthermore all of the AU's bodies are expected to 'complement and support' the work of these three bodies. However, such a 'collaborative approach' failed to materialise in the AU's early years leading to a human rights strategy in 2011 that highlighted the 'inadequate coordination and collaboration', 'insufficient implementation and enforcement' and the 'limited capacity of human rights institutions'.[151]

Despite the intentions behind the strategy, the African human rights system continues to be affected by 'poor coordination'[152] and 'institutional and structural challenges' that limit its effectiveness, particularly in relation to socio-economic rights.[153] Like the Inter-American system, funding is a particular issue,[154] and ensuring 'additional and sustainable funding' has been acknowledged as one of the 'main challenges' faced by the ACtHPR.[155] Nevertheless, it is laudable that a legal aid fund has been established to enhance access to justice.[156] The delivery of justice, however, is affected by the absence of a 'functional monitoring body' like the CoM[157] and 'the lack of political enforcement' by the AU of the decisions made by the ACommHPR and ACtHPR.[158] Like the European and Inter-American systems, the African human rights system has also faced resistance and backlash from state governments.[159] This is compounded by a lack of 'genuine commitment' at state level to human rights protection.[160] Notwithstanding the challenges that it continues to face, the African human rights system, as the result of a 'distinctly post-colonial vision of human rights' that 'imbu[es] the ACtHPR with an unprecedented mandate to hold governments accountable',[161] has done important work in 'exposing human rights violations ... and inspiring legislative and jurisprudential developments'.[162]

---

[150] Ayeni 2023, p 372. AU Constitutive Act, Article 9.

[151] AU (2011) Human Rights Strategy for Africa. https://au.int/en/documents/20111214/human-rights-strategy-africa. Accessed 17 March 2025. Viljoen 2012, p 170.

[152] Ayeni 2023, p 380.

[153] Dersso 2022, pp. 35, 43.

[154] Dersso 2022, p 38.

[155] ACtHPR 2021, paras 32–33.

[156] Statute on the Establishment of Legal Aid Fund for the African Union Human Rights Organs, adopted 30 January 2016. https://au.int/en/treaties/statute-establishment-legal-aid-fund-african-union-human-rights-organs. Accessed 26 March 2025.

[157] Ayeni 2023, p 380.

[158] Dersso 2022, p 38.

[159] Chenwi 2020, pp. 17–19; Ayeni 2023, p 379.

[160] Ayeni 2023, p 377.

[161] Sanchez 2023, p 365.

[162] Dersso 2022, p 31.

1.5 The Arab System

Unlike the African, European and Inter-American systems, the Arab system of human rights currently lacks an operative Court. It is, nevertheless, relevant because the Statute of the Arab Court of Human Rights,[163] adopted in 2014 by Resolution 7790/142 of the League of Arab States (LAS), provides insight into how the Arab Court of Human Rights (ArabCtHR) would work.[164] The Statute, which was first proposed by Bahrain in 2011,[165] will only come into force when it has been ratified by seven LAS member states.

The LAS was established on 22 March 1945, just before the end of the Second World War and a few years before the OAS and the CoE.[166] Membership is based on Arab ethnicity,[167] although the Arab countries may be collectively referred to as the Arab region. Originally comprised of six founding member states, there are currently 22 member states.[168] Its main purpose is to foster political cooperation to further the interests of Arab states while protecting their 'independence and sovereignty'.[169] Although the scope of cooperation was wide, the focus was on the state and the LAS Charter makes no reference to human rights.[170] Their absence from the core purposes of the LAS, along with a lack of political will and 'meaningful' interaction with NGOs,[171] delayed any engagement with human rights until the 1960s, when pressure from the Union of Arab Lawyers NGO and Israel's occupation of Palestinian territory in 1967 persuaded the LAS to establish the Permanent Committee for Human Rights in 1968.[172] The lack of political will persisted and, despite the Permanent Commission's mandate to draft human rights agreements, it was not until 1994 that the doomed first version of the Arab Charter on Human Rights (ArabCHR) was adopted, but languished unratified. Some ten years later the 'significantly revised 2004 version' was adopted, coming into force in 2008.[173] By 2021, the ArabCHR

[163] See the English language version published by the Arab Center for International Humanitarian Law and Human Rights Education. https://acihl.org/texts.htm?article_id=44&lang=ar-SA. Accessed 17 March 2025.

[164] See Almutawa 2023.

[165] International Federation for Human Rights 2013, p 17.

[166] Museum with No Frontiers (2025) Member States. https://www.museumwnf.org/league-of-arab-states/?page=LAS-member-states.php. Accessed 17 March 2025.

[167] Charter (or Pact) of the League of Arab States, opened for signature 22 March 1945, 70 UNTS 237, entered into force 10 May 1945, Article 1.

[168] A seventh state, Yemen, joined on 5 May 1945. Museum with No Frontiers (2025) Member States.

[169] Charter of the LAS, Article 2.

[170] Rishmawi and Comandulli 2010, para 2.

[171] Sadri 2019, pp. 1166–1168.

[172] Donnelly 2013, p 178; Akram 2007, p 147.

[173] Almutawa 2021, pp. 507–508. Arab Charter on Human Rights, opened for signature 22 May 2004, entered into force 15 March 2008.

had been ratified by 16 of the 22 states,[174] but Oman and Comoros have since ratified the Charter bring the total to 18 states parties.[175]

The ArabCHR provides for a wide range of civil and political rights, as well as economic, social and cultural rights, and may be seen as a 'hugely important step in the development of a regional human rights regime'.[176] It also provides for the Arab Human Rights Committee as an independent monitoring body.[177] However, the Charter was criticised for falling short of international standards in other respects, including permitting corporal punishment and the death penalty, the restriction of individual rights through *Sharia* law, weak protection for the rights of women, children and minorities, and the condemnation of Zionism as racist.[178] More crucially, the ArabCHR failed to provide for any enforcement mechanism, which rendered it 'toothless'[179] and arguably contributed to the Arab Spring in 2011.[180] In November 2011, following the Arab Spring and the Bahrain Independent Commission of Inquiry's criticisms of the way in which Bahrain had treated Arab Spring protestors, Bahrain proposed an Arab Court of Human Rights (ArabCtHR).[181] Subsequently the LAS Statute was adopted on 7 September 2014.[182] However, as noted earlier, it has not yet received sufficient ratifications to enter into force and, given the time passed since its adoption, it seems unlikely that this will change unless, and until, the Statute is amended.

Following its adoption, the Statute was subject to scathing criticism, particularly from the International Commission of Jurists, which highlighted, *inter alia*, the lack of transparency and involvement of NGOs in the drafting process, the lack of guaranteed judicial independence, the absence of interim measures provisions, and the lack of a mechanism for monitoring enforcement of the Court's decisions. Most damning was the failure to provide a right of individual petition, which 'defeats' the whole purpose and reason for the existence of a regional human rights court. Consequently, the International Commission of Jurists proposed 17 critical amendments and called on the LAS member states not to ratify the Statute in the meantime.[183] For others, however, the flaws in the Statute were not fatal and many of the issues could be resolved through carefully drafted Rules of Court. For these commentators, it is 'better to implement the LAS Statute and then work to improve it rather than leave'

[174] Almutawa 2021, p. 509.

[175] LAS Human Rights Committee, States Parties. http://www.lasportal.org/ar/humanrights/Committee/Pages/MemberCountries.aspx. Accessed 26 March 2025.

[176] Ibid., p 509.

[177] ArabCHR, Article 45.

[178] Rishmawi 2005, pp. 364–370.

[179] Donnelly 2013, p 178.

[180] Harrelson-Stephens and Callaway 2014, pp. 418–21, 426.

[181] International Federation for Human Rights 2013, p 17.

[182] LAS Resolution No. 7790, Ministerial Council, 142nd Regular Session, EA (142) C 3, 7 September 2104.

[183] International Commission of Jurists 2015, pp. 5–8.

the system without an enforcement mechanism: 'an imperfect Court is better than no Court at all'.[184]

1.6 The Book's Structure

Beyond this introduction, the book is comprised of ten chapters written by a diverse range of authors from Africa, Europe and the Middle East. This allows for different perspectives that shape the comparative analyses of the regional human rights Courts. Each chapter focuses on specific procedural or institutional issues. Concluding with a discussion of the past, present and future of regional human rights protection, the book aims to provide coherent comparative analyses of the key procedural and institutional aspects of the regional human rights Courts.

Before introducing each of the individual chapters, it is worth noting that the concept of legitimacy emerged as relevant to the analyses presented in Chaps 2, 4, 8 and 9. As a normative judgment on the proper use of power, legitimacy engages with three aspects of its use, requiring: procedural justice, the proper authority, and substantive justification.[185] Apart from being a judgment about the rightness of an act, legitimacy is also important because a perception of legitimacy 'encourage[s] normative compliance', which is very relevant to the compliance of states parties with their obligations under the relevant treaties.[186]

In Chap. 2, Wouters and Grossi examine the institutional and procedural framework that governs the judges and their roles within the human rights Court. Noting the importance of institutional safeguards to ensure 'credibility and legitimacy', their analysis focuses particularly on how those arrangements affect judicial independence and impartiality, which they argue are essential for upholding human rights.

In Chap. 3, Naldi compares the Courts' approaches to determining jurisdictional issues for both interstate and individual applications, including consent and withdrawal. While noting that they share many of the 'same basic concepts', he argues that the differences between the Courts are most pronounced in relation to individual applications.

In Chap. 4, Glas comparatively analyses the Courts' approaches to the interpretation of the rights protected by the relevant human rights treaty, or treaties. Using perceived legitimacy as an assessment tool, Glas considers seven different interpretative techniques. While noting the similar approaches taken by the Courts, Glas also highlights the important differences, such as the greater reliance of the ECtHR on domestic laws compared to the IACtHR and ACtHPR, which rely more on international human rights law.

In Chap. 5, Fontanelli and Dzehtsiarou examine the issues of admissibility and access to justice. While also addressing interstate applications, they focus essentially

[184] Almutawa 2021, pp. 512, 531. See also Magliveras 2017.

[185] Almutawa 2020, pp. 245–247.

[186] Ibid., p. 246.

on the admissibility requirements applied to individual applications. They argue that, while there are differences between the approaches of the Courts/Commissions, they share the 'common function' of balancing access to justice against the need to ensure a functionally viable system.

In Chap. 6, Walyemera comparatively analyses the procedural aspects of adjudicating human rights cases at the regional Courts. Bearing in mind the importance of both efficiency and procedural fairness, Walyemera notes the commonalities in the Courts' approaches and argues for the importance of both third-party interventions and legal aid, highlighting the value of the European legal aid scheme.

In Chap. 7, Polymenopoulou considers the Courts' powers to award interim or provisional measures. Bearing in mind their importance, Polymenopoulou highlights their proactive use by the Inter-American Court and Commission, whilst acknowledging the implementation issues faced by the ACtHPR and the less innovative role they play in the European system. The failure of the ArabCtHR Statute to provide for interim measures is noted, but Polymenopoulou suggests that this failure may be rectified through its Rules of Court.

In Chap. 8, Abrusci compares the Courts' powers to provide advisory opinions. Noting the relevance of advisory opinions to the development of human rights law, Abrusci argues that the different strategies adopted by the Courts may be influenced by a concern to enhance their own legitimacy. Thus, she concludes that the ACtHPR has been relatively cautious, while the ECtHR has used its opinions to 'consolidate its legitimacy' by promoting subsidiarity and dialogue with national courts. In contrast, Abrusci concludes that the IACtHR has taken an activist approach, advancing human rights protection but also triggering a backlash from certain affected state parties.

In Chap. 9, Magliveras and Almutawa comparatively assess the issuance of judgments and the provision of reparations. Through consideration of their legal validity and their temporal and procedural aspects, they conclude that the importance of judgments lies not just in the confirmation that a right has been violated, but also in their impact on the legitimacy of the Court, the development of human rights law and the measures that respondent states are required to implement. These measures include the provision of reparations. Here, Magliveras and Almutawa argue that the victim-centred approach of the IACtHR and ACtHPR 'affords greater priority to individual justice' than the corrective justice approach of the ECtHR.

In Chap. 10, Killander and Kibirango examine the execution and supervision of judgments. By considering both specific and general state compliance to remedy individual violations and prevent future violations respectively, they argue that while all the systems experience delays and compliance issues, the lack of political will has pushed the IACtHR and ACtHPR to develop a greater role in supervising the execution of judgments than the ECtHR. They posit that the ArabCtHR, when operational, may also be hampered by a lack of political will. Nevertheless, they suggest that the IACtHR's use of compliance hearings and on-site visits are useful tools for encouraging compliance.

In Chap. 11, Magliveras addresses the past, present and future of regional human rights justice. In so doing, Magliveras considers topical issues such as the interaction between the Courts and other regional bodies that engage with human rights issues; the relationship between the Courts and their founding regional organisations; their complementary relationship to international/regional criminal courts; and the relationship and interactions between the regional human rights Courts. Magliveras draws his discussion to a close by considering the issue of a World human rights Court, arguing that ongoing 'discussion should be kept alive' but that, for political reasons, it is unlikely to be established in the foreseeable future.

References

ACtHPR (2021) Strategic Plan 2021-2025. https://www.african-court.org/wpafc/wp-content/uploads/2021/06/ACtHPR-Strategic-Plan-2021-2025-Deepening-Trust-in-The-African-Court.pdf. Accessed 26 March 2025.

Akram S (2007) The Arab Charter on Human Rights 2004. Boston University International Law Journal 24:147–164.

Almutawa A (2020) The Qatar Crisis, Legitimacy and the use of Sanctions against Terrorist Financing. In: Benson K, King C, Walker C (eds) Assets, Crimes and the State: Innovation in 21st Century Legal Responses. Routledge, London, pp. 244-256.

Almutawa A (2021) The Arab Court of Human Rights and the Enforcement of the Arab Charter on Human Rights. Human Rights Law Review 21:506-532.

Almutawa A (2023) Arab Court of Human Rights. In: Fabri H (ed) Max Planck Encyclopedia of International Procedural Law. Oxford University Press, Oxford.

Ayeni V (2023) The African human rights system: a critical appraisal. In: Andreassen B (ed) Research Handbook on the Politics of Human Rights Law. Edward Elgar, Cheltenham, pp. 365-389.

Bedjaoui M (2012) Brief Historical Overview of Steps to African Unity. In: Yusuf A, Ouguergouz F (eds) The African Union: Legal and Institutional Framework. A Manual on the Pan-African Organization. Brill, Leiden, pp. 9-23.

Boyle K, Hannum H (1974) Individual Applications under the European Convention on Human Rights and the Concept of Administrative Practice: the Donnelly Case. The American Journal of International Law 68:440-453.

Buergenthal T (1980) The American and European Conventions on Human Rights: Similarities and Differences. American University Law Review 30:155-166.

Burgorgue-Larsen L (2024) The 3 Regional Human Rights Courts in Context: Justice That Cannot Be Taken for Granted. Oxford University Press, Oxford.

Caynes M (1945) The Inter-American System and the Conference of Chapultepec. The American Journal of International Law 39:504-517.

Chenwi L (2020) Rights Enforcement in the African Human Rights Court: Restrictiveness, progressivity and resistance. African Yearbook on International Humanitarian Law:15-43.

Contesse J (2016) Contestation and Deference in the Inter-American Human Rights System. Law and Contemporary Problems 79:123-145.

Demir-Gürsel E (2021). For the Sake of Unity: the Drafting History of the European Convention on Human Rights and its Current Relevance. In: Aust H, Demir-Gürsel E (eds) The European Court of Human Rights. Edward Elgar Publishing, Cheltenham, pp. 109-132.

Dersso S (2022) The Future of Human Rights and the African Human Rights System. Nordic Journal of Human Rights 40:28-43.

De Silva N (2018) African Court on Human and Peoples' Rights. In: Hohmann J, Joyce D (eds) International Law's Objects. Oxford University Press, Oxford, pp. 95-105.

Donnelly J (2013) Universal Human Rights: in Theory and Practice, 3rd edn. Cornell University Press, Ithaca.

Donald A, Leach P (2016) Parliaments and the European Court of Human Rights. Oxford University Press, Oxford.
Dörr O (2017) European Convention on Human Rights. In: Schmahl S, Breuer M (eds) The Council of Europe: Its Laws and Policies. Oxford University Press, Oxford, pp. 465-506.
Duranti M (2017) The Conservative Human Rights Revolution: European Identity, Transnational Politics and the Origins of the European Convention. Oxford University Press, Oxford.
European Parliament (1999) Congress of Europe, The Hague, 7-11 May 1948. Publications Office of the European Union, Luxembourg. https://op.europa.eu/en/publication-detail/-/publication/a4687da6-8f11-4520-8f2e-6822d236961a. Accessed 17 March 2025.
Frost L (1992) The Evolution of the Inter-American Court of Human Rights: Reflections of Present and Former Judges. Human Rights Quarterly 14:171-205.
Ghidirmic B (2018) The American Declaration of the Rights and Duties of Man: An Underrated Gem of International Human Rights Law. Journal of Law and Public Administration 31:50-60.
Goldman R (2009) History and Action: The Inter-American Human Rights System and the Role of the Inter-American Commission on Human Rights. Human Rights Quarterly 31:856-887.
Greer S, Williams A (2009) Human Rights in the Council of Europe and the EU: Towards "Individual", "Constitutional" or "Institutional" Justice? European Law Journal 15:462-481.
Hansungule M (2012) The African Charter on Human and Peoples' Rights. In: Yusuf A, Ouguergouz F (eds) The African Union: Legal and Institutional Framework. A Manual on the Pan-African Organization. Brill, Leiden, pp. 417-453.
Harrelson-Stephens J, Callaway R (2014) You Say You Want a Revolution: The Arab Spring, Norm Diffusion, and the Human Rights Regime. Human Rights Review 15:413–431.
Herz M (2011) The Organization of American States (OAS): Global Governance Away from the Media. Routledge, Oxford.
Heyns C (2004) The African Regional Human Rights System: The African Charter. Penn State Law Review 108:679-702.
Hoffmann S-L (2016) Human Rights and History. Past and Present 232:279-310.
International Commission of Jurists (2015) The Arab Court of Human Rights: A Flawed Statute for an Ineffective Court. https://icj.org/wp-content/uploads/2015/04/MENA-Arab-Court-of-Human-Rights-Publications-Report-2015-ENG.pdf. Accessed 12 March 2025.
International Federation for Human Rights (2013) The Arab League and Human Rights: Challenges Ahead. https://www.fidh.org/en/international-advocacy/other-regional-organisations/league-of-arab-states/the-arab-league-and-human-rights-challenges-ahead. Accessed 12 March 2025.
Johnson C (1962) Conferences of Independent African States. International Organization 16:426-429.
Kunz J (1945) The Inter-American Conference on Problems of War and Peace at Mexico City and the Problem of the Reorganization of the Inter-American System. The American Journal of International Law 39:527-533.
Leach P (2009) On reform of the European court of Human Rights. European Human Rights Law Review 6:725-735.
Madsen M (2021) The Narrowing of the European Court of Human Rights? Legal Diplomacy, Situational Self-Restraint, and the New Vision for the Court. European Convention on Human Rights Law 2:180-208.
Magliveras K (2017) Completing the Institutional Mechanism of the Arab Human Rights System: The Arab Court of Human Rights. International Human Rights Law Review 6:30-52.
Magliveras K (2023) Legal and Procedural Issues Arising from the Expulsion of The Russian Federation from the Council of Europe. International and Comparative Law Review 23:95-116.
Miller V (1998) Protocol 11 and the New European Court of Human Rights. House of Commons Research Paper 98/109. https://researchbriefings.files.parliament.uk/documents/RP98-109/RP98-109.pdf. Accessed 17 March 2025.

Naldi G, Magliveras K (1998) Reinforcing the African System of Human Rights: The Protocol on the Establishment of a Regional Court of Human and Peoples' Rights. Netherlands Quarterly of Human Rights 16:431-456.
Parente F (2025) Domestic accountability and non-compliance with international law: Evidence from the Inter-American Court of Human Rights. Journal of Peace Research 62:119-133.
Pinto M (2013) The Role of the Inter-American Commission and Court of Human Rights in the Protection of Human Rights: Achievements and Contemporary Challenges. Human Rights Brief 20:34-38.
Polakiewicz J (2019) Council of Europe, update 2019. In: Peters A, Wolfrum R (eds) Max Planck Encyclopedias of International Law (2008). Oxford University Press, Oxford. https://opil.oup law.com/home/mpil. Accessed 17 March 2025.
Quintana F-J (2023) The (Latin) American Dream? Human Rights and the Construction of Inter-American Regional Organisation (1945-1948). Journal of the History of International Law 25:560-591.
Ramcharan B (2020) A History of the UN Human Rights Programme and Secretariat. Brill, Leiden.
Rishmawi M (2005) The Revised Arab Charter on Human Rights: A Step Forward? Human Rights Law Review 5:361-376.
Rishmawi M, Comandulli M (2010) League of Arab States (LAS). In: Wolfrum R (ed) The Max Planck Encyclopedia of Public International Law. Oxford University Press, Oxford. www.mpe pil.com. Accessed 12 March 2025.
Risini I (2018) The Inter-State Application under the European Convention on Human Rights: Between Collective Enforcement of Human Rights and International Dispute Settlement. Brill/ Nijhoff, Leiden.
Romano C (2021) The Origins of the Right to Science: The American Declaration on the Rights and Duties of Man. In: Porsdam H, Porsdam Mann S (eds) The Right to Science: Then and Now. Cambridge University Press, Cambridge, pp. 33-53.
Sadri A (2019) The Arab human rights system: achievements and challenges. International Journal of Human Rights 23:1166–1182.
Sanchez M (2023) The African Court on Human and Peoples' Rights: forging a jurisdictional frontier in post-colonial human rights. International Journal of Law in Context 19:352-366.
Stiansen Ø, Voeten E (2020) Backlash and Judicial Restraint: Evidence from the European Court of Human Rights. International Studies Quarterly 64:770-784.
Sweet A, Sandholtz W (2024) The Law and Politics of International Human Rights Courts. Oxford University Press, Oxford.
Viljoen F (2012) International Human Rights in Africa. Oxford University Press, Oxford.
Wassenberg B (2013) History of the Council of Europe. Council of Europe Publishing, Strasbourg.
Weiβ N (2017) Origin and Further Development. In Schmahl S, Breuer M (eds) The Council of Europe: Its Laws and Policies. Oxford University Press, Oxford, pp. 3-22. https://opil.ouplaw. com. Accessed 28 December 2023.
Welch C (1991) The Organisation of African Unity and the Promotion of Human Rights. The Journal of Modern African Studies 29:535-555.
Whelan D (2010) Indivisible Human Rights: A History. University of Pennsylvania Press, Philadelphia.
Wildhaber L (2014) Rule of law: "Constitutional Court" or "guardian of individuals"? In: Proceedings of the Conference on the long-term future of the European Court of Human Rights. Council of Europe, Oslo, pp. 92-97. https://edoc.coe.int/en/conferences-on-the-future-of-the-european-court-of-human-rights/7307-conference-on-the-long-term-future-of-the-european-court-of-human-rights-oslo-7-8-april-2014.html. Accessed 17 March 2025.
Yeshanew S (2010) Is there a Human Rights Organ of the African Union? The Status of Specialised Human Rights Monitoring Bodies within the Structure of the African Union. Nordic Journal of Human Rights 28:80-100.

Chapter 2
The Judges, The Bench, and The Rules of Court

Zoë Grossi and Jan Wouters

Contents

2.1 Introduction 26
2.2 Internal Functioning of the Courts 27
  2.2.1 Composition of the Courts 27
  2.2.2 The Working of the Courts 32
2.3 Appointment of Judges 33
  2.3.1 Professional Qualifications 33
  2.3.2 The Election Process 36
  2.3.3 Vacancies 39
2.4 Conditions of Tenure 41
2.5 Incompatibilities 42
2.6 Privileges and Immunities 45
2.7 Concluding Remarks 46
References 46

Abstract Independence and impartiality are essential criteria for courts to contribute to the rule of law and uphold human rights. Judges must be free from any form of external pressure and may not hold any personal prejudice or bias. Additionally, the institutional framework of the human rights Courts must contain sufficient safeguards to ensure their independence and impartiality. This chapter provides a comparative analysis of the organisational structure, Statutes and Rules of Court governing the judges within the ECtHR, the ACtHPR, the IACtHR and the ArabCtHR from the perspective of the principles of independence and impartiality. It delves into the various facets of judges' professional life, examining such matters as appointment procedures, dismissal, tenure, privileges and immunities as well as restrictions on external activities. The chapter aims to discern the commonalities and divergences between the regional human rights Courts. It argues that, despite positive steps taken by the Courts, there is still room for improvement.

Z. Grossi · J. Wouters (✉)
Institute for International Law, KU Leuven, Leuven, Belgium
e-mail: jan.mf.wouters@kuleuven.be

Z. Grossi
e-mail: zoe.grossi@kuleuven.be

A. Almutawa and K. D. Magliveras (eds.), *A Comparison of the European, Inter-American, African and Arab Human Rights Courts: Institutional Aspects*,
https://doi.org/10.1007/978-94-6265-695-6_2

Keywords Independence · Impartiality · Appointment of judges · Tenure · Dismissal of judges · Incompatibilities · Privileges and immunities

2.1 Introduction

Judicial independence and impartiality lie at the heart of the protection of human rights and upholding the rule of law. The imperative of these principles remains uncontested within the regional human rights Courts ('RHR Courts'), namely the ECtHR, ACtHPR, IACtHR and ArabCtHR. Upon assuming office, judges must make a declaration undertaking to perform their functions independently and impartially, to hold legal opinions without any external influence and to remain free from bias or prejudice.[1]

However, to ensure their credibility and legitimacy, it is crucial for the Courts to incorporate institutional safeguards upholding such guarantees.[2] Therefore, the governing Statutes and Rules of Court address the requirements necessary to ensure judicial independence and impartiality. According to the ECtHR: "To establish whether a tribunal can be considered as 'independent', regard must be had, *inter alia*, to the manner of appointment of its members and their term of office, the existence of guarantees against outside pressures and ... whether the body presents an appearance of independence".[3]

This chapter explores judicial independence and impartiality in the four Courts by comparing their judicial procedural rules. It delves into their internal functioning (Sect. 2.2) and focuses on their composition (Sect. 2.2.1) and workings (Sect. 2.2.2). The chapter also considers the appointment to the bench (Sect. 2.3) and the conditions of tenure (Sect. 2.4), judicial incompatibilities (Sect. 2.5), as well as privileges and immunities (Sect. 2.6). Finally, concluding remarks are offered (Sect. 2.7).

---

[1] ACtHPR Protocol, art. 16; ACtHPR Rules of Court, rule 3; ArabCtHR Statute, art. 10; ECtHR Rules of Court, rule 3; IACtHR Statute, art. 11.

[2] Cardamone 2019, p. 96; Dzehtsiarou and Coffey 2014.

[3] ECtHR, Application No. 22107/93, *Findlay v. United Kingdom*, Judgment, 25 February 1997, para. 73, further cited in ECtHR, Application No. 22678/93, *Incal v. Turkey*, Judgment, 9 June 1998, para. 65; ECtHR, Application No. 5312/11, *Beg S.P.A. v. Italy*, Judgment, 20 May 2021, para. 128, etc. See, further, International Law Association Study Group 2004.

2.2 Internal Functioning of the Courts

2.2.1 Composition of the Courts

RHR Courts are typically composed of a prefixed number of judges. The ECtHR comprises as many judges as the High Contracting Parties to the ECHR.[4] After the expulsion of the Russian Federation from the Council of Europe (CoE), the number of judges were decreased by one to forty-six. The IACtHR and the ArabCtHR are both composed of seven judges,[5] while the ACtHPR has eleven judges.[6] However, the number of judges in the ArabCtHR can increase to eleven when so requested by it and approved by the Assembly of State Parties.[7] For those Courts consisting of fewer judges than the number of State Parties,[8] there are concerns on potential competition between States for judicial positions, and the politicisation of the election processes.[9]

The Courts elect among their members a President and Vice-President. The President and Vice-President are typically elected for a two-year term and may be re-elected once.[10] For the ECtHR, however, the President and the two Vice-Presidents of the plenary Court serve a single renewable three-year term, while the Presidents and Vice-Presidents of the Sections serve a single renewable two-year term.[11]

Shared characteristics pertaining to the Presidency lie in the inherent full-time character of their tenures and their residence at the seat of the Courts.[12] Generally, the President's tasks consist in directing the Court's work and supervising its administration, representing it before judicial authorities or third parties, presiding at Court meetings or sessions and Chambers, promoting its activities, presenting a detailed annual report on the Court's activities, and any other tasks envisaged in the Rules of Court.[13]

---

[4] ECHR, art. 20.

[5] ArabCtHR Statute, art. 5; IACHR, art. 52; IACtHR Statute, art. 4(1).

[6] ACtHPR Protocol, art. 11(1).

[7] ArabCtHR Statute, art. 5.

[8] Malleson 2009, pp. 679–680.

[9] See Faúndez Ledesma 1998, p. 187; for practices of vote-trading in the IACtHR, see American Court Independent Panel for the Election of Inter-American Commissioners and Judges 2015, pp. 36–37.

[10] ACtHPR Protocol, art. 21(2); ACtHPR Rules of Court, rule 13(1); ArabCtHR Statute, art. 11(1); IACtHR Statute, art. 12(1); IACtHR Rules of Procedure, art. 3(1).

[11] ECtHR Rules of Court, rule 8. See also ECHR, art. 25(a). See Sect. 2.2.1 *infra* for the explanation of the Sections.

[12] ACtHPR Protocol, art. 21(2); ArabCtHR Statute, art. 11(3); IACtHR Statute, art. 16(2). However, in the ECtHR, all judges sit full-time and reside at its seat in Strasbourg: ECHR, art. 21(4); ECtHR Rules of Court, rule 4(1).

[13] ACtHPR Protocol, arts. 21(3), 31; ACtHPR Rules of Court, rule 14(1); ArabCtHR Statute, arts. 11(2), 29(2); ECtHR Rules of Court, rule 9(1) and (2); IACtHR Statute, art. 12(2); IACtHR Rules of Procedure, art. 4(1).

The Vice-President's responsibilities are to assist the President and replace him/her in case of contingent and temporary absences.[14] When the office of the President becomes vacant and the Vice-President assumes the role of President, a new Vice-President shall be elected to serve out the rest of the term of office.[15] This is different in the ArabCtHR, where the Court elects a new President to fill the vacancy for the remaining term.[16] If both President and Vice-President are absent, other judges replace them according to seniority. Elected judges take precedence according to the date they assumed office. If judges have the same seniority, they take precedence according to age.[17] An analogous procedure is followed at the ECtHR, but consideration will be given to the availability of a Section President before appealing to the other judges in the order of seniority.[18]

To assist the President, the ACtHPR and the ECtHR also have a Bureau, consisting of the President and Vice-President.[19] The ACtHPR Bureau operates on a rotation system,[20] while the ECtHR Bureau is supplemented by the Section Presidents.[21] Beyond assisting the President with any competent administrative or extrajudicial matters,[22] the ECtHR Bureau facilitates the coordination between the Court's Sections, reports on any matter, and makes proposals to the plenary Court.[23] The IACtHR, in contrast, has a Permanent Commission, composed of the President, the Vice-President, and any other Judges that the President deems appropriate to appoint according to the Court's needs.[24] The Permanent Commission similarly assists the President in exercising his/her functions.[25]

To manage multiple cases simultaneously, Courts may organise themselves into Sections, each comprising a President, a Vice-President, and several judges who together form a Chamber. At the ECtHR, these Sections serve as the pool from which a particular Chamber or Committee formation is selected to hear specific cases.[26] Sections will be set up by the plenary Court, upon a proposal by its President, for

[14] ACtHPR Protocol, art. 21(3); ACtHPR Rules of Court, rule 14(2) and 15(1) and (3); ArabCtHR Statute, art. 11(4); ECtHR Rules of Court, rule 10; IACtHR Statute, art. 12(3); IACtHR Rules of Procedure, art. 5(1).

[15] IACtHR Statute, art. 12(3); IACtHR Rules of Procedure, art. 5(1). At the ACtHPR, this role is assumed by the 'Dean of Judges', i.e. 'the longest serving Judge of the Court who is not a member of the Bureau', ACtHPR Rules of Court, rule 15(1).

[16] ArabCtHR Statute, art. 11(4).

[17] ACtHPR Rules of Court, rule 4(2)–(3); ArabCtHR Statute, arts. 11(5), 12; IACtHR Statute, art. 13; IACtHR Rules of Procedure, art. 5(2).

[18] ECtHR Rules of Court, rule 11 uses 'precedence' instead of 'seniority'. ECtHR Rules of Court, rule 5.

[19] ACtHPR Rules of Court, rule 10(1); ECtHR Rules of Court, rule 9A(1)(a).

[20] ACtHPR Rules of Court, rule 10(2).

[21] ECtHR Rules of Court, rule 9A(1)(a).

[22] Ibid., rule 9A(3).

[23] Ibid., rule 9A(4) and (6).

[24] IACtHR Rules of Procedure, art. 6(1).

[25] Ibid.

[26] See in this regard: ECtHR Rules of Court, rule 25–27.

a period of three years.[27] At present, the ECtHR is divided into five Sections.[28] Each judge is a member of a Section and the composition of the Sections must be geographically and gender balanced, as well as reflect the different legal systems among the Contracting Parties.[29]

Furthermore, the ECtHR, due to its complex organisational structure, sits in various formations to adjudicate individual applications. These are: a single-judge, a Committee of three judges, a Chamber of seven judges, and a Grand Chamber of 17 judges.[30] The single-judge formation is used to issue decisions on individual complaints that are clearly inadmissible,[31] while a Committee may rule on the admissibility and merits for cases concerning issues that fall within well-established case law, i.e. case law consistently applied by a Chamber.[32] The Chambers rule on the admissibility and merits of cases that raise issues that have not been ruled on repeatedly.[33] Finally, the Grand Chamber hears cases that have been appealed from or relinquished by a Chamber when they involve important or novel questions.[34] To increase independence and impartiality, a judge sitting in a single-judge formation may not examine any application against the State in respect of which that judge had been elected or against the State of which that judge is a national.[35]

Like the ECtHR, the ArabCtHR, when operative, will also have different formations to adjudicate cases. A single-judge formation will be formed to examine challenges to the Court's jurisdiction,[36] while the subject matter of disputes will be heard by chambers composed of at least three judges.[37] Although not specifically focused on the single-judge formation, judges who are nationals of a State that is a party to a case must recuse themselves.[38] In contrast, the ACtHPR and the IACtHR have a single structure without division into chambers.[39]

Unlike the ACtHPR and the ArabCtHR, the European and American human rights systems also have Judge Rapporteurs. ECtHR Judge Rapporteurs,[40] who are designated from the judges of the relevant Chamber, are tasked with submitting an admissibility report as well as any other documents that may assist the Chamber in inter-State

---

[27] ECHR, art. 25(b); ECtHR Rules of Court, rule 25(1).

[28] ECtHR Rules of Court, rule 25(1) stipulates that there shall be at least four Sections.

[29] Ibid., rule 25(2).

[30] ECHR Protocol No. 14, art. 6(1); ECHR, art. 26(1).

[31] ECHR, art. 27(1); Council of Europe 2004, para. 67.

[32] ECHR, art. 28(1); Council of Europe 2004, paras 68–69.

[33] ECHR, art. 29(1); Harris et al. 2023, p. 118.

[34] ECHR, arts. 30, 31 and 43; ECtHR Rules of Court, rule 72 and 73.

[35] ECHR Protocol No. 14, art. 6(3); ECHR, art. 26(3); ECtHR Rules of Court, rule 27(A)(3).

[36] ArabCtHR Statute, art. 24(1).

[37] Ibid., art. 24(2).

[38] Ibid., art. 24(4).

[39] Phan 2012, p. 216.

[40] ECtHR Rules of Court, rule 1(k) defines 'Judge Rapporteur' as 'a judge appointed to carry out the tasks provided for in Rules 48 and 49'.

cases.[41] For individual petitions, the Judge Rapporteur is designated by the relevant Section President to examine the application. They may request relevant material from the parties, decide whether the application will be considered by a single-judge, a Committee, or a Chamber, and submit reports, drafts and other documents to assist the latter.[42] Regarding the IACtHR, once an application has been received by the Court, it is assigned to a Judge Rapporteur, who will work together with the Secretariat[43] and will present a draft judgment to the Court for its consideration; subsequently, judges will proceed to deliberation.[44]

An issue, in the context of judicial independence, is that of national representation in the composition of the bench. Specifically, this refers to the ECtHR practice whereby the judge of the State Party which is the respondent will automatically participate in the Court formation that will rule on the application.[45] To address this concern, judges at both the ACtHPR and the ArabCtHR are prohibited from sitting in cases involving the respondent State of which they are nationals.[46]

This issue was raised before the IACtHR when Argentina questioned the interpretation of Article 55(1) ACHR during individual petitions. Article 55(1) ACHR states: "[i]f a judge is a national of any of the States Parties to a case submitted to the Court, he shall retain his right to hear that case." Argentina argued that the presence of the national judge could compromise the Court's independence and impartiality, while other States noted that his/her presence facilitates the clarification of domestic law complexities.[47] The IACtHR, acknowledging that Article 55 ACHR was inspired by the State-to-State procedures before the ICJ, and after considering the ACtHPR approach, decided that the *ratio legis* of the provision could only apply to inter-State communications (Article 45 ACHR) and not to cases originated in individual petitions (Article 44 ACHR).[48] Thus, national judges are not allowed to sit in applications lodged by individuals.[49]

The ECtHR remains an exception in allowing the 'national judge' to hear both individual petitions and inter-State applications.[50] The purpose of the 'national judge'

[41] ECtHR Rules of Court, rule 48(1).

[42] Ibid., rule 49(3).

[43] Inter-American Court of Human Rights 2023, p. 15.

[44] Ibid., p. 18.

[45] ECHR, art. 26(4).

[46] ACtHPR Protocol, art. 22; ACtHPR Rules of Court, rule 9(2); ArabCtHR Statute, art. 24(4).

[47] IACtHR, *Article 55 of the American Convention on Human Rights*, Advisory Opinion, 29 September 2009, OC-20/09, Series A No. 20, para. 70.

[48] Ibid., paras 74 *et seq.*, 81–84.

[49] Ibid., paras 83–85; IACtHR Rules of Procedure, art. 19(1).

[50] ECHR, art. 26(4); Parliamentary Assembly of the Council of Europe 2011.

is to benefit the Court with expertise regarding the respondent State's law and practice.[51] Nevertheless, the relevance of this argument is questionable considering that States are not obliged to nominate a judge of their own nationality.[52]

Similar concerns relate to the appointment of ad hoc judges. Where a State has no judge of its own nationality or the 'national judge' has recused himself/herself, respondent States can appoint ad hoc judges. Their role is to bring relevant expertise to the bench, increase the court's legitimacy, and ensure equality between the parties.[53] Nevertheless, the independence and impartiality of ad hoc judges have also been questioned, particularly when they adjudicate on individual petition cases.[54] For instance, before 2009, the IACtHR allowed States to appoint ad hoc judges, for both inter-State and individual applications.[55] Argentina challenged such appointments as far as individual applications were concerned in the abovementioned request for an advisory opinion. Referring to the ordinary meaning of Article 55(3) ACHR, in particular the plural form used ('States Parties'), the IACtHR concluded that the use of ad hoc judges is restricted to inter-State communications.[56] In contrast, because ACtHPR judges are not allowed to sit in a case involving the State of which they are nationals, the issue of ad hoc judges is redundant.[57] A similar conclusion may be drawn for the ArabCtHR.[58]

The ECtHR, however, still allows the appointment of ad hoc judges in both inter-State cases and individual applications. Since each contracting party has its own judge on the bench, an ad hoc judge comes into play when the regular judge of a party may not sit in a case.[59] Prior to 2004, parties were allowed to choose, at their discretion, who would be appointed as ad hoc judge after the proceedings had already begun. Following criticism,[60] the impartiality and independence of the system was improved by Protocol No. 14 to ECHR.[61] Under the new system, the President of the Chamber appoints an ad hoc judge from a list of three to five eligible candidates submitted by the State. Under the Rules of Court, the list must include 'both sexes' and the person appointed serves for a renewable period of four years.[62]

---

[51] Council of Europe 2004, para. 71.

[52] E.g., from 1980 to 1998, Ronald St. John Macdonald, a citizen of Canada, was the ECtHR judge for Liechtenstein.

[53] Kolb 2013, p. 118; Swigart 2010, p. 227.

[54] Dzehtsiarou and Coffey 2014; Feria-Tinta 2004, pp. 84 *et seq.*

[55] ACHR, art. 55(2) and (3); IACtHR Statute, art. 10(2) and (3). See further, IACtHR Rules of Procedure, art. 20 (appointment of ad hoc judges).

[56] IACtHR, *Article 55 of the American Convention on Human Rights*, *supra*, paras 50–51.

[57] ACtHPR Protocol, art. 22.

[58] See ArabCtHR Statute, art. 24(4).

[59] ECtHR Rules of Court, rule 29; Parliamentary Assembly of the Council of Europe 2011.

[60] Parliamentary Assembly of the Council of Europe 2009.

[61] CETS 194, opened for signature on 13 May 2004, entered into force on 1 June 2010. Council of Europe 2004, para. 64.

[62] ECtHR Rules of Court, rule 29(1)(a).

2.2.2 *The Working of the Courts*

The three RHR Courts in operation hold ordinary and extraordinary sessions at their respective seat; it will be the same for the ArabCtHR when it starts operating. Ordinary sessions take place at a regular time and typically serve to hold hearings, make rulings in contentious cases, indicate provisional measures, and handle administrative matters.[63] The ACtHPR holds four ordinary sessions annually, each lasting for at least four weeks, invariably at its seat in Arusha, Tanzania.[64] The IACtHR holds approximately eight ordinary sessions annually. Extraordinary sessions usually serve to decide on urgent matters or handle backlog. For instance, in 2022, it held several extraordinary sessions to continue deliberations on the request for an advisory opinion on 'differentiated approaches to persons deprived of liberty';[65] the opinion was given in May 2022.[66] At the ACtHPR and IACtHR, extraordinary sessions can be convened by the President at his/her own initiative or when requested by a majority of judges.[67]

The situation is different at the ECtHR. Plenary sessions are convened by the President whenever required to perform his/her official functions, when at least one-third of the bench so requests, and annually to consider administrative matters.[68] Generally speaking, these matters include, amending the Rules of Court, electing the Court President, Vice-Presidents, Registrar and deputies, setting-up Sections, and dismissing judges.[69] In contrast, the Grand Chamber, Chambers, and Committees sit full-time. However, when proposed by the President, the Court fixes session periods,[70] outside of which, the Grand Chamber and Chambers may be convened to hear urgent cases.[71]

In most regional Courts, the judgments are taken by a majority of judges present.[72] In the event of a tie, the President casts the deciding vote.[73] At the ECtHR, the mechanism is similar for plenary sessions, but Committees must decide unanimously, while

---

[63] See e.g. IACtHR Rules of Procedure, art. 11.

[64] ACtHPR Rules of Court, rule 22(1) and 24. These ordinary sessions take place in March, June, September and November; African Court on Human and Peoples' Rights 2024, para. 4.

[65] The advisory opinion was requested by the Inter-American Commission on Human Rights, see Press Release, 'I/A Court H.R._PR-29/2022 English', 27 May 2022, https://www.corteidh.or.cr/docs/comunicados/cp_29_2022_eng.pdf. Accessed 1 April 2025.

[66] IACtHR, Advisory Opinion OC-29/22, *Differenciated Approaches with Respect to Certain Groups of Persons Deprived of Liberty*, 30 May 2022, Series A No. 29.

[67] ACtHPR Rules of Court, rule 23; IACtHR Statute, art. 22; IACtHR Rules of Procedure, art. 12.

[68] ECtHR Rules of Court, rule 20(1).

[69] ECHR, art. 25; ECtHR Rules of Court, rules 7 (as amended by the Court on 23 June 2023), 8(1), 15, 16(1), 25(1), 116(1).

[70] ECtHR Rules of Court, rule 21(1).

[71] Ibid., rule 21(2).

[72] ACtHPR Protocol, art. 28(2); ACtHPR Rules of Court, rule 69(2); ArabCtHR Statute, art. 25(2); IACtHR Statute, art. 23(2); IACtHR Rules of Procedure, art. 16(3).

[73] ACtHPR Rules of Court, rule 69(4); IACtHR Statute, art. 23(3); IACtHR Rules of Procedure, art. 16(4).

Chambers and Grand Chamber decisions require a majority.[74] Furthermore, none of the three operating Courts allow abstentions in the final votes on the admissibility and merits of a case.[75]

Depending on the number of judges, there exist different quorums. The ACtHPR has a quorum of seven judges,[76] in the IACtHR it is five judges.[77] Although the IACtHR's constitutive documents are silent on when a quorum is required, in practice it applies to all Court decisions,[78] including orders relating to preliminary objections, monitoring compliance with judgments, adopting judgments or requests for interpretation, and advisory opinions. To preserve quorum, the IACtHR allows the use of substitute ('interim') judges.[79] At the ECtHR, where the number of judges is much larger than in the other Courts, the quorum for the plenary Court is two-thirds of the elected judges in office. If the quorum is not reached, the President shall adjourn the sitting.[80] In the other ECtHR Court formations (Committees, Chambers, and the Grand Chamber), substitute members are always appointed to ensure a full bench of three, seven and seventeen judges respectively.[81] Finally, the ArabCtHR Statute requires at least three judges per Chamber but leaves further details for determination in the Court Rules.[82]

2.3 Appointment of Judges

2.3.1 Professional Qualifications

To guarantee judicial independence and impartiality, legal instruments, such as the UN Basic Principles on the Independence of the Judiciary ('UN Basic Principles')[83] and the Burgh House Principles on the Independence of the International Judiciary,[84]

[74] ECtHR Rules of Court, rule 53, 23(1), (2). Some plenary Court decisions require a two-thirds majority, e.g. the dismissal of judges (rule 7) or the removal of the Registrar or Deputy-Registrar (rule 15(2)).

[75] ACtHPR Rules of Court, art. 69(2); ECtHR Rules of Court, rule 23(2); IACtHR Rules of Procedure, art. 16(1). The ArabCtHR Statute is silent.

[76] ACtHPR Protocol, art. 23; ACtHPR Rules of Court, rule 25.

[77] ACHR, art. 56; IACtHR Statute, art. 23; IACtHR Rules of Procedure, art. 14.

[78] Hennebel and Tigroudja 2022, p. 1236.

[79] IACtHR Rules of Procedure, arts. 2(19), 18. See IACtHR Statute, arts. 6(3), 19(4) for their appointment. Substitute judges are also appointed to replace a judge *ad hoc* in case of disqualification. IACtHR Statute, arts. 10(5), 19(4).

[80] ECtHR Rules of Court, rule 20(2)–(3).

[81] Council of Europe 1994, para. 33. For their specific appointment, see ECtHR Rules of Court, rules 24–27.

[82] ArabCtHR Statute, art. 24.

[83] Seventh United Nations Congress on the Prevention of Crime and the Treatment of Offenders 1985, Principle 10.

[84] International Law Association Study Group 2004, Principle 2.1.

require that international judges are appointed through strict selection criteria, in a transparent manner, and based on their legal skills.[85] For instance, the UN Basic Principles require the procedure for selecting judges to "safeguard against judicial appointments for improper motives".[86]

Most of the constitutive instruments of the RHR Courts are rather vague regarding the requisite qualifications for judges. They often state that judges must be of a high moral character and possess the qualifications required for appointment to high judicial office or be jurisconsults of recognised competence.[87] Regarding the ECtHR, the Convention does not explicitly require candidates to possess relevant experience or knowledge in the field of human rights. Nevertheless, this requirement has been added by the Parliamentary Assembly of the CoE ('PACE').[88] Candidates must be less than 65 years of age at the date by which PACE invites the governments to submit a list of candidates.[89] Furthermore, judges sit in their individual capacity;[90] therefore, they represent neither the High Contracting Parties nor the CoE. Other qualifications have been adopted by the Court, for example judges must possess a good command of one of the two official Court languages (French and English).[91]

Similarly, the election of ACtHPR and IACtHR judges is guided by the appropriateness of candidates. Regarding the ACtHPR, candidates must be nationals of AU Member States (with no more than one judge per Member State), be jurists by profession, possess recognised practical, judicial, or academic competence and experience in the field of human and peoples' rights, and be of a high moral character.[92] *Mutatis mutandis*, the same conditions are required in the IACtHR.[93] Even if not explicitly stated, language skills, especially in the IACtHR's principal working languages (Spanish and English), are also required.[94] In contrast to the ECtHR, there exists no explicit age limit at the ACtHPR and IACtHR. Nevertheless, the reference to "qualifications required for the exercise of the highest judicial functions" at the IACtHR, might allow OAS Member States to impose age limits.[95]

---

[85] International Commission of Jurists 2007, p. 41.

[86] Seventh United Nations Congress on the Prevention of Crime and the Treatment of Offenders 1985, Principle 10.

[87] See e.g. ECHR, art. 21(1).

[88] Parliamentary Assembly of the Council of Europe 1999, para. 6.4; Parliamentary Assembly of the Council of Europe 2004, para. 19(2).

[89] ECHR, art. 21(2).

[90] ECHR, art. 21(3).

[91] ECHR, *Advisory opinion on Certain Legal Questions Concerning the Lists of Candidates Submitted with a View to the Election of Judges to the European Court of Human Rights*, Advisory Opinion, 12 February 2008, A47–2008-00, para. 47; Parliamentary Assembly of the Council of Europe 1999, para. 6.4; Parliamentary Assembly of the Council of Europe 2004, para. 3; Committee of Ministers of the Council of Europe 2012, para. II.3.

[92] ACtHPR Protocol, art. 11.

[93] ACHR, art. 52; IACtHR Statute, art. 4.

[94] Hennebel and Tigroudja 2022, p. 1205.

[95] Dunshee de Abranchas 1980, p. 91.

The ArabCtHR Statute stipulates that judges must be nationals of contracting parties; there cannot be two judges from the same State.[96] Like in the other Courts, candidates must be known for their integrity and commitment to high moral values, as well as have competence and experience in legal or judicial office.[97] In addition, they must possess the qualifications required for appointment to the highest judicial or legal offices in their respective State, such as the position of attorney-general.[98] In contrast to the other Courts, experience in the field of international human rights law is not a requirement, but candidates with such knowledge will be preferred.[99] The provision in an earlier draft of the Statute that required judges to have at least 10 years' experience in the field of human rights was removed, leading to concerns that Arab judges would lack the appropriate skills, training and qualifications.[100] Furthermore, unlike the Statutes of the other Courts, the ArabCtHR Statute does not explicitly state that judges serve in an individual capacity and will not act as State representatives. Although this can be read into the requirement to exercise their duties with impartiality and independence, the failure has been criticised.[101] However, it is clear from Article 15(3) ArabCtHR Statute that the question of judges' independence will be revisited in the Court Rules.

Besides the candidates' appropriateness, the ACtHPR requires a general need for balance. Hence, there must be an adequate gender representation,[102] as well as representation of Africa's five regions and principal legal traditions.[103] This has been further developed by the AU Executive Council in its Decision on the Modalities on Implementation of Criteria for Equitable Geographical and Gender Representation in the AU Organs, which effectively requires that judges come from each of Africa's five regions (East, Central, North, South, and West), and that at least one of the judges from each region be female. The remaining seat is considered a 'floating seat' and rotates by region.[104] PACE has added a similar criterion for gender balance in the ECtHR.[105] The OAS has also taken initiatives to ensure gender parity and consolidate regional geographic representation.[106] Given that the States comprising the Arab world share similar cultural and legal traditions, geographical representation

---

[96] ArabCtHR Statute, art. 5.

[97] Ibid., art. 7.

[98] Ibid., art. 7; Magliveras and Naldi 2016, p. 160.

[99] Ibid., art. 7.

[100] International Commission of Jurists 2015, p. 14.

[101] ArabCtHR Statute, art. 15(1). See in contrast: ACtHPR Protocol, art. 11(1); ECHR, art. 21(3); ACHR, art. 52(1); IACtHR Statute, art. 4(1). International Commission of Jurists 2015, p. 16.

[102] ACtHPR Protocol, arts. 12(2), 14(3); See also AU Constitutive Act, opened for signature on 11 July 2000, entered into force on 26 May 2001, art. 4(1), defining the promotion of gender equality as one of the AU's principles.

[103] ACtHPR Protocol, art. 14(2). The legal traditions are the Islamic/Shari'ah-based system, the common law system, the civil law system, African customary law, traditional law, and the mixed 'Roman-Dutch law' in the southern part of Africa; Viljoen 2012, p. 422.

[104] Executive Council of the African Union 2016.

[105] Parliamentary Assembly of the Council of Europe 2025.

[106] OAS General Assembly 2020, pp. 150–151.

current Member States of the AU represented in the AU Assembly decide on the election of the judges in respect of the 34 States that have ratified the ACtHPR Protocol. Accordingly, the involvement of non-State Parties may serve as an encouragement to the other AU Member States to ratify the Protocol.[120]

IACtHR judges are elected by the State Parties to the ACHR at the OAS General Assembly by secret ballot and by absolute majority from a list of candidates nominated by the State Parties.[121] Like with the ACtHPR, each State Party may nominate up to three candidates, nationals of their State or of any other OAS Member State.[122] Where three judges are nominated, at least one of the candidates must be a national of a State other than the nominating State.[123]

At the ArabCtHR, each State Party may nominate two of its nationals as candidates.[124] The nomination process has been criticised for insufficient transparency safeguards. The Statute does not mandate that national nomination procedures be open to all qualified candidates or require that the nomination be widely publicised.[125] The election of the Arab Court judges will be through a secret ballot of the Assembly of States Parties.[126] A reserve list will be established by the Assembly from among the candidates who were not elected, which is an uncommon feature.[127]

Pursuant to Article 22 ECHR, the election of judges is undertaken by PACE by a majority of the votes cast from a list of three candidates nominated by each High Contracting Party. Unlike the other Courts, the ECtHR has the safeguard of an independent nominations commission, which assesses the candidates' suitability and delivers an opinion to State Parties.[128] The lists of candidates are first examined by the Committee on the Election of Judges, consisting of 22 legal experts, who assess the fairness and transparency of the national procedure, the qualifications of candidates and the gender balance, and make specific recommendations to PACE.[129] During its plenary sessions, PACE votes on the list of candidates as reviewed by this Committee. A candidate is elected if he/she obtains the absolute majority of the votes cast. Failing that, a second round takes place for which a relative majority is sufficient.[130]

[120] Viljoen 2012, p. 421.

[121] ACHR, art. 53(1); IACtHR Statute, arts. 7(1) and 9(1).

[122] ACHR, art. 53(2); IACtHR Statute, art. 7(2). See e.g. the nomination of Professor Thomas Buergenthal, a US national, as a judge by Costa Rica even though the United States had not ratified the American Convention. Nevertheless, this is the only example in IACtHR history.

[123] IACtHR Statute, art. 7(3).

[124] ArabCtHR Statute, art. 6(2).

[125] International Commission of Jurists 2015, p. 15.

[126] ArabCtHR Statute, art. 6(1).

[127] Ibid., art. 6(5).

[128] De Baere et al. 2015, p. 54. For an analysis of the politicisation of the appointment process at the ECtHR before the establishment of the Committee, see Voeten 2007.

[129] Parliamentary Assembly of the Council of Europe 2025, paras 14, 18–22.

[130] Ibid., para. 32.

2.3.3 *Vacancies*

The vacancy of a judge's office may occur due to events such as death, dismissal, resignation, or invalidity.[131] For instance, under the ArabCtHR Statute, a judge's office will be considered vacant in the event of death, dismissal, resignation or an invalidity that prevents the judge from exercising his/her functions on a regular basis.[132] The Statute requires the vacancy to be filled by another judge completing the predecessor's term of office, except when the vacancy occurs six months before the judge's mandate ends. In that case, the President shall designate a judge from the list of reserve judges.[133] The same circumstances are envisaged at the IACtHR.[134] Where possible, the vacancy will be filled at the next session of the OAS General Assembly. As is the case with the ArabCtHR, an election is not necessary when a vacancy occurs within six months of the expiration of a term of office.[135]

In general, judges wishing to resign, shall submit their resignation in writing to the President of the Court.[136] While at the ACtHPR and the ECtHR the notification by the President to the Chairperson of the AU Commission or to the CoE Secretary General is sufficient, a resignation in the IACtHR shall not become effective until the Court has accepted it, and in the ArabCtHR, until the President has approved it.[137] A notable example is the resignation of Judge Roberto F. Caldas from the IACtHR in 2018 following allegations against him of domestic violence.[138] The same procedure applies to incapacity, with the IACtHR itself deciding whether a judge is incapable of performing his functions.[139]

Regarding the dismissal of judges, judges should only be removed for serious misconduct, disciplinary, or criminal offences.[140] International standards require that the investigation and adjudication of said misconduct take place in the context of fair proceedings before a competent, independent and impartial body, respecting the judge's rights.[141] Furthermore, the dismissal must be proportionate.[142] Considering

[131] The terminology differs among the RHR Courts. 'Invalidity' covers concepts such as illness, and physical or mental incapacity.

[132] ArabCtHR Statute, art. 9(1)–(3).

[133] Ibid., art. 9(1). See *supra* Sect. 2.3.2.

[134] IACtHR Statute, art. 6(2).

[135] Ibid., art. 6(2).

[136] ACtHPR Rules of Court, rule 7; ArabCtHR Statute, art. 9(2); ECtHR Rules of Court, rule 6.

[137] ACtHPR Protocol, art. 20(1); ArabCtHR Statute, art. 9(2); ECtHR Rules of Court, rule 6; IACtHR Statute, art. 21(1).

[138] IACtHR Press Release CorteIDH_CP-16/18, 15 May 2018 (in Spanish). https://www.corteidh.or.cr/docs/comunicados/cp_16_18.pdf. Accessed 4 April 2025.

[139] IACtHR Statute, art. 21(2).

[140] International Commission of Jurists 2007, p. 55.

[141] Seventh United Nations Congress on the Prevention of Crime and the Treatment of Offenders 1985, Principles 17–20; African Commission on Human and Peoples' Rights 2003, Principle A(4)(q); International Law Association Study Group 2004, Principles 3.1 and 17; Committee of Ministers of the Council of Europe 2010, para. 69.

[142] Ibid.

their independence, judges cannot face removal for *bona fide* errors or for dissenting with a particular interpretation of the law.[143]

The procedural rules of the RHR Courts only provide in general terms that judges can be removed when they are found to no longer fulfill the prescribed conditions for judicial office. Judges may only be removed by the Courts themselves, typically requiring a unanimous decision of the bench. This procedural safeguard is designed to keep the judicial tenure free from political influence, ensuring that it remains immune to external interferences.[144] The procedure differs for the ECtHR, where the decision requires a two-thirds majority.[145]

For instance, in the ArabCtHR, a judge can be dismissed when the rest of the bench decides that he/she does not meet the requirements for his/her position anymore or does not meet the standards for selection.[146] For the International Commission of Jurists, it is worrying that the Statute lacks a description of the grounds and the procedure according to which judges may be dismissed from office.[147] In their opinion, the Statute should have "specified, well-defined grounds, including reasons of incapacity or behaviour that render judges unfit to discharge their duties".[148] Nevertheless, by comparison to the limited detail in Article 23(3) ECHR and given that the ArabCtHR does not yet have Rules of Court, which may be used to provide the missing details, this criticism may not be justified. Moreover, the formulation of the grounds for dismissal at the ECtHR is equally limited.

By contrast, in the ACtHPR, there is a fair and appropriate procedure for the dismissal of judges. The procedure for dismissal requires that the President or Vice-President inform the judge in a written statement that includes the grounds for dismissal and any relevant evidence. Subsequently, the judge concerned shall have the opportunity to make a statement, submit information or explanations, and answer any questions put at a private session of the Court.[149]

An interesting aspect of the IACtHR, compared to the other RHR Courts, is that its framework also allows for disciplinary action against judges. They are answerable to the Court for their conduct, which should be consistent with the requirements of international judicial office, as well as for any violation, act of negligence, or omission committed in the exercise of their functions.[150] The OAS General Assembly is authorised to discipline judges, but only following a request from the Court itself. The Court, composed of the remaining judges, must present the reasons for the request to the General Assembly.[151]

---

[143] International Commission of Jurists 2007, p. 55.

[144] See ACtHPR Protocol, art. 19(1); ACtHPR Rules of Court, rule 8; ArabCtHR Statute, art. 15(5).

[145] ECHR, art. 23(3); ECtHR Rules of Court, rule 7.

[146] ArabCtHR Statute, art. 15(5).

[147] International Commission of Jurists 2015, p. 17.

[148] Ibid.

[149] ACtHPR Rules of Court, rule 8.

[150] IACtHR Statute, art. 20(1).

[151] Ibid., art. 20(2).

2.4 Conditions of Tenure

Another fundamental requirement for safeguarding judicial independence in general is the security offered by tenure,[152] for otherwise judges become vulnerable to unwarranted influence exerted by those responsible for renewing their mandate.[153] Therefore, life tenure would be the least problematic scenario.[154] Nonetheless, most international standards on the independence of judges stipulate that judges should have security of tenure until a mandatory retirement age or the expiry of their term of office.[155]

In the IACtHR, judges are elected for a six-year term and may be re-elected only once.[156] The same procedure applies for the ACtHPR.[157] The judges in the ArabCtHR will serve a term of office of four years, with the possibility of one renewal.[158] However, to ensure continuity, the term of office of some judges in the first Court formations was shorter.[159] For instance, in the ACtHPR, following the very first election in 2006, only three judges served the full six-year term, while four judges served four years, and another four served two years.[160]

The ECtHR currently stands as an exception.[161] Before 2004, judges served a term of six years, with the possibility of renewal. Unfortunately, the re-election of judges was sometimes used as a tool by governments to discipline the judges. While obedient judges were proposed for re-election, the contrary was true for judges that did not necessarily please their State.[162] There exist two documented examples of judges being denied renewal by their government for political motivations or for ruling against their State.[163] To safeguard judicial independence, judges now serve a single, non-renewable, nine-year term.[164]

---

152 International Law Association Study Group 2004, principle 3.1; Committee of Ministers of the Council of Europe 2010, para. 49.

153 International Commission of Jurists 2007, p. 51.

154 Ibid.; Shelton 2003, p. 38.

155 Seventh United Nations Congress on the Prevention of Crime and the Treatment of Offenders 1985, Principle 12; African Commission on Human and Peoples' Rights 2003, Principle A(4)(l).

156 ACHR, art. 54(1); IACtHR Statute, art. 5(1).

157 ACtHPR Protocol, art. 15(1); ACtHPR Rules of Court, rule 2(3).

158 ArabCtHR Statute, art. 8(1).

159 ACtHPR Protocol, art. 15(1); ArabCtHR, art. 8(1); ECHR version of 1950, art. 40(1), available at https://www.echr.coe.int/documents/d/echr/Archives_1950_Convention_ENG. Accessed 4 April 2025; ACHR, art. 54(1).

160 ACtHPR Protocol, art. 15(1).

161 ECHR, art. 23(1).

162 Lemmens 2015.

163 See Hedigan 2007, p. 245, referring to Austria's refusal to put forward Judge Willi Fuhrmann as a candidate in the 2001 elections, and the withdrawal of Judge Tudor Pantiru from the Moldovan list in 2001.

164 ECHR, art. 23(1). According to the Explanatory Report to Protocol No. 14, this provision, intended to reinforce the independence and impartiality of judges, was desired by the Parliamentary

The arrangement of the term of office in the ECtHR aligns most closely with international standards. These generally postulate a single term of office between 9 and 12 years, since this would curtail inappropriate or unwarranted interferences in the judicial re-election process.[165] Conversely, in the event of a short term of office, international judges will have to look for re-employment in the national administrations or the judiciary after leaving their position, which allows for influence from their government.[166] On the other hand, longer terms of office may raise questions regarding the representativeness of RHR Courts. The rotation and re-election mechanisms cater to the interests of all States aspiring to secure the appointment of their nationals to the bench.[167] Nonetheless, this does not raise issues for the ECtHR, where every State has its own judge on the bench.

2.5 Incompatibilities

The constitutive instruments of RHR Courts also lay down specific rules concerning the compatibility of judges' activities and past affiliations with the exercise of their judicial function. This is reflected in the rules concerning the restrictions or prohibitions on extrajudicial activities while in office, as well as conflict of interest provisions, which may occur, for instance, when the case involves relatives of the sitting judge. A common characteristic of all four Courts is that they prohibit judges from engaging in any activity incompatible with their independence and impartiality, although these concepts are not precisely defined.[168] Nevertheless, the different instruments vary as to the degree of restrictions on such activities.

Within the European human rights system, judges are not allowed to engage in any activity incompatible with their independence, impartiality, or with the demands of a full-time office.[169] According to the ECtHR Rules of Court, judges shall not participate in any incompatible "political or administrative … [or] professional activity", and they must declare any additional activity to the President.[170] At the ArabCtHR, judges may not perform work or activities that might interfere with or affect their impartiality or the requirements of their duty.[171] A similar prohibition

Assembly in its Recommendation 1649 (2004) 'Candidates for the European Court of Human Rights', 30 January 2004.

165 Institut de Droit International 2011, art. 2(1); International Commission of Jurists 2015, p. 17.

166 Engel 2012, p. 448; Flauss 2008; Keller 2023, p. 266; Meron 2005, p. 362; Phan 2012, pp. 212–213.

167 Mackenzie and Sands 2003, p. 279.

168 Although these definitions can be based on the Courts' case law when interpreting the right to a fair trial. See Hennebel and Tigroudja 2022, pp. 1433–1434.

169 ECHR, arts. 21(3), 21(4); See also Plenary Court of the ECtHR 2021.

170 ECtHR Rules of Court, rule 4(1).

171 ArabCtHR Statute, art. 15(3).

applies in the ACtHPR.[172] The ACtHPR Rules of Court add that judges are prohibited from "hold[ing] political, diplomatic or administrative positions or function[ing] as government legal advisors".[173] For the interpretation of incompatibility, the AU Commission, in its 2018 Verbal Note,[174] refers to an early opinion of the Advisory Committee of Jurists on the establishment of the Permanent Court of International Justice, stating:

> "[A] member of government, a Minister or under-secretary of State, a diplomatic representative, a directory of a ministry, or one of his subordinates, or the legal adviser to a foreign office, though they would be eligible for appointment as arbitrators to the Permanent Court of Arbitration of 1899, are certainly not eligible for appointment as judges upon our Court."[175]

The IACtHR Statute includes an extensive list of incompatibilities.[176] The position of judge is incompatible with the position of "[m]embers or high-ranking officials of the executive branch of government, except for those who hold positions that do not place them under the direct control of the executive branch and those of diplomatic agents who are not Chiefs of Missions to the OAS or to any of [OAS State Parties]; [o]fficials of international organizations; [a]ny others that might prevent the judges from discharging their duties, or that might affect their independence or impartiality, or the dignity and prestige of the office."[177] In case of doubt as to incompatibility, it is the Court that decides.[178] Incompatibilities may be a ground for dismissal; however, the acts and decisions in which the judge participated shall not be invalidated.[179]

In addition, a judge's prior involvement with a party or an issue before the Court may give rise to concerns of bias or the appearance thereof. Consequently, the Courts' constitutive instruments commonly prohibit judges from sitting in a case in which they have previously participated in another capacity. This issue assumes particular significance in international courts, including RHR Courts, which are characterised by the interconnected realm of international law. Thus, a judge on a RHR Court might have previously appeared as counsel, acted as an advisor for one of the parties, functioned as a diplomat dealing with issues subsequently brought before the Court, or expressed views in academic writings directly pertinent to a case adjudicated by the Court, etc.[180]

---

[172] ACtHPR Protocol, arts. 17(3), 18; ACtHPR Rules of Court, rule 5(1).

[173] ACtHPR Rules of Court, rule 5(2).

[174] AU Commission 2018.

[175] Permanent Court of International Justice/Advisory Committee of Jurists 1920, pp. 693, 715–716. According to Jorritsma 2017, the Permanent Court of Arbitration (PCA) makes use of 'National Groups'. A National Group is a group of up to four persons appointed by the contracting parties to one or both of the PCA's founding conventions, available to act as arbitrators. National Groups tend to consist of persons from the Ministry of Foreign Affairs (e.g. current or former ministers, legal advisors or diplomats) or the Ministry of Justice, as well as from universities, supreme courts, law firms and bar associations.

[176] See also IACHR, art. 71.

[177] IACtHR Statute, art. 18(1).

[178] Ibid., art. 18(2).

[179] Ibid., art. 18(3); see *supra* Sect. 2.3.3.

[180] Mackenzie and Sands 2003, p. 280.

secure complete freedom of speech and independence, immunity from legal process in respect of words spoken or written persists even after they have ceased their responsibilities and retired from office.[203] All other privileges and immunities will no longer apply. The ECtHR Rules of Court, nevertheless, provide for waiving immunity if it would impede the course of justice and where a waiver is possible without prejudice to the purpose for which the immunity was accorded. The decision shall be taken by the plenary Court with an absolute majority of the elected judges in office.[204]

2.7 Concluding Remarks

The four Courts not only protect the independence and impartiality of judges within the domestic court systems of the contracting parties, but also within the Courts themselves. Their constitutive instruments lay down various safeguards, including requirements in the judicial election process, security of tenure, dismissal proceedings, restrictions on judges' external activities, and the provision of immunities, all aimed at upholding the crucial elements of independence and impartiality. Promising initiatives have been taken, for example, in the areas of gender balance and geographical representation.

Despite their efforts, there remain areas for improvement. For instance, although the constitutive instruments accord considerable significance to the judges' qualifications, specific requirements are vague. The instruments only refer to the need for high moral character and the qualifications necessary for the highest judicial office, without any further detail on how these requirements are to be interpreted. Moreover, the lack of coherent rules for the nomination of judges at the national level and issues with national representation, particularly regarding the appointment of ad hoc judges, continue to be significant concerns. In our opinion, the RHR Courts, by addressing these challenges, would better fulfil their mandate to protect and promote human rights, ultimately contributing to the advancement of justice and the rule of law at both regional and global levels.

References

African Commission on Human and Peoples' Rights (2003) Principles and Guidelines on the Right to a Fair Trial and Legal Assistance in Africa, DOC/OS(XXX)247. https://achpr.au.int/sites/default/files/files/2021-08/achpr33guidefairtriallegalassistance2003eng.pdf. Accessed 2 April 2025.

respect of words spoken or written, privileges in respect of exchange facilities, repatriation facilities in time of international crisis, and the right to import free of duty their furniture and effects.

[203] Ibid., art. 3.

[204] ECtHR Rules of Court, rule 7A.

African Court on Human and Peoples' Rights (2024) Practice Directions. Adopted 5 March 2024. https://www.african-court.org/wpafc/wp-content/uploads/2024/03/EN-Practice-Direction-Adopted-5-March-2024_.pdf. Accessed 2 April 2025.

AU Commission (2018) Verbal Note on the Election of Judges of the African Court on Human and Peoples' Rights. BC/OLC/66.5/502.18. https://au.int/sites/default/files/announcements/34089-annc-502.18_bc-olc-66.5_eng_nv_for_election_for_judges_june-july_2018.pdf. Accessed 4 April 2025.

Cardamone D (2019) Independence of International Courts. In: Pinto de Albuquerque P, Wojtyczek K (eds) Judicial Power in a Globalized World: Liber Amicorum Vincent De Gaetano. Springer, Cham, pp. 91-104.

Committee of Ministers of the Council of Europe (2010) Recommendation CM/Rec(2010)12, Adopted by the Committee of Ministers on 17 November 2010 and explanatory memorandum. Strasbourg, Council of Europe Publishing.

Committee of Ministers of the Council of Europe (2012) Guidelines on the selection of candidates for the post of judge at the European Court of Human Rights, Adopted by the Committee of Ministers on 28 March 2012 at the 1138th meeting of the Ministers' Deputies, CM(2012)40-final.

Consultative Council of European Judges (2001) Opinion No 1 on Standards Concerning the Independence of the Judiciary and the Irremovability of Judges, CCJE (2001) OP N°1. Strasbourg, 23 November 2001.

Council of Europe (1994) Explanatory Report to Protocol No. 11 to the Convention for the Protection of Human Rights and Fundamental Freedoms, restructuring the control machinery established thereby, ETS No. 155.

Council of Europe (2004) Explanatory Report to Protocol No. 14 to the Convention for the Protection of Human Rights and Fundamental Freedoms, amending the control system of the Convention, ETS No. 194.

De Baere G, Chané A-L, Wouters J (2015) The Contribution of International and Supranational Courts to the Rule of Law: A framework for analysis. In: De Baere G, Wouters J (eds) The Contribution of International and Supranational Courts to the Rule of Law. Edward Elgar, Cheltenham, pp. 19-81.

Dunshee de Abranchas CA (1980) The Inter-American Court of Human Rights. American University Law Review 30:79-125.

Dzehtsiarou K, Coffey DK (2014) Legitimacy and Independence of International Tribunals: An Analysis of the European Court of Human Rights. Hastings International and Comparative Law Review 37(2):271-322.

Engel NP (2012) More Transparency and Governmental Loyalty for Maintaining Professional Quality in the Election of Judges to the European Court of Human Rights. Human Rights Law Journal 32:448-455.

Executive Council of the African Union (2016) Modalities on Implementation of Criteria for Equitable Geographical and Gender Representation in the African Union Organs. EX.CL/953(XXVIII).

Faúndez Ledesma H (1998) La independencia e imparcialidad de los miembros de la Comisión y de la Corte: paradojas y desafíos [The Independence and impartiality of the members of the Commission and the Court: paradoxes and challenges]. In: Méndez J, Cox F (eds) El futuro del sistema Interamericano de los Derechos Humanos. Instituto Interamericano de Derechos Humanos, San José, pp. 185-210.

Feria-Tinta M (2004) "Dinosaurs" in Human rights Litigation: The Use of Ad Hoc Judges in Individual Complaints before the Inter-American Court of Human Rights. The Law and Practice of International Courts and Tribunals 3:79-112.

Flauss JF (2008) Les élections de juges à la Cour européenne des droits de l'homme (2005-2008) [The Election of Judges to the European Court of Human Rights (2005-2008)]. Revue trimestrielle des droits de l'homme 75:713-741.

Harris D, O'Boyle M, Bates E, Buckley CM (2023) Law of the European Convention on Human Rights, 5th edn. Oxford University Press, Oxford.

Hedigan J (2007) The Election of Judges to the European Court of Human Rights. In: Kohen MG (ed) Promoting Justice, Human Rights and Conflict Resolution through International Law: Liber Amicorum Lucius Caflisch. Brill, Leiden, pp. 235-253.
Hennebel L, Tigroudja H (2022) The American Convention on Human Rights: A Commentary. Oxford University Press, Oxford.
Independent Panel for the Election of Inter-American Commissioners and Judges (2015) Final Report. 2 June 2015. https://www.justiceinitiative.org/uploads/34b476e4-dd7b-431e-acd4-e25fbff100cc/iachr-panel-report-eng-20150603.pdf. Accessed 2 April 2025.
Institut de Droit International (2011) Resolution on the Position of the International Judge, 6 RES EN FINAL. https://www.idi-iil.org/app/uploads/2017/06/2011_rhodes_06_en.pdf. Accessed 2 April 2025.
Inter-American Court of Human Rights (2023) Annual Report 2023 https://www.corteidh.or.cr/docs/informe2023/ingles.pdf. Accessed 2 April 2025.
International Commission of Jurists (2007) International Principles on the Independence and Accountability of Judges, Lawyers and Prosecutors: A Practitioners Guide. Geneva.
International Commission of Jurists (2015) The Arab Court of Human Rights: A Flawed Statute for an Ineffective Court. Geneva.
International Law Association Study Group on the Practice and Procedure of International Court and Tribunals (2004) The Burgh House Principles On The Independence Of The International Judiciary. https://docs.pca-cpa.org/2020/04/ef1f0fb6-burgh-house-principles.pdf. Accessed 2 April 2025.
Jorritsma R (2017) National Groups: Permanent Court of Arbitration (PCA). Max Planck Institute Luxembourg for Procedural Law Research Paper Series No. 8.
Keller H (2023) How to Improve the Independence and Impartiality of Judges of the European Court of Human Rights. European Convention on Human Rights Law Review 4:259-266.
Kolb R (2013) The International Court of Justice. Hart Publishing, Oxford.
Lemmens K (2015) (S)electing Judges for Strasbourg. In: Bobek M (ed) Selecting Europe's Judges: A Critical Review of the Appointment Procedures to the European Courts. Oxford University Press, Oxford, pp. 120-161.
Mackenzie R, Sands P (2003) International Courts and Tribunals and the Independence of the International Judge. Harvard International Law Journal 44:271-286.
Magliveras KD, Naldi G (2016) The Arab Court of Human Rights: A Study of Impotence. Quebec Journal of International Law 29:147-172.
Malleson K (2009) Promoting Judicial Independence in the International Courts: Lessons from the Caribbean. International & Comparative Law Quarterly 58:671-687.
Meron T (2005) Judicial Independence and Impartiality in International Criminal Tribunals. American Journal of International Law 99:359-369.
OAS General Assembly (2020) 'Promotion and Protection of Human Rights', Resolution AG/RES. 2961(L-O/20). Adopted on 21 October 2020. https://www.oas.org/en/sla/dil/docs/AG-RES_2961_L-O-20_EN.pdf. Accessed 2 April 2025.
Parliamentary Assembly of the Council of Europe (1999) Recommendation 1429 on National procedures for nominating candidates for election to the European Court of Human Rights. Adopted on 24 September 1999. https://assembly.coe.int/nw/xml/XRef/Xref-XML2HTML-en.asp?fileid=16755&lang=en. Accessed 2 April 2025.
Parliamentary Assembly of the Council of Europe (2004) Resolution 1366 on Candidates for the European Court of Human Rights. Adopted on 30 January 2004. https://assembly.coe.int/nw/xml/XRef/Xref-XML2HTML-en.asp?fileid=17194&lang=en. Accessed 4 April 2025.
Parliamentary Assembly of the Council of Europe (2009) Ad hoc judges: a problem for the legitimacy of the European Court of Human Rights, Doc. 11976. 1 July 2009.
Parliamentary Assembly of the Council of Europe (Committee on Legal Affairs and Human Rights) (2011) *Ad hoc* judges at the European Court of Human Rights: an overview, Information report, AS/Jur (2011)36. 19 October 2011. https://assembly.coe.int/CommitteeDocs/2011/ajdoc36_2011.pdf. Accessed 4 April 2025.

Parliamentary Assembly of the Council of Europe (2025) Procedure for the election of judges to the European Court of Human Rights - Memorandum prepared by the Secretary General of the Assembly, SG-AS(2025)01. https://rm.coe.int/procedure-for-the-election-of-judges-to-the-european-court-of-human-ri/1680aa8ddf. Accessed 4 April 2025.
Permanent Court of International Justice/Advisory Committee of Jurists (1920) Procès-verbaux of the Proceedings of the Committee June 16th–July 24th 1920 with Annexes. Van Langenhuysen Brothers, The Hague. https://www.icj-cij.org/sites/default/files/permanent-court-of-international-justice/serie_D/D_proceedings_of_committee_annexes_16june_24july_1920.pdf. Accessed 2 April 2025.
Phan HD (2012) A Selective Approach to Establishing a Human Rights Mechanism in South-East Asia: The Case for a Southeast Asian Court of Human Rights. Brill, Leiden.
Plenary Court of the ECtHR (European Court of Human Rights) (2021) Resolution on Judicial Ethics. https://www.echr.coe.int/documents/d/echr/Resolution_Judicial_Ethics_ENG. Accessed 4 April 2025.
President of the ECtHR (European Court of Human Rights) (2024) Practice Directions: Recusal of judges. Issued 22 January 2024. https://www.echr.coe.int/practice-directions. Accessed 4 April 2025.
Robinson DR (2003) The Role of Politics in the Election and Work of Judges of the International Court of Justice. American Society of International Law Proceedings 97:277-282.
Seventh United Nations Congress on the Prevention of Crime and the Treatment of Offenders (1985) Basic Principles on the Independence of the Judiciary. UN Doc. A/CONF.121/22/Rev.1. Adopted on 6 September 1985. https://www.ohchr.org/en/instruments-mechanisms/instruments/basic-principles-independence-judiciary. Accessed 4 April 2025.
Shelton D (2003) Legal Norms to Promote the Independence and Accountability of International Tribunals. Law and Practice of International Courts and Tribunals 2:27-62.
Swigart L (2010) The "National Judge": Some Reflections on Diversity in International Courts and Tribunals. McGeorge Law Review 42:223-242.
Terris D, Romane CPR, Swigart L (2007) The International Judge: An Introduction of the Men and Women Who Decide the World's Cases. Oxford University Press, Oxford.
Viljoen F (2012) International Human Rights in Africa. Oxford University Press, Oxford.
Voeten E (2007) The Politics of International Judicial Appointments: Evidence from the European Court of Human Rights. International Organization 61:669-701.
Wood M (2007) The Selection of Candidates for International Judicial Office: Recent Practice. In: Ndiaye TM, Wolfrum R (eds) Law of the Sea, Environmental Law and Settlement of Disputes - Liber Amicorum Judge Thomas A. Mensah. Brill, Leiden, pp. 357-368.

Zoë Grossi is a PhD Candidate in International Criminal Law at the Institute for International Law and the Leuven Centre for Global Governance Studies at KU Leuven. She is also a Teaching Assistant at the University of Hasselt.

Jan Wouters is Full Professor of International Law and International Organizations, Jean Monnet Chair *ad personam*, Director of the Institute for International Law and of the Leuven Centre for Global Governance Studies (a Jean Monnet and KU Leuven Centre of Excellence), and Administrator of the America Europe Fund at KU Leuven. He is Adjunct Professor at Columbia University and Visiting Professor at the College of Europe and Paris2. A Member of the Belgian Royal Academy and *Of Counsel* at Omega Law, he has published widely on international and EU law, international organizations, global governance, corporate and financial law.

Parliamentary Assembly of the Council of Europe (2005) Procedure for [illegible] the European Court of Human Rights – Memorandum prepared by the Secretary General of the Assembly, SG-AS (2005) 01, [illegible]

[illegible]

Chapter 3
The Jurisdiction of the Courts

Gino Naldi

Contents

3.1 Introduction 52
3.2 Compulsory Jurisdiction 52
3.2.1 Fourth Instance Doctrine 54
3.2.2 Inter-State Cases 55
3.2.3 Individual Complaints 56
3.2.4 Jurisdictional Requirements 61
3.3 Friendly Settlement 65
3.4 Withdrawal 66
3.5 Conclusions 70
References 71

Abstract In September 2014, the League of Arab States approved the Statute of the Arab Court of Human Rights, finalising a 20-year process to put in place a human rights mechanism resembling those operating in the other regions. All the regional systems provide a platform for the collective enforcement of treaty rights by States but more significantly, they seek to provide individuals, to a greater or lesser extent, with a possibility of redress for any alleged violations of their human rights. The focus of this chapter is on the jurisdiction of the regional Courts, particularly on the procedural conditions on admissibility. It also examines how the regional systems deal with States wishing to release themselves from their human rights obligations.

Keywords Compulsory jurisdiction · Inter-State cases · Individual complaint procedures · Friendly settlement · Withdrawal

---

G. Naldi (✉)
Norwich, UK
e-mail: ginonaldi57@yahoo.co.uk

A. Almutawa and K. D. Magliveras (eds.), *A Comparison of the European, Inter-American, African and Arab Human Rights Courts: Institutional Aspects*,
https://doi.org/10.1007/978-94-6265-695-6_3

applications to a Chamber composed of seven judges,[14] while individual applications, including from NGOs, are usually decided by a three-judge committee,[15] or failing a decision, by a Chamber.[16] Only when individual applications are manifestly inadmissible are single judges competent to decide not to proceed with further examination.[17] Therefore, it seems more appropriate for challenges to the ArabCtHR's jurisdiction to be considered, at least, by a panel of three judges,[18] or by the Court, as in the African system.[19]

3.2.1 Fourth Instance Doctrine

It is a basic principle of the regional human rights architecture that the Courts do not act as a court of appeal in relation to national courts, sometimes known as the fourth instance doctrine.[20] Thus, they cannot "intervene directly in the legal systems of the Contracting States, [they]...must respect the autonomy of those legal systems".[21] While the ECtHR may find a domestic law to be incompatible with the ECHR, that law is not invalidated; it is the national legislatures' responsibility to remedy the deficiencies. The fourth instance doctrine is not spelt out explicitly in the regional treaties but has been recognised through case-law.[22] However, Article 18 ArabCtHR Statute provides that the Court's jurisdiction is complementary to the national judiciary and does not supplant it.

---

[14] ECHR art. 26(1). See also Rule 48 Rules of Court.

[15] ECHR art. 28(1).

[16] Ibid., art. 29(1).

[17] Ibid., art. 27. See also Rule 49(1) Rules of Court.

[18] Provision is made for chambers comprised of at least three judges to hear the subject matter of the dispute, ArabCtHR Statute art. 24(2).

[19] Rule 49(1) ACtHPR Rules of Court. But note Rule 38(2), discussed below. In the American system, petitions from individuals or organisations are initially assessed by the Executive Secretariat of the IACHR for compliance with admissibility requirements, IACHR Rules of Procedure art. 30(1). The IACHR examines those deemed *prima facie* admissible, IACHR Rules of Procedure arts. 30–36. The IACtHR is not bound by the IACHR's decisions on admissibility and may review them, IACtHR, *Velasquez Rodriguez v. Honduras*, Judgment, Preliminary Objections, 26 June 1989, Series C No. 1, para 29. See Pasqualucci 2013, p 101.

[20] ECtHR 2024, Practical Guide, paras 362–369. See further Harris et al. 2023, p 18; Pasqualucci 2013, pp. 125–128.

[21] ECtHR 2024, Practical Guide, para 364. This stance also reflects the principle of subsidiarity, which was inserted into the ECHR Preamble by Protocol No. 15, opened for signature 24 June 2013, CETS No. 213, entered into force 1 August 2021.

[22] But see ECHR art. 19. See, e.g., ECtHR, App. Nos. 1474/62; 1677/62; 1691/62; 1769/63; 1994/63; 2126/64, *Case "Relating to Certain Aspects of the Laws on the Use of Languages in Education in Belgium" v. Belgium*, Judgment, (Merits), 23 July 1968, Series A No. 6; IACtHR, *Palma Mendoza* et al. *v. Ecuador*, Judgment (Preliminary Objection and Merits), 3 September 2012, Series C No. 247, paras 16, 18, (2012) 28 *Inter-American Yearbook on Human Rights* 674; ACtHPR, App. No. 003/2014, *Ingabire Victoire Umuhoza v. Rwanda*, Judgment, 24 November 2017, para 54.

3.2.2 Inter-State Cases

All the regional treaties make provision for inter-State cases.[23] Under Article 33 ECHR, acceptance of the ECtHR's jurisdiction over inter-State cases is of a mandatory nature.[24] In inter-State cases a particular interest need not be proven as applicants share in the "collective enforcement" of the Convention rights.[25] Under the ACtHPR Protocol, the Court can be approached only in specific circumstances. These include where a State Party has lodged a complaint to the African Commission on Human and Peoples' Rights (African Commission);[26] where a State Party against which a complaint has been lodged at the African Commission; and where a State Party whose citizen is allegedly a victim of a human rights violation,[27] which presumably must implead another party to proceed. However, the first scenario is critical because under Article 47 African Charter a State Party can initiate an inter-state complaint if it "has good reasons to believe that another State party…has violated" its provisions. Evidently, the concept of "collective guarantee" is at play and no special interest is needed to have standing. The applicant State then has the opportunity conferred by the Protocol to approach the ACtHPR. But another possible avenue exists. Based on Article 5(1)(a) ACtHPR Protocol and Rule 130(1) of the African Commission's Rules of Procedure,[28] the African Commission could refer the Communication to the ACtHPR, after obtaining the complainant's consent in accordance with Rule 130(2), and before deciding on its admissibility. The ACtHPR received its first inter-state application in 2023.[29]

The ACHR lacks a straightforward provision corresponding to Article 33 ECHR. However, States may approach the IACHR if both parties recognise its competence[30] and the IACHR or the State concerned can thereafter submit the issue to the IACtHR

---

[23] ACHR art. 61(1); ACtHR Protocol art. 5(1)(b)-(d); ArabCtHR Statute art. 19(1).

[24] Risini 2022, pp. 15–18.

[25] ECtHR, App. No. 5310/71, *Ireland v. United Kingdom*, Judgment, 18 January 1978, Series A No. 25, para 239. See Harris et al. 2023, pp. 122–124. This is also the position in the Americas, see, e.g., IACtHR, *Ivcher-Bronstein v. Peru*, Judgment, (Competence), 24 September 1999, Series C No. 54, para 42; *Denunciation of the American Convention on Human Rights and the Charter of the Organization of American States and the consequences for State human rights obligations*, Advisory Opinion OC-26/20, 9 November 2020, Series A No. 26, paras 163–164, (2022) 116 *American Journal of International Law* 409. See further Lixinski 2021.

[26] Its mandate is set out in African Charter art. 45 and includes the protection of human and peoples' rights through its communication procedure, see Magliveras and Naldi 2023, paras 288–293. The procedure regarding inter-state complaints submitted to the African Commission is governed by African Charter arts. 47–49 and is automatic upon ratification. See African Commission, Communication No. 227/99, *Democratic Republic of Congo v. Burundi, Rwanda, Uganda*, May 2003, paras 51–61.

[27] ACtHR Protocol art. 5(1)(b), (c), (d).

[28] As last adopted during its 27th Extra-Ordinary Session (19 February to 4 March 2020).

[29] ACtHPR, App. No. 007/2023, *Democratic Republic of Congo v. Republic of Rwanda*, filed on 21 August 2023. On 7 March 2024, the Court President rejected applicant's request for expedited procedure.

[30] ACHR art. 45.

if it remains unresolved.[31] Additionally, a combined reading of Articles 61(1) and 62(3) ACHR, subject to reciprocity,[32] make it evident that the ACHR includes an inter-State procedure.

The Arab regime is very restrictive. Under Article 19(1) ArabCtHR Statute only States Parties whose 'subjects' claim to be victims of human rights violations by another State Party have the right to submit cases. Inter-State cases are essentially limited to diplomatic protection.[33] Accordingly, if State X is a repressive State that imprisons political dissenters, assuming they are all State X nationals, State Y would have no cause before the ArabCtHR. But if one such dissenter was a State Y national, then State Y would have standing before the ArabCtHR. The Statute thus joins the other regional human rights systems in making provision for inter-state cases, but only rarely does a State launch proceedings against another State due to political and diplomatic considerations.[34] This is certainly the case in the Inter-American and African systems.[35] Usually only in the context of grave or massive violations may States with no direct interest at stake be prevailed upon to lodge an action against another State.[36] However, in recent years there has been a significant increase in inter-state cases submitted to the ECtHR, with fourteen cases currently pending, mostly concerning circumstances of crisis or conflict in Eastern Europe and the Caucasus.[37]

3.2.3 Individual Complaints

An issue that goes to the heart of whether any human rights enforcement mechanism can protect them capably is the degree of access granted to individual complainants. Its effectiveness is the litmus test. Only the ECHR grants direct access, described

[31] Ibid., art. 51(1).

[32] Ibid., art. 62(2).

[33] It may be premature to argue that diplomatic protection no longer has a role to play as a result of developments in international human rights law, International Law Commission 2000, paras 18–31. See ECtHR, App. No. 13255/07, *Georgia v. Russia (I)* [GC], Judgment, 3 July 2014, ECHR 2014-IV, (2014) 53 *International Legal Materials* 810, concerning the arrest, detention and expulsion of a large number of Georgian nationals from Russia.

[34] Harris et al. 2023, p 124.

[35] No inter-State cases have been submitted to the IACtHR. However, the IACHR has considered a handful of such communications, see Coop and Fietta 2022, p 20.

[36] For instance, European Commission on Human Rights, App. No. 176/56, *Government of the Kingdom of Greece v. Government of the United Kingdom of Great Britain and Northern Ireland*, lodged on 7 May 1956 (*First Cyprus Case*); European Commission on Human Rights, App. Nos. 3321–3/67 to 3323/67 and 3344/67, *Denmark, Norway, Sweden and Netherlands v. Greece (I)*, lodged on 20 September 1967; and European Commission on Human Rights, App. Nos. 9940/82 to 9944/82, Denmark, France, Norway, Sweden & Netherlands v. Turkey, lodged on 1 July 1982.

[37] See, e.g., ECtHR, App. No. 42521/20, *Armenia v. Azerbaijan*, lodged on 27 September 2020; ECtHR, App. Nos. 20958/14 and 38,334/18, *Ukraine v. Russia (re Crimea)*, lodged on 13 March 2014 and 11 August 2018; ECtHR, App. No. 55855/18, *Ukraine v. Russia (VIII)*, lodged on 29 November 2018.

as "a key component of the machinery for protecting" human rights[38]; under the other systems access is indirect and/or optional. Article 34 ECHR defines applicants to include not only persons but also associations, NGOs and groups of individuals, allowing the ECtHR to recognise the standing of different legal and juridical entities.[39] However, governmental organisations or public bodies such as regional or municipal authorities, which exercise public functions, do not satisfy this test.[40]

Applicants under Article 34 ECHR must be victims of a violation, either directly, indirectly or potentially, to have standing,[41] *actio populares*, or public interest litigation, not being permissible.[42] Article 19 ArabCtHR Statute also refers to victims. In contrast, Article 44 ACHR allows for greater flexibility as standing is not conditional on victim status. Any person, group of persons or NGO, regardless of victim status, may petition the IACHR to complain of an alleged violation of a victim's rights; petitions based on abstract victims and *actio populares* are inadmissible.[43] The IACtHR has stated that a petition must allege a concrete violation of the human rights of a specific individual.[44] The African system, however, may represent a departure from these positions. Given that the African Commission is authorised to submit cases,[45] and given that it accepts *actio populares* when adjudicating Communications, the possibility exists that it may submit such a case to the ACtHPR.[46] This may also

[38] ECtHR, App. Nos. 46,827/99 and 46,951/99, *Mamatkulov and Askarov v. Turkey* [GC], Judgment, 4 February 2005, ECHR 2005-I, para 122.

[39] ECtHR 2024, Practical Guide, paras 17–23; Harris et al. 2023, pp. 92–93; Dopplinger 2021. In ECtHR, App. No. 53600/20, *Verein Klimaseniorinnen Schweiz and Others v. Switzerland* [GC], Judgment, 9 April 2024, para 498, the existing law on the standing of associations, in the specific context of climate change, seems to have been relaxed so that it may be possible for an association to have standing even if it cannot itself claim to be the victim of a violation.

[40] ECtHR, App. No. 53984/00, *Radio France* et al. *v. France*, Judgment, 30 March 2004, ECHR 2004-II; ECtHR, App. No. 55346/00, *Ayuntamiento de Mula v. Spain*, Decision, 1 February 2001, ECHR 2001-I.

[41] ECtHR 2024, Practical Guide, paras 24–86; ECtHR, App. Nos. 29,381/09 and 32,684/09, *Vallianatos and Others v. Greece*, Judgment, 7 November 2013, ECHR 2013-VI, para 47; ECtHR, App. No. 53600/20, *Verein Klimaseniorinnen Schweiz v. Switzerland*, above n. 39, paras 463, 465–477.

[42] ECtHR, App. No. 47848/08, *Centre for Legal Resources on behalf of Valentin Câmpeanu v. Romania* [GC], Judgment, 17 July 2014, ECHR 2014, para 101; ECtHR, *Verein Klimaseniorinnen Schweiz v. Switzerland*, above n. 39, para 460. However, Judge Eicke observed that the ECtHR had opened the door to "*actio popularis* type complaints", Separate Opinion by Judge Eicke, ibid., para 45.

[43] Pasqualucci 2013, p 134; Rodriguez Pinzón 2001, pp. 372–376.

[44] IACtHR, *International Responsibility for the Promulgation and Enforcement of Laws in Violation of the Convention (Arts. 1 and 2 of the American Convention of Human Rights)*, Advisory Opinion OC-14/94, 9 December 1994, Series A, No. 14, paras 45–46.

[45] ACtHPR Protocol art. 5(1)(a).

[46] African Commission, Communication No. 275/2003, *Article 19 v. Eritrea*, May 2007, para 65; African Commission, Communication No. 155/96, *The Social and Economic Rights Action Center and the Center for Economic and Social Rights v. Nigeria*, 27 October 2001, para 49.

be the case with African inter-governmental organisations (IGOs),[47] which have unconditional access, and NGOs and individuals under Article 5(3) Protocol.

In contrast, there is no direct access to the IACtHR: individuals must first submit their complaints to the IACHR,[48] only States and the IACHR are entitled to bring cases before the IACtHR.[49] However, the IACtHR has taken a more restrictive approach than the ECtHR as Article 1(2) ACHR provides that 'person' means a human being; legal entities, including businesses, are not holders of ACHR human rights and freedoms. Nevertheless, in accordance with the Protocol of San Salvador,[50] indigenous and tribal communities as well as unions and federations, may appear before it.[51] Finally, corporations could become bearers of human rights through the individuals who are their legal representatives.[52]

Under Article 5(3) ACtHPR Protocol, the ACtHPR *may* allow individuals and NGOs to bring cases directly before it,[53] clearly an exercise of discretion whether to accept an application.[54] But Article 5 does not expressly list legal persons as amongst those having access, except for NGOs in certain circumstances. The definition of 'applicant' under Rule 1(a) ACtHPR Rules of Court includes any entity initiating proceedings before it under Article 5, which presumably includes NGOs. However, African Commission Rule 115(1) refers to communications submitted under Article 55 African Charter by any natural or *legal person* (emphasis added). In one case, one of the applicants was a company but the case was dismissed on the ground that the respondent State had not accepted the ACtHPR's personal jurisdiction.[55]

[47] ACtHPR Protocol art. 5(1)(e). In ACtHPR, Request No. 002/2013, *Request for Advisory Opinion by the African Committee of Experts on the Rights and Welfare of the Child on the Standing of the African Committee of Experts on the Rights and Welfare of the Child before the African Court of Human and Peoples' Rights*, Advisory Opinion, 5 December 2014, paras 60–76, 94, since said Committee was not specifically listed in art. 5(1), it was concluded that it did not meet the definition of an IGO and, consequently, had no standing.

[48] Cf. ACHR art. 44.

[49] ACHR art. 61(1).

[50] Additional Protocol to the American Convention on Human Rights in the Area of Economic, Social, and Cultural Rights, opened for signature 17 November 1988, OAS Treaty Series No. 69, entered into force 16 November 1999, art. 19(6).

[51] IACtHR, *Entitlement of Legal Entities to Hold Rights under the Inter-American Human Rights System*, Advisory Opinion OC-22/16, 26 February 2016, Series A, No. 22, paras 85–105.

[52] Ibid., paras 111, 119. See Pasqualucci 2013, pp. 135–136.

[53] ACtHPR, App. No. 013/2011, *Beneficiaries of late Norbert Zongo, Abdoulaye Nikiema alias Ablasse, Ernest Zongo and Blaise Ilboudo & the Burkinabe Human and Peoples' Rights Movement v. Burkina Faso*, Judgment (Merits), 28 March 2014, para 49. The right extends to groups of individuals, ACtHPR, App. No. 042/2016, *Collectif des Anciens Travailleurs du Laboratoire ALS v. Mali*, Ruling (Jurisdiction & Admissibility), 28 March 2019, para 16.

[54] The term "can consider" was used in ACtHPR, App. Nos 009/2011 and 011/2011, *Tanganyika Law Society and the Legal and Human Rights Centre & Reverend Christopher Mtikila v. United Republic of Tanzania*, Judgment, 14 June 2013, para 86.

[55] ACtHPR, App. No. 002/2012, *Delta International Investments SA, Mr AGL de Lange and Mrs M. de Lange v. South Africa*, Decision, 30 March 2012.

Article 5(3) ACtHPR Protocol restricts access to NGOs that have observer status with the African Commission. Several cases have failed to progress beyond this point as the applicant NGO has not been accredited with the African Commission.[56] Curiously, in one case an application lodged by a trade union was dismissed on this ground, not because it was not an NGO.[57] In 2022 the African Commission stirred controversy by rejecting the applications for observer status of three NGOs committed to protecting the rights of LGBTQ persons because “sexual orientation is not an expressly recognized right or freedom under the African Charter …and …contrary to the virtues of African values”.[58] However, the chief impediment to ACtHPR’s jurisdiction over a particular contracting State is that it depends on that State’s prior acceptance of its jurisdiction, in accordance with Article 34(6) of the Protocol, discussed further below.

Article 19(1) of the ArabCtHR Statute on standing is disappointing as individuals have no right to approach it directly, only States Parties do. Since LAS Member States are unwilling to grant individuals direct access to the ArabCtHR, consciously eschewing the precedence of the other regional HR systems, it might have been possible to follow the example of other regional systems and have a treaty-based organ act as a filter mechanism, endowing it with the competence to process petitions from individuals with the power either to dismiss them or refer them to the ArabCtHR. The current position in the Americas is based on a two-tier structure, virtually identical to the original system that prevailed in Europe: under the aforementioned Article 44 ACHR, the IACHR receives and examines petitions from individuals and NGOs, issuing a report on whether or not a violation had occurred, dismissing inadmissible cases and referring those worthy of further consideration to the IACtHR.[59] In Africa, the option for those with grievances against States that have not ratified the ACtHPR Protocol or made separate declarations under Article 34(6) thereof is the African Commission’s automatic competence under Articles 55 and 56 African Charter, given that it may submit cases to the ACtHPR under Article 5(1)(a) ACtHPR Protocol.[60] This arrangement provides a possible avenue for complaints originating in, or concerning, African LAS Member States, such as Libya, to come before the ACtHPR.[61] The Arab Human Rights Committee could have been mandated with this task.[62] In keeping with international practice, the procedural conditions of admissibility could have been extended to individuals to ensure that ill-founded cases be

---

[56] ACtHPR, App. No. 006/2011, *Association Juriste d’Afrique pour la Bonne Gouvernance v. Ivory Coast*, Decision, 16 June 2011, paras 7–9.

[57] ACtHPR, App. No. 012/2011, *National Convention of Teachers Trade Union v. Gabon*, Decision, 15 December 2011.

[58] African Commission on Human and Peoples’ Rights, Final Communiqué, 73rd Ordinary Session, 20 October to 9 November 2022, para 58.

[59] IACHR Rules of Procedure art. 45. Until its dissolution in 1998, the European Commission on Human Rights played a similar role, Merrills and Robertson 2022, pp. 271–282.

[60] Magliveras and Naldi 2023, para 337.

[61] See ACtHPR, App. No. 004/2011, *African Commission on Human and Peoples’ Rights v. Great Socialist People’s Libyan Arab Jamahiriya*, lodged on 3 March 2011.

[62] See Arab Charter art. 45.

dismissed without having to encumber the ArabCtHR. Such safeguards are in place in other jurisdictions.[63] Regrettably, a draft that conferred upon the Arab Committee the mandate to consider individual complaints did not proceed.[64]

Whereas there is no right of individual access, individuals may have been granted an indirect means of approaching the ArabCtHR through Article 19(2) Statute. This stipulates that States Parties may recognise that NGOs, accredited and working in the field of human rights in the State Party whose subjects allege human rights violations, will have standing. This option is discretionary; NGOs will have direct access to the ArabCtHR contingent on a State's prior acceptance of its jurisdiction. This procedure most closely resembles that of the African system, where experience reveals that NGOs can play an invaluable role in protecting human rights.[65] The position of NGOs under the Statute raises the question of the *bona fides* of States Parties and how many would be willing to accept this discretionary option and how free from state interference NGOs would be to carry out their work. Another obvious difficulty is that NGOs must be recognised by the State in question. The domestic legal system of contracting states will need to recognise NGOs as legal entities capable of acting on account of third persons and there must also be provisions on the recognition of NGOs for the specific purpose of bringing cases before the ArabCtHR. State Parties can easily evade this possible irritant by the simple expedient of refusing or withdrawing accreditation.

As previously seen, under Article 19(1) ArabCtHR Statute only States Parties whose 'subjects' claim to be victims of human rights violations by another State Party can submit cases to the ArabCtHR.[66] Another translation refers instead to 'citizens',[67] but whether or not there is any substantive difference between the two terms the more important question is whether jurisdiction is restricted to the nationals of State Parties. If permanent residents, migrant workers, refugees, are excluded, this would run counter to the other regional systems, where States are obliged to secure the rights of all persons within their jurisdiction regardless of nationality, assuming a "jurisdictional link".[68] Indeed, this is the situation under Article 3(1) Arab Charter, which makes this particular wording odd since it would mean that States must take the necessary domestic measures to guarantee the rights and freedoms enshrined therein to all individuals subject to their jurisdiction, who would have no recourse to the ArabCtHR. Another question is whether the definition of 'subject' rather than 'citizen' extends to legal entities/persons such as private corporations or whether it is

---

[63] Harris et al. 2023, pp. 52–83; Magliveras and Naldi 2023, paras 304–321; Pasqualucci 2013, pp. 85–101.

[64] International Commission of Jurists 2015, p 26.

[65] Mbelle 2008.

[66] International Commission of Jurists 2015.

[67] See the translation made by the Arab Center for International Humanitarian Law and Human Rights Education, https://acihl.org/texts.htm?article_id=44&lang=ar-SA. Accessed 2 April 2025.

[68] ACHR art. 1(1); African Charter art. 1; ECHR art. 1. See further, ACtHR, *Denunciation of the American Convention*, above n. 25, para 53; African Commission, Communication No. 294/2004, *Zimbabwe Lawyers for Human Rights and IHRDA (on behalf of Andrew Barclay Meldrum) v. Zimbabwe,* Decision, 30 March-3 April 2009; ECtHR 2024, Practical Guide, para 2.

limited to natural persons. It can be argued that the term 'subject' rather than 'citizen' implies the former. The jurisprudence from other human rights jurisdictions differs somewhat on this issue. It may be that the Rules of the ArabCtHR will clarify these apparent inconsistencies.[69]

3.2.4 Jurisdictional Requirements

3.2.4.1 Competence *Ratione Personae*

The exercise of the competence *ratione personae* (personal jurisdiction) by the Courts is dependent on the respondent State being bound by the treaty in question and/or to any protocols for otherwise the applications will be held inadmissible. Article 32(1) ECHR refers just to the ECHR and the relevant Protocols. On the contrary, in the Americas jurisdiction shall also be exercised over other related OAS treaties ratified by respondent States.[70] Under Article 34(6) ACtHPR Protocol contracting States must make a separate declaration accepting the ACtHPR's competence to receive petitions.[71] In its first case, the ACtHPR explained: "The effect of … [Articles 5(3) and 34(6) of the Protocol], read together, is that direct access to the Court by an individual is subject to the deposit by the respondent State of a special declaration authorizing such a case to be brought before the Court".[72] For the ACtHPR to exercise jurisdiction the respondent State Party must have deposited the declaration under Article 34(6).[73] In the absence of such a declaration the ACtHPR was unable to entertain the case.[74] Nevertheless, the case could be transferred to the

---

[69] The ArabCtHR is authorised to draft its own Rules, ArabCtHR Statute art. 28.

[70] ACHR art. 62(3); IACHR Rules of Procedure art. 23. See, e.g., Inter-American Convention on Forced Disappearance of Persons, opened for signature 9 June 1994, 2716 UNTS 3, entered into force 28 March 1996, art. XIII; IACtHR, *Heliodoro Portugal v. Panama*, Judgment, Preliminary objections, merits, reparations and costs, 12 August 2008, Series C No. 186, para. 117. Also, the Inter-American Convention to Prevent and Punish Torture, opened for signature 9 December 1985, OAS Treaty Series A-67, entered into force 28 February 1987, IACtHR, *Heliodoro Portugal v. Panama*, ibid., para 63. And Inter-American Convention Against All Forms of Discrimination and Intolerance, opened for signature 5 June 2013, OAS Treaty Series A-69, entered into force 20 February 2020, art. 15(iii). See further Pasqualucci 2013, pp. 122–124.

[71] ACtHPR, App. No. 007/2013, *Mohamed Abubakri v. Tanzania*, Judgment, 3 June 2016, para 33; ACtHPR, App. No. 001/2012, *Omary and Others v. Tanzania*, Judgment, 28 March 2014, para 80. And only States may be respondents, ACtHPR, App. No. 001/2011, *Femi Falana v. African Union*, Jurisdiction, 26 June 2012, Separate Opinion by Judge Mutsinzi.

[72] ACtHPR, *Michelot Yogogombaye v. Senegal*, above n. 10, para 34.

[73] Ibid., paras 35–37; ACtHPR, *Tanganyika Law Society v. Tanzania*, above n. 54, para 86.

[74] ACtHPR, *Michelot Yogogombaye v. Senegal*, above n. 10, para 37. See also, ACtHPR, App. No. 002/2011, *Soufiane Ababou v. Algeria*, Decision, 16 June 2011, paras 5–11; ACtHPR, App. No. 005/2011, *Daniel Amare and Mulugeta Amare v. Republic of Mozambique and Mozambique Airlines*, Decision, 16 June 2011, paras 6–8.

African Commission in accordance with Article 6(3) ACtHPR Protocol.[75] Furthermore, under Rule of Court 38(2), should an application involving a State that has neither ratified the Protocol nor made the Article 34(6) declaration be submitted to the ACtHPR, the Registry shall inform the applicant that the ACtHPR lacks jurisdiction and inform the applicant that s/he may approach the African Commission.[76] It appears that this has occurred on a number of occasions.[77] The question that arises is whether it is appropriate for the Registry to exercise what is considered a judicial function in other jurisdictions. At the time of writing, eight States have valid Article 34(6) declarations: Burkina Faso, Gambia, Ghana, Guinea-Bissau, Malawi, Mali, Niger, and Tunisia. Several applications submitted to the regional human rights Courts have been dismissed either because the respondent State had not ratified the treaty in question[78] or because the respondent was not actually a State.[79]

3.2.4.2 Competence *Ratione Materiae*

For the Courts to be able to exercise jurisdiction *ratione materiae* (subject matter jurisdiction), the right or freedom invoked by the applicant must be guaranteed or recognised by the treaty regime, otherwise the case will be dismissed. Article 32(1) ECHR extends jurisdiction to all cases concerning the interpretation and application of the ECHR and relevant Protocols,[80] whereas under Article 62(1) ACHR the IACtHR's jurisdiction covers "all matters relating to the interpretation or application" of the ACHR. As stated above, other OAS treaties may also confer jurisdiction upon the IACtHR.[81] The ACtHPR's jurisdiction reaches beyond the African Charter and the Protocol on the ACtHPR to "any other relevant human rights instrument which

---

[75] See, e.g., ACtHPR, *Soufiane Ababou v. Algeria*, above n. 74; ACtHPR, App. No. 008/2011, *Alexandre v. Cameroon*, Decision, 23 September 2011.

[76] This rule seems to express the oft-expressed view of Judge Ouguergouz that applications where the ACtHPR 'manifestly lacks jurisdiction' should be treated by the Registry as a purely administrative matter and dismissed by a letter of rejection rather than given judicial consideration, see, e.g., *Alexandre v. Cameroon*, above n. 75, Separate Opinion of Judge Ouguergouz, paras 2–6.

[77] Makunya 2021, p 1234.

[78] ECtHR, App. No. 27535/04, *De Saedeleer v. Belgium*, Judgment, 24 July 2007, paras 68–69 (Belgium had not ratified Protocol No. 7 ECHR); IACtHPR, *Baena-Ricardo* et al. *v. Panama*, Judgment, Merits, Reparations and Costs, 2 February 2001, Series C No. 72, para 99 (Panama had not ratified the Protocol of San Salvador); ACtHPR, *Youseff Ababou v. Morocco*, above n. 5 (Morocco was not at the time a member of the AU).

[79] ACtHPR, *Femi Falana v. African Union*, above n. 71 (complaint lodged against AU); ACtHPR, App. No. 059/2016, *Akwasi Boateng & 351 others v. Ghana*, Ruling (Jurisdiction), 27 November 2020, para 35 (complaint lodged against respondents who were individuals).

[80] ECtHR 2024, Practical Guide, paras 348–354. See, e.g., ECtHR, App. No. 9697/82, *Johnston and Others v. Ireland*, Judgment, 18 December 1986, Series A No. 102; ECtHR, App. No. 22414/93, *Chahal v. United Kingdom* [GC], Judgment, 15 November 1996, ECHR 1996-V, para 73.

[81] The IACtHR held that it can apply the Convention on Torture although it is silent on the matter of its jurisdiction, IACtHR, *Heliodoro Portugal v. Panama*, above n. 70, para 63.

a State has ratified".[82] This provision is exceptionally broad in scope and has been described as conferring an "almost unlimited substantive jurisdiction".[83] Indeed, the ACtHPR has assumed jurisdiction over not only other AU treaties[84] but also universal and regional human rights treaties to which the respondent State is a party, including the International Covenant on Civil and Political Rights[85] and ECOWAS treaties.[86]

Similarly, Article 16(1) ArabCtHR Statute states that it has jurisdiction over the application and interpretation of the Arab Charter *or* any other Arab human rights treaty to which a disputing Member State is a party (emphasis added). The substantive provisions of the Arab Charter, which many commentators consider comparable to international standards,[87] therefore assume an increased importance.[88] However, prior acceptance of the Arab Charter, as opposed to the Statute, may not be a condition precedent. It does not appear that the ArabCtHR's ability to assume jurisdiction on the basis of another Arab treaty would be dependent on the State being a prior party to the Arab Charter. The Statute does not elaborate as to which these 'Arab treaties' might be. A broad reading could extend to any relevant universal or regional human rights instrument that a State Party has ratified, such as the African Charter or the UN Convention on the Rights of the Child.[89] But the difference in wording between the ArabCtHR Statute and the ACtHPR Protocol is crucial. Therefore, the reference might only concern LAS treaties, the Arab Convention on Refugees being one.[90] An interesting question is whether the LAS Charter itself could come within the ArabCtHR's remit. The ACtHPR has held that it has competence over the human rights provisions of the AU's Constitutive Act,[91] but the LAS Charter is silent on the subject and that possibility therefore seems unlikely.

---

[82] ACtHPR Protocol art. 3(1).

[83] Harrington 2002, p 318. See, e.g., ACtHPR, App. No. 003/2011, *Urban Mkandawire v. Malawi*, Judgment, 21 June 2013, para 34.

[84] Such as the African Charter on Democracy, Elections and Governance, opened for signature 30 January 2007, entered into force 15 February 2012. See, e.g., ACtHPR, App. No. 001/2014, *Actions pour la Protection des Droit de l'Homme (APDH) v. Côte d'Ivoire*, Judgment, 18 November 2016, para 151; ACtHPR, App. No. 062/2019, *Sébastien Germain Marie Aikoué Ajavon v. Benin*, Judgment, 4 December 2020, para 257.

[85] See, e.g., ACtHPR, App. No. 006/2013, *Wilfred Onyango Nganyi & 9 Others v. Tanzania*, Judgment, 18 March 2016, para 165.

[86] See, e.g., ACtHPR, *APDH v. Côte d'Ivoire*, above n. 84. See Rachovitsa 2019.

[87] Magliveras 2017, p 34; Naskou-Perraki 2009; Rishmawi 2005.

[88] Robertson and Merrills 1996, pp. 202–205, 249–260.

[89] UN Convention on the Rights of the Child, opened for signature 20 November 1989, 1577 UNTS 3, entered into force 2 September 1990.

[90] Arab Convention on the Status of Refugees in Arab Countries, opened for signature 27 March 1994, not yet in force; Arab Charter of Women's Rights, opened for signature 9 October 2019, not yet in force.

[91] ACtHPR, App. No. 007/2013, *Mohamed Abubakri v. Tanzania*, Judgment, 3 June 2016, para 51. Constitutive Act of the African Union, opened for signature 11 July 2000, 2158 UNTS 3, entered into force 26 May 2001, art. 4(m).

3.2.4.3 Competence *Ratione Temporis*

All the regional human rights treaties apply the principle of temporal jurisdiction, or *ratione temporis*, based on the non-retroactivity of treaties.[92] Thus a respondent State is not bound by any treaty or protocol relating to any circumstance which occurred before their entry into force regarding that State.[93] However, the ACtHPR has taken a more expansive approach. In *Mkandawire v. Malawi* one issue was whether it could have jurisdiction over alleged violations that took place after the African Charter had come into force and been ratified by the Respondent State but before the ACtHPR Protocol had done so. For the ACtHPR it was crucial that at the time of the alleged incidents the African Charter was already binding on the Respondent.[94] It was the ratification of the African Charter rather than the Protocol that was the decisive factor.

An important principle embedded in international and regional human rights law is the concept of 'ongoing' or 'continuing violations', that is, that jurisdiction will not be declined even though the violation began before the State had become a party to the treaty because its effects continued to impact beyond that time.[95] The question arises whether the ArabCtHR will adopt this principle when it becomes operational. This concept has the potential to play a crucial role regarding the ongoing conflicts in Libya, Syria or Sudan (assuming the ArabCtHR has jurisdiction over these States).

3.2.4.4 Competence *Ratione Loci*

The principle of competence *ratione loci* (by reason of place) is also well-established in international and regional human rights law.[96] A violation must therefore have

---

[92] Vienna Convention on the Law of Treaties, opened for signature 22 May 1969, 1155 UNTS 331, entered into force 27 January 1980, art. 28 (VCLT).

[93] ACHR art. 62(1); ArabCtHR Statute art. 17. ECtHR 2024, Practical Guide, paras 316–346; ECtHR, App. No. 59532/00, *Blečić v. Croatia* [GC], Judgment, 8 March 2006, ECHR 2006-III, para 70; IACtHR, *González Medina and Family v. Dominican Republic*, Judgment, Preliminary objections, merits, reparations and costs, 27 February 2012, Series C No. 240, para 46; ACtHPR, *APDH v. Côte d'Ivoire*, above n. 84, para 68.

[94] ACtHPR, *Mkandawire v. Malawi*, above n. 83, para 32.

[95] ECtHR, App. No. 15318/89, *Loizidou v. Turkey* [GC], Judgment, 18 December 1996, ECHR 1996-VI, paras 46–47; IACtHR, *Blake v. Guatemala*, Preliminary Objections, 2 July 1996, Series C No. 27, paras 39–40; IACtHR, *Ticona Estrada* et al. *v. Bolivia*, Judgment, Merits, reparations and costs, 27 November 2008, Series C No. 191, paras 29–30; ACtHPR, App. No. 013/2011, *Zongo and Others v. Burkina Faso*, Preliminary Objections, 21 June 2013, para 73. See ECtHR 2024, Practical Guide, paras 331–334; Harris et al. 2023, pp. 100–102; Pasqualucci 2013, pp. 138–141.

[96] ECHR art. 1; ACHR art. 1(1). See ECtHR, *Loizidou v. Turkey*, above n. 95, paras 52–56. See ECtHR 2024, Practical Guide, paras 305–311; Harris et al. 2023, pp. 103–107; Pasqualucci 2013, pp. 146–149.

taken place within the respondent State's jurisdiction or in territory under its effective control.[97] The ECtHR has repeatedly stated that a State's jurisdictional competence is "primarily territorial",[98] although there may be exceptions in extraordinary circumstances for the application of extra-territorial jurisdiction, such as exercising "effective control" over the territory of another State.[99] The IACtHR has similarly adopted the position that extraterritorial application is exceptional.[100] The *ratione loci* concept is incorporated in Article 3(1) Arab Charter: State Parties undertake to ensure to all individuals subject to its jurisdiction the right to enjoy the rights and freedoms therein. It is not mentioned as such in the ArabCtHR Statute but seems implied in Article 19(1) as previously discussed. It does not, however, feature *per se* in the African instruments. The ACtHPR has to date simply satisfied itself, without too much reflection, that the violations took place in the respondent State's territory.[101]

3.3 Friendly Settlement

All the regional Courts have a part to play in the friendly or amicable settlement of cases, which must be compatible with respect for human rights and justice. Rule 64(5) ACtHPR Rules of Court provides explicitly that, in the interest of justice or to preserve public interest or order, it may decide to proceed with a case notwithstanding that an amicable settlement has been reached by the parties. While the ECtHR may place itself at the parties' disposal for an amicable resolution at any stage of the proceedings,[102] Rule 62 Rules of Court lessens the discretionary element as the Registrar must enter into contact with the parties to secure a friendly settlement once an application has been declared admissible, and the Chamber must take appropriate steps to facilitate it. Article 9 ACtHPR Protocol and Rule 64(1) Rules of Court are similar and confer a discretionary proactive role. Additionally, Rule 64(2) permits the parties at any stage of the proceedings to request the ACtHPR's involvement to settle their dispute. Article 22(1) ArabCtHR Statute is similar in that at any stage the Court can 'cooperate' with the parties to reach a settlement. Moreover, Article 22(4)

[97] See, e.g., ECtHR, *Ilaşcu v. Moldova and Russia*, above n. 3, paras 313–316; ECtHR, App. No. 38263/08, *Georgia v. Russia (II)* [GC], Judgment, 29 January 2021.

[98] See, e.g., ECtHR, *Ilaşcu v. Moldova and Russia*, above n. 3, para 312; ECtHR, App. No. 55721/07, *Al-Skeini and Others v. United Kingdom* [GC], Judgment, 7 July 2011, ECHR 2011-IV, paras 138–140.

[99] See, e.g., ECtHR, *Al-Skeini v. United Kingdom*, above n. 98, paras 132–137.

[100] IACtHR, *The Environment and Human Rights (States Obligations in Relation to the Environment in the Context of the Protection and Guarantee of the Rights to Life and to Personal Integrity: Interpretation and Scope of Articles 4(1) and 5(1) in Relation to Articles 1(1) and 2 of the American Convention on Human Rights)*, Advisory Opinion OC-23/17, 15 November 2017, Series A No. 23, para 81. One writer has therefore commented that, "The jurisprudence of human rights bodies has shifted away from territorial limits on the scope of human rights obligations", Cerone 2021, p 141

[101] See, e.g., ACtHPR, *APDH v. Côte d'Ivoire*, above n. 84, para 67.

[102] ECHR art. 39(1). See Harris et al. 2023, pp. 135–139.

states that an amicable settlement must be referred to the Assembly of States Parties to monitor its execution. Under its Rules of Procedure, the IACtHR must approve any friendly settlement; otherwise, it has no other involvement.[103]

3.4 Withdrawal

With the sole exception of the African Charter,[104] the other regional instruments make provision for withdrawal subject to notice and other procedural conditions. Article 58(1) ECHR allows denunciation subject to six months' notice.[105] The ACHR specifies twelve months,[106] whereas under the ArabCtHR Statute withdrawal becomes effective one year after written notice is given to the LAS Secretary-General.[107] But there exists another possible route to withdrawal, which is leaving the organisation in the context of which each of the regional systems operates. Article 18 LAS Charter specifies one year's notice. A Member State may withdraw from the CoE by notifying the Secretary General, such withdrawal taking effect at the end of the financial year in which it is notified.[108] However, according to Article 58(3) ECHR terminating membership results in ceasing to be a party to the ECHR "under the same conditions." This specification must be read in light of Article 58(2) ECHR, which provides that denunciation does not release a Party from its obligations before the denunciation became effective. It therefore seems that the six months' notice requirement, as well as other procedural conditions, extends to Article 7 CoE Statute.[109] This conclusion is supported by the IACtHR Opinion in the *Denunciation Case* that all

---

[103] Rules of Procedure art. 63. See generally Pasqualucci 2013, pp. 175–177.

[104] Nevertheless, notice would be required if a State wished to denounce the African Charter, African Commission, Communication No. 129/94, *Civil Liberties Organization v. Nigeria*, March 1995, para 12.

[105] On 15 March 2022, Russia informed the Secretary General of its withdrawal from the CoE in accordance with its Statute, Statute of the Council of Europe, opened for signature 5 May 1946, ETS No. 001, entered into force 3 August 1949, art. 7, and of its intention to denounce the ECHR. However, in keeping with the Statute art. 8, Russia ceased to be a member of the CoE as from 16 March 2022 and ceased to be a party to the ECHR as from 16 September 2022, Committee of Ministers Resolution CM/Res(2022)2 on the cessation of the membership of the Russian Federation to the Council of Europe, 16 March 2022, Committee of Ministers Resolution CM/Res(2022)3 on legal and financial consequences of the cessation of the membership of the Russian Federation in the Council of Europe, 23 March 2022, and Resolution of the European Court of Human Rights on the consequences of the cessation of membership of the Russian Federation to the Council of Europe in light of Article 58 of the European Convention on Human Rights, 22 March 2022. See (2023) 62 *International Legal Materials* 295.

[106] ACHR art. 78(1). For denunciations of the ACHR, see http://www.oas.org/dil/treaties_B-32_American_Convention_on_Human_Rights_sign.htm. Accessed 2 April 2025.

[107] ArabCtHR Statute art. 35. By contrast, the Arab Charter does not contain a withdrawal clause.

[108] CoE Statute art. 7.

[109] This follows from the CoE's reaction to Russia's invasion of Ukraine in February 2022, see above n. 105.

OAS Charter obligations remain unchanged during the transition period, including all human rights obligations.[110] Article 143 OAS Charter stipulates that withdrawal takes effect two years after the declaration.[111] However, withdrawal from the OAS does not automatically lead to the denunciation of other regional treaties; hence the IACtHR has stated that they remain in force and that OAS membership is not required for the continuity of these obligations.[112]

An alternative scenario is whether a State Party could withdraw its acceptance of the Court's compulsory jurisdiction and yet remain a party to the Convention in question. This is not possible under the ECHR and the ordinary meaning of Article 35 ArabCtHR Statute would suggest not. Indeed, as a general rule, international law requires withdrawal from the whole treaty rather than permitting the denunciation of specific provisions.[113] Accordingly, the IACtHR has held that, given the object and purpose of a human rights treaty, and the fact that the ACHR does not expressly permit States Parties to withdraw their declaration of recognition of its binding jurisdiction, a State Party may only release itself by renouncing the treaty as a whole.[114] However, the ACtHPR has taken a diametrically opposed position, presumably because the African Charter and the ACtHPR Protocol lack withdrawal clauses. In *Umuhoza v. Rwanda*, the ACtHPR had to determine its jurisdiction in light of the respondent's withdrawal of its declaration recognising the right of individual access.[115] Relying primarily on the principle of state sovereignty, with no attention paid to the special character of human rights treaties emphasised by other regional Courts,[116] the ACtHPR has ruled that the declarations are unilateral acts of States and therefore, unlike the Protocol itself, not subject to the VCLT and also optional in nature. Thus, the declarations are separable from the Protocol and may be withdrawn without denouncing it. However, Rwanda's discretion to withdraw was "not absolute", as it did not have immediate effect but was subject to a notice period of one year to provide legal certainty.[117] The trend in Africa is concerning because, of

---

[110] ACtHR, *Denunciation of the American Convention*, above n. 25, paras 149–152.

[111] Charter of the Organization of American States, opened for signature 30 April 1948, 119 UNTS 3, entered into force 13 December 1951. In November 2021 Nicaragua gave notice of its decision to withdraw from the OAS, https://www.oas.org/en/sla/dil/docs/A-41_letter_denounce_Nicaragua_11-19-2021.pdf. Accessed 2 April 2025.

[112] ACtHR, *Denunciation of the American Convention*, above n. 25, para 154.

[113] VCLT art. 44(1).

[114] See, e.g., *Constitutional Court v. Peru*, above n. 12, paras 38–39, 41–42, 49–50.

[115] ACtHPR, App. No. 003/2014, *Ingabire Victoire Umuhoza v. Rwanda*, Ruling on Jurisdiction, 3 June 2016, paras 54–59; ACtHPR, App. No. 016/2020, *Hossou and Adelakoun v. Benin*, Ruling, 2 December 2021, paras 29–33, 201 *International Law Reports* 89. See Enabulele 2018, pp. 234–239; Windridge 2018.

[116] See, e.g., IACtHR, *Ivcher Bronstein v. Peru*, Judgment (Competence), 24 September 1999, Series C No. 54, paras 42–49 and authorities cited therein; IACtHR, *Denunciation of the American Convention*, above n. 25, paras 48, 51–58.

[117] ACtHPR, *Ingabire Victoire Umuhoza v. Rwanda*, above n. 115, paras 61–66. The principle of good faith "requires a reasonable time for withdrawal from or termination of treaties that contain no provision regarding the duration of their validity", ICJ, *Military and Paramilitary Activities*

conventions and protocols,[132] some of which it has subsequently denounced.[133] In Africa, the AU Constitutive Act contains a withdrawal clause.[134] The majority of African human rights treaties, including the African Charter, but also the African Charter on the Rights of the Child,[135] and the Protocol on the Rights of Women,[136] are silent on the issue of withdrawal, but notice is still required for denunciation,[137] whereas the Protocol on Older Persons,[138] and the Protocol on Persons with Disabilities in Africa,[139] do have withdrawal clauses.

3.5 Conclusions

All the regional regimes share the same basic concepts on admissibility criteria relating to jurisdiction, such as incompatibility *ratione personae* or *ratione materiae*. The ECtHR and IACtHR jurisprudence on these conditions is extensive; that of the ACtHPR is not yet as developed. How the ArabCtHR will approach these issues remains to be seen but certain of the Statute's defects could be remedied by its Rules. Several jurisdictional issues of the ACtHPR have been ironed out in this manner. However, the Rules cannot realistically be expected to create a right of individual petition where none exists in the parent instrument. Of course, it is theoretically possible for the LAS to expand the ArabCtHR's mandate in an amended protocol.

The ECHR is the only instrument that allows individual access to the Court without preconditions, which brings with it associated problems in terms of numbers of applications.[140] At the other end of the spectrum, the ArabCtHR Statute's provisions on

---

[132] Ibid.

[133] Secretariat General of the Council of Europe (Treaty Office), Notification - JJ9589C Tr./157–54 - Russian Federation - Denunciation of the Framework Convention for the Protection of National Minorities (ETS No. 157) - 11 January 2024.

[134] AU Constitutive Act art. 31.

[135] African Charter on the Rights and Welfare of the Child, opened for signature 1 July 1990, (1989) 28 *International Legal Materials* 1456, entered into force 29 November 1999.

[136] Protocol to the African Charter on Human and Peoples' Rights on the Rights of Women, opened for signature 1 July 2003, 3269 UNTS, entered into force 25 November 2005.

[137] African Commission, *Civil Liberties Organization v. Nigeria*, above n. 104, para 12; ACtHPR, *Ingabire Victoire Umuhoza v. Rwanda*, above n. 115, paras 61–66.

[138] Protocol to the African Charter on Human and Peoples' Rights on the Rights of Older Persons in Africa, opened for signature 31 January 2016, art. 30.

[139] Protocol to the African Charter on Human and Peoples' Rights on the Rights of Persons with Disabilities in Africa, opened for signature 29 January 2018, art. 42.

[140] ECtHR 2024, Practical Guide, paras 2–3.

jurisdiction, particularly its restrictive *locus standi* terms, arguably render it fundamentally flawed and have attracted significant criticism.[141] Its leading failing unquestionably must be the lack of a right of individual petition. These faults, in addition to a lack of democratic values among the Statute's drafters, has therefore resulted in the ArabCtHR being described as having "weak legitimacy".[142]

References

Almutawa A (2021) The Arab Court of Human Rights and the Enforcement of the Arab Charter on Human Rights. Human Rights Law Review 21:506–532.

Cerone J (2021) The Abandonment of *Ratione Loci* in International Human Rights Jurisprudence. Boston University International Law Journal 39:109-142.

Coop G, Fietta V (2022) Other Inter-state Communication Procedures. In: Reilly R, Trout H (eds) Inter-State Complaints in International Human Rights Law. British Institute of International and Comparative Law, pp. 19-23. https://www.biicl.org/publications/inter-state-complaints-in-international-human-rights-law. Accessed 2 April 2025.

Dopplinger L (2021) Legal Persons as Bearers of Rights Under the ECHR. University of Vienna Law Review 5:1-46.

Enabulele A (2018) The problems of jurisdiction by optional declaration: reflections on Articles 5(3) and 34(6) of the Protocol of the African Court on Human and Peoples' Rights. Australian Journal of Human Rights 24:223-243.

European Court of Human Rights (ECtHR) (2024) Practical Guide on Admissibility Criteria, 31 August 2024. https://prd-echr.coe.int/web/echr/d/admissibility_guide_eng. Accessed 2 April 2025.

Harrington J (2002) The African Court on Human and Peoples' Rights. In: Evans M, Murray R (eds) The African Charter on Human and Peoples' Rights: The System in Practice, 1986–2000. Cambridge University Press, Cambridge, pp. 305–334.

Harris DJ, O'Boyle M, Bates EP, Buckley CM (2023) Harris, O'Boyle and Warbrick: Law of the European Convention on Human Rights, 5th edn. Oxford University Press, Oxford.

International Commission of Jurists (2015) The Arab Court of Human Rights: A Flawed Statute for an Ineffective Court. http://www.icj.org/arab-court-of-human-rights-comprehensive-amendments-required-before-ratification-new-report/. Accessed 2 April 2025.

International Law Commission (2000) First Report on Diplomatic Protection. UN Doc. A/CN.4/506.

Lixinski L (2021) The 'collective guarantee' of international human rights: Creating, reinforcing, and undoing legitimacies and mandates between law and politics. QIL, Zoom-in 80:5-19.

Magliveras K (2017) Completing the Institutional Mechanism of the Arab Human Rights System. International Human Rights Law Review 6:30-52.

Magliveras K, Naldi G (2016) The Arab Court of Human Rights: A Study in Impotence. Revue québécoise de droit international 29:147-172 [Quebec Journal of International Law].

Magliveras K, Naldi G (2023) The African Union: History, Institutions, and Activities. Kluwer Law International, Alphen aan den Rijn.

Makunya T (2021) Decisions of the African Court on Human and Peoples' Rights during 2020: Trends and Lessons. African Human Rights Law Journal 21:1230-1264.

[141] Magliveras and Naldi 2016; Sadri 2019; International Commission of Jurists 2015. Almutawa 2021 and Magliveras 2017 take a more optimistic view, arguing that despite its flaws the ArabCtHR can still play a positive role.

[142] Almutawa 2021.

Mbelle N (2008) The Role of Non-governmental Organisations and National Human Rights Institutions at the African Commission. In: Evans M, Murray R (eds) The African Charter on Human and Peoples' Rights: The System in Practice, 1986–2006, 2nd edn. Cambridge University Press, Cambridge, pp. 289-315.

Merrills J G, Robertson A H (2022) Human Rights in Europe, 4th edn, reprint. Manchester University Press, Manchester.

Naldi G, Magliveras K (2013) Human Rights, The Denunciation of Treaties and Withdrawal from International Organisations. Polish Yearbook of International Law 33:95-127.

Naskou-Perraki P (2009) The Arab Charter on Human Rights: A New Start for the Protection of Human Rights in the Arab World. Revue Hellénique de Droit International 62:117-136 [Hellenic Review of International Law].

Pasqualucci J M (2013) The Practice and Procedure of the Inter-American Court of Human Rights, 2nd edn. Cambridge University Press, Cambridge.

Quintana J J (1995) Los Procedimientos Incidentales ante la Corte Interamericana de Derechos Humanos Revista. [Interim Measures before the Inter-American Court of Human Rights] IIDH 21:121-148.

Rachovitsa A (2019) On New 'Judicial Animals': The Curious Case of an African Court with Material Jurisdiction of a Global Scope. Human Rights Law Review 19:255–289.

Rishmawi M (2005) The Revised Arab Charter on Human Rights: A Step Forward? Human Rights Law Review 5:361-376.

Risini I (2022) The European System. In: Reilly R, Trout H (eds) Inter-State Complaints in International Human Rights Law. British Institute of International and Comparative Law, pp. 15-18. https://www.biicl.org/publications/inter-state-complaints-in-international-human-rights-law. Accessed 2 April 2025.

Robertson A H, Merrills J G (1996) Human Rights in the World, 4th edn. Manchester University Press, Manchester.

Rodriguez Pinzón D (2001) The "Victim" Requirement, The Fourth Instance Formula and the Notion of "Person" in the Individual Complaint Procedure of the Inter-American Human Rights System. ILSA Journal of International& Comparative Law 7:369-383.

Sadri A (2019) The Arab human rights system: achievements and challenges. International Journal of Human Rights 23:1166-1182.

Viljoen F (2012) International Human Rights Law in Africa, 2nd edn. Oxford University Press, Oxford.

Windridge O (2018) Assessing Rwexit: the impact and implications of Rwanda's withdrawal of its article 34(6)-declaration before the African Court on Human and Peoples' Rights. African Human Rights Yearbook 2:243-258.

Chapter 4
Sources of Law

Lize R. Glas

Contents

4.1 Introduction 74
4.2 A Note on Legitimacy 75
4.3 The Principle of Effectiveness 76
4.4 The Principle of Subsidiarity 79
4.5 The Margin of Appreciation 81
4.6 Systemic Interpretation 83
4.7 Consensus 87
4.8 Evolutive Interpretation 88
4.9 Autonomous Interpretation 90
4.10 Conclusion 91
References 93

Abstract The wording of human rights treaty provisions can be characterised as vague. Consequently, interpretation is particularly important when applying human rights to actual cases. This chapter discusses seven interpretative techniques on which the regional Courts rely and compares how their operationalisation by these Courts enhances or diminishes their legitimacy. Legitimacy is defined here as diffuse support for a Court among the states parties to a regional human rights treaty. The chapter demonstrates that the Courts have much in common by relying on considerations of effectiveness and on an evolutive, autonomous and systemic interpretation. However, their approaches, particularly those of the ECtHR and the IACtHR, differ in important respects as well. Whereas domestic laws are an important source for the former when interpreting the ECHR, the IACtHR and the ACtHPR rely more heavily on international human rights law. Additionally, whereas the ECtHR leaves some room for the states parties to make their own decisions, the IACtHR's *pro persona* approach leads it to emphasise the responsibilities of states. These differences make it easier for the ECtHR to address legitimacy challenges compared to the IACtHR.

L. R. Glas (✉)
Radboud University, Nijmegen, The Netherlands
e-mail: lize.glas@ru.nl

A. Almutawa and K. D. Magliveras (eds.), *A Comparison of the European, Inter-American, African and Arab Human Rights Courts: Institutional Aspects*,
https://doi.org/10.1007/978-94-6265-695-6_4

Keywords Interpretation · Subsidiarity · Effectiveness · Margin of appreciation · Systemic interpretation · Consensus · Evolutive interpretation · Autonomous interpretation

4.1 Introduction

The regional human rights Courts are confronted with a myriad of difficult legal questions. Do embryos have the right to life prior to implantation through in-vitro fertilisation? Does the right to property include communal property of indigenous communities? Can persons be detained based on international humanitarian law (IHL) at variance with the human right to liberty? These questions must be answered through interpretation, because human rights treaties do not provide conclusive answers as to how they should be applied to 'real life'.[1] Although interpretation is key to virtually all legal texts, it is particularly important to these treaties, because they are 'often drafted in a distinctive, open-textured manner'.[2] Put more squarely, they are inherently 'vague'[3] and, moreover, their meaning evolves over time.[4] A discussion of interpretative techniques helps to clarify which sources of law are most important to the regional Courts.

This chapter describes, compares and comments on the methods and principles that these Courts use to interpret the treaty or treaties of which they are the guardian. The comments are based on the concept of legitimacy, as explained in Sect. 4.2. The chapter does not engage in a semantic discussion as to whether a certain interpretative technique is a method, a principle, or something else, and uses these terms interchangeably.[5]

Each of Sects. 4.3–4.9 addresses one interpretative technique: effectiveness, subsidiarity, the margin of appreciation (MoA),[6] systemic, consensus, evolutive and autonomous interpretation. This is not an exhaustive list of interpretative techniques,[7] although they are the ones most relevant to understanding these Courts' case law. Where possible, each section introduces the relevant interpretative technique with reference to the Vienna Convention on the Law of Treaties (VCLT),[8] as it applies

---

[1] Björgvinsson 2018, p. 235.

[2] Rachovista 2009, p. 558.

[3] Killander 2010, p. 145; Gardiner 2017, p. 474. See also Çalı 2020, p. 508.

[4] Section 4.8.

[5] For elaboration, see Senden 2011, pp. 44–46, 72.

[6] While MoA may be a standard of review, not an interpretative technique (Polgári 2021, p. 83), it was included here, because not only is it important to understand ECtHR case law but it is also closely connected to effectiveness and consensus and associated with legitimacy.

[7] E.g. Serghides 2017, pp. 4–6, 11–12.

[8] Vienna Convention on the Law of Treaties, opened for signature 23 May 1969, 1155 *UNTS* 331, entered into force 27 January 1980.

to human rights treaties[9] and has been invoked by the Courts themselves.[10] The operationalisation of these techniques has developed in their case-law over time. Therefore, only few insights can be given into how the ArabCtHR might interpret the Arab Charter on Human Rights (ArabChHR). Section 4.10 considers whether any general conclusions can be drawn about how the interpretative techniques increase or decrease the Courts' legitimacy.

4.2 A Note on Legitimacy

Relying on De Londras and Dzehtsiarou, legitimacy is here regarded as *perceived* legitimacy: the perceptions that stakeholders, e.g. the states parties, applicants, NGOs, the academic community and the public, hold of a regional court.[11] Perceived legitimacy is based on the stakeholders' 'conviction' that a Court adopts consistent rulings based on 'clear and transparent evidence', and respects its jurisdiction as well as the nature of the human rights treaty.[12] Maintaining such legitimacy necessitates 'diffuse support', which is support for the institution as such that persists through any discontent among (certain) stakeholders over a specific ruling.[13]

Diffuse support among the states parties stimulates them to comply with the rulings adopted against them.[14] Since states must execute the rulings, it is particularly important for the effective functioning of a regional system that they perceive the regional court as legitimate. This is also true, because they determine the future of the Courts in question, by establishing their budget and by potentially reforming their founding treaty and the international organisation of which they are part.[15] At the same time, particularly from the perspective of the states, the Courts start 'with a legitimacy deficit'.[16] In fact, the three functioning Courts have been confronted with serious legitimacy questions, to the extent that states have withdrawn from the jurisdiction of the IACtHR and have withdrawn their special declarations allowing individuals and NGOs to bring cases directly to the ACtHPR.[17] The states parties to the ECHR have not withdrawn from the jurisdiction of the ECtHR, but are anxious

[9] Gardiner 2017, p. 474.

[10] Christoffersen 2009, p. 37; Killander 2010, p. 145.

[11] Dzehtsiarou 2015, pp. 143, 145; Dzehtsiarou and De Londras 2018, p. 2 (writing on the ECtHR).

[12] Dzehtsiarou and De Londras 2018, p. 2.

[13] Ibid.

[14] Ibid; Dzehtsiarou and De Londras 2015, p. 526.

[15] Dzehtsiarou and De Londras 2015, p. 527.

[16] Dzehtsiarou and De Londras 2018, p. 2.

[17] See Plagis 2020a; Soley and Steininger 2018.

to ensure that it retains its subsidiary role.[18] The legitimacy deficit stems from three difficulties, which are outlined now.[19]

First, in a comparable manner to domestic courts, the regional Courts potentially review decisions made by democratically elected parliaments. This is the well-known counter-majoritarian difficulty. For this reason, the national executive, legislature and judiciary are in principle best placed to decide human rights questions as primary decision-makers.[20] Second, domestic authorities are also better placed to decide these questions, because they are more knowledgeable than the regional Courts of the particularities of the national situation in which the human rights treaties are implemented. I call this the knowledge-gap difficulty.[21] Third, the Courts adopt judgments that potentially impose (minimum) uniform standards across the states, whereas the individual states are diverse in terms of legal systems, policies and (cultural and religious) practices and are concerned about their sovereign right to make decisions as they deem fit. I call this the unifying-diversity difficulty.[22]

Since legitimacy as perceived by the states parties is particularly important for the Courts' effective functioning, and since they may lack such perceived legitimacy, this chapter reflects on how the methods of interpretation impact on the states' perceived legitimacy of the Courts. The way in which they interpret human rights treaties can clearly be a source of increased or decreased perceived legitimacy.[23] The relationship between legitimacy and interpretation is not a one-way street, however. Perceived legitimacy can also influence a Court's boldness.[24]

4.3 The Principle of Effectiveness

The effectiveness principle is not included in the VCLT as such. It is discussed first nevertheless, because it is an 'underlying principle' of the VCLT and intertwined with various other methods of interpretation,[25] including autonomous and evolutive interpretation.[26] Narrowly construed, effectiveness signifies interpretation in light of the *effet utile* or useful/appropriate effect of a norm[27] and is known under the

---

[18] Glas 2020, p. 125.

[19] Dzehtsiarou and De Londras 2018, p. 2. See also Dzehtsiarou 2015, p. 144. The second reason given here, is not as such given by Dzehtsiarou and De Londras 2018.

[20] Dzehtsiarou 2015, p. 144; Glas 2016, p. 110.

[21] Glas 2016, pp. 110–111.

[22] Ibid., p. 111. See also Dzehtsiarou 2015, p. 144. Dzehtsiarou emphasises 'a State's fierce protection of its sovereignty'; I emphasise diversity. Arguably, we both mean to emphasise that states want to make their *own* decisions.

[23] Dzehtsiarou and De Londras 2015, p. 528; Dzehtsiarou and De Londras 2018, pp. 2, 7.

[24] Dzehtsiarou and De Londras 2018, p. 2.

[25] Rietiker 2019.

[26] Rietiker 2010, p. 267; Çalı 2020, p. 512.

[27] Rietiker 2010, p. 256.

Latin maxim *ut res magis valeat quam pereat* ('to give effect to the matter rather than having it fail').[28] Thus construed, the principle dictates that, when different interpretations are possible, a treaty must be interpreted so as to realise its effectiveness.[29] An interpretation 'which gives a term some meaning rather than none'[30] is preferred therefore and a treaty cannot be interpreted so as to render parts of it redundant.[31] In a broader sense, the principle requires interpreting a treaty in the manner that contributes most to achieving its object and purpose.[32] This is in line with the VCLT, which dictates that a treaty must be interpreted 'in the light of its object and purpose'.[33] In international human rights law (IHRL), effectiveness is an 'overarching' principle of interpretation[34] and, in its broader meaning, favours the effective protection of human rights[35] as opposed to interpreting these rights restrictively.[36]

Although the object and purpose of the AChHPR is protecting and promoting the rights in the treaty,[37] the ACtHPR does not seem to have elaborated on the principle of effectiveness in connection with this object and purpose. Still, one can find manifestations of the principle in the AChHPR and the ACtHPR's case law. That the AChHPR does not require the exhaustion of domestic remedies which are obviously 'unduly prolonged' can be regarded as such a manifestation,[38] particularly because it has ruled that the remedies must 'meet the criteria of availability, *effectiveness* and sufficiency' (emphasis added).[39]

Since the object and purpose of the ECHR is the protection of individual human rights, the ECtHR interprets it 'so as to make its safeguards practical and effective',[40] rather than 'theoretical and illusory'.[41] With the effectiveness principle in mind, the

---

[28] Gardiner 2017, p. 179.

[29] Rietiker 2010, p. 256.

[30] Gardiner 2017, p. 179.

[31] WTO Appellate Body, *European Communities v Korea - Definitive Safeguard Measure on Imports of Certain Dairy Products*, Report, 14 December 1999, WT/DS98/AB/R, paras 80–81.

[32] Dissenting Opinion of Judge Read in ICJ, *Interpretation of Peace Treaties with Bulgaria, Hungary and Romania (Second Phase)*, Advisory Opinion, 18 July 1950, ICJ Reports 1950, pp. 231, 235–236.

[33] Article 31(1) VCLT.

[34] Çalı 2020, p. 512.

[35] Wewerinke 2015, p. 73; Çalı 2020, p. 512.

[36] Dilton 2016, p. 5; Rietiker 2019, p. 259.

[37] ACommHPR, *Hossam Ezzat & Rania Enayet (represented by Egyptian Initiative for Personal Rights & INTERIGHTS) v The Arab Republic of Egypt*, Decision, 25 February 2016, Communication 355/07, para 163; Amin 2021, p/ 210.

[38] Article 56(5) AChHPR in conjunction with Article 6(2) of the Protocol to the AChHPR on the Establishment of an ACtHPR.

[39] ACtHPR, *Tanganyika Law Society, The Legal and Human Rights Centre & Reverend Christopher R. Mtikila v Tanzania*, Judgment, 14 June 2013, App. Nos. 009/2011 & 011/2011, para 82.1.

[40] ECtHR, *Rantsev v Cyprus and Russia*, Judgment, 7 January 2010, App. No. 25965/04, para 275. See also ECtHR, *Saadi v The United Kingdom*, Judgment, 29 January 2008, App. No. 13229/03, para 62.

[41] ECtHR, *Scoppola v Italy (No. 2)*, Judgment, 17 September 2009, App. No. 10249/03, para 104.

ECtHR subjects respondent states to relatively strict scrutiny,[42] interpreting the rights expansively and their limitations narrowly, and looks behind appearances.[43] Consequently, an effective interpretation of the ECHR means an interpretation that favours the rightsholders[44] and has also led the ECtHR to impose positive obligations.[45] The exceptions that the ECtHR allows to the exhaustion of domestic remedies rule[46] are also manifestations of the principle.[47] Excessively lengthy remedies do not need to be exhausted for example.[48]

The object and purpose of the ACHR is 'the *effective* protection of the human person' (emphasis added).[49] Consequently, the IACtHR interprets it 'in favor of the individual'.[50] This approach is also based on Article 29 ACHR, which establishes standards of interpretation, and requires that it can neither be interpreted as restricting the exercise of rights laid down in domestic law or in another treaty to which a state is a contracting party, nor as limiting the effect of the American Declaration of the Rights and Duties of Man and comparable international acts.[51] This *pro persona* or 'most favourable'[52] interpretation governs the IACtHR's interpretation 'at all times',[53] extends to both substantive rights and procedural provisions,[54] and can be at the expense of (con)textual interpretation.[55] The influence of this approach on the procedural provisions can be exemplified by the following IACtHR dictum: 'the rule of prior exhaustion must never lead to a halt or delay that would render international action in support of the defenseless victim ineffective'.[56]

The principle of effectiveness in its broader sense underlies each regional human rights treaty, and presumably the ArabCHR as well, considering their similar object and purpose. The principle plays a more pronounced role in the Inter-American and the European systems than in the African system and has been particularly influential in the Americas in the form of *pro persona* interpretation. Since it is so closely connected to the object and purpose of the treaties, reliance by the Courts on the principle as such probably does not decrease their legitimacy: it is unlikely that states

---

[42] Glas 2016, p. 30.

[43] Serghides 2017, p. 3.

[44] Ibid.

[45] ECtHR, *Cossey v The United Kingdom*, Judgment, 29 August 1990, App. No. 10843/84, para 36.

[46] Article 35(1) ECHR.

[47] Glas 2016, pp. 30–31.

[48] ECtHR, *Mc Farlane v Ireland,* Judgment, 10 September 2010, App. No. 31333/06, para 123.

[49] IACtHR, *Murillo* et al. *v Costa Rica,* Judgment, 28 November 2012, Series C No. 257, para 173.

[50] IACtHR, *In the Matter of Viviana Gallardo* et al., Advisory Opinion, Series A, No. G 101/81, 13 November 1981, para 16. See also Lixinski 2010, p. 588.

[51] Ibid.

[52] Killander 2010, p. 147.

[53] Medina 2016, p. 52.

[54] Negishi 2017, p. 471.

[55] Çalı 2020, p. 510.

[56] IACtHR, *Velasquez-Rodriguez v Honduras,* Judgment, 26 June 1987, Series C No 1, para 93. See also Article 46(2) ACHR as noted by Pasqualucci 2003, p. 134.

parties will disagree with the need, *in abstracto*, to protect human rights effectively. It is only when this principle is combined with other interpretative techniques, such as evolutive interpretation, and leads to specific outcomes in individual cases, that it may raise questions of legitimacy, as will become clear when discussing these other techniques.

4.4 The Principle of Subsidiarity

The subsidiarity principle is a foundational principle of IHRL.[57] In its 'simplest form', it holds that this body of law is 'best implemented at the lowest level of government that can effectuate' it.[58] This is desirable due to the counter-majoritarian and knowledge-gap difficulties.[59] The principle has a procedural and substantive component.[60] The former concerns a regional Court's *competence* to review[61] and is reflected, for example, in the exhaustion of domestic remedies rule.[62] Substantive subsidiarity qualifies a Court's *intensity* of review[63] and includes the MoA.[64] Substantive subsidiarity is also reflected in the fourth-instance doctrine. This doctrine implies that a regional Court does not rule on errors of fact or law of domestic courts, unless such an error caused a human rights violation.[65]

Although not referring to the concept as such, the African and Arab systems are subsidiary in nature, for they both recognise the exhaustion of domestic remedies rule.[66] Moreover, the ACtHPR has relied on the MoA and the fourth-instance doctrine.[67] Additionally, the Statute of the ArabCtHR reads: 'The jurisdiction of the Court is complementary to the national judiciary and does not supplant it',[68] which can be regarded as a reference to the subsidiarity principle.[69]

Since 2021, the ECHR's preamble has stipulated that contracting parties, 'in accordance with the principle of subsidiarity, have the primary responsibility' to

[57] Carozza 2003, p. 38; Carter 2009, p. 319.

[58] Carter 2009, p. 319.

[59] Sect. 4.2.

[60] ECtHR, Background paper, 30 January 2015, para 7. https://www.echr.coe.int/documents/d/echr/seminar_background_paper_2015_eng. Accessed 10 March 2025.

[61] Bessons 2016, p. 78.

[62] Article 35(1) ECHR; Article 46(1)(a) ACHR; ArabChHPR Article 56(5); Article 18(a) ArabCtHR Statute as unofficially translated in International Commission of Jurists 2015, p. 39.

[63] Bessons 2016, p. 78.

[64] Section 4.5.

[65] Contesse 2019, p. 226.

[66] Above n. 62.

[67] Jonas 2020, p. 744.

[68] Article 18(a) ArabCtHR Statute as unofficially translated in International Commission of Jurists 2015, p. 39.

[69] Ghantous 2022, para 15.

secure the ECHR rights. This amendment originated in the Brighton Declaration (2012), adopted against the backdrop of discontent with the ECtHR's perceived lack of respect for the principle.[70] The discontentment arose even though the ECtHR has generally applied a strong version of subsidiarity since its start,[71] meaning that it strongly prefers decision-making by domestic authorities and that it only steps in for 'strong reasons in exceptional cases'.[72] Recently, the ECtHR seems to have expressed increased respect for the principle and its substantive and procedural components, likely a response to states' discontent.[73]

The preamble to the ACHR provides that the regional system 'reinforce[s] or complement[s] the protection' by domestic law. The IACtHR applies a weak version of subsidiarity nevertheless,[74] which has led some authors to conclude that it is actually reluctant 'to embrace subsidiarity'.[75] Although it prefers domestic decision-making, it will step in much more easily than its European counterpart: for 'any reason that makes [its action] appear advantageous, be it for the sake of efficiency, efficacy, or justice'.[76] Understanding the IACtHR's application of the subsidiarity principle thus helps explain why it relies on the principle as a rationale for conventionality control.[77] Conventionality control requires the domestic authorities to interpret domestic law in line with the IACtHR's interpretation of the ACHR.[78]

The state is the primary guarantor and the Court the subsidiary guarantor of human rights in each system.[79] However, whereas the IACtHR focuses on one side of the coin—the states' primary responsibility –, the ECtHR focuses on the other side—its own subsidiary role –, which results in a weak and a strong form of subsidiarity respectively. It is, therefore, perhaps better to use the terms primarity[80] or complementarity[81] rather than subsidiarity for the Inter-American system. This difference in emphasis has consequences for how both Courts interpret 'their' treaty, as becomes apparent when discussing the MoA in the next section. It also has consequences for

[70] Glas 2020, pp. 125, 127, 136. Discontent was prevalent in the UK and Denmark, see ibid., p. 125.

[71] Jachtenfuchs and Krisch 2016, p. 20.

[72] Ibid, p. 8. See also Carozza 2003, p. 44.

[73] Glas 2023, p. 82.

[74] Carozza 2003, p. 44; Contesse 2016, p. 145; Jachtenfuchs and Krisch 2016, p. 20.

[75] Contesse 2016, p. 138. See also Dulitzky 2015, p. 55; Kanetake 2016, p. 278; Lixinski 2017, pp. 88–89, 95.

[76] Jachtenfuchs and Krisch 2016, p. 8.

[77] IACtHR, *Santo Domingo Massacre v Colombia*, Judgment (Preliminary objections, merits and reparations), 30 November 2012, Series C No. 259, para 142.

[78] See Burgorgue-Larsen 2018a, para 2.

[79] Eventually, certain states will come under the jurisdiction of both the ACtHPR and the ArabCtHR. For the time being, this remains a theoretical possibility, given that only one (non-African) state (i.e. Saudi Arabia) has ratified the ArabCtHR Statute, whereas seven ratifications are required for its entry into force (Article 33 ArabCtHR Statute; Almutawa 2021, p. 507). Presently, only one of the states that has accepted the ACtHPR jurisdiction is also a member of the League of Arab States, Tunisia; see https://www.african-court.org/wpafc/declarations/ Accessed 5 March 2025.

[80] Christoffersen 2009, p. 360.

[81] See also the preamble to the ACHR.

what each regional Court expects of domestic courts: whereas the IACtHR requires conventionality control, the ECtHR does not require domestic courts to 'interpret legislation in a Convention-compliant way',[82] not even when domestic law requires them to consider potential ECHR violations 'of their own motion'.[83] Due to the ECtHR's focus, the subsidiarity principle and its components can be a source of legitimacy in the European system; they lead to *reining in the ECtHR* and giving room to the states parties to take their own decisions. This effect should not be overstated, considering that the states parties have still questioned the ECtHR's legitimacy. However, their protests probably would have been more intense had the ECtHR not applied strong subsidiarity. By contrast, the IACtHR's focus on the states' primary responsibility can decrease its legitimacy in the eyes of the states, because it emphasises what *the states must do*, despite the difficulties recounted in Sect. 4.2. Conventionality control, for example, can be regarded as problematic because of the counter-majoritarian difficulty.[84]

4.5 The Margin of Appreciation

The different systems have been discussed in alphabetical order so far. This section starts with the ECHR system however, because it is where the MoA originated.[85] The ECtHR has used the doctrine in relation to an increasing number of rights[86] and mentions the doctrine increasingly often since its first mention in 1958.[87] In 2021, a reference to the doctrine was even added to the ECHR's preamble.[88] The MoA enables the ECtHR to afford the states a varying degree of discretion when implementing the ECHR. A broad MoA gives a state much leeway to, for example, decide how to restrict a right. Consequently, the ECtHR shows deference, normally only establishing whether the state made a manifestly unreasonable decision. When the MoA is narrow, the ECtHR scrutinises the decisions of the respondent state more intensely.[89] In addition to a broad and a narrow MoA, the ECtHR may grant the state a (not so clear) 'certain' MoA[90] or show full deference.[91]

---

[82] ECtHR, *Peacock v The United Kingdom*, Decision, 5 January 2016, App. No. 52335/12, para 39.

[83] ECtHR, *Gouda Sallam v The Netherlands*, Decision, 11 December 2012, App. No. 20328/08, para 15.

[84] Engstrom 2017, p. 1266.

[85] Yourow 1996, p. 15, referring to a report of the European Commission of Human Rights in *Greece v The United Kingdom*, Report, 26 September 1958, App. No. 176/56 ('Application of the Convention for the Protection of Human Rights and Fundamental Freedoms to the Island of Cyprus'), p. 138.

[86] Gerards 2018, pp. 500–501.

[87] Madsen 2018, pp. 199, 206, 220.

[88] See Protocol 15 ECHR.

[89] Gerards 2023, pp. 248, 249–250.

[90] ECtHR, *Stoll v Switzerland*, Judgment, 10 December 2007, App. No. 69698/01, para 107.

[91] Arnardóttir 2016, p. 50.

The MoA's scope depends on a number of factors. A broad MoA applies, for example, when the states do not agree on the relative importance of the interest at stake and when the domestic authorities are best placed to decide on a human rights question, which normally applies when a case concerns moral, ethical, socioeconomic or health issues.[92]

Although the ECtHR itself has not theorised elaborately about the doctrine,[93] it has relied on the subsidiarity principle and on the knowledge-gap difficulty[94] to justify its recourse to the doctrine.[95] For scholars reflecting on the doctrine, handling the unifying-diversity difficulty[96] seems to be the most important legitimation of the doctrine.[97] Considering these possible justifications for the doctrine, it clearly has legitimacy-enhancing potential (especially when a broad MoA applies).

The ACommHPR endorses the MoA as developed by the ECtHR.[98] The ACtHPR agrees with the ACommHPR's legitimation of the doctrine, which is the knowledge-gap difficulty.[99] Still, the ACtHPR is hesitant to show deference.[100] It has referred to two factors that the ECtHR also relies on to determine the MoA's scope: the nature of the aim of the restriction and of the right involved.[101] More specifically, the ACtHPR has granted states a MoA when making choices pertaining to the design of their criminal justice systems.[102]

The IACtHR's standard of review has evolved and can be qualified as 'non-deferential' currently.[103] Consequently, it rejects the MoA.[104] This stance can be explained with reference to the context in which it functions of (especially in the past) the gross human rights violations, relatively weak democracies and (related to that) not so independent and well-functioning domestic judiciaries.[105] Its rejection of the MoA can also be read into the doctrine of conventionality control, which can be

[92] Gerards 2023, pp. 256–272.

[93] Legg 2021, p. 15.

[94] Section 4.2.

[95] ECtHR, *Handyside v The United Kingdom*, Judgment, 7 December 1976, App. No. 5493/72, para 48.

[96] Section 4.2.

[97] E.g. Arnardóttir 2016, p. 40; Legg 2021, p. 38; Gerards 2023, p. 243.

[98] Killander 2010, p. 152.

[99] ACtHPR, *Jebra Kambole v Tanzania*, Judgment, 15 July 2020, App. No. 018/2018, para 80.

[100] Rachovitsa 2020, para 33.

[101] ACtHPR, *Legal & Human Rights Centre and Tanzanian Human Rights Defenders Coalition v Tanzania*, Judgment, 13 June 2023, App. No. 039/2020, para 149.

[102] ACtHPR, *Benedicto Daniel Mallya v Tanzania,* Judgment, 26 September 2019, App. No. 018/2015, para 61.

[103] Ibid., paras 4–5. See for previous approaches, including references to the MoA, ibid., paras 7–49.

[104] Contesse 2016, p. 124; Contesse 2019, p. 227; Falcón 2022, paras 50, 77.

[105] Contreras 2012, p. 29; Dulitzky 2015, p. 51; Contesse 2016, p. 145; Pascual-Vives 2019, p. 181; Falcón 2022, para 80. Cf McGoldrick 2014, pp. 359–362.

regarded as the opposite of the MoA because it leaves no discretion to the domestic authorities.[106]

Considering the findings regarding subsidiarity in Sect. 4.4, it is not surprising that the ECtHR has developed and embraced the MoA, whereas the IACtHR has not. The IACtHR refers to the doctrine, but does not necessarily exercise restraint. For the ECtHR, the MoA is a tool that contributes to enhancing its legitimacy as perceived by the contracting parties. Affording a broad MoA, leads to respect for diversity between the states and leaves room for the domestic authorities to take decisions based on their knowledge and democratic processes. The difference between the European and the Inter-American Courts can largely be explained by the different contexts in which they function (or used to function).[107] Consequently, the IACtHR may have less trust in the national authorities than the ECtHR,[108] which translates into granting them less leeway than the latter.[109] Still, some authors have argued that the IACtHR should also adopt a doctrine of deference.[110] They have made their call in response to allegedly too far-reaching case law and against the background of backlash against the IACtHR and even withdrawals from the system.[111] In 2019, five states (Argentina, Brazil, Chile, Colombia, and Paraguay) asked the IACtHR to show more deference to no avail.[112] In the African system, Tanzania has also requested more deference.[113] The ECtHR's MoA can function as a source of inspiration in case the other Courts want to respond to the critical states; in Europe, the doctrine is the flagship of critical states.[114]

4.6 Systemic Interpretation

Article 31(3)(c) VCLT stipulates that 'any relevant rules of international law applicable in the relations between the parties' must be considered when interpreting a treaty. This rule requires interpretation by reference to the 'normative environment' of international legal obligations,[115] which includes treaties, custom and potentially soft law.[116] When confronted with opposing rules, a court must first determine whether they can be interpreted harmoniously and, if not, which rule trumps the other.[117]

---

[106] Barreiros 2014.

[107] See also Sect. 4.10.

[108] But see McGoldrick 2014, pp. 344–345.

[109] Kanetake 2016, p. 278.

[110] Contreras 2012, pp. 63–64; McGoldrick 2014, pp. 344–345, 353; Contesse 2019, p. 227.

[111] See generally Soley and Steininger 2018.

[112] Steininger 2022.

[113] Rachovista 2020, para 35.

[114] E.g. Brighton Declaration (2012), para 12(a).

[115] International Law Commission 2006, para 413.

[116] Peters 2017, p. 693.

[117] International Law Commission 2006, paras 36, 220.

The jurisdiction of the ACtHPR extends 'to all cases and disputes submitted to it concerning the interpretation and application of the Charter, this Protocol and any other relevant Human Rights instrument ratified by the States concerned'.[118] This provision goes beyond the use of other treaties as a source of inspiration; it requires the ACtHPR to interpret these treaties and to find violations of them, as it has done with, the ICCPR, for example.[119] This broad jurisdiction 'may lead to divergence in jurisprudence and to forum shopping, where quasi- judicial and judicial institutions are compared and played off against one another'.[120] The ACtHPR has even gone beyond the text of the relevant provision by finding a violation of the UDHR, even though the latter cannot be ratified because it is a non-binding declaration.[121] However, it has refused to find violations of the ACHR and the ECHR—treaties that an African state cannot ratify because of their limited geographical scope.[122] The ACtHPR is also instructed to apply as sources of law 'the provisions of the Charter and any other relevant human rights instrument ratified by the States concerned'.[123] This provision 'seems to dramatically and unnecessarily limit the sources of law' that the ACtHPR can use in interpreting the AChHPR, since it refer to *treaties ratified* by the states parties.[124] However, the ACtHPR has not felt constrained by this provision by invoking two other provisions. Articles 60 and 61 AChHPR require the ACommHPR to 'draw inspiration from' IHRL and to rely as a subsidiary means of interpretation on 'other general or special international conventions, laying down rules expressly recognized by' the OAU member states. Although addressed to the ACommHPR, the ACtHPR relies on this instruction when invoking, for example, a UN HRC general comment,[125] albeit rarely expressly.[126] As these instructions suggest, the ACtHPR relies heavily on IHRL, including (regional) human rights treaties and rulings of UN bodies and other regional Courts.[127] In response, some scholars have raised the question whether its heavy reliance on, in particular, its European and Inter-American counterparts is 'disproportionate', because it restricts the development of an African body of case law.[128]

---

118 Article 3(1) Protocol to the AChHPR on the Establishment of an ACtHPR.

119 E.g. ACtHPR, *Anudo Ochieng Anudo v Tanzania*, Judgment, 22 March 2018, App. No. 012/2015, para 106.

120 Viljoen 2012, p. 354. See also Heyns 2001, p. 167.

121 E.g. ACtHPR, *Anudo v Tanzania*, App. No. 012/2015, above note 119, para 88.

122 Murray 2019, p. 824.

123 Article 7 Protocol to the AChHPR on the Establishment of an ACtHPR.

124 Heyns 2001, p. 169.

125 ACtHPR, *Tanganyika Law Society, The Legal and Human Rights Centre v Tanzania*, above n. 39, para 107.3.

126 Rachovista 2016, p. 77.

127 Brems 2017, p. 9; Burgorgue-Larsen 2018b, pp. 194–195; Rachovista 2016, pp. 77, 82; Rachovista 2019, p. 278; Plagis 2020b.

128 Rachovista 2019, p. 284.

The ArabCHR aims 'to entrench the principle that all human rights are universal, indivisible, interdependent and interrelated'.[129] Its Preamble reaffirms the principles of the UN Charter, the UDHR, the ICCPR and the ICESCR. Additionally, Article 43 ArabCHR provides that it may not be interpreted as impairing the rights protected by domestic laws as well as by international and regional human rights instruments ratified by states parties, including the rights of women, children and minorities. Despite this universalistic outlook,[130] the formulations of the rights tell a different story: one of inconsistencies with IHRL.[131] Article 7(1) ArabCHR, for example, does not prohibit the imposition of the death penalty on children when provided for in domestic law, whereas Article 37(a) of the Convention on the Rights of the Child (CRC) prohibits it.[132] Mattar has argued, based on Article 43 ArabCHR, that the ArabCtHR must interpret such provisions in line with IHRL, taking into consideration any reservations that the contracting state has made to the relevant treaty.[133]

In line with Article 31(3)(c) VCLT,[134] the ECtHR does not interpret the ECHR 'in a vacuum', but rather 'in a spirit of systemic harmonisation', using external documents as a source of inspiration,[135] including rulings of the Inter-American and (to a lesser extent) the African institutions.[136] The ECtHR also relies on treaties that the respondent state has not ratified and soft law, although it attaches more weight to hard law and finds external sources particularly authoritative if most states have accepted them.[137] It may also go further than relying on external sources for inspiration, for example, by harmonising the ECHR with IHL to the extent that it prioritises the latter over the former[138] and turning the CRC into a formal source of law.[139]

Comparable to the ACtHPR, the jurisdiction of the IACtHR extends beyond the ACHR in case a state ratified any of the specialised Inter-American human rights

[129] Article 1(4) ArabCtHR as translated by the UN, at https://digitallibrary.un.org/record/551368?v=pdf. Accessed 5 March 2025.

[130] Almutawa 2021, p. 509.

[131] Rishmawi 2010, p. 170; Sadri 2019, p. 1172.

[132] Rishmawi 2010, p. 171. Convention on the Rights of the Child, opened for signature 20 November 1989, entered into force 2 September 1990, 3 *UNTS* 1577.

[133] Mattar 2013, pp. 106–108, 126–127. Except for Malaysia's reservation regarding the whole of article 37, which declared that 'the said provisions shall be applicable only if they are in conformity with the Constitution, national laws and national policies', there are no reservations under Article 37(a) CRC, see https://treaties.un.org/Pages/ViewDetails.aspx?src=TREATY&mtdsg_no=IV-11&chapter=4&clang=_en#EndDec. Accessed 5 March 2025.

[134] ECtHR, *Demir and Baykara v Turkey*, Judgment, 12 November 2008, App. No. 34503/97, para 67.

[135] ECtHR, *Al-Dulimi and Montana Management Inc. v Switzerland*, Judgment, 21 June 2016, App. No. 5809/08, para 134.

[136] Papaioannou 2014, p. 1046.

[137] Gerards 2023, p. 163; Nilsson 2023, p. 259.

[138] Rachovista 2009, p. 577; Peters 2017, p. 693, citing as an example ECtHR, *Hassan v The United Kingdom*, Judgment, 16 September 2014, App. No. 29750/09.

[139] Ibid., p. 572. See also Burgorgue-Larsen 2018b, pp. 199–200.

treaties, such as, the Inter-American Convention to Prevent and Punish Torture or the Inter-American Convention on Forced Disappearance of Persons.[140] When it comes to the interpretation of these treaties, the IACtHR takes a 'universalistic' approach, relying on the entire *corpus juris* of (soft) IHRL.[141] This approach is based Article 31(3) VCLT[142] and Article 29(b) ACHR,[143] which provides that the ACHR shall not be interpreted as restricting rights recognised in domestic law or in a treaty acceded to by a state party. This provision forbids the IACtHR to interpret the ACHR rights restrictively.[144] Put differently, when the ACHR and another (international or domestic) norm apply, 'the rule most favorable to the individual must prevail'.[145] Consequently, the IACtHR has extensively relied on UN and regional instruments and decisions,[146] including the ECtHR's judgments.[147] In a comparable manner to the ECtHR, the IACtHR has integrated requirements from other treaties, such as the CRC, into the ACHR.[148] Additionally, it has converted 'global soft law into regional hard law'.[149]

The three functioning regional Courts pay due respect to Article 31(3)(c) VCLT and even go beyond the letter of that provision by relying on instruments that are not binding (on the respondent state) and on judgments of their counterparts. Thus, they broaden the scope and contribute to the systemic integration of IHRL and keep IHRL relevant in ever changing circumstances.[150] The ECtHR stands out, because it has relied on external sources that express concerns other than fundamental rights, leading to less protection than would the ECHR when not relying on these external sources. This could enhance the ECtHR's legitimacy, because it leaves room for the states (and their parliaments) to abide by other international obligations. The IACtHR, in contrast, largely disregards such other obligations, unless they conform to the ACHR.[151] However, reliance on instruments that are not binding (on the respondent state) could be regarded as lacking legitimacy, due to the counter-majoritarian difficulty: the states (and their parliaments) did not consent to be bound by these

---

[140] Either the treaty (except the Inter-American Convention on the Elimination of all Forms of Discrimination Against Persons with Disabilities) 'provide[s] for an individual complaint procedure before the Commission and ultimately before the Court' or the IACtHR has ruled that it has jurisdiction, see Rodríguez-Pinzón and Martin 2006, p. 37.

[141] Killander 2010, p. 163.

[142] IACtHR, *Murillo* et al. *v Costa Rica,* above n. 49, para 191.

[143] Neuman 2017, p. 88; Burgorgue-Larsen 2018b, p. 193. Cf Rachovista 2016, p. 91.

[144] IACtHR, '*Mapiripán Massacre' v Colombia,* Judgment, 15 September 2005, Series C No. 134, para 188.

[145] IACtHR, *Juridical Condition and Rights of Undocumented Migrants,* Advisory Opinion OC-18/03, 17 September 2003, para 156.

[146] Pasqualucci 2003, p. 13; Killander 2010, p. 163.

[147] Neuman 2008, p. 109.

[148] Rachovista 2009, p. 570.

[149] Neuman 2008, p. 111.

[150] See also Lixinski 2010, p. 603; Burgorgue-Larsen 2018b, p. 188; Nilsson 2023, p. 259.

[151] Rachovista 2009, p. 578.

instruments.[152] The ACtHPR's practice of finding violations of the ICCPR in respect of states that did not ratify the first Optional Protocol, may also undermine its legitimacy because it disregards the decision of states not to ratify a treaty and sidelines parliaments and the role they may play in a ratification process.

4.7 Consensus

Consensus interpretation mainly surfaces in the ECtHR's case law. Dzehtsiarou has usefully identified four types of consensus in its case law. The first is European or regional consensus, which emerges from domestic laws[153] and reflects the 'wealth of differences in historical development, cultural diversity, political thought and, consequently, democratic vision' in Europe.[154] Interpretation based on regional consensus finds support in Article 31(3) VCLT,[155] which requires considering 'subsequent agreement between the parties', 'subsequent practice' and, as was noted in Sect. 4.6, 'relevant rules of international law applicable' between the parties. Second, and as Sect. 4.6 also explained, the ECtHR can rely on international consensus: IHRL and decisions of international Courts and other interpretative bodies based thereon. The third type of consensus is the opinion of the people in the respondent state[156] but the ECtHR does not rely on it often. Lastly, the ECtHR relies on consensus among experts to account for scientific developments.[157]

In the ECtHR's case law, consensus is either a factor determining the width of the MoA, as was explained in Sect. 4.5, or a method of interpretation.[158] In the latter function, the finding that consensus exists can lead the ECtHR to adopt a new definition of a right, thus widening its scope and at the same time updating the ECHR.[159] This method of interpretation is often associated with evolutive interpretation.[160]

As Sect. 4.6 clarified, the ACtHPR and the IACtHPR rely on the second type of consensus distinguished above. The IACtHR's reliance on regional consensus is 'negligible' however,[161] and such consensus is never its only interpretative tool.[162]

---

[152] Burgorgue-Larsen 2018b, p. 188; Rachovista 2009, p. 583. Cf Peters 2017, p. 693.

[153] Dzehtsiarou 2015, p. 40.

[154] ECtHR, *Animal Defenders International v The United Kingdom*, Judgment, 22 April 2013, App. No. 48876/08, para 123.

[155] Lixinski 2017, p. 74; Polgári 2021, p. 93; Gerards 2023, p. 159.

[156] E.g. ECtHR, *Marckx v Belgium*, Judgment, 13 June 1979, App. No. 6833/74, para 41, referring to 'attitudes'.

[157] Dzehtsiarou 2015, pp. 45, 49, 55.

[158] Senden 2011, p. 226.

[159] See also Sect. 4.9.

[160] Gerards 2023, pp. 109–110, 159. See Sect. 4.8.

[161] Killander 2010, p. 151. See also Neuman 2008, p. 107; Lixinski 2017, p. 68; Burgorgue-Larsen 2018b, p. 190.

[162] Lixinski 2017, p. 68.

The IACtHR even expressly rejected relying on a lack of regional consensus 'regarding full respect for the rights of sexual minorities', adding that it 'must refer solely and exclusively to the stipulations of the international obligations arising from a sovereign decision by the States to adhere to the' ACHR.[163] Its lack of enthusiasm is in part because this method does not always lead to a *pro persona* interpretation.[164] Additionally, 'the comparative prevalence of systematic human rights abuses directed against the core of the protected rights' in the Americas may be part of the explanation, since relying on regional consensus could lead to limited protection.[165]

As noted above, consensus and in particular regional consensus is principally a tool used by the ECtHR. When recalling that it is also mainly this Court that uses the MoA and that consensus is a factor establishing the MoA,[166] this finding was to be expected. However, consensus in its other function, as a method of interpretation, is also primarily used by the ECtHR. The IACtHR's reluctance to use this method might also be expected based on the discussion in Sect. 4.6, which described the IACtHR's universalistic outlook. Moreover, it may be interpreted as it being 'in a position largely out of sync with Member States'.[167] Reliance on regional consensus is a means for the ECtHR to enhance its legitimacy,[168] because diverse practices in the states can be a reason either not to broaden the scope of a right or to leave a MoA to the respondent state and thus to address the unifying-diversity difficulty. Additionally, by relying on regional consensus as expressed in domestic laws, the ECtHR bases itself on the laws that democratically elected majorities adopted, thus addressing the counter-majoritarian difficulty.

4.8 Evolutive Interpretation

The synonyms evolutive interpretation, dynamic interpretation or living instrument doctrine[169] denote that treaty terms do not have a static meaning.[170] Instead, the human rights Courts update the meaning of these terms in response to societal and technical developments that that the drafters could not have foreseen.[171] Consequently, these Courts are increasingly firm in addressing human rights violations.[172]

---

[163] IACtHR, *Atala Riffo and Daughters v Chile*, Judgment (Merits, Reparations and Costs), 24 February 2012, *Series* C No. 239, para 92. See IACtHR, *Murillo* et al. *v Costa Rica,* above n. 49, paras 170, 316.

[164] Lixinski 2017, p. 68.

[165] Neuman 2008, p. 107. See also McGoldrick 2014, p. 354.

[166] Section 4.5.

[167] Lixinski 2017, p. 70. See also Neuman 2008, p. 123.

[168] See also Dzehtsiarou 2015, pp. 175–176; Ziemele 2018, p. 24.

[169] Helmersen 2013, p. 128 especially footnote 1.

[170] Gardiner 2017, p. 467.

[171] Pascual-Vives 2019, p. 92.

[172] ECtHR, *Selmouni v France*, Judgment, 28 July 1999, App. No. 25803/94, para 101.

Although not mentioned by the VCLT as such,[173] its 'proper application' results in evolutive interpretation,[174] since *inter alia* the principles of good faith and effectiveness and the need to take the context, object and purpose of a treaty into account necessitate evolutive interpretation.[175]

Human rights treaties are, according to the IACtHR, 'live instruments whose interpretation must adjust to the changing times and, specifically, to current living conditions'.[176] Its application of evolutive interpretation can be characterised as 'generous'[177] and can be justified with reference to Article 29 ACHR.[178] Thanks to this method of interpretation, IHRL has 'made great headway' according to the IACtHR.[179] This method goes hand in hand with the *pro persona* approach[180] and is based on specialised OAS human rights treaties adopted after the ACHR and on external sources.[181]

Although neither the ACtHPR, nor the ACommHPR have expressly invoked the concept of evolutive interpretation,[182] some of their rulings are nevertheless evolutive in nature.[183] This approach can be grounded in Articles 60 and 61 AChHPR, as described in Sect. 4.6.[184]

It is 'crucial' for the ECtHR to interpret the ECHR in line with the effectiveness principle,[185] since it is a 'living instrument'.[186] The aspects of private life protected by Article 8 ECHR have, for example, come to include sexual life,[187] while acts classified as 'inhuman and degrading treatment' have become 'torture' under Article 3 ECHR.[188] If necessary to adapt the ECHR to new circumstances, the ECtHR is prepared to overrule previous judgments.[189] Additionally, it has broadened the scope of protection to include rights that the contracting parties have decided to exclude

---

[173] Pascual-Vives 2019, p. 92.

[174] Gardiner 2017, p. 467. See also Helmersen 2013, pp. 166–167; IACtHR, *The Right to Information on Consular Assistance in the Framework of the Guarantees of the Due Process of Law,* Advisory Opinion OC-16/99, 1 October 1999, para 114.

[175] Gardiner 2017, p. 473; Pascual-Vives 2019, p. 79; IACtHR, *Indigenous Communities of the Lkaka Honat (Our Land) Association v Argentina*, Judgment (Merits, reparations and costs), 6 February 2020, Series C No. 420, para 197.

[176] IACtHR, *Mayagna (Sumo) Awas Tingni Community v Nicaragua*, Judgment Merits, reparations and costs), 31 August 2001, Series C No. 79, para 146.

[177] Neuman 2008, p. 114.

[178] Hennebel and Tigroudja 2022, p. 837.

[179] IACtHR, Advisory Opinion OC-16/99, above n. 174, para 114.

[180] Lixinski 2010, pp. 588–589. See also Sect. 4.3.

[181] Neuman 2008, p. 108.

[182] Killander 2010, p. 150 (writing about the ACommHPR).

[183] Çalı et al. 2018, p. 113; Matusse 2020, p. 77.

[184] Heyns 2001, p. 157.

[185] ECtHR, *Scoppola v Italy (No. 2)*, above n. 41, para 104.

[186] ECtHR, *Bayatyan v Armenia*, Judgment, 7 July 2011, App. No. 23459/03, para 102.

[187] ECtHR, *X. and Y. v The Netherlands*, Judgment, 26 March 1985, App. No. 8978/80, para 22.

[188] ECtHR, *Selmouni v France*, above n. 2, para 101.

[189] Dzehtsiarou 2011, p. 1731.

from protection.[190] Regional and international consensus may be a reason either to interpret the ECHR in an evolutive manner or a reason not to do so.[191]

Evolutive interpretation has been relied upon in all systems but plays the most prominent role in the European and the Inter-American systems. Although the goal served by evolutive interpretation is the same—effective protection of human rights—the underlying source is mainly regional consensus in the European system and mainly international consensus in the Inter-American system. Thus, the ECtHR is less prone to legitimacy challenges when using evolutive interpretation than the IACtHR, because it bases itself on domestic laws adopted by parliaments. Still, the states parties may criticise the ECtHR for protecting rights that the contracting parties have deliberately excluded.

4.9 Autonomous Interpretation

The autonomous meaning of a term denotes a meaning 'independent of what [it] may mean in another context', such as, domestic law.[192] It can be regarded as a manifestation of the textual approach. It is, therefore, different from the interpretation based on Article 31(4) VCLT, which provides that a 'special meaning shall be given to a term if it is established that the parties so intended'.[193] Additionally, interpretation in the light of the object and purpose of a treaty, which includes the effective protection of human rights laid down in regional human rights treaties,[194] can form a basis for autonomous interpretation. The opposite of autonomous interpretation, i.e. when states define treaty terms at will, would undermine a treaty's effectiveness.[195]

Since the terms of the ACHR have an autonomous meaning,[196] the IACtHR normally refers to international instruments.[197] The meaning of the term 'property', for example, goes beyond what domestic law defines as 'property', namely 'both the private property of individuals and communal property of the members of the indigenous communities'.[198] The ACtHPR does not seem to have elaborated on the concept of autonomous interpretation.[199]

[190] Letsas 2010, p. 518. E.g. the right not to be compelled to join an association under Article 11 ECHR, see ibid., pp. 518–519.

[191] ECtHR, *Demir and Baykara v Turkey*, above n. 4, para 85; Dzehtsiarou 2011, p. 1731.

[192] Gardiner 2017, p. 336.

[193] Ibid. Cf Senden 2011, p. 78; Killander 2010, p. 148.

[194] See Sect. 4.3.

[195] Killander 2010, p. 148; Gardiner 2017, p. 335; Rietiker 2019, p. 271.

[196] IACtHR, *The Word 'Laws' in Article 30 of the American Convention on Human Rights,* Advisory Opinion OC-6/86, 9 May 1986, para 19.

[197] Killander 2010, p. 148.

[198] IACtHR, *Yakye Axa Indigenous Community v. Paraguay*, Judgment, 17 June 2005, Series C No. 125, para 143.

[199] Searching https://africanlii.org with the keyword 'autonomous' did not result in any relevant cases.

Certain ECHR terms, such as ‘criminal charge’ and ‘home’, have an autonomous meaning so states cannot freely define them in a way that is incompatible with its object and purpose.[200] Autonomous interpretation also helps the ECtHR to ensure ‘uniformity of treatment’ despite national differences.[201] Domestic law definitions are of some relevance nevertheless, because their ‘common denominator’[202] is the ‘starting point’[203] for defining the ECHR terms. The interpretations of certain terms by international bodies can also be a source of inspiration.[204] The ECtHR does not engage in autonomous interpretation when the domestic-law definition of a term provides more protection than the ECHR, when the ECHR refers to domestic law[205] and, exceptionally, when there is a lack of consensus on a term.[206]

All three regional human rights Courts rely on autonomous interpretation, although the ACtHPR not expressly. When comparing the Inter-American and the European approach, it again becomes apparent that international instruments play a more important role in the Americas, whereas domestic law plays a more important role in Europe.[207] By allowing, even exceptionally, diversity in domestic laws to be a reason not to interpret an ECHR term autonomously, the ECtHR has allowed room for diversity and has incorporated the views of national parliaments, which are (at least in part) responsible for defining domestic law terms. In this way, the ECtHR enhances the legitimacy of its rulings.

4.10 Conclusion

This chapter has demonstrated that the three functioning regional Courts have a fair bit in common: the interpretation of ‘their’ human rights treaty is underpinned by effectiveness considerations, and they rely on evolutive, autonomous and systemic interpretation. Still, their approach differs in other respects. Before sketching the differences between the ECtHR and the IACtHR, it should be noted that the ACtHPR has not yet elaborated extensively on its interpretative techniques, although it relies on these techniques. While it relies on the principles of subsidiarity and effectiveness and uses autonomous and evolutive interpretation, its lack of elaboration hinders reaching conclusions vis-à-vis its perceived legitimacy.

An important source for the ECtHR’s interpretation of the ECHR is the law of the states parties, due to the significant role that regional consensus plays in evolutive

200 ECtHR, *Chassagnou and Others v France*, Judgment, 29 April 1999, App. No. 25088/94, para 100; Letsas 2004, pp. 282–283.

201 Serghides 2017, p. 10.

202 ECtHR, *Engel v The Netherlands*, 8 June 1976, Judgment, App. No. 5100/71, para 82.

203 ECtHR, *Chassagnou and Others v France,* above n. 200, para 100.

204 Gerards 2023, p. 129.

205 This applies to the question of scope.

206 Gerards 2023, pp. 129–132.

207 Killander 2010, p. 148; Gismondi 2016, p. 49.

and autonomous interpretation and in determining the MoA's scope. Still, the ECtHR also engages with IHRL when interpreting the ECHR in a systemic and evolutive way. The ECtHR also relies on international external sources that express concerns other than fundamental rights protection when engaging in systemic interpretation. Another important characteristic of the ECtHR's approach is that it leaves room for the domestic authorities to make their own decisions up to a certain level, due to the strong version of subsidiarity that it applies and its extensive use of the MoA. The ECtHR also engages in *pro persona*/effective and in systemic interpretation, but the influence of these techniques is less evident than in the Inter-American system, due the ECtHR's application of subsidiarity and the MoA. In short, the ECtHR's interpretative techniques help it to address the difficulties outlined in Sect. 4.2. By basing itself on domestic laws, it addresses (at least in part) both the counter-majoritarian and the knowledge-gap difficulty, and by leaving room for the states parties to make their own decisions, these two difficulties may not arise within the confines of a single case. Moreover, allowing states parties to make their own decisions addresses the unifying-diversity difficulty.

The IACtHR relies heavily on IHRL, which influences the autonomous meaning of ACHR terms and is relevant to evolutive interpretation; the IACtHR does not put domestic laws in the spotlight by relying on regional consensus extensively. Systemic interpretation is, therefore, of great importance, provided this technique leads to a *pro persona* interpretation, which is an important distinctive element of its case law. Other important characteristics are that it does not shy away from emphasising the primary responsibility of states parties and that it does not currently use the MoA. Contrary to the European approach, the operationalisation of interpretative techniques by the IACtHR probably causes legitimacy questions rather than addresses them. The emphasis on *pro persona* interpretation and on international instruments sidelines domestic laws, the knowledge of domestic authorities and leads to the imposition of uniform rather than diverse solutions for IHRL questions.

These differences between the Inter-American and the European systems are not so surprising, considering the different contexts in which they started functioning. The IACtHR was confronted with gross human rights violations and relatively weak democracies in its first years.[208] In contrast, its European counterpart started operating in relative quietness, being confronted with 'highly technical issues'[209] and 'relatively minor and discrete conflicts of interests prevalent in any complex society'.[210] The contexts arguably have grown increasingly comparable, with the ECtHR being confronted with serious violations caused by war and internal strife.[211] Additionally, among its states parties is a 'consolidated authoritarian regime' (Azerbaijan),[212] rulers of one of its states parties have become 'increasingly authoritarian'

[208] Sections 4.5 and 4.7.

[209] Ryssdal 1996, p. 22.

[210] Helfer 2008, p. 129.

[211] Conflicts in e.g. Chechnya, South-Eastern Turkey, Nagorno-Karabakh, Georgia and Ukraine.

[212] According to Freedom House, at https://freedomhouse.org/countries/nations-transit/scores. Accessed 5 March 2025. See also European External Action Service 2023, pp. 34–35.

(Turkey)[213] and there is a serious decline of respect for the rule of law in Hungary among others.[214] Still the 'context-specific path dependencies',[215] probably have explanatory force. Another way to explain the different approaches may be found in the dissimilar philosophies on which the systems are based: the Inter-American on 'human dignity as the foundation of human rights', the European on 'the (philosophy of) liberty'.[216]

The aforementioned differences determine in part whether it is relatively easy for the Courts to address legitimacy questions. This is the case for the ECtHR, whereas the IACtHR's approach may exacerbate legitimacy challenges that are inherent in a regional system of human rights protection anyway. With this conclusion, the author does not mean to make the normative point that the IACtHR should change its course, in part because the notion of legitimacy was defined narrowly as perceived legitimacy in the eyes of the states.

References

Almutawa A (2021) The Arab Court of Human Rights and the enforcement of the Arab Charter on Human Rights. Human Rights Law Review 21:506-532.

Amin A (2021) A teleological approach to interpreting socio-economic rights in the African Charter: Appropriateness and methodology. African Human Rights Journal 21:204-233.

Arnardóttir M O (2016) Rethinking the two margins of appreciation. European Constitutional Law Review 12:27-53.

Barreiros L E (2014) Emerging voices: Freedom or restraint? On the comparison between the European and Inter-American human rights courts. Opinio Juris. http://opiniojuris.org/2014/08/11/emerging-voices-freedom-restraint-comparison-european-inter-american-human-rights-courts/. Accessed 5 March 2025.

Besson S (2016) Subsidiarity in international human rights law-what is subsidiary about human rights? American Journal of Jurisprudence 61:69-107.

Björgvinsson D T (2018) Reflections on legal reasoning in the case law of the European Court of Human Rights. In: Bencze M, Ng G Y (eds) How to measure the quality of judicial reasoning. Springer, Cham, 251-268.

Brems E (2017) Introduction: Rewriting Decisions from a Perspective of Human Rights Integration. In: Brems E (ed) Integrated Human Rights in Practice. Edward Elgar Publishing, Cheltenham, pp. 1-27.

Burgorgue-Larsen L (2018a) Conventionality Control: Inter-American Court of Human Rights. In: Ruiz Fabri H (ed) Max Planck Encyclopedia of International Procedural Law. Oxford University Press, Oxford.

Burgorgue-Larsen L (2018b) 'Decompartmentalization': The key technique for interpreting regional human rights treaties. International Journal of Constitutional Law 16:187-213.

Çalı B (2020) Specialized Rules of Treaty Interpretation. Human rights. In: Hollis D B (ed) The Oxford Guide to Treaties 2nd edn. Oxford University Press, Oxford, pp. 504-523.

[213] According to Freedom House, at https://freedomhouse.org/country/turkey/freedom-net/2023. Accessed 5 March 2025. See also European Commission 2023a, p. 5.

[214] European Commission 2023b, pp. 37, 45.

[215] Çalı 2020, p. 520.

[216] Lubarda 2020, p. 98.

Çalı B, Madsen M R, Viljoen F (2018) Comparing regional human rights regimes: Defining a research agenda. International Journal of Constitutional Law 16:128-135.

Carozza P G (2003) Subsidiarity as a structural principle of international human rights law. American Journal of International Law 97:38-79.

Carter W M (2009) Rethinking subsidiarity in international human rights adjudication. Hamline Journal of Public Law and Policy 30:319-333.

Christoffersen J (2009) Impact of General Principles of Treaty Interpretation. In: Kamminga M T, Scheinin M (eds) The Impact of Human Rights Law on General International Law. Oxford University Press, Oxford, pp. 37-61.

Contesse J (2016) Contestation and deference in the Inter-American Human Rights System. Law and Contemporary Problems 79:123-145.

Contesse J (2019) Resisting the Inter-American Human Rights System. The Yale Journal of International Law 44:179-237.

Contreras P (2012) National discretion and international deference in the restriction of human rights: A comparison between the jurisprudence of the European and the Inter-American Court of Human Rights. Northwestern Journal of International Human Rights 11:28-82.

Dilton R (2016) The *pro homine* principle as a fundamental aspect of international human rights law. Journal of Global Studies 47:1-9.

Dulitzky A E (2015) An Inter-American constitutional court—The invention of the conventionality control by the Inter-American Court of Human Rights. Texas International Law Journal 50:45-94.

Dzehtsiarou K (2011) European consensus and the evolutive interpretation of the European Convention on Human Rights. German Law Journal 12:1730-1745.

Dzehtsiarou K (2015) European Consensus and the Legitimacy of the European Court of Human Rights. Cambridge University Press, Cambridge.

Dzehtsiarou K, De Londras F (2015) Managing judicial innovation in the European Court of Human Rights. Human Rights Law Review 15:523-547.

Dzehtsiarou K, De Londras F (2018) Great Debates on the European Convention on Human Rights. Bloomsbury, London.

Engstrom P (2017) Reconceptualising the impact of the Inter-American Human Rights system. Direito & Práxis revista 8:1250-1285.

European Commission (2023a) Commission Staff Working Document Türkiye 2023 Report, *Accompanying the document* Communication from the Commission to the European Parliament, the Council, the European Economic and Social Committee and the Committee of the Regions 2023 Communication on EU Enlargement policy, SWD(2023) 696 final, 8 November 2023.

European Commission (2023b) Communication from the Commission to the European Parliament, the Council, the European Economic and Social Committee and the Committee of the Regions, 2023 Rule of Law Report, CoM (2023) 800 final, Brussels, 5 July 2023.

European External Action Service (2023) EU annual report on human rights and democracy in the world. 2022 country updates. https://www.eeas.europa.eu/eeas/2022-human-rights-and-democracy-world-country-reports_en. Accessed 5 March 2025.

Falcón G C (2022) Standards of Review: Inter-American Court of Human Rights. In: Ruiz-Fabri H (ed) Max Planck Encyclopaedia of International Procedural Law. Oxford University Press, Oxford.

Gardiner R K (2017) Treaty Interpretation, 2nd edn. Oxford University Press, Oxford.

Gerards J H (2018) Margin of appreciation and incrementalism in the case law of the European Court of Human Rights. Human Rights Law Review 18:495-515.

Gerards J H (2023) General Principles of the European Convention on Human Rights, 2nd edn. Oxford University Press, Oxford.

Ghantous M (2022) Arab Court of Human Rights. In: Binder C and others (eds) Elgar Encyclopedia of Human Rights. Edward Elgar Publishing, Cheltenham, pp. 145-149.

Gismondi G (2016) Denial of Justice: The latest indigenous land disputes before the European Court of Human Rights and the need for an expansive interpretation of Protocol 1. Yale Human Rights & Development Law Journal 18:1-58.
Glas L R (2016) The theory, potential and practice of procedural dialogue in the European Convention on Human Rights System. Intersentia, Antwerp.
Glas L R (2020) From Interlaken to Copenhagen: What has become of the proposals aiming to reform the functioning of the European Court of Human Rights? Human Rights Law Review 2020:121-151.
Glas L R (2023) The age of subsidiarity? The ECtHR's approach to the admissibility requirement that applicants raise their Convention complaint before domestic courts. Netherlands Quarterly of Human Rights 41:75-96.
Helfer L R (2008) Redesigning the European Court of Human Rights: Embeddedness as a deep structural principle of the European human rights regime. European Journal of International Law 19:125-159.
Helmersen S T (2013) Evolutive treaty interpretation: Legality, semantics and distinctions. European Journal of Legal Studies 6:161-188.
Hennebel L, Tigroudja H (2022) The American Convention on Human Rights. A Commentary. Oxford University Press, Oxford.
Heyns C (2001) The African regional human rights system: In need of reform? African Human Rights Law Journal 1:155-174.
International Commission of Jurists (2015) The Arab Court of Human Rights: A flawed Statute for an ineffective Court. International Commission of Jurists, Geneva.
International Law Commission (2006) Report of the Study Group of the International Law Commission, finalized by Mr. Martti Koskenniemi, 13 April 2006, A/CN.4/L.682 and Add.1. https://legal.un.org/ilc/documentation/english/a_cn4_l682.pdf. Accessed 5 March 2025.
Jachtenfuchs M, Krisch N (2016) Subsidiarity in global governance. Law and Contemporary Problems 79:1-26.
Jonas O (2020) *Res interpretata* principle: Giving domestic effect to the judgments of the African Court on Human and Peoples Rights. African Human Rights Law Journal 20:736-755
Kanetake M (2016) Subsidiarity in the Practice of International Courts. In: Kanetake M, Nollkaemper A (eds) The Rule of Law at the National and International Levels: Contestation and Deference. Hart Publishing, Oxford, pp. 445-460.
Killander M (2010) Interpreting regional human rights treaties. International Journal of Human Rights 7:145-170.
Legg A (2021) The Margin of Appreciation in International Human Rights Law: Deference and Proportionality. Oxford University Press, Oxford.
Letsas G (2004) The truth in autonomous concepts: How to interpret the ECHR. European Journal of International Law 15:279-305.
Letsas G (2010) Strasbourg's interpretive ethic: Lessons for the international lawyer. European Journal of International Law 21:509-541.
Lubarda B A (2020) From the interpretation of norms to social change: Human rights treaties as living instruments in light of reality. In: Inter-American Court of Human Rights, Dialogue between regional human rights courts, pp. 85-106. https://www.corteidh.or.cr/sitios/libros/todos/docs/dialogo-en.pdf. Accessed 5 March 2025.
Lixinski L (2010) Treaty interpretation by the Inter-American Court of Human Rights: Expansionism at the service of the unity of international law. European Journal of International Law 21:585-604.
Lixinski L (2017) The consensus method of interpretation by the Inter-American Court of Human Rights. Canadian Association of Comparative and Contemporary Law 3:65-95.
Madsen M R (2018) Rebalancing European human rights: Has the Brighton Declaration engendered a new deal on human rights in Europe? Journal of International Dispute Settlement 9:199-222.
Mattar M Y (2013) Article 43 of the Arab Charter on Human Rights: Reconciling national, regional and international standards. Harvard Human Rights Journal 26:91-148.

Matusse Â (2020) From the interpretation of norms to social change: Human rights treaties as living instruments in light of reality. In: Inter-American Court of Human Rights, Dialogue between regional human rights courts, pp. 77-82. https://www.corteidh.or.cr/sitios/libros/todos/docs/dialogo-en.pdf. Accessed 5 March 2025.
McGoldrick D (2014) Affording states a margin of appreciation: Comparing the European Court of Human Rights and the Inter-American Court of Human Rights. In: Buckley C M, Donald A, Leach P (eds) Towards convergence in international human rights law. Brill Nijhoff, Leiden, pp. 323-365.
Medina C (2016) The American Convention on Human Rights. Crucial rights and their theory and practice, 2nd edn. Intersentia, Cambridge.
Murray R (2019) The African Charter on Human and Peoples' Rights. Oxford University Press, Oxford.
Negishi Y (2017) The *pro homine* principle's role in regulating the relationship between conventionality control and constitutionality control. European Journal of International Law 28:457-481.
Neuman G L (2008) Import, export, and regional consent in the Inter-American Court of Human Rights. European Journal of International Law 19:101-123.
Neuman G L (2017) Standing Alone or Together: The Human Rights Committee's Decision in *A.P. v Russian Federation*. In: Brems E, Desmet E (eds) Integrated Human Rights in Practice. Edward Elgar Publishing, Cheltenham, pp. 71-99.
Nilsson I (2023) On the path to universalism? The role of external instruments in the European Court of Human Rights jurisprudence. Nordic Journal of International Law 92:249-282.
Papaioannou M (2014) Harmonization of International Human Rights through Judicial Dialogue: The Indigenous Rights' Paradigm. Cambridge Journal of International and Comparative Law 3:1037-1059.
Pascual-Vives F (2019) Consensus-based interpretation of regional human rights treaties. Brill Nijhoff, Leiden.
Pasqualucci J M (2003) The Practice and Procedure of the Inter-American Court of Human Rights. Cambridge University Press, Cambridge.
Peters A (2017) The refinement of international law: From fragmentation to regime interaction and politicization. International Journal of Constitutional Law 15:671-704.
Plagis M (2020a) The beginning of the end of a home-grown African Court? 20 May 2020. Asser Institute. https://www.asser.nl/about-the-asser-institute/news/blog-post-the-beginning-of-the-end-of-a-home-grown-african-court/. Accessed 5 March 2025.
Plagis M (2020b) Regional courts and their sources: The practice of the African court and 'others'. 4 February 2020. The ACtHPR Monitor. https://www.acthprmonitor.org/regional-courts-and-their-sources-the-practice-of-the-african-court-and-the-others/. Accessed 5 March 2025.
Polgári E (2021) The role of the Vienna rules in the interpretation of the ECHR. A normative basis or a source of inspiration? Erasmus Law Review 14:82-95.
Rachovista A (2009) The principle of systemic integration in human rights law. International and Comparative Law Quarterly 66:557-588.
Rachovista A (2016) Treaty clauses and fragmentation of international law: Applying the more favourable protection clause in human rights treaties. Human Rights Law Review 16:77-101.
Rachovista A (2019) On new 'judicial animals': The curious case of an African court with material jurisdiction of a global scope. Human Rights Law Review 19:255-289.
Rachovista A (2020) Balancing Test (ACtHPR). In: Ruiz-Fabri H (ed) Max Planck Encyclopaedia of International Procedural Law. Oxford University Press, Oxford.
Rietiker D (2010) The principle of 'effectiveness' in the recent jurisprudence of the European Court of Human Rights: Its different dimensions and its consistency with public international law—no need for the concept of treaty *sui generis*. Nordic Journal of International Law 79:245-277.
Rietiker D (2019) Effectiveness and Evolution in Treaty Interpretation. In: Oxford Bibliographies. Oxford University Press, Oxford.

Rishmawi M (2010) The Arab Charter on Human Rights and the League of Arab Nations: An update. Human Rights Law Review 10:169-178.
Rodríguez-Pinzón D, Martin C (2006) The Prohibition of torture and ill-treatment in the Inter-American Human Rights System. A handbook for victims and their advocates. World Organisation Against Torture, Geneva.
Ryssdal R (1996) The coming of age of the European Convention on Human Rights. European Human Rights Law Review 1:18-29.
Sadri A (2019) The Arab human rights system: Achievements and challenges. The International Journal of Human Rights 23:1166-1182.
Senden H C K (2011) Interpretation of fundamental rights in a multilevel legal system: An analysis of the European Court of Human Rights and the Court of Justice of the European Union. Intersentia, Antwerp.
Serghides G A (2017) The principles of effectiveness in the European Convention on Human Rights, in particular its relationship to other Convention principles. Hague Yearbook of International Law 30:1-15.
Soley X, Steininger S (2018) Parting ways or lashing back? Withdrawals, backlash and the Inter-American Court of Human Rights. International Journal of Law in Context 14:237-257.
Steininger S (2022) Harder, better, faster, stronger. 1 October 2022. Verfassungsblog. https://verfassungsblog.de/harder-better-faster-stronger/. Accessed 5 March 2025.
Viljoen F (2012) International Human Rights Law in Africa, 2nd edn. Oxford University Press, Oxford.
Wewerinke M J (2015) State responsibility, climate change and human rights under international law. European University Institute (PhD thesis), Florence.
Yourow H C (1996) The margin of appreciation doctrine in the dynamics of the European Court of Human Rights jurisprudence. Martinus Nijhoff Publishers, Dordrecht.
Ziemele I (2018) European Consensus and International Law. In: Van Aaken A, Motoc I (eds) The European Convention on Human Rights and General International Law. Oxford University Press, Oxford, pp. 23-40.

Lize Glas is an associate professor of international and European law at the Radboud University (the Netherlands).

Rishmawi, M. (2010) The Arab Charter on Human Rights and the League of Arab States: An update. Human Rights Law Review 10(1):169-178.
Rodríguez Pinzón, D., Martin, C. (2014) The Prohibition of Torture and Ill-treatment in the Inter-American Human Rights System: A Handbook for Victims and their Advocates. World Organisation Against Torture.
[illegible]

Chapter 5
Admissibility Criteria and Access to Justice in Regional Human Rights Jurisdictions

Filippo Fontanelli and Kanstantsin Dzehtsiarou

Contents

5.1 Introduction 100
5.2 Admissibility of Claims in International Litigation 100
5.2.1 Inadmissibility at the ICJ 101
5.2.2 Customary Notions of Inadmissibility in Diplomatic Protection and State Responsibility 102
5.3 Individual Applications in Human Rights Courts/Commissions: Access to Justice and Admissibility 103
5.4 Specific Courts and Commissions 105
5.4.1 The European Court of Human Rights 105
5.4.2 The System of the American Convention on Human Rights 112
5.4.3 The African Commission and the African Court on Human and Peoples' Rights 115
5.4.4 The Arab Court of Human Rights 119
5.5 Comparative Reflections 119
5.5.1 Common Traits 120
5.5.2 Differences 121
5.6 Conclusions 122
References 122

Abstract In litigation proceedings before regional human rights Courts and Commissions, only applications meeting admissibility requirements can reach the merits stage. While claims' admissibility is an established notion in public international law, human rights regimes have developed rules and implementation approaches that are specific to this field of litigation. A comparative analysis of the case-law of the four regional human rights systems reveals that the law and practice of admissibility has a common function across the different models, which transcends the idiosyncrasies and historical trajectory of each. In establishing and

F. Fontanelli
School of Law, University of Edinburgh, Edinburgh, UK
e-mail: filippo.fontanelli@ed.ac.uk

K. Dzehtsiarou (✉)
School of Law and Social Justice, University of Liverpool, Liverpool, UK
e-mail: k.dzehtsiarou@liverpool.ac.uk

A. Almutawa and K. D. Magliveras (eds.), *A Comparison of the European, Inter-American, African and Arab Human Rights Courts: Institutional Aspects*,
https://doi.org/10.1007/978-94-6265-695-6_5

applying admissibility requirements, the regional human rights systems try to strike a balance between the individual's access to justice and the viability of their work.

Keywords Admissibility · Jurisdiction · Human rights · International tribunals · Exhaustion of domestic remedies

5.1 Introduction

When individuals bring applications against States, their claims' admissibility determines their access to international justice,[1] particularly before human rights Courts. This chapter assesses the inadmissibility requirements of regional human rights Courts, comparing them against each other and the general international law notion, to highlight their common core and discrepancies.

Admissibility is a claim's *attribute*, permitting competent adjudicators to examine its merits, and respondents can allege that a claim is inadmissible to have it rejected, irrespective of its merit. 'Inadmissibility', therefore, denotes generally the *procedural label* for the claim's rejection, but can also indicate the circumstances warranting it (inadmissibility grounds). This premise matters: human rights Courts can reject claims as inadmissible also for non-admissibility-related grounds (e.g., for exceeding their competence).

Section 5.2 extols the admissibility notion in general international law and dispute settlement. Section 5.3 introduces its peculiarities in human rights litigation. Section 5.4 compares the regional human rights systems. Section 5.5 summarises the findings and Sect. 5.6 concludes briefly.

5.2 Admissibility of Claims in International Litigation

In general international law, objections to the claim's admissibility differ from those to the courts' jurisdiction (or competence). They share the goal of defeating claims at the bar—irrespective of their merits—but their rationale and function differ.

Jurisdictional objections question the courts' powers' extent, deriving from the parties' consent to compulsory jurisdiction. Respondent States claim to have not consented to adjudicating disputes like that introduced by the applicant; thus, the application is misdirected and the tribunal cannot resolve it. Rejections on jurisdictional grounds amount to responding 'sorry, wrong number'.

Conversely, admissibility objections hinge on flaws other than the absence of consent. They warrant the application's dismissal even if it falls within the court's competence *ratione personae*, *materiae*, *temporis*, *loci* and *voluntatis*.

[1] For a comparative study, see Hampson et al. 2018.

Unless *lex specialis* treaty rules govern admissibility, its operation follows international general principles and customary rules (*lex generalis*). The International Court of Justice (ICJ)'s practice and the documents reflecting customary law illustrate these general rules.

In turn, this section addresses the ICJ's usage (Sect. 5.2.1) and the customary rules governing inadmissibility in the field of diplomatic protection (Sect. 5.2.2).

5.2.1 Inadmissibility at the ICJ

For the ICJ, respondents' jurisdictional objections allege their lack of consent to its jurisdiction, whereas inadmissibility objections target other concerns (i.e., non-consent-related).[2] Accordingly, jurisdictional and inadmissibility circumstances differ, the latter assuming the ICJ's competence, but precluding its exercise.

The ICJ Statute does not list pre-determined inadmissibility grounds, but has upheld these on occasion[3]: the claim's indeterminacy; a genuine legal dispute's absence or mootness; *res judicata* or *lis pendens*; the failure to exhaust local remedies[4] or a mismatch between the applicant State and the victim's nationality (in diplomatic protection); an indispensable State party missing from the proceedings; the applicant's acquiescence to the wrongdoing.[5] This list is open-ended.[6] For instance, the ICJ stated that claims can be inadmissible for abuse of process, but did not elaborate.[7]

These grounds—unconnected to the parties' consent to confer jurisdiction to the ICJ[8]—involve procedural or substantive fairness. They are established by general principles and provide courts with the inherent power to activate emergency safeguards when litigation itself apparently delivers injustice rather than justice.

---

[2] ICJ, *Oil Platforms* (*Iran v USA*), Judgment, Merits, 6 November 2003, ICJ Reports 2003, p 161, para. 29.

[3] Kolb 2014, pp. 173–175.

[4] ICJ, *Elettronica Sicula S.P.A.* (*USA v Italy*), Judgment, 20 July 1989, ICJ Reports 1989, p. 15, para. 50.

[5] ICJ, *Certain Phosphate Lands in Nauru (Nauru v Australia)*, Judgment (Preliminary Objections), 26 June 1992, ICJ Reports 1992, p 240, para. 32.

[6] ICJ, *Application of the Convention on the Prevention and Punishment of the Crime of Genocide (Croatia v Serbia)*, Judgment (Preliminary Objections), 18 November 2008, ICJ Reports 2008, p 412, para. 120.

[7] ICJ, *Immunities and Criminal Proceedings (Equatorial Guinea v France)*, Judgment (Preliminary Objections), 6 June 2018, ICJ Reports 2018, p 336, para. 150.

[8] ICJ, *Certain Questions of Mutual Assistance in Criminal Matters (Djibouti v France)*, Judgment, 4 June 2008, ICJ Reports 2008, p 177, para. 48: 'in determining the scope of the consent expressed by one of the parties, the Court pronounces on its jurisdiction and not on the admissibility of the application'.

5.2.2 *Customary Notions of Inadmissibility in Diplomatic Protection and State Responsibility*

The ICJ has clarified several admissibility criteria, some specific to diplomatic protection (when a State espouses its citizens' grievance against another State and brings inter-State action), other applicable to all invocation of State responsibility. Diplomatic protection, arguably, foreshadows the modern systems of human rights-protection,[9] and State responsibility rules apply to all breaches of international obligations—including human rights ones. These customary criteria are thus relevant for this study.

Article 44 of the International Law Commission (ILC) Articles on the Responsibility of States for Wrongful Acts ('Admissibility of claims') does not list general criteria, but acknowledges two requirements for invoking State responsibility specific to certain obligations. The first is 'the nationality of claims': State claims are admissible with respect to that State's citizens only. The second is the 'exhaustion of local remedies': the aggrieved citizens must have tried all remedies of the respondent State. These rules condition all invocation of responsibility, including through diplomatic exchanges or the methods listed in Article 33(1) UN Charter (conciliation, mediation, good offices, adjudication, arbitration).[10] Naturally, when invocation occurs in international proceedings, they constitute positive admissibility requirements, screening unviable claims and elevating grievances actionable before foreign courts into international claims.

The ILC's Articles on Diplomatic Protection stipulate that exhaustion of local remedies conditions the State's lodging of international claims in respect of a national's injury.[11] Nationality-matching also affects invocation, regulating standing: '[t]he State entitled to exercise diplomatic protection is the State of nationality.'[12]

Each human rights system has its particularities in terms of admissibility, and may repurpose, or deviate, from these general rules.

---

[9] Amerasinghe 2008, pp. 73–78; Dugard 2005.

[10] UN General Assembly, Resolution 56/83, 12 December 2001, Annex; Pellet 2013; Fontanelli and Sthoeger 2024.

[11] International Law Commission 2006, Article 14. Article 15 contains the exceptions to the rule of exhaustion.

[12] Ibid., Article 3.1.

5.3 Individual Applications in Human Rights Courts/ Commissions: Access to Justice and Admissibility

International human rights courts generally draw from the 'procedural common law'[13] of all international jurisdictions. However, the applicable provisions and the relevant practice of each can sidestep this template, also regarding claims' admissibility.[14] Our analysis concerns mostly these system-specific features.

The four human rights systems examined give individuals access to supranational adjudicators, but use different processes. Approximately, they appear at different stages of a similar trajectory, going from reserving individual applications only to quasi-judicial 'commissions' to envisaging only a 'court'. Intermediate models exist, granting concurrent competence to both (with a system for allocating cases), or allowing States to opt-in to courts' competence besides commissions' one. Each system's basic features are explored,[15] and their apparent discrepancy can occasionally reflect a different level of advancement along this common journey, rather than a meaningful difference.

The focus here is not on the (*ratione*-something) jurisdictional features, unless it is relevant to explaining admissibility's operation. Naturally, the competence of each court/commission has a direct bearing on individuals' access to justice. For instance, there is a significant diversity in how different systems limit standing using requirements *ratione personae.*[16] While the European system almost exclusively accepts applications brought by alleged victims, the American one accepts claims brought on behalf of a group (by any member thereof), and the African one even accepts petitions by NGOs representing victims (a scenario available for opt-in in the Arabic system). This variation affects which cases proceed in each system and, in turn, influences the formulation of admissibility filters for caseload management.

Across human rights regional systems, three types of admissibility criteria have been theorised: requirements 'anchor[ing] the relevant treaty in international law generally or [reflecting] the legitimate interests of states', those relating to the applicant's behaviour and those relating to the application's substance.[17]

The exhaustion requirement applies across all systems,[18] and is codified in the treaties establishing the courts/commissions' powers. Conversely, nationality-matching is inherently unfit for systems processing individual applications. In diplomatic protection, it seeks to associate the concerned applicant State to the aggrieved individual. Obviously, applicant-victim matching is unnecessary when they are the

[13] Brown 2007; Fontanelli and Busco 2016.

[14] Inter-State claims' admissibility is not addressed in-depth (see Leckie 1988) and neither is the operation of monitoring bodies supervising compliance with UN human rights treaties, despite its similarity with adjudicative proceedings.

[15] See also Hampson et al. 2018, p 179.

[16] Ibid., pp. 180–182.

[17] Ibid., p 171.

[18] Differently from the practice in investor-State arbitration, the purpose of which is to spare applicants from domestic proceedings.

same person, like individual applicants before human rights courts. Thus, applicants need not have any specific nationality, because States owe human rights obligations to everyone within their jurisdiction, irrespective of their nationality.[19] Moreover, this requirement typically does not apply even to inter-State claims. With the notable exception of the Arab Court of Human Rights ('Arab Court'[20]), applicant States can address the condition of non-citizens.[21]

Thus, the customary admissibility criteria of diplomatic protection claims were either codified (exhaustion) or dropped (nationality-matching). Normally, other criteria acknowledged by the ICJ also apply in human rights proceedings, but human rights-specific admissibility criteria apply more often, effectively crowding out customary ones.

Indeed, all human rights jurisdictions enforce stipulated admissibility criteria additional to the customary ones, with the common goal to reduce the aggregate number of applications processed in full. Accordingly, they employ several procedural and substantive filters, like subsidiarity (exhaustion), strict time-frames, and *de minimis* assessment. While these requirements narrow down individuals' access to international justice, they are normally designed to balance between this right and competing interests: the viability of the courts' work, the State's right to remedy its own wrongdoing, legal certainty and other rule of law safeguards. For instance, the conditions concerning exhaustion and time-bars do not remove altogether the individual's right to seize an international tribunal or commission, but screen—respectively—premature or belated applications.

The admissibility conditions used by human rights tribunals and commissions are normally stipulated in the treaties that establish their jurisdictional powers. Formally, therefore, these criteria specify that the tribunal cannot hear certain categories of applications, thus carving them out from the tribunal's competence through express treaty provisions. In other words, treaty-contained admissibility criteria seem indistinguishable from jurisdictional limitations, a blur that contradicts the ICJ's taxonomy.

In this chapter, we do not question the formal—and express—characterisation of these treaty-based requirements as concerning claims' admissibility. However, it is helpful to wonder the reason for this counterintuitive label. First, possibly the admissibility tag depends on these filters' specific function (i.e., sheltering Courts from too many applications), which does not align intuitively with the typical function of jurisdictional boundaries (i.e., tracking the stipulated extent of the Court's powers). Second, several of these common admissibility requirements in human rights instruments might inherit their characterisation from comparable admissibility criteria in municipal laws. For instance, in several jurisdictions, issues of claim's timeliness

---

[19] Conversely, in investment arbitration nationality matters, because the applicable treaties grant substantive and procedural rights only to the nationals of the contracting States.

[20] ArabCtHR Statute, Article 19.1.

[21] ECommHR, Application nos 3321/67 to 3323/67 and 3344/67, *Denmark, Norway, Sweden and the Netherlands v Greece*, Decision, 31 May 1968.

or *res judicata* are described in terms of inadmissibility.[22] This analogy could have influenced the denomination in human rights treaties, at the expense of theoretical accuracy.

Another issue worth flagging is that, in some systems, the claim's *rejection* for inadmissibility is available to sanction flaws that are unquestionably of jurisdictional nature (e.g., failing to meet the treaty's requirements *ratione personae*). In such cases, indicated below, the procedural flaw is correctly characterised, but the distinction between inadmissibility flaws and the rejection for inadmissibility must be remembered, because the latter can be administered without the former occurring.

5.4 Specific Courts and Commissions

This section surveys the four systems in turn, bringing out commonalities and distinctions.

5.4.1 The European Court of Human Rights

5.4.1.1 General Overview

ECtHR is the busiest human rights Court in the world by number of applications pending and decisions issued, and has had numerous opportunities to address admissibility. ECtHR's admissibility criteria shape the applicants' access to it, as they prescribe which applications can reach the merit. Concurrently, admissibility criteria allow the ECtHR to manage its docket more effectively, increasingly an existential necessity. In 2011, the backlog of pending cases exceeded 150,000.[23] Unsurprisingly, reform efforts strived then to establish new filters, including admissibility conditions. For instance, Article 12 of Protocol 14 ECHR in 2010 introduced a new *de minimis* admissibility criterion. Protocol 15 ECHR in 2018 simplified its application, shortening from 6 to 4 months the time-window during which applications can be submitted after local remedies are exhausted, and introduced a simplified procedure for dismissing inadmissible applications. Reforms also concerned the organisational arrangements: before Protocol 14 ECHR, a three-judge Committee handled clearly inadmissible applications; afterwards, this power was vested with single judges. These efforts resulted in reducing the backlog to around 68,000 pending applications by late 2023.[24]

[22] E.g., Article 122 of the French Code of Civil Procedure.

[23] ECtHR, Analysis of statistics 2011, January 2012. https://www.echr.coe.int/d/stats_analysis_2011_eng?p_l_back_url=%2Fsearch%3Fq%3D2011. Accessed 28 March 2025.

[24] ECtHR, Analysis of statistics 2023, January 2024. https://www.echr.coe.int/documents/d/echr/stats-analysis-2023-eng?download=true. Accessed 29 March 2025.

The ECtHR declares many applications inadmissible. According to official reports, in 2023, '31,329 applications were declared inadmissible or struck out of the list of cases by a single judge, a Committee, a Chamber or a Grand Chamber, a 12% decrease compared with 2022 (35,402)'.[25] For reference, in 2023, the ECtHR allocated 34,650 applications to a judicial formation. Roughly, over 90% of applications were declared inadmissible.

Generally, ECtHR's admissibility criteria are perceived as formalities used to discard clearly inadmissible cases, but this might not be true. Admissibility decisions can dispose of delicate and important cases and even the Grand Chamber[26] issues them.[27] Moreover, the ECtHR has significant discretion in applying admissibility requirements, to the point of disregarding them when there is sufficient justification.[28] Arguably, 'in truth there are *no* admissibility criteria that would exclude discretionary decision making'.[29]

Early on, the Court would even weigh reasons of 'European public order' to justify hearing otherwise inadmissible complaints.[30] More recently, references to European public order in this context have disappeared, but the ECtHR still demonstrates certain flexibility. For instance, in *Centre for Legal Resources on behalf of Valentin Câmpeanu*, the ECtHR considered whether an NGO had standing on behalf of the deceased victim (an orphan without relatives). Normally, only victims have standing, but the ECtHR argued as follows:

> …in the exceptional circumstances of this case and bearing in mind the serious nature of the allegations, it should be open to [the NGO] to act as a representative of Mr. Câmpeanu, notwithstanding the fact that it had no power of attorney to act on his behalf and that he died before the application was lodged under the Convention. To find otherwise would amount to preventing such serious allegations of a violation of the Convention from being examined at an international level, with the risk that the respondent State might escape accountability under the Convention as a result of its own failure to appoint a legal representative to act on his behalf as it was required to do under national law […]. Allowing the respondent State to escape accountability in this manner would not be consistent with the general spirit of the Convention, nor with the High Contracting Parties' obligation under Article 34 of the Convention not to hinder in any way the effective exercise of the right to bring an application before the Court.[31]

Thus, the ECtHR can eschew admissibility's binary logic, using creative interpretation if necessary. While creative tactics do not and should not occur often, the backlog's pressure discourages the ECtHR from accepting applications that could be rejected.

---

[25] Ibid., p 3. For the most recent statistics, ECtHR, Analysis of statistics 2024, January 2025. https://www.echr.coe.int/documents/d/echr/stats-analysis-2024-eng. Accessed 29 March 2025.

[26] The Grand Chamber has 17 judges.

[27] ECtHR, Application no. 52207/99, *Banković and Others v Belgium and Others*, Decision (Admissibility), 12 December 2001.

[28] Tickell 2011; de Londras and Dzehtsiarou 2015, pp. 61–66.

[29] de Londras and Dzehtsiarou 2015, p 61 (emphasis in the original).

[30] Dzehtsiarou 2021, pp. 46–52.

[31] ECtHR, Application no. 47838/08 [GC], *Centre for Legal Resources on behalf of Valentin Câmpeanu v Romania*, Judgment, 17 July 2014, para. 112.

The ECtHR deals with two types of contentious cases: individual applications under Article 34 and inter-state applications under Article 33 ECHR. Not all criteria of admissibility used in individual complaints apply to inter-state ones. For instance, the ECtHR cannot declare the inter-state applications manifestly ill-founded.[32] Even as regards the other requirements (inter-state complaints must fall within the jurisdiction of the Court, applicant states need to have exhausted national remedies, and the four-month time-bar must be observed), their application must be tailored to inter-state cases.[33] This chapter focuses on individual applications' admissibility.

5.4.1.2 The Process of Application of Admissibility Criteria

Preliminarily, it must be recalled that admissibility is not the only obstacle to the ECtHR's jurisdiction on the merits. Before ascertaining admissibility, the ECtHR checks administratively whether applications comply with Rule 47 of the Rules of Court, setting out the formal parameters (i.e., the *seisin* requirements). If it finds irregularities, the ECtHR will not register the application and will return it to the authors, inviting them to revise and re-submit it. If the application is not resubmitted properly within 4 months after the exhaustion of national remedies (a time-limit that is neither suspended nor restarted by the application bouncing), it will be rejected administratively. In 2023, 10,600 applications fell in this category, down from 14,400 in 2022 (almost a fourth of that year's submissions).[34]

The ECtHR can consider an application's admissibility in a separate decision, before addressing its merits.[35] However, this happens rarely, only in complex admissibility cases. Usually, the ECtHR decides on admissibility and merits in the same judgment. The ECtHR can declare the whole application inadmissible, or it can consider some parts admissible while some others inadmissible. The decision on admissibility is final and cannot be changed unless there was a factual mistake, a very rare occurrence.

Initially, the applicant must demonstrate the application's *prima facie* admissibility. Upon receiving it, the ECtHR checks whether the application seems admissible. If so, the application can be 'communicated' to the respondent government under Rule 54(2) of the Rules of Court. Thereafter, it is for the government to raise any preliminary objections, including any challenging admissibility.

---

[32] ECommHR, Application nos 9940–9944/82, *France, Norway, Denmark, Sweden and Netherlands v Turkey,* Decision (Admissibility), 6 December 1983, pp. 160–162.

[33] However, the non-exhaustion requirement does not apply if the complaint concerns legislation or administrative practices in the respondent State, see ECtHR, Application no. 13255/07, *Georgia v Russia* (I), Decision (Admissibility), 30 June 2009, para. 125.

[34] Analysis of statistics 2023.

[35] ECtHR, Application no. 15318/89, *Loizidou v Turkey*, Judgment (Preliminary Objections), 23 March 1995.

5.4.1.3 Types of Inadmissibility

Articles 34 and 35 ECHR list the admissibility criteria for individual applications. In its Practical Guide on Admissibility, the ECtHR divides them into three types.[36] First, procedural grounds for inadmissibility. These include non-exhaustion of domestic remedies; failure to comply with the four-month limit for the application; and anonymous applications, applications which are substantively the same as those previously submitted to the ECtHR or other international judicial body, and applications abusing the right to petition. Second, grounds relating to the ECtHR's jurisdiction, including the material, territorial and temporal jurisdiction and the victim status requirement. Finally, merits-based inadmissibility. This criterion clearly straddles the line between admissibility and merits—one that sometimes is not easy to draw. In principle, the application can be rejected for being manifestly ill-founded or when the applicant did not suffer significant disadvantage, if these circumstances can be ascertained without complete consideration of the case's merits.

The following subsections consider the most illustrative examples of these inadmissibility types.

Procedural Inadmissibility

Providing a detailed overview of procedural inadmissibility exceeds the scope of this chapter. Many complaints are dismissed because they are premature or late: submitted before the exhaustion of domestic remedies or more than 4 months thereafter. Article 35(1) ECHR clearly establishes these requirements:

> The Court may only deal with the matter after all domestic remedies have been exhausted, according to the generally recognised rules of international law, and within a period of four months from the date on which the final decision was taken.

This rule reflects the principle of procedural subsidiarity, namely that the ECtHR should only hear complaints if national authorities have had a chance to address them to redress the underlying violations. The four-month limit seeks to promote legal certainty and, indirectly, contributes to making the ECtHR's docket manageable.

These two requirements are intrinsically connected: the four-month limit starts when the applicant exhausts the final effective domestic remedy. The ECtHR exercises wide discretion in interpreting 'effectiveness',[37] which can depend on the functions and features of particular remedies in particular States. Accordingly, remedies with the same name (for instance, resorting to a constitutional court) can be effective in one State and ineffective elsewhere. Moreover, the remedy's effectiveness sometimes depends on the field at hand. For instance, in the context of extradition or

[36] ECtHR, 'Practical Guide on Admissibility Criteria', updated on 31 August 2024. https://www.echr.coe.int/web/echr/d/admissibility_guide_eng. Accessed 28 March 2025.

[37] ECtHR, Application no. 2614/65, *Ringeisen v Austria*, Judgment, 16 July 1971, para. 89.

deportation effective remedies should have suspensive effect, preventing the deportation before they reach an outcome.[38] After exhaustion, the applicant has 4 months to submit the application. If the applicant chooses to resort to an ineffective remedy, the ECtHR will count the time-limit after the last effective one, and might reject the application for being submitted after the deadline.[39]

Under Article 35(2) ECHR, the application cannot be anonymous, and applicants must include their real name on its frontpage. The respondent State must know the applicant's identity to defend itself. Even if applicants request that their name be kept confidential,[40] the State will be informed. The ECtHR has applied some discretion even in this seemingly straightforward criterion. Occasionally, it has rejected applications made under a pseudonym;[41] however, at least once, it used a more flexible approach to admit one such application.[42]

Under Article 35(2), the ECtHR may deal with applications which are substantively the same as one submitted previously before another procedure of international investigation. This requirement's rationale is to maintain legal certainty and prevent forum-shopping when multiple international bodies can hear the same matter. To decide whether two complaints are substantively the same, the ECtHR considers whether applicants, complaint and underlying facts correspond.[43] The international investigation mechanism should be functionally comparable to the ECtHR (i.e., a judicial or quasi-judicial institution). The UN Human Rights Committee ('HRC') or the UN Working Group on Arbitrary Detention would qualify under this test,[44] unlike the UN Special Rapporteurs.[45]

Finally, the ECtHR can declare an application inadmissible for abuse of the right of application under Article 35(3) ECHR. This rubric can apply widely: from applications providing false information to those using offensive language. This criterion is applied rarely, but it serves as a safety valve when rejection through other criteria is unwarranted. For example, the ECtHR rejected a well-known Russian LGBTI activist's application:

> in reaction to the Court's judgment in the case of *Alekseyev and Others v Russia*, the applicant, a well-known LGBT activist and a public figure whose social networking accounts have hundreds of followers, published on [social media] accounts the virulently and personally offensive and threatening statements about the Court and its judges. Those statements clearly exceeded the limits of normal, civic and legitimate criticism... The Court … found that by

[38] ECtHR, Application nos. 40,503/17, 42,902/17 and 43,643/17, *M.K. and Others v Poland*, Judgment, 23 July 2020, paras. 142–148.

[39] ECtHR, Application no. 44898/10, *Jeronovičs v Latvia*, Judgment, 5 July 2016, para. 75.

[40] Rule 47(4) Rules of Court.

[41] ECtHR, Application no. 7245/09, *'Blondje' v the Netherlands*, Decision, 15 September 2009.

[42] ECtHR, Application no. 36378/02, *Shamayev and Others v Georgia and Russia*, Judgment, 12 April 2005; de Londras and Dzehtsiarou 2015, pp. 65–66.

[43] ECtHR, Application no. 32772/02, *Verein gegen Tierfabriken Schweiz (VgT) v Switzerland* (no. 2), Judgment, 30 June 2009, para. 63.

[44] See ECtHR, Application no. 25326/03, *Patera v Czech Republic*, Judgment, 26 April 2007 and ECtHR, Application no. 81553, *Hilal Mammadov v Azerbaijan*, Judgment, 4 February 2016.

[45] ECtHR, Application no. 29590/96, *Yağmurdereli v Turkey*, Judgment, 4 June 2002.

> continuing to publish insults about the Court and its judges after the warning, the applicant has shown disrespect to the very institution to which he had applied for the protection of his rights. His conduct constituted "a vexing manifestation of irresponsibility and a frivolous attitude towards the Court", amounting to contempt, and is therefore contrary to the purpose of the right of individual application, as provided for in Articles 34 and 35 [ECHR]. It constituted an abuse of the right of application within the meaning of Article 35 § 3 (a) [ECHR].[46]

Admissibility Based on Jurisdiction

Under Article 35(3) ECHR:

> The Court shall declare inadmissible any individual application submitted under Article 34 if it considers that: (a) the application is incompatible with the provisions of the Convention or the Protocols thereto.

The ECtHR interprets this provision as stipulating that the application must fall within the scope of one of the Convention's substantive rights, and refer to circumstances within the jurisdiction of one Contracting Party; furthermore, it needs to be submitted by the victim of the alleged violation, which must have occurred while the ECHR was binding the respondent State. The scholarship on the ECtHR's jurisdiction is extensive.[47] Hence, it is discussed briefly, also in light of this hybrid inadmissibility ground (for lack of jurisdiction).

One key jurisdiction-based admissibility requirement is that application be submitted by the victim of the violation. In abovementioned *Centre for Legal Resources on behalf of Valentin Câmpeanu*, the ECtHR approached the requirement of standing and victim status flexibly. However, in applications regarding covert operations, applicants often cannot conclusively show that they were subjected to practices such as wire-tapping[48] or technology-assisted facial recognition.[49] Since applicants bear the burden of proof, they can submit circumstantial evidence,[50] or the ECtHR accepts to review the domestic legislation allowing such covert operations *in abstracto*, regardless of whether specific victims can be identified. The ECtHR has stated clearly that such abstract review is not within its competence.[51] However, the approach in relation to covert operations has required flexibility to ensure effective human rights protection. In *Roman Zakharov v Russia*, the ECtHR therefore stated:

---

[46] ECtHR, Application nos 26,624/15 and 76 others, *Alekseyev and Others v Russia*, Judgment, 16 January 2020, paras. 7–8. The in-quote reference is to ECtHR, Applications nos. 14,988/09 and 50 others, *Alekseyev and Others v. Russia*, Judgment, 27 November 2018.

[47] See Wallace 2019; Forde 2024.

[48] ECtHR, Application no. 47143/06, *Roman Zakharov v Russia*, Judgment, 4 December 2015.

[49] ECtHR, Application no. 11519/20, *Glukhin v Russia*, Judgment, 4 July 2023.

[50] In *Glukhin*, the applicant was arrested at the underground station only 30 minutes after the police visited his home.

[51] ECtHR, Application nos 12,244/86, 12,245/86; 12,383/86, *Fox, Campbell and Hartley v The United Kingdom*, Judgment, 30 August 1990, para. 45.

> Having regard to the secret nature of the surveillance measures provided for by the contested legislation, the broad scope of their application, affecting all users of mobile-telephone communications, and the lack of effective means to challenge the alleged application of secret surveillance measures at domestic level, the Court considers an examination of the relevant legislation *in abstracto* to be justified. The Court therefore finds that the applicant is entitled to claim to be the victim of a violation of the Convention, even though he is unable to allege that he has been subject to a concrete measure of surveillance in support of his application.[52]

So, it transpires clearly that for the application to be admissible it must fall within the ECtHR's jurisdiction. Pursuant to Article 32 ECHR, the ECtHR itself decides on its jurisdiction, and this power grants the ECtHR some latitude in accepting applications that seem inadmissible when human rights protection warrants doing so.

Inadmissibility Based on Merits

The remaining admissibility criteria allow the ECtHR to review merits *prima facie*. If the complaint has manifestly no merit, it can declare the application inadmissible. Unsurprisingly, there is sometimes a fine line between such inadmissibility decisions and proper judgments on merits.

Under Article 35(3) ECHR, the ECtHR should declare applications which are manifestly ill-founded inadmissible. Without a more specific definition, this standard has been interpreted relatively broadly,[53] to include cases of clear absence of a violation, and of unsubstantiated or far-fetched complaints. The ECtHR can also declare the application manifestly ill-founded when it is treated as a fourth instance court,[54] for instance when it is invited to reconsider the evidence submitted in the domestic proceedings. Because its role is only to ascertain whether the national authorities violated the ECHR, these applications are rejected as ill-founded.

The newest admissibility criterion in the ECHR, which was added by Protocol 14 ECHR in 2010 and amended by Protocol 15 ECHR in 2018, is the *de minimis* criterion, which also relates to the merits of the application. Under Article 35(3) ECHR:

> The Court shall declare inadmissible any individual application submitted under Article 34 [ECHR] if it considers that: ... (b) the applicant has not suffered a significant disadvantage, unless respect for human rights as defined in the Convention and the Protocols thereto requires an examination of the application on the merits.

The ECtHR has clarified that both subjective and objective factors matter in determining whether the applicant suffered significant disadvantage:

---

[52] *Roman Zakharov v Russia,* n. 48, paras 178–179.

[53] De Londras and Dzehtsiarou 2015, pp. 62–64.

[54] See, ECtHR, Application no. 17621/91, *Kemmache v France (no. 3),* Judgment, 24 November 1994, para. 44.

> The assessment of this minimum level is relative and depends on all the circumstances of the case. The severity of a violation should be assessed by taking into account both the applicant's subjective perception and what is objectively at stake in a particular case.[55]

The ECtHR has considered both financial and non-financial disadvantage for the purposes of this criterion of admissibility. Although it is impossible to identify a fixed sum of money beyond which the ECtHR will find an application inadmissible, it is fair to point out that inadmissibility is an unlikely outcome if the damages sought exceeds 500 euro.[56] Smaller amounts can still be significant, depending on the personal circumstances of the applicant. It is even more difficult to establish a significance threshold for non-financial disadvantage. The ECtHR has held, for example, that an expulsion of short duration from school did not constitute significant disadvantage,[57] nor did the expropriation of a small piece of land.[58]

5.4.2 The System of the American Convention on Human Rights

5.4.2.1 Overview of Admissibility Review

In the Inter-American system, individuals cannot access the IACtHR but only the IACommHR, which reviews all applications' admissibility.[59] The process resembles the European system before 1998, when Protocol 11 ECHR came into effect.

Admissibility is addressed normally in a separate decision but, sometimes, the Commission reviews it with the merits, if the facts underlying both are inextricable, or for reasons of urgency warranting the case's immediate referral to the Commission for adjudication.[60] In 2020, the IACommHR published a '*Digesto*' on admissibility, to systematise its practice and, concurrently, reduce the mounting backlog.[61] This document provides a helpful primer on this notion.

---

[55] Practical Guide on Admissibility Criteria, n. 36, para. 83.

[56] Ibid., para. 85.

[57] ECtHR, Application no. 300/11, *C.P. v United Kingdom*, Decision, 21 December 2010.

[58] ECtHR, Application no. 14501/12, *Borg and Vella v Malta*, Decision, 3 February 2015.

[59] The IACtHR reviews individual applications only upon the Commission's referral, after the latter's report on the merits, and if certain requirements are met, namely, that the respondent State must have accepted the IACtHR's jurisdiction, and must have failed—in the Commission's view—to follow its recommendations. IACommHR Rules of Procedure, Article 43.

[60] Ibid., Article 36.3.

[61] Organization of American States 2020, p 9.

5.4.2.2 Backlog Management

The division of labour between the various bodies of the Inter-American system is worth describing, before focusing on their admissibility scrutiny, and bearing in mind the system's struggle to manage its caseload.[62]

Remarkably, all applications are screened twice under 'the same competency and admissibility requirements', but '[w]ith a different level of strictness in the analysis.'[63] The first vetting—the so-called 'Initial Review'—is performed by the Commission's Executive Secretariat which screens the applications' content;[64] the second review occurs (if and) when they pass to the IACommHR, after notifying the State.

Somewhat differently from the European practice, the preliminary screening has increased, rather than reduced, the backlog. Thus, the IACommHR has rearranged its internal bureaucracy repeatedly, including by devoting more resources and personnel to the Initial Review.[65] Furthermore, the Commission has adopted several resolutions to streamline the process using blunt measures, e.g. by rejecting requests to re-examine dismissed petitions.[66] In 2022, it notified collectively 3357 apparently inactive petitioners that their applications would be archived if they failed to respond within 2 months.[67] These measures allowed the IACommHR, in 2023, to eliminate the backlog of applications stuck in the Initial Review stage.

The backlog at the subsequent stage (the IACHR's review of admissibility) warranted other bold measures. In 2016, the IACHR expedited 360 applications that had remained unreviewed at the admissibility stage for more than 10 years, using its power, discussed above, to join the analysis of admissibility with the merits, thus automatically advancing these cases to adjudication.[68]

Moreover, the IACHR piloted a template admissibility report for cases relating to the same underlying situation (for instance, petitions on due process in relation to death penalty sentencing; petitions on the right to appeal criminal convictions and pre-trial detention).[69]

5.4.2.3 The Applicable Criteria

Like the ECtHR, the IACommHR reviews its own competence at this 'admissibility' stage. Therefore, inadmissibility grounds intended widely also include cases in which

[62] On various backlog-reducing policies, see de Oliveira Biazatti 2023.

[63] Organization of American States 2020, p 11.

[64] IACommHR Rules, Articles 26, 28 and 29.

[65] de Oliveira Biazatti 2023.

[66] IACommHR, Resolution 1/19 on the Initial Review of Petitions, 29 October 2019.

[67] IACommHR, Resolution 1/22 on Inactive Petitions Archive, 19 January 2022.

[68] IACommHR, Resolution 1/16, 18 October 2016.

[69] Organization of American States 2018.

the petition falls outside the IACommHR's jurisdiction under the ACHR (*ratione materiae, loci, temporis, personae*).

No textual baseline justifies conflating admissibility and jurisdictional requirements (as opposed to ECHR's Article 35(3)(a), discussed above). Apparently, the IACommHR simply refers to inadmissibility as an *outcome*, whenever applications fail before reaching the merits.[70] However, our analysis here focuses on the non-jurisdictional admissibility requirements.

The IACommHR's Rules of Procedure list the inadmissibility grounds: a) the applicant failed to exhaust domestic remedies, unless mitigating factors intervene;[71] b) more than 6 months have passed since such exhaustion;[72] c) the application duplicates another one pending before, or conclusively examined by, the Commission itself or other international organisations;[73] d) the petition fails to state the facts establishing the alleged breach;[74] e) the petitioner's statements indicate that the claim is 'manifestly groundless or out of order'.[75] Certain circumstances warrant a specific analysis.

For instance, when applying *res judicata*, the IACommHR has held that decisions of UN bodies competent to hear individual applications (like the Human Rights Committee and the Committee against Torture) can render the application inadmissible.[76] However, bodies like the ICJ, or the UN Human Rights Council, the UN Working Groups and Special Rapporteurs do not count for this criterion, since their decisions do not concern individual cases, or are non-judicial.[77] Interestingly, the IACommHR also held that a decision by the Committee on Freedom of Association of the International Labour Organisation would not constitute *res judicata*, because it was not binding and, in any case, did not cover the full range of rights of the American Convention.[78]

---

[70] Besides the hypothesis of 'manifestly groundless' petitions, which properly pertains to admissibility despite its merits-based content.

[71] This seems a pre-condition to the admissibility review, IACommHR Rules, Article 31. The exceptions are: the State's failure to afford due process remedies; denial of justice; excessive delay.

[72] Ibid., Article 32.1.

[73] Articles 46(1)(c) and 47(d) ACHR; IACommHR Rules, Articles 28(9), 33. Article 33(2) lists two exceptions: when the previous case only focused on the State's general conduct rather than the specific applicant's claim, and when it was brought by an applicant with neither link nor mandate from the posterior one. For instance, this occurs if the IACommHR has already addressed a pattern of conduct in its general country reports, see IACommHR, Application no. 11.227, *Jusé Bernardo Diaz et al 'Unión Patriótica' v Colombia*, Report No. 5/97, Admissibility, 12 March 1997, paras 69, 72 and 74.

[74] IACommHR Rules, Article 34(a).

[75] Ibid., Article 34(b).

[76] See, respectively, IACommHR, Application no. 11.827, *Peter Blaine v Jamaica*, Report No. 96/98, Inadmissibility, 17 December 1998, paras 46, 65; IACommHR, Application no. 12.103, *Cecilia Rosana Nuñez Chipana v Venezuela*, Report No. 89/05, Inadmissibility, 24 October 2005, para. 37.

[77] Organization of American States 2020, pp. 30–31.

[78] IACommHR, Application no. 384–08, *Workers dismissed from Ecopetrol v Colombia*, Report No. 49/17, Admissibility, 25 May 2017, para. 15; IACommHR, Application no. 142–04, *José Tomás*

The IACommHR has developed a detailed practice on prior exhaustion. In light of the generous standing criteria (allowing applications by NGOs and large groups), the formalist triple identity test gives way to a substantive test, i.e., whether the *purpose* of exhaustion was met:

> [i]f an alleged victim pursued the matter through one of the valid and appropriate options in accordance with the domestic legal system, and the State had the opportunity to remedy the matter in its jurisdiction, the objective of international law has been achieved.[79]

Besides available, remedies must be adequate and effective. Moreover, the IACommHR has frequently held that the State has the burden of proving the applicant's failure (and must indicate the relevant remedies and their adequacy).[80]

Moreover, the petition must not be 'manifestly groundless', a requirement redolent of the European 'manifestly ill-founded' one, which the IACommHR applies to discard applications with no chances of success, using the 'assessment of colourable claims'.[81] While recognising that this assessment 'does not imply a prejudgment of the merits',[82] the IACommHR has used it for underdefined or overbroad claims,[83] or attempts to re-litigate final domestic judgments (so-called 'fourth-instance' applications).[84]

5.4.3 The African Commission and the African Court on Human and Peoples' Rights

5.4.3.1 The Approach of the African Court to Admissibility

The ACtHPR started operating in 2006. It has issued more than 200 decisions since 2009 and adjudicates cases brought by the African Commission, State parties, and African Intergovernmental Organisations. Conversely, individuals and NGOs can bring applications only against those contracting parties which have agreed by

---

Tenorio Morales and others (Ervin Abarca Jimenez Union for Higher Education Professionals of the National Engineering University) v Nicaragua, Report No. 41/16, 11 September 2016, para. 53.

[79] IACommHR, Application no. 884–07, *Victoria Piedad Palacios Tejada de Saavedra v Peru*, Admissibility, Report No. 16/18, 24 February 2018, para. 12.

[80] IACommHR, Application no. 151–08, *José Francisco Cid v Argentina*, Report No. 83/17, Admissibility, 7 July 2017, para. 17; IACommHR, Application no. 491–98, *Néstor Rolando López and others v Argentina*, Report No. 3/11, Inadmissibility, 5 January 2011, para. 26.

[81] Organization of American States 2020, p 58.

[82] IACommHR, Application no. 681–00, *Guillermo Patricio Lynn v Argentina*, Report No. 69/08, Admissibility, 16 October 2008, para. 48.

[83] IACommHR, Application no. 11.214, *Pedro Velásquez Ibarra v Argentina*, Report No. 40/06, Admissibility, 15 March 2006, para. 54; IACommHR, Application no. 1057–07, *Thelmo Reyes Palacios v Mexico*, Report No. 14/18, Admissibility, 24 February 2018, para. 11.

[84] IACommHR, Application no. 11.671, *Carlos García Saccone v Argentina*, Report No. 8/98, Admissibility, 2 March 1998, para. 53.

a specific declaration to the ACtHPR's compulsory jurisdiction.[85] Alongside the ACommHPR-specific track (similar to the Inter-American and pre-1998 European systems) a growing practice exists of direct applications to the Court against States that have opted-in. The African Commission and the African Court use the same admissibility criteria.[86]

The ACtHPR follows the ICJ's approach (see Sect. 5.2), addressing separately questions relating to its jurisdiction/competence and challenges to the application's admissibility.[87] It has settled into this approach after some hesitation, partly because the judges struggled to reconcile the public international law admissibility's template with the ECtHR's eccentric approach (whereby jurisdictional requirements are a subset of admissibility criteria, see Sect. 5.4.1).[88]

5.4.3.2 The Applicable Admissibility Criteria

Despite rejecting the ECtHR's practice, the ACtHPR applies similar treaty-based admissibility criteria. Specifically, Article 56 ACHPR establishes seven admissibility requirements that are largely comparable to those envisaged in Article 35(2) ECHR.[89] These are: (1) the prohibition of anonymous applications; (2) compatibility with the ACHPR and the AU Constitutive Act;[90] (3) the prohibition of disparaging language; (4) the prohibition against applications exclusively based 'on news disseminated through the mass media'; (5) the exhaustion of local remedies; (6) the requirement of a reasonably prompt submission after the exhaustion; (7) the prohibition to submit cases already settled by other procedures.

Notably, unlike the ECtHR, the ACtHPR has not used the second requirement to handle jurisdictional questions within the admissibility review. Regarding the other requirements, its practice largely aligns with that of the ECtHR, and a short comparative discussion suffices.

The most-often invoked admissibility requirements are exhaustion and timeliness. The ACtHPR's test to ascertain exhaustion and its exceptions builds on the African Commission's practice[91] and comprises several elements: only ordinary domestic remedies count (not extraordinary ones like applications for executive pardons),[92]

[85] Articles 34(6) and 5(3) ACtHPR Protocol. Presently, eight out of 34 ratifying States have accepted the African Court's jurisdiction on individual applications.

[86] Plagis 2021. On the Commission' work and use of admissibility criteria, see Jimoh 2022.

[87] E.g., ACtHPR, Application no. 003/2011, *Mkandawire v Malawi*, Ruling, 21 June 2013, paras. 32 and 33, and Joint Dissenting Opinion of Judges Gerard Niyungeko and El Hadji Guisse, para. 3.

[88] For a chronology of this debate, see Plagis 2021, para. 5.

[89] Article 56 ACHPR is referred to in Article 6(2) ACtHPR Protocol (referring expressly to 'admissibility') and is replicated in Rule 40 Rules of Court.

[90] Originally, the OAU Charter.

[91] Udombana 2003; Chenwi 2019.

[92] ACtHPR, Application no. 034/2016, *Juma Haruna v Tanzania*, Ruling, 7 November 2023, para. 39; ACtHPR, Application no. 023/2015, *Laurent Munyandilikirwa v Rwanda*, Ruling, 2 December

and they must be available, effective[93] and sufficient.[94] The requirement that the application be brought within a reasonable time is apparently looser than the strict four- or six-month time-bars applied in Europe and America. The ACtHPR has clarified that this requirement must be assessed considering each case's circumstances,[95] including 'the applicant's situation, the fact that he or she is in prison, is lay, did not benefit from legal assistance, and is indigent or illiterate.'[96] Applicants, however, enjoy no presumption: besides these circumstances' existence, they must prove that they caused the delay.

Some circumstances can justify long delays, e.g. if an applicant fled the respondent State,[97] or an indigent and incarcerated applicant received the court records belatedly.[98] However, justification is not easily accorded. For instance, the ACtHPR rejected a claim brought more than 6 years after the respondent state had lodged its declaration accepting individual applications. While the applicant in this case had proved his incarceration during that period, he 'failed to explain why he waited for [so long] to file the Application'.[99] Likewise, the ACtHPR rejected another applicant's argument that the delay (more than 6 years) was justifiable because the Court's existence was unknown in the Tanzanian prison where he served his sentence, since his ignorance was not decisive and rather evinced negligence.[100] This decision reflects the Court's strict approach in assessing mitigating circumstances for lengthy delays: in 2019, it had expressly mentioned the scenario of the applicant's ignorance that the Court existed as potentially justifying the extension of the reasonable delay.[101]

Inadmissibility due to *res judicata* (or *lis pendens*) appears to be motivated by the operation of other international fora in the region,[102] and normally hinges on the triple identity between the cases (parties, cause of action, remedy). However, the generous standing conditions—permitting NGOs to bring applications before the

---

2021, para. 74; ACtHPR, Application no. 005/2013, *Alex Thomas v Tanzania*, Ruling, 20 November 2015, para. 64.

[93] ACtHPR, Application no. 062/2019, *Sébastien Germain Ajavon v Benin*, Ruling, 4 December 2020, para. 86; Application no. 009/2016, *Mamadou Diakité and Another v Mali*, Ruling, 28 September 2017, para. 42.

[94] ACtHPR, Application no. 054/2019, *Mama Seidou Samiratou v Benin*, Ruling, 5 September 2023, para. 36.

[95] ACtHPR, Application no. 013/2011, *Beneficiaries of late Norbert Zongo and Others v Burkina Faso*, Ruling, 28 March 2014, para. 92; ACtHPR, Application no. 032/2015, *Kijiji Isiaga v Tanzania*, Ruling, 21 March 2018, para. 56; *Thomas v Tanzania*, n. 92, para. 73.

[96] *Haruna v Tanzania*, n. 92, para. 47.

[97] ACommHPR, Application No. 307/05, *Chinhamo v Zimbabwe*, Decision, 28 November 2007, paras. 88–89.

[98] *Thomas v Tanzania*, n. 92, para. 74.

[99] *Haruna v Tanzania*, n. 92, para. 50.

[100] ACtHPR, Application no. 026/2017, *Mauridi Swedi alias Mswezi Kalijo v Tanzania*, Ruling, 7 November 2023, para. 58

[101] ACtHPR, Application no. 015/2015, *Godfred Anthony and Ifunda Kisite v Tanzania*, Ruling, 26 September 2019, para. 48.

[102] For an overview, see Gathii and Otieno Mbori 2020.

African Court—require relaxing this test.[103] For instance, the African Court held an application inadmissible because the same matter had been brought against the same State before the African Committee of Experts on the Rights and Welfare of the Child.[104] Even if the applicants before the other forum were different (namely, other NGOs), the African Court recognised that both cases were instances of public interest litigation. Therefore:

> the identity of parties in different Applications can be considered as being similar to the extent that they both aim to protect the interest of the public at large, rather than only specific private interests.[105]

In another case, the African Court applied the same inadmissibility grounds noting that the applicant had brought a case before the HRC, under a provision of the International Covenant on Civil and Political Rights comparable to one of the African Charter. It held that the views of the HRC, which is not a judicial body, settled the case triggering the application's inadmissibility, and that whether the respondent State had followed or not the HRC's recommendations—possibly engaging in a continued breach—was immaterial.[106]

The prohibition of disparaging language is, understandably, rarely decisive, and the African Court has tempered it with the freedom of expression granted under Article 9(2) ACHPR, particularly when the applicant is a politician.[107] Inadmissibility of media-disseminated allegations is peculiar to the African system, and has never been applied.[108] This ground apparently seeks to prevent NGO-driven litigation from channelling unsubstantiated cases based exclusively on propaganda.

Interestingly, applications must not be *prima facie* grounded on the merits, unlike in Europe and America, where 'manifestly ill-founded' and 'manifestly groundless' applications are inadmissible. Instead of this *de minimis* requirement, the African

---

[103] For reference, the ECtHR requires that the cases concern the 'same persons, facts and complaints': ECtHR, Application no. 23205/08, *Karoussiotis v Portugal*, Judgment, 1 February 2011, para.63.

[104] Established under the African Charter on the Rights and Welfare of the Child, adopted on 1 July 1990, entered into force on 29 November 1999.

[105] ACtHPR, Application no. 042/2020, *Tike Mwambipile & Equality Now v Tanzania*, Ruling, 1 December 2022, para. 50. Interestingly, the ECtHR concluded differently in *Folgerø v Norway*, noting that the victims of an alleged violation were not exactly the same as for the application before the HRC, so the case was admissible even if the facts were identical. This flexible use of the criterion 'prevent[ing] forum shopping' seemingly aligns with the ECtHR's more rigorous approach to standing: ECtHR, Application no. 15472/02, *Folgerø and Others v Norway*, Judgment, 29 June 2007.

[106] ACtHPR, Application no. 016/2017, *Dexter Eddie Johnson v Ghana*, Ruling, 28 March 2019, para. 54. For a critique, see Novak 2019.

[107] ACtHPR, Application no. 013/2020, *Komi Koutché v Benin*, Ruling, 22 September 2022, paras. 37–38.

[108] ACommHPR, Communication nos. 147/95–149/96, *Sir Dawda K Jawara v The Gambia*, Decision, 11 May 2000, paras. 24–26.

Court had to overcome a peculiar '*de maximis*' objection, i.e. that cases alleging 'a series of serious or massive violations' cannot be heard by the Court.[109]

5.4.4 *The Arab Court of Human Rights*

The Arab Court could not receive individual applications even if it were operative. Complaints may be brought by States—including some which are also parties to the ACtHPR Protocol—and, subject to a specific declaration, by accredited human rights NGOs.[110] Therefore, admissibility requirements provide only a textual comparator, and do not shape individuals' access to international justice, a prospect foreclosed in the Arab system.[111]

The Arab Court's Statute lists three admissibility requirements: exhaustion of local remedies, non-duplication of cases before another regional human rights court (*lis pendens* and *res judicata*), and a six-month time-bar.[112]

Besides some doubts on the interpretation of the requirement about external proceedings (it seemingly excludes non-regional bodies, like the HRC, and quasi-judicial entities like the ACommHPR),[113] the only relevant comment relates to the pithiness of these admissibility rules. Compared to all other regional systems, these clauses seem rather unspecific, also considering their recent drafting. Normally, lack of precision should favour claims' admissibility, but the exclusionary rules of standing and the absence of cases make all assessment ultimately speculative, also since the Rules of Court will have to be drafted by the Arab Court, if it will be established.

5.5 Comparative Reflections

Admissibility in human rights litigation forecloses merits adjudication for some applications, and risks eroding the applicants' right to access international judges. Accordingly, admissibility in practice is the result of tinkering and compromise, rather than strictly applied rules:

---

[109] ACtHPR, Application no. 006/2012, *The African Commission on Human and Peoples' Rights v Republic of Kenya*, Ruling, 26 May 2017, para. 53. See Article 58 ACHPR: when it appears to the ACommHPR that are special cases revealing the existence of serious human rights violations, the Commission shall draw the attention of the African Union's Assembly of Heads of State and Government (without however establishing an inadmissibility or jurisdictional criterion).

[110] ArabCtHR Statute, Article 19.2.

[111] Arguably, the Arab Court would be effective despite its limited jurisdiction, see Almutawa 2021. *Contra*, International Commission of Jurists 2015.

[112] ArabCtHR Statute, Article 18.

[113] Magliveras and Naldi 2016, pp. 165–166; Ghantous 2022.

> admissibility criteria, which might constitute a significant barrier to access to the regional machinery, do not generally appear to do so in practice. The relevant bodies have largely taken seriously the admissibility criteria but have not been overly formalistic in their application.[114]

Some observations drawn from the comparative survey are possible.

5.5.1 Common Traits

First, two admissibility rules apply across the board: exhaustion of local remedies and time-bars. Exhaustion derives from a rule of admissibility applicable in the field of diplomatic protection, and reflects human rights systems' subsidiarity. The latter strikes belated (but otherwise good) claims. Their combined application creates a narrow window of opportunity, before and after which claims can become inadmissible, and requires applicants' meaningful diligence.

Second, in all human rights systems admissibility requirements are codified in treaties. This model deviates from the presumption that express limitations to a court's consent-based jurisdiction are, instead, jurisdictional. This conceptual blur is mostly inconsequential, and the practice seems to have digested these treaty-based admissibility conditions with ease. Arguably, this unorthodox usage aligns with the apparent difference between classic *rationes*-based jurisdictional limits and express admissibility requirements; the latter's core rationale is rather to reduce the flow of viable applications, than disempower the judges.

Third, in all human rights systems admissibility requirements' design promotes legal certainty and subsidiarity (through time limitations and exhaustion). However, their application, evolution and update in the 'busier' systems (the European and American) were driven apparently by caseload-management concerns, i.e. to prevent and/or address surges of applications that could overburden the system. This function is dormant in the Arab system (which awaits establishment of a Court), but permeates the African one, where inadmissibility is routinely used to dismiss belated applications. This goal explains the subsequent reforms in Europe and in America and the apparent inroad of admissibility requirements into the merits (stipulating *de minimis* review, or introducing 'manifest groundless/ill-founded' thresholds), both pursuing the goal of sustainability. Ultimately, admissibility requirements are pressure-points used to safeguard institutional processes vulnerable to overload, without resorting to alternative means that would be equally effective (like restricting the systems' jurisdiction) but raise the prospect of human rights-backsliding.

Fourth (and resultantly), all systems somehow position the admissibility check along a sequence of procedural steps preceding the merits. Some of these steps anticipate or duplicate the admissibility analysis, under cover of reviewing administratively the applications' completeness or validity. In each system, the entire process must be appreciated to identify admissibility's precise role and weight therein; to compare the admissibility practice of two systems without acknowledging their specific contexts

[114] Hampson et al. 2018, p 185.

can yield confusing information. For instance, the ECtHR rejects more than seventy per cent of the applications at the admissibility stage, while the IACHR rejects a minority.[115] This superficial difference is misleading since, before the admissibility stage, the IACHR's Secretariat runs a pre-admissibility check using the same criteria, rejecting the vast majority of applications. While the systems have over time adopted different organisational models, their overall aim with regards to the ultimate purpose (of selecting carefully how many applications should reach the merits) is similar, and similarly handled.

5.5.2 Differences

Despite several differences across them, the regional human rights systems are essentially comparable as regards the establishment of admissibility criteria and their application. However, the following distinctions are noteworthy.

First, the ECtHR has determined that the right of access to justice includes the right to have duly submitted applications rejected by judges (not administrative staff). Instead, the American and African systems accept that applications can be dismissed administratively after a *prima facie* admissibility check. This principled divide transpires from the different set-up and division of labour of the systems examined.[116] This means that the European system at least formally relies on judicial decision-making at the admissibility stage, unlike the other systems discussed. In practice, a significant proportion of such decision-making is effectively performed by the ECtHR Registry lawyers, and the Single Judge's role is often for confirmation only, a circumstance that reduces the effective relevance of this distinction.

Second, the specific language of their admissibility clauses reflects each system's peculiarities and history, revealing local flavours and concerns through minor variations or additions. For instance, the concern with unbridled propaganda and uncontrolled dissemination of fake news in the African continent shaped the 'mass media allegations' criterion in the African system; conversely, awareness of an endemically modest legal literacy has shaped the 'reasonable' characterisation of time-bars (instead of fixed ones); attention to indigenous peoples' collective rights motivated the softening of the victim requirement in the American and African systems and in turn the tests of *res judicata* or *lis pendens*. In Europe, tasking the ECtHR with processing thousands of applications has led to the creation of the additional *de minims* filter of 'significant disadvantage', to reduce the workload. In the Arab system, the rudimentary language of the applicable clauses might reflect the regional lack of experience with enforcing human rights claims in supra-national fora.

Third, as explained above, the European and American systems accept some overlap between admissibility and jurisdiction and use the label of inadmissibility

[115] Ibid., p 171.

[116] Before 1998, a Commission performed the preliminary screening of applications in Europe, but it was dissolved by Protocol 11.

to characterise the rejection of applications for jurisdictional flaws. Conversely, the African system opted for the clear-cut distinction reflected in the ICJ's case-law. Ultimately, there is limited practical difference between the two approaches; all treaty-based admissibility conditions operate effectively as limits to the jurisdiction of the forum seised, and adopting a unified procedural label for the decisions with which the claims are dismissed seems practical.

5.6 Conclusions

The rules on admissibility in regional human rights courts and commissions have a common core. However, its precise codification and practice vary, and understandably so. These systems have faced different challenges and admissibility tools are systematically honed or applied to address them. These differences result not only in textual variations, but also in how similar provisions apply differently in the practice. Admissibility rules are largely perceived as administrative or formal criteria, but their application is not always automatic, and in practice the various institutions maintain a margin of discretion.

Besides the variations between the regional systems, a further difference has emerged between the notion of inadmissibility stipulated in general international law and the usage in most regional systems, which elides the distinction with jurisdiction. The arguable causes of this field-specific approach are: the legacy of diplomatic protection, the analogy with domestic legal cultures, and the caseload-management function that admissibility often discharges.

References

Almutawa A (2021) The Arab Court of Human Rights and the Enforcement of the Arab Charter on Human Rights. Human Rights Law Review 21:506-532.

Amerasinghe CF (2008) Diplomatic Protection. Oxford University Press, Oxford.

Brown C (2007) The Common Law of International Adjudication. Oxford University Press, Oxford.

Chenwi L (2019) Exhaustion of local remedies rule in the jurisprudence of the African Court on Human and Peoples' Rights. Human Rights Quarterly 41:374-398.

de Londras F, Dzehtsiarou K (2015) Great Debates on the European Convention on Human Rights. Palgrave, London.

de Oliveira Biazatti B (2023) Overcoming the Backlog in the Initial Review of Petitions in the Inter-American Commission on Human Rights. EJIL:Talk! 27 October 2023. https://www.ejiltalk.org/overcoming-the-backlog-in-the-initial-review-of-petitions-in-the-inter-american-commission-on-human-rights/. Accessed 29 March 2025.

Dugard J (2005) Diplomatic protection and human rights: the draft articles of the International Law Commission. Australian Yearbook of International Law 24:75-91.

Dzehtsiarou K (2021) Can the European Court of Human Rights Shape European Public Order? Cambridge University Press, Cambridge.

Fontanelli F, Busco P (2016) The Function of Procedural Justice in International Adjudication. The Law and Practice of International Courts and Tribunals 15:1-23.

Fontanelli F, Sthoeger E (2024) Alternative and Atypical Dispute Settlement Resolution Methods. In: Gomula J, Wittich S (eds) Research Handbook of International Procedural Law. Edward Elgar, Cheltenham, pp. 578-597.
Forde A (2024) European Human Rights Grey Zones: The Council of Europe and Areas of Conflict. Cambridge University Press, Cambridge.
Gathii JT, Otieno Mbori H (2020) Reference Guide to Africa's International Courts: An Introduction. In: Gathii JT (ed) The Performance of Africa's International Courts: Using Litigation for Political, Legal and Social Change. Oxford University Press, Oxford, pp. 300-344.
Ghantous M (2022) Arab Court of Human Rights. In: Binder C et al (eds) Elgar Encyclopaedia of Human Rights. Edward Elgar, Cheltenham, pp. 145-149.
Hampson F et al (2018) Inaccessible apexes: Comparing access to regional human rights courts and commissions in Europe, the Americas, and Africa. International Journal of Constitutional Law 18:161-186.
International Commission of Jurists (2015) The Arab Court of Human Rights: A Flawed Statute for an Ineffective Court. https://www.icj.org/wp-content/uploads/2015/04/MENA-Arab-Court-of-Human-Rights-Publications-Report-2015-ENG.pdf. Accessed 28 March 2025.
Jimoh MA (2022) A critique of the seizure criteria of the African Commission on Human and Peoples' Rights. African Human Rights Law Journal 22:362-378.
Kolb R (2014) The Elgar Companion to the International Court of Justice. Edward Elgar, Cheltenham.
Leckie S (1988) The inter-state complaint procedure in international human rights law: hopeful prospects or wishful thinking? Human Rights Quarterly 10:249-301.
Magliveras K, Naldi G (2016) The Arab Court of Human Rights: a study in impotence. Revue Québécoise de droit international 29:147-172.
Novak A (2019) A missed opportunity on the mandatory death penalty: a commentary on *Dexter Eddie Johnson v Ghana* at the African Court on Human and Peoples' Rights. African Human Rights Yearbook 3:456-469.
Organization of American States (2018) 'IACHR completes 2 years of its Procedural Backlog Reduction Program and announces new actions approved following a second round of its participatory process of consultations'. Press Release No. 257/18, 5 December 2018. https://www.oas.org/en/iachr/media_center/preleases/2018/257.asp. Accessed 29 March 2025.
Organization of American States (2020) Digest of the Inter-American Commission on Human Rights on its Admissibility and Competence Criteria. OEA/Ser.L/V/II.175 Doc. 20, 4 March 2020. https://www.oas.org/en/iachr/reports/pdfs/DigestoADM-en.pdf. Accessed 28 March 2025.
Pellet A (2013) Peaceful Settlement of International Disputes. In: Oxford Encyclopaedia of Public International Law. Oxford University Press, Oxford. https://opil.ouplaw.com/home/mpil. Accessed 28 March 2025.
Plagis MA (2021) Jurisdiction and Admissibility: African Court on Human and Peoples' Rights (ACtHPR). In: Oxford Encyclopaedia of Public International Law. Oxford University Press, Oxford. https://opil.ouplaw.com/home/mpil. Accessed 28 March 2025.
Tickell A (2011) Dismantling the iron-cage: the discursive persistence and legal failure of a "bureaucratic rational" construction of the admissibility decision-making of the European Court of Human Rights. German Law Journal. 12(10):1786-1812.
Udombana NJ (2003) So Far, So Fair: The Local Remedies Rule in the Jurisprudence of the African Commission on Human and Peoples' Rights. American Journal of International Law 97:1-37.
UN International Law Commission (2006) Draft Articles on Diplomatic Protection, ILC Yearbook 2006, vol II, pt 2.
Wallace S (2019) The Application of the European Convention on Human Rights to Military Operations. Cambridge University Press, Cambridge.

Chapter 6
The Processes and the Procedures of Hearing a Case

Daniel M. Walyemera

Contents

6.1 Introduction 126
6.2 The Courts' Power to Determine Their Jurisdiction Under the Principle of *Kompetenz-Kompetenz* 127
6.2.1 Interpretation of International Instruments and the Jurisdiction of Human Rights Courts 128
6.2.2 Principle of *Kompetenz-Kompetenz* 129
6.2.3 Jurisdiction of Regional Human Rights Courts 130
6.3 The Commencement and Management of Proceedings 131
6.3.1 Institution of Court Proceedings and Admissibility of Applications 131
6.3.2 The Management of Court Proceedings 133
6.3.3 Effective Participation of the Parties 135
6.4 Representation of Litigants and Role of Amicus Curiae and Other Third-Party Interventions 136
6.4.1 Representation of Litigants 136
6.4.2 Third-Party Intervention Including *Amicus Curiae* 137
6.5 The Joinder of Court Proceedings and Preliminary Objections 138
6.5.1 The Joinder of Court Proceedings 138
6.5.2 Preliminary Objections 139
6.6 Management of Evidence at Regional Human Rights Courts 140
6.6.1 Rules of Adducing Evidence Before the Courts 140
6.6.2 Role of In-Situ Visits Undertaken by the Courts 141
6.7 The Ending of Proceedings 142
6.7.1 Dismissal of Applications 142
6.7.2 Non-Appearance of Parties and Default Judgments 143
6.8 Legal Costs, Legal and Financial Aid 144
6.9 Conclusion 146
References 146

Abstract This chapter provides a comparative analysis of processes and procedures in adjudicating human rights disputes at the Arab, African, Inter-American, and European Human Rights Courts. It includes the complex undertaking of the regional human rights courts' power to determine their jurisdiction. The chapter

---

D. M. Walyemera (✉)
College of Law, University of South Africa (UNISA), Pretoria, South Africa
e-mail: walyedm@unisa.ac.za

A. Almutawa and K. D. Magliveras (eds.), *A Comparison of the European, Inter-American, African and Arab Human Rights Courts: Institutional Aspects*,
https://doi.org/10.1007/978-94-6265-695-6_6

also addresses: the institution of, management, and conclusion of court proceedings; the representation of the litigants; the role of *amicus curiae* and third-party interventions; the value of investigations, inquiries, and *in-situ* visits undertaken by the courts. Moreover, it considers the issue of filing fees at the commencement of an application and the payment of legal costs after a case is concluded. The value of a legal aid scheme to the effectiveness of a regional human rights court is underscored. This is especially so for the legal aid scheme of the European Court of Human Rights, which has developed effective mechanisms for enabling access to justice for vulnerable communities within its jurisdiction.

Keywords *Kompetenz-Kompetenz* · Legal costs · Legal aid · Third-party intervention · *Amicus curiae* · Rules of evidence · Investigations

6.1 Introduction

Protecting human dignity is a core obligation of regional human rights law. Consequently, promoting and protecting human dignity is the basic mandate of regional human rights courts (regional courts). The preambles of numerous human rights instruments emphasise human dignity as their fundamental object and purpose.[1] This normative value is central to interpreting any human rights instrument worldwide.

Without the regional courts, the international human rights system would face significant obstacles in the execution of its core mandate.[2] These obstacles include regional customs, values, and cultural practices that can be difficult to interpret and enforce within the international human rights system. The regional human rights mechanisms are vital to member states' compliance with international human rights standards. Consequently, the Arab, African, Inter-American, and European human rights systems are important enablers in promoting and protecting human rights. Three of the four regional human rights systems have operational human rights courts embedded in their structures.[3] The Arab Court of Human Rights (ArabCtHR) is not yet operational.[4] The Statute that establishes the ArabCtHR has also met with criticism because its provisions conflict with several international human rights standards.[5]

---

[1] UDHR, preambular para 1; ICCPR, preambular para 1; African Charter, preambular paras 1 & 2; ECHR, Art. 1; ACHR, preambular paras 1, 2.

[2] European Parliament 2010, p 5.

[3] As a United Nations-designated region, the Asia-Pacific has not established a regional human rights court.

[4] International Commission of Jurists 2015; Magliveras and Naldi 2016; Almutawa 2021.

[5] Ibid.

Following this introductory section, Sect. 6.2 of the chapter considers the regional human rights Courts' power to determine its jurisdiction otherwise known as the principle of *Kompentenz-Kompentenz*. The commencement and management of proceedings are discussed in Sect. 6.3. Section 6.3 also discusses the effective participation of the parties. Section 6.4 discusses the representation of litigants and the role of *amicus curiae* and other third-party interventions. The joinder of proceedings and preliminary objections are reviewed in Sect. 6.5. Section 6.6 deals with the management of evidence at the four Courts. The non-appearance of parties, dismissal of applications, and default judgments are examined in Sect. 6.7. Section 6.8 discusses the management of legal costs, legal and financial aid. The end of court proceedings is discussed in Sect. 6.9. The chapter is concluded in Sect. 6.9. Interim measures and advisory opinions are not considered in this chapter because they are addressed in Chaps. 7 and 9 of this book.

6.2 The Courts' Power to Determine Their Jurisdiction Under the Principle of *Kompetenz-Kompetenz*

International courts of justice derive their jurisdiction from the instruments that establish them.[6] Regional human rights courts are no exception to this rule. It is however important to note that human rights instruments that establish the jurisdiction of the regional courts must abide by the general rules of interpretation found in the Vienna Convention on the Law of Treaties (Vienna Convention).[7]

Jurisdiction is a fundamental concept for all international courts. How international courts interpret their jurisdiction is the same, with slight variations due to the rules of procedure, object, and purpose for which they were created.[8] There are, however, common procedural practices that have now attained *jus cogens* status under international law. They are part of international customary law rules of procedure in international adjudication.[9] Under international law, consent to a court's jurisdiction is a fundamental prerequisite.[10] There are three major forms of consent: optional, jurisdictional, or compromissory.[11] "Optional" means the state party may consent to the court's jurisdiction at a later stage after signing a treaty.[12] "Jurisdictional" refers to the capacity of an international court to decide specific disputes with binding force

[6] Jardón 2013, p 102.

[7] Vienna Convention on the Law of Treaties, opened for signature 23 May 1969, 1155 *UNTS* 331, entered into force 27 January 1980, Part III.

[8] Jardón 2013, p 123.

[9] Brown 2007; Gray 1987.

[10] African Court Protocol, Article 34(4); ACHR, Article 45; ECHR (Protocol No 11), Article 46; Pellet 2008, p 286.

[11] Jardón 2013, p 125.

[12] Ulfstein 2023.

based on the state parties' past consent to its jurisdiction.[13] "Compromissory" refers to a state party's consent to a treaty that clothes an international court with jurisdiction, which may not be expressed in any form.[14] The form of the state parties' consent may be ascertained as a result of "whether the actions or omissions of the Respondent complained of by the Applicant fall within the treaty allegedly violated".[15]

6.2.1 Interpretation of International Instruments and the Jurisdiction of Human Rights Courts

Regarding the interpretation of international instruments and the jurisdiction of international courts, one school of thought argues that human rights are part of international law and not a separate international legal system and, therefore, must be interpreted by the international law system.[16] It follows that any human rights system that is developed to undermine state sovereignty, which is the fundamental foundation of international law, is intended to destabilise the international human rights system itself. This is so because states are the source of international law and, consequently, of international human rights law as well. Therefore, the general rules of interpretation as laid down in the Vienna Convention should be applied to human rights treaties.

The other school of thought argues that the departure from the general rules of interpretation of international law instruments is justified when interpreting human rights treaties.[17] This school of thought emphasises the element of human rights and not the element of state sovereignty.[18] It is argued that the traditional rules of interpretation cannot be applied to human rights treaties because they are adopted for a specific purpose.[19] Consequently, context-specific rules of interpretation for only human rights instruments should be adopted. The debate between these two schools of thought is still alive and developing.[20]

[13] Szafarz 2023, p 1.

[14] ICJ, *Allegations of Genocide under the Convention on the Prevention and Punishment of the Crime of Genocide* (Ukraine V. Russian Federation: 32 States Intervening), Judgment (Preliminary Objections), 2 February 2024, paras 135–136; Also see de Vries-Zou 2023, pp. 338–364.

[15] ICJ, *Ukraine v. Russian Federation*, para 136.

[16] Jardón 2013, p 102.

[17] Ibid.

[18] Crema 2010, p 694.

[19] Schwelb 1976, p 263.

[20] ECtHR, Application No. 4451/70, *Golder v. United Kingdom*, Judgment, 21 February 1975, para. 31; IACtHR, *Cabrera-García and Montiel-Flores v. Mexico*, Judgment (Preliminary Objections, Merits, Costs), 26 November 2010, Series C No. 220, para 23; ACtHPR, Application No. 001/2008, *Michelot Yogogombaye v Senegal*, Judgment (Preliminary Objections), 21 June 2013, paras. 36–37, 46. Enabulele 2018.

6.2.2 Principle of Kompetenz-Kompetenz

Given the aforementioned discourse, a regional human rights court has the power to ascertain its jurisdiction under the principle of *Kompetenz-Kompetenz* (also known as 'compétence de la compétence').[21] It originated from the case law of the Federal Constitutional Court in Germany.[22] The English translation is "competence – competence". This principle means that a court of law or tribunal can decide as to the extent of its competence or jurisdiction to hear a matter before it.[23] Article 16(2) of the ArabCtHR Statute provides that "the Court shall decide any dispute related to its jurisdiction in examining suits, petitions or cases at hand". Further, under Article 24(1) of the ArabCtHR Statute, challenges to the jurisdiction of the Court are decided by a single judge. Article 3(2) of the Protocol to the African Charter on Human and Peoples' Rights on the Establishment of an African Court on Human and Peoples' Rights (African Court Protocol) provides that "In the event of a dispute as to whether the Court has jurisdiction, the Court shall decide".[24] Interestingly, neither temporal nor territorial jurisdiction is provided for in any of the three instruments governing this Court's administration.[25] In the absence of a statutory provision, the Court has developed case law under Article 3(2) of its Protocol to guide it.[26] Using its discretionary power under Article 3(2), in *Frank David Omary and Others v. Tanzania* it held that the Universal Declaration of Human Rights (UDHR) had attained *jus cogens* status under international customary law.[27] The Court concluded that the UDHR could be cited "as long as the alleged violation is provided for by a treaty ratified by the state concerned".[28]

In the event of a dispute regarding its jurisdiction, the ECtHR is authorised to rule on it.[29] Equally, Article 62 ACHR provides for the IACtHR's power to decide on its own jurisdiction.[30] Thus, in *Gonzalez* et al. *('Cotton Field') v. Mexico*, a preliminary objection was raised regarding its jurisdiction over the applicant's claim.[31] The respondent state argued that the IACtHR did not have jurisdiction to determine

---

[21] Amerasinghe 2003, p 121.

[22] Federal Constitutional Court of Germany, BVerfG, Judgment of the Second Senate of 30 June 2009–2 BvE 2/08 - paras 1–421, para 233. https://www.bverfg.de/e/es20090630_2bve000208en.html. Accessed 3 April 2025.

[23] Shihata 1965.

[24] See, further, African Court Rules, Rule 49(1); ACtHPR, Application No. 001/2011, *Femi Falana v. African Union*, Judgment (Preliminary Objections), 26 June 2012, para 57.

[25] The ACHPR, the African Court Protocol, and the ACtHPR Rules of the Court.

[26] Plagis 2021, para 9.

[27] ACtHPR, Application No. 001/2012, *Frank David Omary and Others v. Tanzania*, Judgment (Jurisdiction), 28 March 2014, paras 73–74.

[28] Ibid.

[29] ECHR, Article 32(2).

[30] IACtHR, *Case of the Constitutional Court v Peru*, Judgment (Competence), 24 September 1999, Series C No. 55. Vienna Convention 1969, Articles 31 and 32.

[31] IACtHR, *Gonzalez* et al. *('Cotton Field') v. Mexico*, Judgment, 16 November 2009, Series C No. 205, paras 31, 32, 35–42.

violations of the Belém do Pará Convention[32] but the Court disagreed and held that it had the power to determine its jurisdiction.[33]

6.2.3 *Jurisdiction of Regional Human Rights Courts*

There is a criterion set by the constitutive instrument of a regional human rights court to exercise its jurisdiction over a matter to determine its merits. The regional court must determine that it has jurisdiction *ratione personae* and *ratione materiae* at the commencement of proceedings. *Ratione personae* refers to the ability to exercise its jurisdiction over a person. *Ratione materiae*, on the other hand, refers to whether the acts complained of, violate the constitutive instrument of the court, and consequently, whether it has been lawfully seized to hear the complaint.

The regional court's jurisdiction to hear a claim may also be challenged based on time and place. This is known as *ratione loci* and *ratione temporis. Ratione loci* requires the court to determine whether the alleged violations occurred in the territory of a contracting party whereas *ratione temporis* refers to the power of the court to exercise jurisdiction after its constitutive instrument came into force. If any of the parties' object to the court's jurisdiction, they must argue within the boundaries of the four forms of jurisdiction to succeed.[34] A regional court's jurisdiction should be distinguished from its admissibility criteria. Admissibility relates to the prerequisites that are set by the court before a matter is heard on its merits. Determining the jurisdiction of a regional court is complicated.[35] It depends on the analysis of the facts of a case. It also depends on the constitutive instrument of the regional court.

It is important to note that whether expressly provided for in the constitutive instrument of a regional court or not, all regional human rights courts follow the same rules on the interpretation of jurisdiction as provided for by the Vienna Convention. Reliance on the previous decisions of a regional court, the court's concept of jurisdiction, and the procedure of adjudicating at a particular court may vary. This does not mean that the regional courts are not following the rules of interpretation as laid down by the Vienna Convention. It simply means the court is adapting to the cultural, economic, political, and social context under which it is functioning.[36] While the debate between cultural relativism and international human rights is old,[37] it remains relevant to the interpretation of human rights in different cultural contexts.[38]

[32] Inter-American Convention on the Prevention, Punishment, and Eradication of Violence against Women (Belém do Pará Convention), adopted on 9 June 1994, entered into force on 5 March 1995, 33 *ILM* 1534 (1994).

[33] Supra, note 31.

[34] Thirlway 2006, para 5.

[35] Jardón 2013, pp. 123–142.

[36] Palombo 2020, pp. 143–171.

[37] Dundes Renteln 2013.

[38] Fagan 2017.

In conclusion, the interpretation of a regional court's jurisdiction is an arduous affair where the court has to assess the facts, its procedure, and its substantive requirements to determine whether it has jurisdiction over a matter. A detailed discussion of jurisdiction is offered in Chap. 3 of this book.

6.3 The Commencement and Management of Proceedings

6.3.1 Institution of Court Proceedings and Admissibility of Applications

All regional human rights Courts have strict criteria for the commencement of proceedings,[39] whose non-observance may lead to the dismissal of the application.[40] The ACtHPR examines an application brought before it to determine whether it has jurisdiction and whether it is admissible according to its Rules.[41] The admissibility Rules of the IACtHR and the ECtHR have slight variations from those of the ACtHPR.[42] The ArabCtHR is open only to the contracting states of the Statute;[43] individual access is not permitted.[44] However, contracting states have the discretion, when ratifying or acceding to the Statute or at any time later, to declare that human rights NGOs accredited in the state, whose citizen claims to be a victim of a human rights violation, have access to the Court.

Experience from other regional human rights systems shows that contracting states do not usually institute court proceedings given the challenges this may create to the states' economic, diplomatic, and political relations.[45] The inability of individuals to access the ArabCtHR is a major shortcoming because it is individuals who are harmed and require remedies.[46] The right of access to file individual petitions is a desirable practice for any human rights court since individuals are usually the principal victims. The ACtHPR has different admissibility criteria.[47] The persons eligible to institute cases are the African Commission on Human and Peoples' Rights,[48] NGOs with

---

[39] African Court Protocol, Article 34(6); ACHPR, Article 56; African Court Rules, Rule 40 on the admissibility of cases; ACHR, Article 20(c); IACtHR Rules of Procedure, Articles 28, 35, 36 & 38; and ECHR, Articles 34 & 35.

[40] ACtHPR Rules of Court, Rules 48 & 65(1)(a)-(b); IACtHR Rules of Procedure, Articles 28, 35, 36, 38; and ECHR, Article 37.

[41] African Court Protocol, Articles 6(2), 34(6); ACHPR, Article 56; ACtHPR Rules of Court, Rule 50(1) on the admissibility of cases.

[42] Ibid; IACtHR Rules of Procedure, Articles 28, 35, 38 & 39; ECHR, Articles 34 & 35.

[43] ArabCtHR Statute, Article 19.

[44] Rishmawi 2005, p 364. Also see AL-HAQ 2014.

[45] Magliveras and Naldi 2016, pp. 161–162.

[46] International Commission of Jurists 2015.

[47] ACHPR, Article 56; African Court Protocol, Articles 6 & 34(6).

[48] African Court Protocol, Article 5(1)(a).

observer status before the African Commission, or an African Organisation seeking an advisory opinion.[49] An individual or a legal entity who is situated within the jurisdiction of a state party can file a matter before the ECtHR.[50] Only the InterAmerican Commission (IACommHR) and state parties to the ACHR can bring cases before the IACtHR.[51] However, individuals may submit their evidence and can be allowed to make oral testimony.[52] The other key criterion on admissibility by all the 4 regional courts is the exhaustion of local remedies.

The basis of claims before the regional courts must emanate from their constitutive instruments.[53] The ACtHPR and the ArabCtHR may also consider other human rights instruments that the respondent state has ratified.[54] The regional courts also have criteria that inform the form and substance of the applications filed.[55] The applications must be admissible following the constitutive instrument of the court. The conditions for admissibility of a case before the ArabCtHR are provided for by Article 18 of the Statute. These include exhaustion of local remedies, that the matter has not been filed before another international forum of dispute settlement, and that the matter has been filed within 6 months from the date of the last judgment given by the competent national court. Perhaps the timeframe within which an applicant should file a case before the ArabCtHR should be interpreted liberally because it is a new human rights court. It could be counter-argued that the principle of equal treatment and security of the law demands that the statutes should be followed to the letter. This, however, is subject to the interpretation rules of the ArabCtHR and its core function to enable access to justice, especially for indigent victims. The ACtHPR has fewer limitations concerning its admissibility criteria compared to the ECtHR and the IACtHR. The ACtHPR has no limits on its temporal jurisdiction[56] whereas the ECtHR and IACtHR do.[57] The ECtHR examines applications to ensure that applicants have not exceeded the six-month time limit. In *Fernie v The United Kingdom*, the ECtHR stated that in determining whether an application has been brought before the Court on time and the applicant has not circumvented the six-month rule, it will assess whether an applicant has not made inappropriate applications to judicial bodies that have no mandate to provide an appropriate redress.[58]

---

[49] African Court Protocol, Article 5, in conjunction with Article 4; ACtHPR Rules of Court, Rule 39(1).

[50] ECHR, Article 35.

[51] African Court Protocol, Article 7.

[52] IACtHR Rules of Procedure, Article 25(1)–(2).

[53] African Court Protocol, Article 3; ECHR, Articles 34 & 35; ACHR, Article 61(1).

[54] African Court Protocol, Article 7; ArabCtHR Statute, Article 16.

[55] ECHR Questions and Answers. http://www.echr.coe.int/Documents/Questions_Answers_ENG.pdf. Accessed 3 April 2025. ECHR, Articles 34 & 35; ACHR, Article 61(1); IACtHR Rules of Procedure, Articles 28, 34, 35, 36, 37, 38 & 39; ACtHPR Rules of Court, Rules 39(1) & 50(1).

[56] ACtHPR, Application No. 003/2011, *Urban Mkandawire v. Malawi*, Judgment (Preliminary Objections), 21 June 2013, para 32.

[57] ECHR, Article 35(1); Sanchez 2023, pp. 1–15.

[58] ECtHR, Application No. 14881/04, *Fernie v The United Kingdom*, Decision (Admissibility), 5 January 2006.

6.3.2 The Management of Court Proceedings

The Rules of Procedure of all regional courts are drafted in a manner that ensures a fair trial. After an application has been deemed admissible by the ACtHPR, it sets a hearing date. Applicant may commence their pleadings by filing the applicable forms.[59] The details on the applicable forms include the name and contact details of the legal representative; one paragraph indicating the nature of the claim and the relief/s sought from the Court; a list of authorities and copies of the judgment/s to be relied on; and the language preferred in presenting the arguments.[60] Coinciding with the COVID-19 pandemic ravaged the world, the ACtHPR amended its Rules of Court to enhance access to justice, with the assistance of technology.[61] Some of the amendments included the commencement of the proceedings by electronic filing of applications.[62]

Matters can only be referred to the IACtHR by state parties or the IACommHR.[63] Individuals and NGOs can file petitions indirectly through the IACommHR, which may refer the matter on to the Court after its own procedures have been exhausted.[64] Whether the Commission refers the case to the IACtHR is governed by the need to secure justice, but where the state fails to comply with the recommendations in its Report on the matter (see below), then the IACommHR must, in the absence of an absolute majority decision to the contrary, refer the case to the IACtHR.[65] The Commission appears before the IACtHR in all cases.[66] The IACommHR or a contracting party to the ACHR may only petition the IACtHR if the respondent state has accepted its jurisdiction.[67]

Under Articles 35 and 36 of the IACtHR Rules of Procedure, the IACommHR or a contracting party to the ACHR shall file a case with the Court's Secretariat. If it is a contracting party applying, it shall state its grounds of objection to the opinion of the IACommHR.[68] If the application was filed by the IACommHR, it shall file the report under Article 50 of the ACHR, which stipulates that the IACommHR must file a report outlining the facts and conclusions of the application as adjudicated by it. The IACommHR is also required to send to litigant parties a statement of the facts, supporting evidence, legal arguments, conclusions, and the purpose of the application.[69] Upon receipt of the application either by the contracting party or the

[59] ACtHPR Practice Directions, sections 6–13.

[60] Ibid.

[61] African Court Protocol, Article 33. See Odum 2020.

[62] ACtHPR Rules of Court, Rule 40(5).

[63] ACHR, Article 61(1).

[64] ACHR, Articles 61(2) & 48–50.

[65] IACommHR Rules of Procedure, Article 45.

[66] ACHR, Article 57.

[67] ACHR, Article 62.

[68] IACtHR Rules of Procedure, Article 41.

[69] IACtHR Rules of Procedure, Article 35.

IACommHR, the Court Secretariat must notify the following[70]: the Presidency and judges, the respondent state, the IACommHR,[71] the alleged victim, the victim's representatives, or the victim's Inter-American Defender. An Inter-American Defender is "a person or group of persons, appointed by the Court in cases in which the alleged victims do not have duly accredited legal representation".[72] Rule 47 provides for the form and substance in which applications should be filed. In addition, the applicants must also show that the matter being filed has not been filed before any other international court for consideration.[73] Other international "courts" include the United Nations (UN) Human Rights Committee and other UN human rights treaty bodies. This requirement also applies to the ACtHPR[74] and to the IACtHR.[75] The framers of international human rights treaties sought to prevent duplication of duties by international human rights mechanisms by incorporating the *lis pendens* rule in the procedural rules of adjudication before these courts.[76] *Lis pendens* is a Latin phrase that means "a pending suit" and means that one court cannot consider a case that is already pending before another court.[77]

The ACtHPR holds four ordinary sessions annually.[78] It may also hold extraordinary sessions to handle urgent matters.[79] It conducts its proceedings in public unless the interests of public order or public morality dictate otherwise.[80] The ACtHPR sessions held virtually due to *force majeure*, are deemed to have been held at the seat of the Court.[81] The decisions of the ACtHPR taken in a virtual session, have the same effect as those held in a physical session at Arusha, Tanzania.[82] The IACtHR holds regular sessions as is required to execute its mandate every year.[83] But special sessions can be held on request by the Court President or a majority of the judges.[84] The IACtHR also holds its sessions in public save for special circumstances.[85] Unlike

[70] IACtHR Rules of Procedure, Article 39.

[71] When the IACommHR has not presented the case itself.

[72] Inter-American Court of Human Rights (2024) What is the I/A Court H.R.? https://corteidh.or.cr/que_es_la_corte.cfm?lang=en. Accessed 3 April 2025.

[73] ECtHR Rules of Court, Rule 47. See Rule 46 on Inter-state applications.

[74] ACtHPR Rules of Court, Rule 50. See also ACtHPR, Application No. 004/2013, *Lohe Issa Konate v. Burkina Faso*, Judgment (Merits), 5 December 2014; ACtHPR, Application Nos. 009/2011 & 011/2011; *Tanganyika Law Society and Others v. Tanzania*, Judgment (Merits), 14 June 2014.

[75] ACHR, Article 46(1).

[76] Galand 2023, p 2. Also see the *res judicata* rule - to prevent re-litigation, and the *electa una via* clause—to prevent duplication at commencement of an application at international human rights courts.

[77] The Law Dictionary 2024.

[78] The sessions are held in March, June, September and November.

[79] ACtHPR Practice Directions, section 4.

[80] African Court Protocol, Article 8; ACtHPR Rules of Court, Rules 52(2) & 57.

[81] ACtHPR Practice Directions, section 5.

[82] Ibid.

[83] IACtHR Rules of Procedure, Articles 11 & 12.

[84] Ibid.

[85] IACtHR Rules of Procedure, Article 15(1).

the ACtHPR and the IACtHR, the ECtHR sits full-time,[86] while, under Rule 20, its plenary sessions shall be convened by the Court President. Even though hearings are public,[87] it may in exceptional circumstances hold them *in camera*, for example, for the welfare of a child, or public morals, national security, and privacy concerns.[88] The ArabCtHR provides for public hearings, except where it is in the parties' "best interests" to hold them in private.[89]

6.3.3 Effective Participation of the Parties

The Rules of Procedure of the regional courts encourage full and effective participation of the parties who have filed applications before them.[90] At the ACtHPR, parties can represent themselves, but they can also select a legal representative of their choice to act on their behalf during the proceedings. Individuals and NGOs can file applications before the ACtHPR. However, as has been explained in other chapters of this book (especially in Chap. 10), individual and NGO applications shall be heard by the Court only if the respondent state has made a declaration under Article 34(6) of the African Court Protocol.[91] Article 5 of the African Court Protocol also provides for the other bodies that may file matters before the Court. Beyond these entities, the ACtHPR can also admit *amicus curiae* and third-party interveners on its own motion or on application by third parties, as earlier discussed. The ACtHPR also allows effective participation in court proceedings by the parties by observing the rules of a fair hearing. Rule 44C of the ECtHR Rules of Court provides that where an individual or a contracting party fails to effectively participate in the hearing of their application, it may lead the Court to handle the application as it deems appropriate. Equally, when a contracting respondent state fails to effectively participate in the proceedings, it does not mean that the ECtHR will discontinue them.[92] Neither the ArabCtHR nor the IACtHR provide for a direct individual complaints system, which may deter the effective participation of the victims of human rights violations.[93] It is however submitted that the strengthening of indirect access by accredited NGOs would ameliorate the lack of individual access thus enabling effective participation of the victims at both these Courts.

---

[86] ECtHR Rules of Court, Rule 21(1).

[87] ECtHR Rules of Court, Rule 63(1).

[88] ECtHR Rules of Court, Rules 63(2)–(3).

[89] ArabCtHR Statute, Article 23(1).

[90] See, for example, ACtHPR Rules of Court, Rules 52–56.

[91] ACtHPR, *Michelot Yogogombaye v Senegal*, supra note 20, para 39; and ACtHPR, Application No. 007/2012, *Baghdadi Ali Mahmoudi v. Tunisia*, Judgment (Jurisdiction), 26 June 2012, para 12.

[92] ECtHR Rules of Court, Rule 44C(1).

[93] Rishmawi 2005 p. 365.

6.4 Representation of Litigants and Role of Amicus Curiae and Other Third-Party Interventions

6.4.1 Representation of Litigants

All four courts allow the representation of the applicants in their individual capacity or by a legal representative or any entity.[94] Article 23(5) of the ArabCtHR Statute provides that "The witnesses and the representatives of the Parties shall enjoy legal and material protection as indicated in the Rules of Court, all facilitations shall be provided to them to carry out their role before the Court". This may be a legal or non-legal representation. Article 10(2) of the African Court Protocol provides that parties to are "entitled to legal representation of their choice". It also provides that legal representation may be given to a party where the interests of justice so dictate. Sections 6, 35(a), and 40 of the ACtHPR Practice Directions provide that a non-legal representative may represent a party in Court proceedings.

Under Articles 25 and 37 of the IACtHR Rules of Procedure, alleged victims are allowed to have an audience before the Court. They may also have legal representation as well as submit briefs. The victims' access to legal representation at the IACtHR has been recently improved.[95] Previously, only the IACommHR or NGOs with specific interests were allowed to represent the victims. Following the amendment of the Rules of Procedure, 'Inter-American Defenders', reference to whom was already made, are trained to act as *pro bono* justice professionals and to be available to represent those alleged victims, who elect not to be represented by an attorney, the IACommHR or NGOs.[96]

An individual, a group of individuals, or an NGO can apply to the ECtHR.[97] The individual(s) or NGO must have a physical address within the jurisdiction of a state party to the ECHR. Individuals or NGOs affected by the state party's extraterritorial acts may also be able to file an application against that state party before the ECtHR.[98]

---

[94] See, for example, ArabCtHR Statute, Article 23.

[95] United Nations Democracy Fund, Training defenders before Inter-American Court of Human Rights. https://www.un.org/democracyfund/news/training-defenders-inter-american-court-human-rights. Accessed 3 April 2025.

[96] IACommHR Rules of Procedure, Article 37; United Nations Democracy Fund, supra note 95.

[97] ECHR, Articles 34 & 35.

[98] ECtHR, Application Nos. 21,034/05 and 7 others, *Sandu and Others v. The Republic of Moldova and Russia*, 17 July 2018.

6.4.2 *Third-Party Intervention Including* Amicus Curiae

Third-party intervention before the regional courts is an important mechanism through which human rights standards can be maintained and developed consistently. All the regional courts provide for third-party intervention including *amicus curiae* except for the ArabCtHR.[99] Perhaps the ArabCtHR Rules of Procedure will provide for third-party intervention when it becomes operational.

Rule 61(2) of the ACtHPR Rules provides that the Court may hear *amicus curiae* if it deems fit. NGOs have taken advantage of this legal provision by filing several requests to be admitted as *amicus curiae*, including other third-party interventions.[100] Moreover, under Rule 61(2), the Court may invite any individual or organisation to express an opinion or submit a report at any time during proceedings. In terms of the procedure for applying for *amicus curiae*, the ACtHPR Practice Directions provide that an individual or an organisation may request to become *amicus curiae* of the Court by stating the specific contribution it intends to make.[101] The decision on whether to grant a request is at the sole discretion of the ACtHPR.[102] Once it has exercised its discretion and granted the request, it provides the *amicus curiae* with all relevant pleadings and submissions. The *amicus curiae* are required to file written submissions and may be called upon to make oral submissions,[103] as happened in *Lohe Issa Konate v. Burkina Faso.*[104]

The ACHR does not specifically provide for *amicus curiae* briefs. The IACtHR can, however, receive requests for third-party interventions and *amicus curiae* under Article 44 ACHR, which provides for the general mandate of the Court. The IACtHR has adopted a very liberal attitude towards the admission of *amicus* briefs. In its first advisory opinion, the Court reviewed the initial amicus briefs concerning the scope of its advisory jurisdiction.[105] Notably, amicus briefs were submitted by CSOs, Organisation of American States (OAS) organs, and state parties to the ACHR. The IACtHR has amended its Rules of Procedure to enable a formal procedure for *amicus* briefs.[106] If the *amicus* briefs have political connotations and are not legal arguments, the IACtHR is duty-bound to reject them. The Court may only consider legal disputes. This, however, does not mean that it will not consider an *amicus* brief that concerns a legal dispute with political undertones. The Court will consider the legal arguments

---

99 ACHR, Article 44; ACtHPR Rules of Court, Rule 61; ECHR, Articles 44 & 48.

100 ACtHPR, Application No. 004/2013, *Lohe Issa Konate v. Burkina Faso*, Judgment (Preliminary Objections; Amicus curiae; Merits), 5 December 2014, paras 20–21, 25, 27, 141–144; several NGOs filed an *amicus* brief with the Court.

101 ACtHPR Practice Directions, section 25.

102 ACtHPR Practice Directions, section 27.

103 ACtHPR Practice Directions, sections 28–30.

104 ACtHPR, *Lohe Issa Konate v. Burkina Faso*, supra note 100.

105 IACtHR, *'Other Treaties' subject to the Consultative Jurisdiction of the Court*, Advisory Opinion OC- 1/82, 24 September 1982, para 5.

106 IACtHR Rules of Procedure, Article 44.

and decide only on them. Several *amicus* briefs have been filed in the exercise of the IACtHR's contentious jurisdiction.[107]

The ECtHR did not have a statutory provision for *amicus curiae* or any third-party interventions before 1983.[108] After 1994, Articles 44 and 48 of the ECHR were amended by Protocol No. 9, which made provision for the appearance of individuals, groups of individuals, and NGOs before the Court.[109] Protocol No. 9 was subsequently repealed by Protocol No. 11, which replaced the text of Articles 19–51 and allowed for third-party intervention under the new Article 36.[110] The Rules of Court, as amended, maintain the statutory provision on third-party interveners including *amicus curiae*.[111]

6.5 The Joinder of Court Proceedings and Preliminary Objections

6.5.1 The Joinder of Court Proceedings

A joinder of court proceedings takes place when pending applications with claims for the same or similar remedies are consolidated into a single set of applications before a court. Its purpose is to enable the efficient management of court matters, to reduce the case backlog, and to avoid handing down judgments with different findings in cases that are similar in content, among other reasons.

The ACtHPR is empowered to join applications on its own motion or on request by litigants. Moreover, it may either join or separate applications or the parties to the application/s. This is done if it is deemed that the joinder or disjoinder is in the interests of justice.[112] The underlying goal is to enable the Court to dispense justice cost-effectively. The ACtHPR is also empowered by Rule 62(2) to seek the opinion of the parties on the joinder or disjoinder of the court proceedings.[113] A similar provision is found in Article 30(3) of the IACtHR Rules of Procedure regarding the joinder of the court proceedings, which the IACtHR is empowered to do where the applications are interrelated by "commonality of parties, subject matter, and

[107] See, for example, IACtHR, *I.V. v. Bolivia,* Judgment, 30 November 2016, Series C No. 329, in which the Court received six briefs.

[108] See ECtHR Rules of Court [amendment of Rules dated 1 January 1983], Rule 37(2) to include third-party interventions.

[109] Protocol No. 9 to the Convention for the Protection of Human Rights and Fundamental Freedoms, opened for signature 6 November 1990, ETS 140, entered into force 1 October 1994.

[110] Protocol No. 11 to the Convention for the Protection of Human Rights and Fundamental Freedoms, opened for signature 11 May 1994, ETS 155, entered into force 1 November 1998.

[111] ECtHR Rules of Court, Rule 44.

[112] ACtHPR Rules of Court, Rule 62(2).

[113] Ibid.

applicable law".[114] The IACtHR may also direct the joinder of written or oral court proceedings of several similar applications in one court hearing.[115]

Rule 42(1) of the ECtHR Rules of Court provides that: "The Chamber may, either at the request of the parties or its own motion, order the joinder of two or more applications". In circumstances where there is a 'mass influx' of applications filed with the Court due to grave human rights violations in a state party, the Court may take administrative measures, including joinder of applications, to manage them more efficiently.[116]

6.5.2 *Preliminary Objections*

Preliminary objections are useful tools in the efficient management of court proceedings. Preliminary objections are legal protestations that are made to a court at the commencement of a matter. If the court is convinced by the preliminary objections of an opposing party, it will not proceed to full trial, to hear the matter on its merits. The procedures of the regional courts provide for the management of preliminary objections. Article 42(4) of the IACtHR Rules of Procedure provides that preliminary objections must be responded to, by the victims, their representatives, or the state, by filing their objections, within 30 days after the Court's notification.[117] The preliminary objections shall be filed with the Court stating the facts on which the objections are based, the relevant legal arguments, and any supporting documents that the objector may wish to produce.[118] *Amicus curiae* may also file briefs regarding the preliminary objections before the Court.[119] The filing of the preliminary objections shall not cause the suspension of the hearing of the merits of the main court proceedings. The Court may decide to join the preliminary objections to the main court proceedings or may decide to rule on them in a special hearing if it deems it appropriate.[120] Rule 60 of the ACtHPR Rules of Court has a similar wording to Article 42 of the IACtHR Rules. The other proceedings on the filing and exchange of pleadings in applications for preliminary objections in the ACtHPR mirror those of the IACtHR.[121] Rule 55 of the ECtHR Rules provides for pleas of inadmissibility. The respondent state may raise a preliminary objection about the application either orally or in written form. These objections will be considered by the Court during the admissibility proceedings under Rules 51 and 54, which set down the procedure

114 IACtHR Rules of Procedure, Article 30(1).

115 IACtHR Rules of Procedure, Article 30(2).

116 ECHR, Article 34; ECtHR Rules of Court, Rule 61.

117 IACtHR Rules of Procedure, Article 42(4).

118 IACtHR Rules of Procedure, Article 42(2).

119 IACtHR Rules of Procedure, Article 44(1).

120 IACtHR Rules of Procedure, Article 42(5), (6).

121 ACtHPR Rules of Court, Rules 60(1), (2), (3), (4) & (5).

for inter-state and individual applications respectively. The ECtHR approach to the admissibility of applications is the same as that of the other regional Courts.[122]

6.6 Management of Evidence at Regional Human Rights Courts

6.6.1 *Rules of Adducing Evidence Before the Courts*

Since the ArabCtHR has yet to be established, there are no rules for presenting evidence.[123] The ACtHPR and IACtHR have statutory rules or rules of practice on adducing evidence before them. The ECtHR, however, has not developed any rules for presenting evidence. For the ECtHR, this position is aptly captured in *Husayn (Abu Zubaydah)* v. *Poland,* where it stated that "In the proceedings before the Court, there are no procedural barriers to the admissibility of evidence or pre-determined formulae for its assessment".[124] This is an admission from the ECtHR that it has yet to adopt a clear approach to the admissibility of evidence. The concepts of the standard of proof and burden of proof are yet to be fully concretised in their practice.[125]

Article 26(1) of the African Court Protocol provides that the Court may hear written or oral submissions from all parties and, if necessary, hold an inquiry. This may include expert evidence. During its oral proceedings, the ACtHPR may call upon witnesses it deems necessary to testify.[126] This provision of the ACtHPR Rules of Court is similar to Article 58(a) of the IACtHR Rules of Procedure.[127] Where a child witness is involved in a hearing, the hearing may be held *in camera* to protect the identity and the interests of the child.[128] Expert witnesses and any other witnesses may be examined and cross-examined.[129] The Court may at any stage of the court proceedings request the opinion of *amicus curiae* or any third-party intervener on

[122] IACtHR Rules of Procedure, Rules 28, 34–39; ACtHPR Rules of Court, Rules 39 & 50 (1); ECHR, Articles 34 & 35.

[123] It is likely that the Rules on adducing evidence will be provided for in the Rules of Court once it becomes operational. The ArabCtHR Statute also does not provide for the procedure for the management of witnesses.

[124] ECtHR, Application No. 7511/13, *Husayn (Abu Zubaydah)* v. *Poland*, Judgment, 24 July 2014, para 394. Also see para 396.

[125] Gunn 2020, p. 201.

[126] ACtHPR Rules of Court, Rules 55(1) and 56(1). Also see Rule 45(3) on enquiries by the Court at any time during proceedings.

[127] See IACtHR Rules of Procedure, Article 58(a), (b) that mirror Rule 55(1) of the ACtHPR Rules of Court.

[128] ACtHPR Rules of Court, Rule 52(3). Also see IACtHR, Advisory Opinion OC-17/2002, IACommHR, Juridical Condition and Human Rights of the Child, 28 August 2002, paras 3–4.

[129] ACtHPR Rules of Court, Rule 54 (4) & (5); IACtHR Rules of Procedure, Rules 51 & 52.

any specific issue before it.[130] The ACtHPR has discretion on whether to admit any person as a witness once a litigant party objects.[131] It is important to note that, of all the regional courts, the IACtHR is the only one that is compelled to refer instances of non-appearance of witnesses, of perjury, and of violation of oath to the 'State with jurisdiction over the witness' so that it can take 'appropriate action'.[132]

6.6.2 Role of In-Situ Visits Undertaken by the Courts

The Courts may on their own motion undertake *in-situ* visits to carry out investigations to ascertain facts on matters before them. Under Rule 2(b) and (c) of the Annexure on Evidentiary Matters of the Practice Directions of the ACtHPR and Rule 55(3) of the ACtHPR Rules of Court, the Court may assign one or more judges to ascertain specific facts or events. The assigned judge(s) may visit a scene and take evidence or testimony during the investigation. Article 58(d) of the Rules of Procedure of the IACtHR is couched in similar words to the aforementioned Rule 55(3). The IACtHR may carry out investigations to collect evidence at any location in the territory of OAS Member States.[133] The ArabCtHR is yet to adopt the Rules of Court,[134] which would ordinarily provide for the Court's investigative powers.

The ECtHR Rules of Court provide for investigations.[135] The ECtHR may appoint one or more judges to carry out on-site investigations and collect evidence.[136] The Court can also appoint other persons and organisations to assist the judges in collecting evidence.[137] The contracting state and the Applicant have a duty to assist the Court delegation during its investigations in the territory of a contracting state.[138] This assistance may be in the form of security for the Court delegation, witnesses, and any other person or institutions engaged in the Court's investigations.[139] The contracting party should also ensure the free movement of the Court delegation in its territory, while the Court's delegation collects evidence.[140] The Rules provide for the parties and the procedure of appearing before the Court delegation as well as for

---

[130] ACtHPR Rules of Court, Rule 54 (4) & (5).

[131] ACtHPR Rules of Court, Rule 56(5).

[132] IACtHR Rules of Procedure, Article 54. In the previous 2002 version of the ECtHR Rules of Court, Rule 69 was similar to Article 54, but that rule has since been deleted leaving only the current Rule 65 on a failure to appear, which simply provides that the ECtHR may proceed with the hearing in absence of the witness. The ArabCtHR Statute does not address these issues, but they could be addressed by the Rules of Court when it becomes operational.

[133] Ibid.

[134] ArabCtHR Statute, Article 28.

[135] See Rules A1 - A8 of Annex to the ECtHR Rules of Court.

[136] Rule A1(3) of Annex to the ECtHR Rules of Court.

[137] Ibid.

[138] Rule A2 of Annex to the ECtHR Rules of Court.

[139] Ibid.

[140] Ibid.

the appearance of both witnesses and experts.[141] The ECtHR Registrar must compile a verbatim record of the investigations carried out by the Court delegation.[142] This verbatim record shall be signed by the head of the delegation, which shall constitute a certified record of Court proceedings.[143]

A literal interpretation of the aforementioned provisions on Court investigations shows that the purpose is to enable the Courts to ascertain for themselves the facts of a case before they make any decisions. This is without any bias from any of the litigant parties appearing before the Court.

6.7 The Ending of Proceedings

6.7.1 Dismissal of Applications

The ACtHPR is empowered to dismiss applications in two broad instances. First, where it considers that the application is "manifestly unfounded", it will dismiss the application by giving reasons for its decision, without summoning the parties involved.[144] In the case of *Ababou v Morocco,*[145] the ACtHPR held that it did not have jurisdiction to hear the application because Morocco was not a state party to the African Court Protocol. The Court also stated that Morocco was not a member state of the African Union. Relatedly, the ACtHPR has the power to strike out an application, if the applicant indicates to the Court that they do not intend to proceed with the application or if the application has not been submitted within the stipulated timelines.[146] Such a struck-out application may be reinstated to the case list of the Court if exceptional circumstances are shown to the Court.[147] Secondly, the ACtHPR will dismiss an application where a state has not ratified the African Court Protocol or has not deposited a declaration within the meaning of Article 34(6) thereof. In *Yogogombaye v Senegal*, the Court held that Senegal had not deposited an Article 34(6) declaration.[148] The Court, therefore, had no jurisdiction to receive applications from individuals for consideration. This was the first-ever application filed before the ACtHPR. Relatedly, in *Atemnkeng v African Union,*[149] the applicant sought to

---

[141] See Rules A5, A6, A7 of Annex to the ECtHR Rules of Court.

[142] Rule A8(1)–(3) of Annex to the ECtHR Rules of Court.

[143] Rule A8(4) of Annex to the ECtHR Rules of Court.

[144] ACtHPR Rules of Court, Rules 48.

[145] ACtHPR, Application No. 007/2011, *Youssef Ababou v Kingdom of Morocco*, Decision (Preliminary Objection), 2 September 2011, para 12.

[146] ACtHPR Rules of Court, Rules 65(1) (a)-(b).

[147] ACtHPR Rules of Court, Rule 65(3).

[148] Supra note 20.

[149] ACtHPR, Application No. 014/2011, *Ataborg Denis Atemnkeng v The African Union*, Judgment, 15 March 2013. See also ACtHPR, *Femi Falana v. African Union*, supra note 24, which was also a majority decision.

sue the African Union. In a majority decision, the ACtHPR held that the African Union was not a party to the African Court Protocol and that only contracting states could be sued.

Article 61 of the IACtHR Rules of Procedure is similar to Rules 65 of the ACtHPR Rules of Court. It provides for the "discontinuance" of applications if the applicants indicate to the Court that they do not intend to pursue their applications to conclusion. This provision also applies where the parties have reached an amicable settlement and consequently notified the Court.[150] Notwithstanding the statutory provisions, the IACtHR may consider, that given its core mandate to protect human rights, it may proceed to consider the application on its merits.[151] Under Article 37 ECHR, the ECtHR may strike out an application for various reasons. These include the fact that an applicant does not intend to pursue his application or that the matter has been amicably resolved.[152] This statutory provision is fortified by Rules 43(1) of the ECtHR Rules of Court, which also provides that it may at any time during proceedings strike out an application from its list of cases, under Article 37 of the ECHR.

6.7.2 Non-Appearance of Parties and Default Judgments

The ArabCtHR Statute does not provide for consequences when a litigant party fails to appear. Perhaps the Rules of Court will provide for it when the Court becomes operational. In the other three Courts, the situation is as follows. In case one of the parties fails to appear at the ACtHPR, Rule 54(7) of the Rules of Court provides that the Court shall proceed to hear the matter, if there was effective service on the absent party for the scheduled Court date. Where both parties do not appear in Court, what would the ACtHPR do? A literal construction of Rule 54(7) shows that the Court may proceed to deliver a default judgment, if the Court records show proof of service of the application to the parties. The Court under Rule 63(1) may enter a judgment in default against a party on its own motion or on application by another litigant party, provided that the Court record shows that the defaulting party was served with the application. The ACtHPR may set aside the default judgment within 1 year if the defaulting party shows sufficient cause, provided the other party has been notified and allowed to respond accordingly.[153]

The IACtHR is also empowered to proceed in the event of the non-appearance of parties in a scheduled hearing. The Court may "take the measures necessary to conduct the proceedings to their conclusion".[154] The absent party may join the Court

---

150 IACtHR Rules of Procedure, Article 63.

151 IACtHR Rules of Procedure, Article 64.

152 ECHR, Article 37(1)(a)-(b).

153 ACtHPR Rules of Court, Rule 63(2) & (3).

154 IACtHR Rules of Procedure, Article 29(1).

proceedings at a later stage but before judgment has been pronounced.[155] Rule 44E of the ECtHR Rules of Court provides that the Court may strike out an application if either the applicant or a respondent state does not pursue it.[156] Rule 65 of the ECtHR Rules of Court is similar to Article 29 of the IACtHR Rules of Procedure regarding the discontinuance and restoration of applications on the Courts' case list.

6.8 Legal Costs, Legal and Financial Aid

All regional human rights Courts provide for legal costs, in some form or another. The general rule at the ACtHPR is that each party will bear its legal costs but there are exceptions.[157] Under Rules 32 of the ACtHPR Rules of Court and Practice Direction No. 11, there shall be no court filing fees for applicants. The IACtHR and ECtHR do not charge court filing fees for submitted applications. The ArabCtHR, as indicated earlier, is not yet operational.[158]

Article 10(2) of the African Court Protocol provides for legal aid to litigants who need it. Rules 31(2) of the ACtHPR Rules of Court provides that the Court shall provide legal assistance within its available financial resources, while Rule 31(3)–(4) fortifies the right to a fair hearing by establishing a legal aid fund for the African Union human rights organs. The legal aid fund of the ACtHPR was established in 2012.[159] It was revised in 2016 and in 2020.[160] Members States of the African Union are the key funders of the legal aid scheme, which is administered by the legal aid unit, under the superintendency of the ACtHPR Registrar. Rules 31 of the Rules of ACtHPR mandates the Court to cooperate with the African Union (AU) Commission in administering the legal aid fund for the AU Human Rights Organs.[161] The ACtHPR maintains a roster of registered counsel who may be called upon to provide legal aid to litigants upon request. Under Rule 31(1), one does not need to be a lawyer to represent an applicant before the Court. Costs for legal expenses are awarded by the ACtHPR where the interests of justice so demand.[162] For example, in *Konate v.*

155 IACtHR Rules of Procedure, Article 29(1)–(2).

156 ECtHR Rules of Court, Rule 43.

157 ACtHPR, Application No. 004/2013, *Lohe Issa Konate v. Burkina Faso*, Judgment (Merits), 5 December 2014, paras 9, 16 & 60; African Court Protocol, Article 27(1); ACtHPR Rules of Court, Rules 40(4) & 69(3) on reparations.

158 When the ArabCtHR becomes operational, it is unlikely to charge fees for the submission and examination of applications, considering that the practice of other regional human rights Courts is to not charge any fees to enable unhindered access to justice.

159 ACtHPR, 'Fees and Legal Aid'. https://www.african-court.org/wpafc/fees-and-legal-aid/. Accessed 3 April 2025.

160 Ibid.

161 Ibid.

162 ACtHPR Rules of Court, Rule 32(2).

Burkina Faso the Court ordered the respondent state to pay damages and expenses to the applicant.[163]

The IACtHR considers equality and non-discrimination as *jus cogens* norm without exceptions.[164] This is because access to justice and non-discrimination are normative human rights standards that the IACtHR is enjoined to enforce.[165] Despite this commitment to equality and non-discrimination, which is inherent in respect for human rights and is given expression in Article 1(1) of the ACHR, until 2010 the IACtHR did not have a legal aid fund to enable vulnerable victims of human rights violations access to it.[166] Even though resisted by some OAS Member States, a legal aid fund for victims was established with the purpose of enabling access to the IACtHR by indigent victims who cannot afford the costs involved in pursuing a claim before it.[167] The fund's operational budget comes from voluntary donations; Denmark and Norway are significant donors.[168] This is due to the fact it is not included in the OAS formal budget owing to scarcity of funds.[169] The fund is managed by the IACtHR Secretariat.

Rules 105 of the ECtHR Rules of Court provides for legal aid, if a litigant has meagre means to pay for the expenses required to file an application and participate in the proceedings. The Court may provide free legal aid to such applicants, when the interests of justice so require. Rule 108(2) of the Rules of Court of the ECtHR reflects a commitment to fair and equal access to justice that is similarly reflected in Article 6 of the ECHR. In terms of procedural fairness, the provision of legal aid to an indigent applicant protects the indigent applicant's right to a fair hearing. It provides that legal aid may cover the legal representative's expenses. For an indigent litigant to qualify for legal aid, the Court has set up benchmarks.[170] Furthermore, the legal aid fund of the ECtHR covers expenses for the applicant's witnesses.[171] The ECtHR also provides for other expenses of the applicant, their appointed representative, and witnesses.[172] Without these legal aid schemes, the regional human rights courts would have fewer matters filed at their court registries. This is because oftentimes, it is the indigents who are vulnerable to human rights violations. It is expensive to litigate at any regional human rights court. Therefore, all regional human rights

---

[163] ACtHPR, Application No. 004/2013, *Lohe Issa Konate v. Burkina Faso*, Judgment (Merits), 5 December 2014, paras 9, 16 & 60.

[164] IACtHR, *Case of the Mapiripán Massacre v. Colombia*, Judgment (Merits, Reparations and Costs), 15 September 2005, Series C No. 134, para 178.

[165] ACHR, Articles 1(1) & 24.

[166] IACtHR Rules of Procedure, Article 79(2).

[167] IACtHR, 'Victims' Legal Assistance Fund'. https://www.corteidh.or.cr/fondo_asistencia_legal_victimas.cfm?lang=en. Accessed 3 April 2025.

[168] Ibid.

[169] Ibid.

[170] ECtHR Rules of Court, Rules 105, 106, 107, 108, 109 & 113.

[171] ECtHR Rules of Court, Rules 105, 106, 107, 108 & 113.

[172] ECtHR Rules of Court, Rules 95 & 105–110.

courts must have legal aid schemes. This is essential for most of the victims who are economically disempowered.

Once an application has been deemed admissible, the Courts examine its merits and determine the outcome by making a judgment.[173] An extensive comparative analysis of the procedure on judgments is considered in Chap. 8 of this book.

6.9 Conclusion

Overall, the importance of fair court proceedings cannot be underestimated in enabling functional and effective regional courts. A comparative analysis of the institution of, management, and adjudication of human rights cases has been carried out for the Arab, African, InterAmerican, and European Human Rights Courts. In numerous instances the procedures of instituting, managing, and concluding a case in these courts are similar.

The role of *amicus curiae* and other party interventions was discussed. It was found that third-party interventions significantly facilitate the effective functioning of the Courts because they benefit from specialised expertise in the adjudication of specific matters before them. The management of legal costs was considered. The costs of litigation can be a hindrance to the promotion and protection of human rights. Various mechanisms have been established to deal with prohibitive litigation costs. They include legal aid schemes, whose importance to indigent litigants cannot be underestimated. The administration of legal aid schemes by the Courts was also assessed. Legal aid is a key pillar in the protection of human rights and a fundamental enabler of regional and international peace.

References

AL-HAQ (2014) Re: Ministerial Council Meeting and the adoption of the draft Statute of the Arab Statute Court of Human Rights. https://www.alhaq.org/advocacy/6608.html. Accessed 3 April 2025.

Almutawa A (2021) The Arab Court of Human Rights and the Enforcement of the Arab Charter on Human Rights. Human Rights Law Review 21:506-532.

Amerasinghe CF (2003) Jurisdiction of International Tribunals. Kluwer Law International, The Hague.

Brown C (2007) A Common Law of International Adjudication. Oxford University Press, Oxford.

Crema L (2010) Disappearance and New Sightings of Restrictive Interpretation(s). European Journal of International Law 21:681-700.

de Vries-Zou IT (2023) An Innovation in the Test for Material Jurisdiction under Certain Compromissory Clauses. The Law & Practice of International Courts and Tribunals 22:338-364.

Dundes Renteln A (2013) International Human Rights: Universalism Versus Relativism. Quid Pro Books, New Orleans.

173 ACHR, Article 66.

Enabulele A (2018) The Problems of Jurisdiction by Optional Declaration: Reflections on Articles 5(3) and 34(6) of the Protocol of the African Court on Human and Peoples' Rights. Australian Journal of Human Rights 24:223–243.
European Parliament (2010) The Role of Regional Human Rights Mechanisms. EXPO/B/DROI/2009/25. PE 410.206. November 2010. https://www.europarl.europa.eu/RegData/etudes/etudes/join/2010/410206/EXPO-DROI_ET(2010)410206_EN.pdf. Accessed 3 April 2025.
Fagan A (2017) Human Rights and Cultural Diversity: Core Issues and Cases. Edinburgh University Press, Edinburgh.
Galand AS (2023) Defer or Revise? Horizontal Dialogue Between UN Treaty Bodies and Regional Human Rights Courts in Duplicative Legal Proceedings. Human Rights Law Review 23 https://doi.org/10.1093/hrlr/ngad009.
Gray C (1987) Judicial Remedies in International Law. Oxford University Press, Oxford.
International Commission of Jurists (2015) Arab Court of Human Rights: A Flawed Statute for an Ineffective Court. International Commission of Jurists, Geneva.
Jardón L (2013) The Interpretation of Jurisdictional Clauses in Human Rights Treaties. Anuario Mexicano de Derecho International 13:99-143.
Magliveras K, Naldi G (2016) The Arab Court of Human Rights: A Study in Impotence. Revue québécoise de droit international 29:148-170.
Odum UN (2020) The Revised Rules of the African Court 2020: towards a more effective African Court. https://africanlii.org/articles/2020-10-02/usani-nicholas-odum/the-revised-rules-of-the-african-court-2020-towards-a-more-effective-african-court#. Accessed 3 April 2025.
Palombo D (2020) Human Rights Adjudication: Between Hopes and Failures. In: Wouters J, Lemmens K, Van Poecke T et al (eds) Can We Still Afford Human Rights? - Critical Reflections on the 70th Anniversary of the Universal Declaration of Human Rights. Edward Elgar Publishing, Northampton, pp. 143-171.
Pellet A (2008) The Anatomy of Courts and Tribunals. The Law & Practice of International Courts and Tribunals 7:275-287.
Plagis M (2021) Jurisdiction and Admissibility: African Court on Human and Peoples' Rights (ACtHPR) Max Planck Encyclopedia of International Procedural Law [MPEiPRO]. https://opil.ouplaw.com/display/10.1093/law-mpeipro/e3760.013.3760/law-mpeipro-e3760. Accessed 3 April 2025.
Rishmawi M (2005) The Revised Arab Charter on Human Rights: A Step Forward? Human Rights Law Review 5:361-376.
Sanchez MA (2023) The African Court on Human and Peoples' Rights: Forging a Jurisdictional Frontier in Post-Colonial Human rights. International Journal of Law in Context, 19:352-366.
Schwelb E (1976) The Law of Treaties and Human Rights. In: Reisman WM, Weston BH (eds) Towards World Order and Human Dignity: Essays in Honor of Myres S McDougal. The Free Press, New York, pp. 266-272.
Shihata IF (1965) The Power of the International Court to Determine its Own Jurisdiction: Compétence de la Compétence. Martinus Nijhoff, The Hague.
Szafarz R (2023) The Compulsory Jurisdiction of the International Court of Justice. Martinus Nijhoff, Dordrecht/Boston/London.
The Law Dictionary (2024) https://thelawdictionary.org/, (featuring Black's Law Dictionary, 2nd edn.). Accessed 3 April 2025.
Thirlway H (2006) Preliminary Objections. In: Wolfrum R, Bogdandy AV, Lachenmann F (eds) The Max Planck Encyclopaedia of Public International Law. Oxford University Press, Oxford, pp. 405-412. https://opil.ouplaw.com/display/10.1093/law:epil/9780199231690/law-9780199231690-e73. Accessed 3 April 2025.
Ulfstein G (2023) Farewell to Compulsory Jurisdiction. British Yearbook of International Law, pp. 1-9. https://doi.org/10.1093/bybil/brad003.

Daniel M. Walyemera is a Postdoctoral Researcher at the College of Law, University of South Africa (UNISA) and an Advocate of the High Court of Uganda. The author has been admitted to the Lists of Counsel of the African Court on Human and Peoples Rights (ACtHPR) and the International Criminal Court (ICC), where he occasionally practices law.

Chapter 7
Interim and Provisional Measures

Eleni Polymenopoulou

Contents

7.1 Introduction 150
7.2 Interim Measures in the Context of the European Human Rights System 151
7.2.1 The Power of the Court to Issue Interim Measures 151
7.2.2 Interim Measures Protecting a Variety of Rights 153
7.2.3 Compliance with Provisional Measures 154
7.3 Provisional Measures in the Context of the Inter-American Human Rights System 154
7.3.1 The Powers of the Inter-American Commission on Human Rights to Order Precautionary Measures (*Medidas Cautelares*) 155
7.3.2 The Powers of the Inter-American Court to Order Provisional Measures 157
7.4 Provisional Measures in the Context of the African Human Rights System 161
7.4.1 The Powers of the African Commission (ACommHPR) to Order Provisional Measures 161
7.4.2 The Powers of the ACtHPR to Order Provisional Measures 163
7.5 Provisional Measures in the Context of the Arab Human Rights System 165
7.6 Conclusion 165
References 167

Abstract The chapter discusses how the mechanism of provisional or interim measures of protection is interpreted and applied in the context of the four main regional systems—with more extensive references to the work of the Courts and Commissions in the Inter-American and African Human Rights systems. The analysis in the chapter explores whether and when interim and provisional measures are available, the authority for ordering them, the rules regulating their use, the reasons underlying their request, their legal validity and binding nature, the difficulties of implementing them and the question of their enforcement. The chapter also provides some examples, considering the use of those measures in situations of extreme urgency, such as pending executions and expulsions.

E. Polymenopoulou (✉)
College of Law, Qatar Foundation, Hamad Bin Khalifa University, Education City Doha, Qatar
e-mail: epolymenopoulou@hbku.edu.qa

A. Almutawa and K. D. Magliveras (eds.), *A Comparison of the European, Inter-American, African and Arab Human Rights Courts: Institutional Aspects*,
https://doi.org/10.1007/978-94-6265-695-6_7

Keywords Interim measures · Provisional measures · Judicial protection · Imminent harm · Irreparable harm · Extreme urgency · Regional human rights courts

7.1 Introduction

The concept of provisional measures, as a form of judicial protection in situations of extreme urgency, is present in virtually all domestic legal systems in both criminal and civil law areas.[1] Such measures are typically ordered in the course of proceedings, with a view to offering urgently needed protection, and to avoid an otherwise imminent, and possibly irreparable harm—including damage to the applicant's life, personality, integrity, or even property.[2] Other rights, however, may also risk being harmed, including, for example, freedom of expression, the right to health and the right to education. Provisional protection is, therefore, naturally also possible at the international level, based on interim relief prescribed in the institutional rules of an international court or tribunal. The purpose of this power is both 'the preservation of the respective rights of the parties pending the decision on the merits' and 'the safeguarding of the jurisdiction of the international court to render a judgment which is effective'.[3]

Provisional measures were conceived already in the context of the jurisdiction of the Permanent Court of International Justice (PCIJ).[4] In its 1931 Rules of Procedure provisional measures 'were regarded as designed to preserve rights claimed in an action at law, sometimes their object was to re-establish or safeguard the *status quo ante*'.[5] At present, many international courts and commissions that are competent in specific matters have such power (for example, the International Tribunal for the Law of the Sea, and UN Commissions such as the UN Commission on International Trade Law).

International human rights entities, including the four regional human rights Courts, provide for the possibility to order provisional measures—or interim measures as they are called in the context of the European system for human rights protection. The function of these measures is precisely to provide interim relief and conserve the respective rights of the parties pending adjudication. The Commissions of the Inter-American and African systems have also this competence, given that these two systems are a two-step process for individuals to access the relevant Court of Justice: the first step is the application before the Commission, the second

---

[1] Brown 2007, p. 21 (noting that 'many international courts have held that there is a general principle of law whereby parties to litigation must abstain from any act which might exercise a prejudicial effect on any future judgment, or aggravate or extend the dispute'); Bantekas and Ullah 2022, p. 250.

[2] See, generally, Palombino et al. 2021; Miles 2017.

[3] Brown 2007, p. 121.

[4] Brown 2007; Wolfrum 2012; Miles 2017, p. 15ff.

[5] Cerna 2021, p. 44; Brown 2007; Rosenne 2005, p. 4.

concerns access to the Court itself. Inter-American bodies have used the procedure far more extensively.[6] Nonetheless, many common features can be found in the way all regional mechanisms have used it, especially regarding urgency[7] and irreparable harm.[8]

7.2 Interim Measures in the Context of the European Human Rights System

7.2.1 The Power of the Court to Issue Interim Measures

Interim measures are not explicitly addressed in the ECHR. They are, however, provided for in Rule 39 Rules of the Court, as presently in force.[9] They are evident in the practice of ECtHR, and the (now defunct) European Commission of Human Rights (ECommHR),[10] even before 1974.[11] Such measures may be ordered by the ECtHR only in case of an imminent risk of irreparable harm.[12] In particular, the following conditions must apply cumulatively: the situation must be imminent and exceptional, there must no longer be any suspensive domestic remedy available against the disputed act, a high degree of probability must exist that the disputed act contravenes the ECHR, and a risk of irreparable damage must be shown.[13]

Under Rule 39, interim measures are intended to prevent 'irreparable harm to a Convention right' where the nature of the harm is such that it 'would not be susceptible to reparation, restoration or adequate compensation'. This is a 'high threshold of seriousness' that should be evidenced in the application, which must

[6] Rieter 2010, p. 1091; Haeck et al. 2011, p. 403.

[7] Brown 2007, p. 142ff; Miles 2017, p. 131ff (discussing international law). Comparisons are in fact abundant in the scholarship, also between the regions, see Burbano-Herrera and Viljoen 2014, p. 157–177.

[8] Brown 2007, p. 139; Rieter 2012, p. 171–172; generally, Rieter 2010, p. 943ff.

[9] ECtHR Rules of Court, Rule 39(1)–(2), last amended on 22 January 2024. See also Wolfrum 2012, p. 1; Cerna 2021, p. 39–40; Haeck et al. 2008, p. 42. The amended Rules were adopted in the context of wider procedural reforms; on 26 June and 6 November 2023, the Plenary Court adopted several decisions clarifying and codifying its existing practice on interim measures, see Changes to the procedure for interim measures, Press Release, ECHR 308 (2023), 13 November 2023.

[10] In *Cruz Varas and Others v. Sweden*, the ECommHR issued an interim order on 6 October 1989 to stay the enforcement of the applicants' expulsion, which was not observed; see ECtHR, *Cruz Varas and Others v. Sweden*, Application no. 15576/89, Judgment, 20 March 1991, paras 52 et seq.; cf. Pasqualucci 1993, p. 818ff. See Saccucci 2021; Marti 2018.

[11] ECommHR Rules of Procedure, entered into force on 13 December 1974, Rule 36; ECommHR, Application no. 3321/67, *Denmark v. Greece*; Application no. 3322/67, *Norway v. Greece*; Application no. 3323/67, *Sweden v. Greece*; Application no. 3344/67, *Netherlands v. Greece*; Council of Europe/Conseil de l'Europe 1972; Marti 2018.

[12] Harris 2023, p. 138ff; Haeck et al. 2008, p. 43; Dzehtsiarou and Tzevelekos 2021, p.1.

[13] Rieter 2010, p. 1092.

set out the grounds justifying the request. In particular, the application must provide a 'detailed description of the current situation', an explanation of the 'nature of the alleged imminent risk of irreparable harm' and all the relevant documents required to support the application and satisfy the ECtHR that the 'high threshold' has been reached.[14]

High-profile cases in which interim measures were ordered arose in extradition cases, particularly those involving fear of torture and exposure to the death row phenomenon (e.g. *Soering*[15] and *Öcalan*[16]) whereas others concerned alleged involvement in terrorist attacks.[17] Most requests have concerned the suspension of expulsion and deportation cases, especially of persons whose asylum applications or immigration requests were rejected by national immigration tribunals.[18] At least two thirds of interim measures concerned immigration in 2023,[19] although from these only a small number (18%) were actually granted.[20] The reason for this rejection could arguably be the fear that 'the European Court was becoming a fourth instance appeal body against national immigration tribunals'.[21] In asylum cases, other reasons arguably include a change of circumstances in the applicants' status as

[14] Practice Direction, Requests for interim measures, annexed to the Rules of the Court, January 2024, pp. 62, 65. https://www.echr.coe.int/documents/d/echr/rules_court_eng (accessed 2 April 2025).

[15] ECtHR, *Soering v. the United Kingdom*, Application no. 14038/88, Judgment, 7 July 1989, Series A no. 161 (finding that the UK would be violating ECHR rules if Soering is extradited to the USA, where he would be facing capital punishment, as he risked being subjected to inhuman and degrading treatment due to the conditions on death row. The ECtHR had indicated interim measures to stay Soering's execution, paras 44–45).

[16] ECtHR, *Öcalan v. Turkey* [GC], Application no. 46221/99, Judgment, 12 May 2005, ECHR 2005-IV (finding Turkey in breach of the ECHR because of a failure to comply with fair trial guarantees. The case concerned the sentence to the death penalty of the Kurdistan Workers' Party's (PKK) leader following his arrest by the Turkish Security forces, despite Turkey's long standing moratorium on the implementation of the death penalty. The ECtHR had indicated interim measures, namely to take steps and stay the execution 'so as to enable the Court to proceed effectively with the examination of the admissibility and merits of the applicant's complaints under the [ECHR]', paras 5 and 170.

[17] ECtHR, *Babar Ahmad and Others v. the United Kingdom*, Applications nos. 24,027/07, 11,949/08, 36,742/08, 66,911/09 and 67,354/09, Judgment, 10 April 2012, (2013) 56 ECHR 1.

[18] E.g. ECtHR, *Abdollahi v. Turkey*, Application no. 23980/08, Decision (strike-out), 3 November 2009 (applicant had complained against a deportation order to Iran alleging exposure to a real risk of death or ill-treatment.); ECtHR, *F.H. v. Sweden*, Application no. 32621/06, Judgment, 20 January 2009 (Iraqi applicant alleged risk of being subjected to inhuman and degrading treatment in the case of deportation); ECtHR, *F.G. v. Sweden* (GC), Application no. 43611/11, Judgment, 23 March 2016 (Iranian applicant had asylum request rejected).

[19] According to the ECtHR's statistics department, 91% of the requests (1297) addressed immigration concerns in Belgium. Notably, 94% of approved requests were for non-expulsion or extradition-related matters; see Analysis of statistics 2023, January 2024, p. 4, at: https://www.echr.coe.int/documents/d/echr/stats-analysis-2023-eng. Accessed 28 March 2025.

[20] Ibid.

[21] Cerna 2021, p. 44 (discussing earlier statistics at: https://www.echr.coe.int/documents/d/echr/Stats_analysis_2010_ENG. Accessed 28 March 2025).

potential victim of persecution in their home country.[22] It is also not uncommon for requests to be the product of heated political debates, specifically in connection with migration and asylum in Europe. For example, on 14 June 2022, the ECtHR issued an interim measure against the UK, before that individual's case had been decided by UK courts, preventing his removal to Rwanda under the (highly controversial) UK-Rwanda Migration and Economic Partnership.[23]

7.2.2 Interim Measures Protecting a Variety of Rights

The protection offered by the ECHR over the years has been enhanced not only through the various Protocols attached to it, but also through its dynamic interpretation of the ECHR. For example, a number of socio-economic and cultural rights, including in particular access to healthcare[24] and protection against forced evictions,[25] have been deduced from the text of Article 8 ECHR, which has been interpreted to cover an extremely broad construction of 'private life'. Hence, interim measures, have been ordered, *inter alia*, to protect persons in custody with existing medical conditions.[26] In cases related to risk of violence inflicted by non State actors the approach of the ECtHR has been hesitant. For example, the ECtHR has refrained from indicating interim measures in the context of domestic and Gender-Based Violence (GBV) through interim measures.[27]

[22] See, e.g., ECtHR, *M.E. v. Sweden*, Application no. 71398/12 [GC], Judgment (strike out), 8 April 2015 (finding that the persecution of the applicant in Libya due to his homosexuality was no longer plausible). Cf. ECtHR, *A.S.B. v. the Netherlands,* Application no. 4854/12, Decision (strike out), 10 July 2012 (finding that there was no longer a risk of expulsion in Jamaica); ECtHR, *M. v. the United Kingdom*, Application no. 16081/08, Decision (strike out), 1 December 2009 (finding that there was no longer a risk of victimhood of human trafficking and sexual exploitation).

[23] ECtHR, *N.S.K. v. the United Kingdom*, Application no. 28774/22, Communicated Case, 5 April 2023; following the UK High Court's judgment, the ECtHR lifted the interim measure on 6 February 2023. See further UK Parliament 2024.

[24] ECtHR, *Vavřička and Others v. the Czech Republic* [GC], Application No 47621/13, Judgment, 8 April 2021 (noting that contracting parties have positive obligations to protect the right to health, stemming from articles 2 and 8 ECHR). Cf. ECtHR, *A.D. v. Greece*, Application No. 55363/19, Judgment, 4 April 2023 (concerning refugees, including pregnant women and children who had arrived on the Greek island of Samos and had to live in tents or containers).

[25] E.g. ECtHR, *Hasanali Aliyev and Others v. Azerbaijan,* Application no. 42858/11, Judgment, 9 June 2022; ECtHR, *Ivanova and Cherkezov v. Bulgaria,* Application no. 46577/15, Judgment, 21 April 2016.

[26] E.g. ECtHR, *N v UK* [GC], Application no. 26565/05, Judgment, 27 May 2008 (prohibition to return a person due to the deterioration of health exacerbated by the treatment for which the British authorities were held responsible).

[27] Evans 2022, p. 12–13.

7.2.3 Compliance with Provisional Measures

Sadly, respondent States have not always been willing to comply with orders on provisional measures. In some cases, they have purely ignored them.[28] A question that arises is whether non-compliance amounts to an additional violation of the ECHR.[29] Until the early 2000s, the ECtHR confined itself in finding a certain type of 'aggravated' State responsibility for violation of the same substantial right concerned,[30] because the harmful impact could have been reasonably prevented.[31] More recently, however, the ECtHR has taken the view that non-compliance of States with provisional measures entails rather a violation of the effective exercise of individual petition, guaranteed by Article 34 ECHR.[32] This is precisely because of the 'failure by the Contracting State to comply with interim measures' which hence 'prevent[s]the Court from effectively examining the applicant's complaint and as hindering the [effective exercise of Article 34]'.[33]

7.3 Provisional Measures in the Context of the Inter-American Human Rights System

The adoption of provisional and precautionary measures is part of the existing framework of mechanisms to address human rights violations in the Americas, complementing the system of individual complaints, on-site visits, annual reports, thematic mandates, and others. While of vital importance for individuals and communities in need of protection, provisional measures also provide 'an early warning mechanism of situations that could compromise the consolidation of democracy and rule of law, while at the same time protecting individual rights when they are not guaranteed at the domestic level'.[34] They have been, therefore, rightly described as a 'major innovation of the Inter-American system' and a 'key element of international human

---

[28] E.g. ECtHR, *Al-Saadoon and Mufdhi v. the United Kingdom*, Application no. 61498/08, Judgment, 2 March 2010; Rieter 2012, p. 198 (discussing the importance of persuasiveness for an effective follow-up).

[29] Haeck et al. 2008.

[30] Ibid., p. 44, n. 22 (pointing, *inter alia*, to ECtHR, *Cruz Varas v. Sweden*).

[31] E.g. ECtHR, *Kılıç v. Turkey*, Application no. 22492/93, Judgment, 28 March 2000 (concerning the killing of a journalist following the bombing of the pro-Kurdish journal Ozgur Gundem in South East Turkey); ECtHR, *Osman v. the United Kingdom*, Application No. 14037/88, Judgment, 28 October 1998, *Reports of Judgments and Decisions* 1998-VIII (found that contracting parties need to take measures to protect family life when there is a 'real and immediate risk' from a third party).

[32] Haeck et al. 2008, p. 44–45.

[33] ECtHR, *Mamatkulov and Askarov v. Turkey* [GC], Application No 46827/99, Judgment, 3 February 2005, para. 201.

[34] Burgogue-Larsen and De Torres 2011, p. 129.

rights protection' not only within the Inter-American system itself but beyond its borders too.[35]

7.3.1 *The Powers of the Inter-American Commission on Human Rights to Order Precautionary Measures (***Medidas Cautelares***)*

Pursuant to Article 25 of its Rules of Procedure, the IACHR has the power to order measures *prior* to the referral of a petition to the IACtHR.[36] Indeed, the Commission has always adopted such measures in the form of a report containing recommendations to States, although this ability is not hinged on an express provision of the ACHR.[37] The IACHR's protection orders in such cases are known as precautionary measures (*medidas provisionales*). The Commission has repeatedly reiterated the twofold nature of the measures, noting, first, that they 'seek to avoid irreparable harm and preserve the exercise of human rights' (i.e. the provisional function) and, secondly, 'they preserve legal situations while they are under consideration by the IACHR' (i.e. the precautionary function).[38] It has also interpreted the three requirements to be fulfilled (urgency, seriousness and irreparable harm) as follows: 'serious situation' refers to a grave impact that an action or omission can have on a protected right or on the eventual effect of a pending decision in a case or petition before the organs of the Inter-American system; 'urgent situation' refers to risk or threat that is imminent and can materialize, thus requiring immediate preventive or protective action; and 'irreparable harm' refers to injury to rights which, due to their nature, would not be susceptible to reparation, restoration or adequate compensation.[39]

Unlike procedures before the IACtHR, the IACHR mechanism is also pertinent in cases against OAS Member States *not* parties to the ACHR. This is an especially

[35] Ibid., p. 193ff. Cf. Pasqualucci 2012, p. 251ff; Rodríguez-Pinźon 2013, p. 13; Dulitzky 2011, p. 129; Burbano-Herrera 2010, p. 603–606; Pasqualucci 1993, p. 806ff.

[36] Rules of Procedure, arts. 25–29; Cerna 2010, p. 597–619. Further, in 'serious and urgent cases', the Commission, acting under art. 48(2) ACHR, has the power to 'conduct an investigation with the prior consent of the state in whose territory a violation has allegedly been committed'.

[37] Under Article 50 ACHR, the IACHR will subsequently publish a report stating its conclusions, which is transmitted to the State concerned, along with conclusions and recommendations. See also Pasqualucci 1993, p. 843; Piacentini de Andrade 2012, p.2.

[38] See, e.g., IACtHR, *Matter of Bámaca-Velásquez v Guatemala*, Order (Provisional Measures and Monitoring Compliance with Judgment), 27 January 2009.

[39] IACommHR, Resolution to lift precautionary measures 65/202, No. 440–16, *Zaheer Seepersad regarding Trinidad and Tobago*, 15 October 2023; see also IACtHR, *Case of the Miguel Castro-Castro Prison v. Peru,* Judgment, 25 November 2006, Series C No. 160.

important function, given that, unlike other regional human rights systems, membership in OAS neither entails automatically participation in the ACHR,[40] nor acceptance of IACtHR's jurisdiction.[41] Furthermore, the Commission follows up with the implementation of its measures, in accordance with Article 25(8) of its Rules of Procedure. Nonetheless, the IACHR's precautionary measures may not be as effective as those of the IACtHR. As argued, 'the binding nature of provisional measures contrasts with the lack of mandatory character of the Commission's precautionary measures, which in practice makes them less effective'.[42] A fine example of this is the action taken by the Commission against the USA in the case of grave human rights violations committed against all those detained in the facilities in Guantánamo Bay, Cuba.[43] In particular, in 2006 the Commission issued a key resolution on the horrendous situation of detainees in the naval base, involving extremely severe torture; trials by military tribunals; and the lack of judicial review of judgments, including those ordering indefinite detention.[44] The Commission had previously examined (and this illustrates the 'synergy that is produced between the political and promotional activities of the IACHR and the processing of individual petitions')[45] a request for precautionary measures lodged by hundreds of detainees, concerning the conditions of their confinement. In these cases, it found that the risk of 'irreparable harm' to all detainees was the result of the US refusal to treat them as prisoners of war.[46]

The Inter-American Commission has also issued other measures that revealed additional mischiefs of the CIA. One such case is Al-Hawsawi, a national of Saudi Arabia abducted by the CIA in the context of its secret rendition, detention and interrogation programmes on the ground of being allegedly involved in the 9/11 bombings.[47] The IACHR ordered the United States to take the necessary measures to improve Hawsawi's detention conditions and allow access to healthcare, since his

---

[40] Presently, 23 out of the 35 OAS Member States have ratified the Convention (the USA, Canada and the English-speaking Caribbean countries are not among them); see https://www.oas.org/dil/treaties_b-32_american_convention_on_human_rights_sign.htm, accessed 28 March 2025.

[41] For example, Dominica, Grenada and Jamaica have ratified the ACHR but have not accepted the IACtHR's jurisdiction.

[42] Piacentini de Andrade 2012, p. 12.

[43] Cerna 2021, p. 37.

[44] IACHR, Resolution No. 2/06, 28 July 2006 'On Guantanamo Bay Precautionary Measures', at: https://www.cidh.org/Comunicados/English/2006/27.06eng.htm, accessed 28 March 2025. See further, IACHR, Towards The Closure of Guantanamo, OAS/Ser.L/V/II., Doc. 20/15, 3 June 2015, at: https://www.oas.org/en/iachr/reports/pdfs/Towards-Closure-Guantanamo.pdf, accessed 28 March 2025. Burbano-Herrera and Haeck 2019, p. 89–113.

[45] Dulitzky 2011, p. 161.

[46] IACHR, *Persons Detained by the USA in Guantanamo Bay,* Resolution 64/23, 25 February and March 12 2002. See also IACHR, 'Precautionary Measures regarding Guantanamo', at: https://www.oas.org/en/iachr/pdl/decisions/GuantanamoMC.asp, accessed 28 March 2025.

[47] IACHR, Matter of Mustafa Adam Al-Hawsawi regarding the United States of America, Resolution 24/2015, Precautionary Measure 422--14, 7 July 2015, para. 3 See also, UN Human Rights Council, Opinions adopted by the Working Group on Arbitrary Detention at its seventy-first session (17–21 November 2014), No. 50/2014 (United States of America and Cuba), Communication addressed to the Government of the United States of America on 25 August 2014 and to the

'detention in interrogation had caused severe damage to his health',[48] which included 'symptoms of cancer and hepatitis C'.[49] Similar requests have also been lodged with the Commission against other States that are not ACHR contracting parties. By way of illustration, in 2017, the IACHR granted precautionary measures in favour of a person with disabilities, who was about to be admitted to a psychiatric hospital, despite requiring special care and the risk of aggravating his medical condition.[50] More recently, the Commission has dealt with many cases involving freedom of expression and other rights of human rights defenders. One such case is *Leaders of the 19 de Abril Carazo Movement*, who were censored for being critical of the government on social media amidst turmoil in Nicaragua,[51] and also the complaint of the family of Ángel Eduardo Gahona, who was murdered while streaming on Facebook live from his smartphone the protests against President Daniel Ortega.[52] In those cases, protection orders were issued to protect the next of kin.

7.3.2 *The Powers of the Inter-American Court to Order Provisional Measures*

The IACtHR is the primary judicial body that deals with 'all matters relating to the interpretation or application of the ACHR'.[53] Its power to order provisional measures is based on Article 63(2) ACHR, which enables it to monitor compliance with the orders, by means of submission of State reports. Provisional measures (*medidas provisionales*) shall be adopted as the Court deems 'pertinent', and only 'in cases of extreme gravity and urgency, and when necessary to avoid irreparable damage

Government of Cuba on 15 September 2014 concerning Mustafa al Hawsawi, UN Doc. A/HRC/WGAD/2014/50, 13 February 2015.

48 Ibid., paras 2–3.

49 Ibid., para. 3.

50 IACHR, *Matter of Zaheer Seepersad v Trinidad and Tobago*, Precautionary Measure No. 440–16, 4 August 2017.

51 IACHR, Precautionary Measures, Resolution 52/2018, 840/18, 841/18 and 779/18, *Leaders of the 19 de Abril Carazo Movement and others,* Nicaragua, 17 September 2018; IACHR, *Yerling Marina Aguilera Espinoza and 17 other human rights defenders,* Resolution 70/18, Precautionary Measures 939/18 and 1067/18, Nicaragua.

52 IACHR, Precautionary Measures, Resolution 41/2018, *Migueliuth Sandoval Cruz y familiares del periodista Ángel Eduardo Gahona,* Nicaragua, 669/18, 12 June 2019 (granting precautionary measures to Gahona's widow).

53 ACHR art 62(3): 'The jurisdiction of the Court shall comprise all cases concerning the interpretation and application of the provisions of this Convention that are submitted to it, provided that the States Parties to the case recognize or have recognized such jurisdiction'.

to persons'.[54] Following the request, the IACtHR will explain the reasons for either acceptance or denial of the measures in light of these criteria.[55]

Requests for provisional measures to the IACtHR may be presented by the Commission, in accordance with Rule 76 IACHR Rules of Procedure, 'in cases of extreme seriousness and urgency, when it becomes necessary to avoid irreparable damage to persons'. The Court may also seize the power *proprio motu,* or, at the request of the victim in accordance with the provisions of Article 27 of its own Rules of Procedure. With respect to the general *locus standi* and *ratione materiae* requirements for such requests, petitions must abide by the conditions set out in Articles 44 and 45 ACHR. Both the Court and the Commission may entertain *actio popularis.* An example of this last function is a request for provisional protection lodged by NGOs to order Canada to identify anonymous asylum seekers, 'John Does', and to verify their situation and status as well as to process any outstanding claim for asylum they may wish to present, so as to stop their refoulement to the USA.[56]

The Court has ruled on the existence of irreparable harm, for example, in respect of violations to the right to life in the case of pending executions (e.g. James v. Trinidad and Tobago prior to the respondent State's denunciation of the ACHR).[57] Also, in the *Haitians* case, the Court ordered measures to suspend mass expulsions and deportation of Haitians and Haitian-origin Dominicans by the Dominican Republic in order to prevent the risk of family separation, and leave underage children unaccompanied.[58] Many cases concern prison violence. For instance, in *Mendoza Prisons,* the Court ordered Argentina to improve the conditions prevailing in two penitentiary centres to protect the life and integrity of inmates, following evidence of solitary confinement and torture, and a number of suspicious deaths.[59] Other cases concern Orders to prevent violation of indigenous' collective rights, including land rights. For example, in the matter of the *Mapiripán Massacre*, the Court ordered the respondent State to take necessary measures to protect the life and personal integrity of

[54] ACHR, art.63(2): 'In cases of extreme gravity and urgency, and when necessary to avoid irreparable damage to persons, the Court shall adopt such provisional measures as it deems pertinent in matters it has under consideration. With respect to a case not yet submitted to the Court, it may act at the request of the Commission'; Inter-American Commission on Human Rights, 'About precautionary measures', https://www.oas.org/en/IACHR/jsForm/?File=/en/iachr/decisions/MC/about-precautionary.asp, accessed 28 March 2025.

[55] Piacentini de Andrade 2012, p.4.

[56] IACHR, Case 12.586, *John Doe et al v. Canada*, Report No. 78/11 (Merits), 21 July 2011.

[57] IACtHR, Matter of *James* et al. *regarding Trinidad and Tobago*, Order (Provisional Measures), 27 May 1999. See further, the Order (Provisional Measures) issued on 2 December 2003.

[58] IACtHR, *Expelled Dominicans and Haitians v. Dominican Republic*, Judgment (Preliminary Objections, Merits, Reparations and Costs), 28 September 2004, Series C No. 282; on other discrimination against Haitians, see IACtHR, *The Girls Yean and Bosico v. Dominican Republic*, Judgment (Preliminary Objections, Merits, Reparations and Costs), 8 September 2005, Series C No. 130.

[59] IACtHR, Provisional Measures regarding Argentina, Matter of Mendoza Prisons, P1231/04, Order, 30 March 2006 (concerning the Mendoza Provincial Prison and the Gustavo André Unit, located in Lavalle). A further Order was issued on 1 July 2011.

twenty beneficiaries and their next of kin.[60] Interim protection was also offered to the *Kankuamo* indigenous people,[61] and also the *Curbaradó* and *Jiguamiandó* communities of Colombia, which were dislocated during the conflict, and later subjected to 'indiscriminate internment' (while further suffering appropriation of their lands by oil firms).[62] A similar situation arose with the *Kichwa Sarayaku* Indigenous People in Ecuador, whose lands had been appropriated by oil companies in 2004–2005,[63] and many other cases concerning land rights.[64]

Other cases where interim measures have been ordered relate to the protection of health and personal integrity. In one such case against El Salvador, which concerned abortion, the IACtHR ordered the respondent State to adopt the necessary measures for doctors to perform the necessary procedures to avoid irreparable harm to the expectant mother's right to life, personal integrity and health.[65] In a few cases, journalistic freedom has also been indirectly concerned. For example, in La Nacion (the Newspaper case), concerning the condemnation of journalist Mauricio Herrera Ulloa for libel-related offences in Costa Rica, the IACtHR ordered the respondent State to suspend the execution of the condemnatory judgment, as well as to abstain from executing any action aimed at affecting the journalist's (and the journal's) freedom of speech.[66]

Many provisional measures cases granted by the IACtHR had also already been subject to protective precautionary measures by the Inter-American Commission. For example, in *Comuna 13,* a case concerning violence, killings and arbitrary detention of community leaders and activists in Medellín, Colombia, the petitioners had requested the Commission for protective measures to protect the life and personal integrity of their family members from actions of paramilitary groups,[67] two years prior to bringing their case before the Court.[68] Moreover, in 1997, the IACHR issued precautionary measures to protect the life and integrity of the members of the Peace Community of San José de Apartadó, in Colombia, and prevent harassment acts and

[60] IACtHR, *Provisional Measures regarding Colombia. Matter of the Kankuamo Indigenous People,* Order, 3 April 2009.

[61] IACtHR, *Provisional Measures regarding Colombia. Matter of the Mapiripán Massacre*, Order, 27 June 2005.

[62] IACtHR, Provisional Measures regarding Colombia. Matter of the Communities of Jiguamiandó and Curbaradó, Order, 22 May 2013.

[63] IACtHR, Provisional Measures regarding the Republic of Ecuador. Matter of Kichwa Indigenous People of Sarayaku, Order, 4 February 2010.

[64] IACtHR, Provisional Measures Regarding Nicaragua. Case of the Mayagna (Sumo) Awas Tingni Community, Order, 26 November 2007 (ordering Nicaragua to demarcate the Awas Tingni property and grant title).

[65] IACtHR, Provisional Measures with Regard to El Salvador. Matter of B., Order, 19 August 2013.

[66] IACtHR, *"La Nación" Newspaper Case (Costa Rica)*, Order, 7 February 2001 (noting also a distinction between the 'preventive' and 'protective' function of the measures). See Cerna 2021, p. 53ff.

[67] IACHR, *Precautionary measures regarding Colombia*, Report 46/07, Admissibility, *Mery Naranjo* (Comuna 13), 22 October 2004.

[68] IACtHR, Provisional Measures regarding Colombia. Matter of *Mery Naranjo et al* (Comuna 13), Case 231–05, Order, 5 July 2006.

violence by paramilitary groups.[69] In October 2000, the IACHR filed to the IACtHR a request for provisional measures in favour of the people living in said Community. The Court ordered them promptly, and extended and re-ordered them by virtue of Resolutions issued in November 2000, June 2002, November 2004, March 2005, February 2006, February 2008, and August 2010.[70] Some overlap between the powers of the two bodies appears unavoidable in this case. This, however, has been partially addressed with updating of IACHR Rules of Procedure in 2013, which attempted to resolve the problem by limiting the powers of the Commission (and allowing victim standing during the proceedings).[71]

It is common to request modification or amplification of provisional measures. For example, in *Comuna 13*, the IACtHR issued in the following years additional measures, ordering Colombia to protect other relatives and next of kin of those community leaders, including children and grandchildren, whose life was also endangered because of the violence.[72] It is also common, sadly, for respondent States to ignore the Orders issued. In 1998, for example, Trinidad and Tobago maintained the mandatory imposition of the death penalty for all capital offenses. In *Hilaire,* thirty-two persons had been convicted to death for capital offences 'regardless of the form of conduct that caused the death'.[73] The IACtHR did order the stay of the executions, but the detainees were executed in total defiance of the relevant Order.[74] Shortly after, Trinidad and Tobago denounced the ACHR. It could be argued, therefore, that akin to the recent developments in the ECHR, discussed earlier, in cases of non-compliance, State responsibility could be triggered for violation of the right to individual petition. This is also corroborated by the fact that provisional measures are explicitly mentioned in article 63 ACHR.[75]

---

[69] IACHR, *Precautionary measures regarding Colombia*, 17 December 1997, mentioned in IACHR, Report No. 61/16, Petition 12.325, Admissibility, *Peace Community of San José de Apartadó*, Colombia, 6 December 2016, OEA/Ser.L/V/II.159, para. 7.

[70] Ibid., para. 8.

[71] IACHR Rules of Procedure, art. 25 (Precautionary Measures) at: https://www.oas.org/en/IACHR/jsForm/?File=/en/iachr/mandate/basics/rulesiachr.asp, accessed 28 March 2025. Piacentini de Andrade 2012 p. 4–5.

[72] IACtHR, Report no. 86/13, Cases 12.595, 12.596 and 12.621, Merits, *Ana Teresa Yarce* et al. Comuna 13, Colombia, 4 November 2013.

[73] IACtHR, *Hilaire, Constantine and Benjamin* et al. *v. Trinidad and Tobago,* Judgment (Merits, Reparations and Costs, Judgment), 21 June 2002, Series C No. 94 (finding that mandatory executions violated art 4 ACHR). Goldman 2009, p. 880.

[74] Ibid.

[75] On this argument cf. Pasqualucci 1993, p. 823; Haeck et al. 2008, p. 45–46.

7.4 Provisional Measures in the Context of the African Human Rights System

7.4.1 The Powers of the African Commission (ACommHPR) to Order Provisional Measures

Under Article 45(1)(3) ACHPR, the Commission is mandated to interpret the Charter 'at the request of a State party, an institution of the Organisation of African Unity [now, African Union], or an African Organization recognized by the Organisation of African Unity [now, African Union'].. The ACHPR does not expressly mention the power of the Commission to order provisional measures . The latter contains rather a provision concerning 'communication[s] from States', according to which 'if a state party to the present Charter has good reason to believe that another state party to this Charter has violated the provisions of the Charter, it may draw, by written communication, the attention of that state to the matter'.[76] Individual communications may be therefore considered by the Commission in accordance with the Charter's provision that states that 'Communications other than those of state parties to the Charter however, may also be transmitted to the members of the Commission'.[77]

In relation to urgent situations, the only option of the Commission under the Charter involves primarily political solutions. Article 58(3) ACHPR states that 'a case of emergency duly noticed by the Commission shall be submitted to the Chairman of the Assembly of Heads of State and Government who may request an in-depth study'.[78] The Commission, however, is independently able to order appropriate provisional measures, by virtue of its Rules of Procedure, whether on 'its own initiative or at the request of a party to the communication'.[79] In any event, any communications that reach the Commission must contain formal requirements mentioned in the Charter, including the exhaustion of domestic legal remedies and submission within a 'reasonable period' of time after exhaustion.[80]

An illustration of the lack of teeth of the Commission is reflected in the procedures before and after the execution of Ken Saro Wiwa and another eight individuals (members of the *Ogoni 9)* by Nigeria.[81] The Commission had decided in an extraordinary session in 1995, to have the executions stayed, although shortly after, the *Ogoni 9* were executed by hanging. Subsequently, a claim was brought before the

[76] ACHPR, art. 47.

[77] Ibid., art. 55.

[78] Viljoen and Louw 2004, p. 3; Murray 2019.

[79] ACommHPR, Rules of Procedure, Rule 100; see also Information Sheet No. 2: Guidelines of the submission of Communications, at: https://archives.au.int/handle/123456789/2071. Accessed 28 March 2025.

[80] ACHR, art. 56. The requirements in fact include both usual (e.g. exhaustion of local remedies) and unusual ones (e.g. complaints should not be 'written in disparaging or insulting language directed against the State' and that 'they are not based exclusively on news disseminated through the mass media').

[81] Coomans 2003.

Commission by three international NGOs, and *Civil Liberties Organisation* against Nigeria. In its decision, the ACommHPR found violations of a number of articles of the Charter,[82] but essentially remained helpless before the interests of the synergy between Nigeria and Shell, incapable of protecting the activists against the imminent harm and their eventual demise. In this case, the Commission even held Nigeria responsible for violating the Charter precisely because it failed to comply with its previous orders.[83] Other cases also illustrate a lack of follow up and enforcement. Suffice to mention a case against Eritrea, in which the Commission had ordered it to release political figures who were unduly imprisoned for criticising Eritrean policies;[84] and a case against Zambia, whereby the Commission found that the deportation of prominent political figures (John Chinula and William Banda) to Malawi was a breach of the African Charter in many respects including freedom of association and freedom of movement.[85] The Commission however has been putting a lot of effort to persuade States to comply, and the Commission has also issued a resolution in this respect.[86] In many ways, the political situation in State parties is so turbulent that makes this follow up difficult.[87] The Commission however may also be at fault, since 'the language the African Commission uses in its findings does not always assist the state in identifying what it should practically do to implement the decision, even if the state were willing to do so'.[88] It does seem however that in many cases related to socio-economic and cultural or collective rights, the Commission has undoubtedly taken a more firm approach, which has been inspiring for other courts around the world.[89] Examples are *Ogoni* (Nigeria)[90] and *Endorois* (Kenya),[91] concerning forced displacement, severe pollution, and other violations of socio-economic and collective rights.

---

[82] ACommHPR, *International PEN, Constitutional Rights Project, Civil Liberties Organisation and Interights (on behalf of Ken Saro-Wiwa Jnr.) v. Nigeria*, 31 October 1998, Application Nos 137/94, 139/94, 154/96 and 161/97.

[83] Viljoen and Louw 2004, p. 8–9.

[84] ACommHPR, *Liesbeth Zegveld and Messie Ephrem v. Eritrea*, 20 November 2003, Communication No. 250/2002; Juma 2012, p. 360.

[85] ACommHPR, *Amnesty International v Zambia*, Communication No. 212/98, 5 May 1999, paras 48ff, 13 and 14.

[86] Murray and Mottershaw 2014, p. 357 (pointing to ACommHPR, 'Resolution on the Importance of Implementing the Recommendations of the African Commission on Human and Peoples' Rights by States Parties', adopted in 2006, reproduced in Secretariat of the African Commission on Human and Peoples' Rights 2017, p. 181).

[87] Ibid. at 359.

[88] Ibid., at 355.

[89] See e.g. Pentassuglia 2013, p. 74–75; Juma 2012, p.358–362.

[90] ACommHPR, *The Social and Economic Rights Action Center for Economic and Social Rights v. Nigeria,* Communication No. 155/96 (2001); Dankwa 2003, p. 121–123.

[91] ACommHPR, *Centre for Minority Rights Development (Kenya) and Minority Rights Group International on behalf of Endorois Welfare Council v Kenya,* Communication No 276/2003 (2009).

7.4.2 The Powers of the ACtHPR to Order Provisional Measures

The ACtHPR has the power to adopt interim measures 'in cases of extreme gravity and urgency, and when necessary to avoid irreparable harm to persons'.[92] The competence of the Court is generally complementary to those of the Commission under the Court Protocol,[93] for those States that have accepted its jurisdiction. The Court will generally hear cases following a preliminary examination of its jurisdiction, either by reference of the case from the Commission, or *proprio motu*,[94] subsequently deciding on admissibility and on merits. With respect to provisional measures, the Court has decided that it suffices to establish merely '*prima facie* jurisdiction to hear the case—as opposed to jurisdiction over the merits.[95] It may hence order a State to abstain from taking any action that will cause irreparable damage to applicants. As will be recalled from Chapter 4 (Applicable Law / Sources of Law), according to Article 3 of its 1998 Protocol, the ACtHPR's jurisdiction extends beyond the interpretation and application of the ACHPR, to 'any other relevant human rights instrument ratified by the States concerned'.

So far however, the Court has exercised its power rather sparingly, emphasizing the need for a real and imminent likelihood of irreparable harm.[96] According to its case law, the notion of 'urgency', is 'consubstantial with extreme gravity', entails 'real and imminent likelihood that irreparable harm will be caused before it renders its final decision', while this real risk 'excludes the purely hypothetical risk and explains the need to remedy it immediately'.[97] A noticeable example of 'prompt action' is its interim measures order against Libya, following referral by the ACommissionHPR.[98]

Overall, the Court has overall minimally contributed to the problem of impunity in Africa.[99] For example, in a case against Tanzania concerning an individual convicted to execution by hanging for committing murder due to the mandatory imposition of

[92] ACtHPR Protocol, art. 27(2); ACtHPR, Rules of Court, Rule 59.

[93] ACtHPR Protocol, art. 8; see also arts 5(1) and 6(3).

[94] Viljoen and Louw 2004, p. 3.

[95] ACtHPR, *Komi Koutche v. Republic of Benin*, Application No. 020/2019, Ruling (Provisional measures), 2 December 2019, para. 14; ACtHPR, *Ayadhi Fathi and Others v. Republic of Tunisia*, Application No. 001/2023, Ruling (Provisional Measures), 17 March 2023, para. 11; ACtHPR, *Houngue Éric Noudehouenou v Republic of Benin and Others*, Application No. 010/2021, Ruling (Provisional Measures), 20 December 2022, para. 14.

[96] For the list of cases involving provisional measures, see https://www.african-court.org/cpmt/latest-decisions/orders, accessed 27 March 2025. See also Teferra 2022, p. 28–62.

[97] ACtHPR, *Noudehouenou*, para. 36; ACtHPR, *Ibrahim Ben Mohamed Ben Ibrahim Belguith v. Republic of Tunisia*, Application No. 017/2021, Judgment (Merits and Reparations), 22 September 2022; ACtHPR, *Sébastien Germain Marie Aikoué Ajavon v. Republic of Benin*, Application No. 062/2019, Ruling (Provisional Measures), 17 April 2020, para. 61.

[98] ACtHPR, In the Matter of African Commission on Human and Peoples' Rights v. Great Socialist People's Libyan Arab Jamahirya, Application 004/2011, Order for Provisional Measures, 25 March 2011; Juma 2012, p. 360. Polymenopoulou 2012, p. 767.

[99] Magliveras 2014.

the death penalty (as in Hilaire), the Court ordered Tanzania 'to set aside the sentence and replace it with any other order that it will deem appropriate within its domestic processes', but without finding the incarceration unlawful per se.[100] Other arguably more important cases against Tanzania are those concerning the electoral process. In both Tangnayika and Mtikila the Court challenged Tanzania's laws prohibiting independent candidates to run for office,[101] ordering it to amend its constitutional and legal framework to allow for independent, fair, and free electoral process following elections in the country.[102] In cases related to indigenous people's rights, the Court has also shown more dynamism in finding State responsibility under the ACHPR—including for lack of implementation of orders of the Commission. More recently, three individuals challenged the elections in Tunisia, alleging violations of the right to participate freely in the government of their country' protected under Articles 13 and 24 ACHPR.[103] They requested the Court to order Tunisia to suspend the relevant domestic law on elections and referenda, as well as 'to postpone the parliamentary elections of 17 December 2022 to a later date', because 'the President of [Tunisia] undertook several illegal and undemocratic acts which truncated constitutional democracy, leading the country into totalitarianism'.[104] The Court declined the request because, in the view of the majority, there was no reasonable likelihood of irreparable harm occurring, and applicant had not managed to show 'manifest prejudice'.[105]

---

[100] ACtHPR, *Ally Rajabu and Others v United Republic of Tanzania*, Application No. 007/2015, Judgment (Merits and Reparations), 28 November 2019; the Order for Provisional Measures was issued on 18 March 2016. Possi 2017, p. 311.

[101] Windridge 2015, p. 299.

[102] ACtHPR, *Tanganyika Law Society and Legal and Human Rights Centre v. The United Republic of Tanzania and Reverend Christopher R. Mtikila and Others v Tanzania*, Application No. 009/2011 and Application No 011/2011, Judgment, 14 June 2013.

[103] ACtHPR, *Fathi*, para 7.

[104] Ibid., para. 4.

[105] But see the Dissenting Opinion by Judge Chafika Bensaoula, whose view, based on art. 27 of the Court Protocol and Rule 59 Rules of Court, was that the application was 'well-founded for the simple reason that it [met] the conditions of urgency required to order provisional measures … requests for provisional measures must be kept in the context of the nature of the request itself and expecting the Applicant to show manifest prejudice is antithetical to the very purpose of the provisional measures mechanism … an application for suspension of an act can only be regarded as temporary and for the purpose of avoiding harm, even if that harm may be strictly immaterial or irreparable pending the judgment on the merits', ibid., paras 14–15 of Dissenting Opinion.

7.5 Provisional Measures in the Context of the Arab Human Rights System

The Arab human rights system, which exists in the context of the League of Arab States, is still not a fully-fledged human rights system. The Arab Charter on Human Rights[106] has still no enforcement mechanism.[107] Discussions during and after the Bassiouni Commission inquiry have been pointing to the establishment of a future ArabCtHR in Manama, Bahrain, in accordance with its Statute.[108]

One beacon of hope in this respect has been the drafting of the Statute of the Arab Court in 2014, the conclusion of which was the principal action to 'fill this enforcement void'.[109] The significance of Article 19(2) of the Statute in particular should not go unnoticed, as it provides for a collective right of individuals to access the Court, acting as NGOs.[110] While the Statute does not contain any reference to provisional or interim measures,[111] in light of Article 28, which states that the ArabCtHR may 'lay down its own rules', there is nothing to preclude developing such mechanism in the future. Since 2014, however, progress has been embryonic. This is despite the obvious seeds of civil society mobilization throughout the Arab region,[112] and the fact that human rights issues are increasingly addressed locally in the Gulf countries and in the broader Middle East.[113]

7.6 Conclusion

Interim measures of protection constitute a general principle of both civil and criminal law procedure all over the world. They are a consistent feature of the institutional frameworks of international courts and tribunals, stemming from the realm of domestic civil procedure. Such measures may be ordered by courts at their sole discretion in the event of urgency and irreparable harm in the context of all international courts and tribunals. Their practice however varies depending on the authority of each and hurdles imposed against potential applicants from gaining access to interim measures. Interim relief mechanisms exist, therefore, naturally also in the context of regional courts. Their function is both protective and preventive, in the sense of protecting the subject matter of litigation (as well as the relevant physical evidence), and preserving the parties' status quo ante. All three functional human

[106] Rishmawi 2005; Vitkauskaite-Meurice 2010; Almutawa 2021a, p. 509ff.

[107] Almutawa 2021b; Almutawa 2021a, p. 510; Magliveras 2017.

[108] ArabCtHR Statute, art. 3.

[109] Almutawa 2021a, p. 506.

[110] ArabCtHR Statute, art. 19.

[111] Almutawa 2021a at p. 511. See also Magliveras and Naldi 2016, p. 147.

[112] Rishmawi 2015; Almutawa 2021a, p. 530.

[113] Polymenopoulou 2024, p. 2.

rights Courts provide for such mechanism, and a similar possibility may also be deduced from the Statute of the nascent ArabCHR. Furthermore, the two Commissions, the IACHR and the ACommissionHPR respectively, have also assumed the authority to order interim and precautionary measures in light of their Rules of Procedure, despite a lack of reference in the respective regional human rights treaties. The IACHR, for example, has also been extremely actively involved in issuing measures of protection that are pertinent even against non-ACHR contracting parties by virtue of the American Declaration on Human Rights. Its role has been complementary to that of the IACtHR, which is the primary judicial body dealing with cases and which possesses the power to order provisional measures in extreme and urgent situations. Both bodies have played a central role in preventing serious, urgent and otherwise irreparable harm in numerous cases of violence, including for the protection of next of kin. Their proactive stance in relation to provisional and precautionary measures has also been vital for the protection of people's rights, and systematic violence perpetrated by paramilitary groups and other non-State actors against indigenous peoples and communities.

In the context of the European system too, interim measures play an important role where there is an imminent risk of irreparable harm and no available domestic remedy. The jurisprudence of the ECtHR in the area of interim measures is more limited and less innovative, compared to that of its counterpart in the Americas. In addition, the effectiveness of interim measures is sometimes hindered by non-compliance from respondent states, raising questions about potential additional violations of the ECHR. A significant contribution of the ECtHR, however, is the recognition that failure to comply with interim measures is a breach of the right to the effective exercise of individual petition (Article 34 ECHR). This approach could provide a fertile paradigm for the other regional systems as well, emphasising the need for states to prevent foreseeable harm and adhere to the Court's orders to ensure the effective protection of human rights.

In the context of the African system, the Court's overall impact on addressing impunity in Africa has been limited. The challenges faced by both the ACommissionHPR and the ACtHPR include states' non-compliance with orders, lack of follow-up mechanisms, and the difficulty in practically implementing decisions. However, noteworthy achievements are observed in cases related to socio-economic and cultural rights, where the Commission has taken a more assertive stance, as seen e.g. in *Ogoni* (Nigeria) and *Endorois* (Kenya).

The Arab human rights system, as embodied in the Arab Charter on Human Rights within the League of Arab states, faces notable challenges in the path to becoming a fully operational human right mechanism. The absence of an enforcement mechanism within Charter has promoted discussions about potential establishment of the ArabCtHR. While the Statute for the court was concluded in 2014, progress towards its effective implementation remains at an early stage.

References

Almutawa A (2021a) The Arab Court of Human Rights and the enforcement of the Arab Charter on Human Rights. Human Rights Law Review 21:506-532.

Almutawa A (2021b) The Failure of the Arab Court of Human Rights and the Conflicting Logics of Legitimacy, Sovereignty, Orientalism and Cultural Relativism. Netherlands International Law Review 68:479-500.

Brown C (2007) A Common Law of International Adjudication. Oxford University Press, Oxford.

Burbano-Herrera C (2010) Provisional Measures in the Case Law of the Inter-American Court of Human Rights. Intersentia, Antwerp/Oxford/Portland.

Burbano-Herrera C, Haeck Y (2019) The Impact of Precautionary Measures on Persons Deprived of Liberty in the Americas. In: Engstrom P (ed) The Inter-American Human Rights System: Impact Beyond Compliance. Springer, Dordrecht, pp. 89-113.

Burbano-Herrera C, Viljoen F (2014) Interim Measures Before the Inter-American and African Human Rights Commissions: Strengths and Weaknesses. In: Haeck Y, Brems E (eds) Human Rights and Civil Liberties in the 21st Century. Springer, Dordrecht, pp. 157-177.

Burgorgue-Larsen L, De Torres A Ú (2011) The Inter-American Court of Human Rights: Case Law and Commentary. Oxford University Press, Oxford.

Cerna C M (2010) The New Rules of Procedure of the Inter-American Commission on Human Rights. International Legal Materials 49:597-619.

Cerna C M (2021) Provisional Measures: How International Human Rights Law is Changing International Law (Inspired by *Gambia v. Myanmar*). Notre Dame Journal of International and Comparative Law 11:34-59.

Coomans F (2003) The Ogoni Case Before the African Commission on Human and Peoples' Rights. International and Comparative Law Quarterly 52:749-760.

Council of Europe/Conseil de l'Europe (1972) Yearbook of the European Convention on Human Rights - Report of the Commission, Chapter I Inter-State Applications Second Greek Case. Brill Nijhoff.

Dankwa V (2003) The African Commission on Human and Peoples' Rights: The Justiciable Indivisibility of Human Rights. In: Litigating Economic, Social and Cultural Rights: Achievements, Challenges and Strategies. Centre on Housing Rights and Evictions, pp. 118- 121. https://www.right-to-education.org/sites/right-to-education.org/files/resource-attachments/COHRE_Litigating_Esc_Rights_2003_en.pdf. Accessed 27 March 2025.

Dulitzky A (2011) The Inter-American Human Rights System Fifty Years Later: Time for Changes. Revue québécoise de droit international (Special Issue, Protecting Human Rights in the Americas: The Inter-American Institutions), pp. 127-164. https://doi.org/10.7202/1068396ar. Accessed 28 March 2025.

Dzehtsiarou K, Tzevelekos V (2021) Interim Measures: Are Some Opportunities Worth Missing? European Convention on Human Rights Law Review 2:1-22.

Evans J (2022) Gender Mainstreaming at the European Court of Human Rights. The University of Miami Inter-American Law Review 54: 1-38.

Goldman R K (2009) History and Action: The Inter-American Human Rights System and the Role of the Inter-American Commission on Human Rights. Human Rights Quarterly 31:856-887.

Haeck Y, Burbano Herrera C, Zwaak L (2008) Non-compliance with a Provisional Measure Automatically Leads To a Violation of the Right of Individual Application… or Doesn't It?: Strasbourg Court Takes Away any Remaining Doubts and Broadens its Pan-European Protection. European Constitutional Law Review 4:41-63.

Haeck Y, Burbano Herrera C, Zwaak L (2011) Strasbourg's Interim Measures under Fire: Does the Rising Number of State Incompliances with Interim Measures Pose a Threat to the European Court of Human Rights?. European Yearbook on Human Rights 11: https://doi.org/10.2139/ssrn.1543945. Accessed 27 March 2025.

Haeck Y, Ruiz-Chiriboga O, Burbano-Herrera C (eds) (2015) The Inter-American Court of Human Rights: Theory and Practice, Present and Future. Intersentia, Cambridge/Antwerp/Portland.

Harris D J, O'Boyle M, Bates E, Buckley C (2023) Law of the European Convention on Human Rights, 5th edn. Oxford University Press, Oxford.
Juma D (2012) Provisional Measures under the African Human Rights System: The African Court's Order against Libya. Wisconsin International Law Journal 30:344-373.
Magliveras K D (2014) Fighting Impunity Unsuccessfully in Africa: A Critique of the African Union's Handling of the Hissène Habré Affair. African Journal of International and Comparative Law 22: 420-447.
Magliveras K D (2017) Completing the Institutional Mechanism of the Arab Human Rights System: The Arab Court of Human Rights. International Human Rights Law Review 6:30-52.
Magliveras K, Naldi G (2016) The Arab Court of Human Rights: A Study in Impotence. Quebec Journal of International Law 29:147-172.
Marti C (2018) Provisional Measures: European Court of Human Rights (ECtHR). In: Ruiz Fabri H (ed) Max Planck Encyclopedia of International Procedural Law. Oxford University Press, Oxford.
Miles C A (2017) Provisional Measures Before International Courts and Tribunals. Cambridge University Press, Cambridge.
Murray R (2019) The African Charter on Human and Peoples' Rights: A Commentary. Oxford University Press, Oxford.
Murray R, Mottershaw E (2014) Mechanisms for the Implementation of Decisions of the African Commission on Human and Peoples' Rights. Human Rights Quarterly 36:349-372.
Palombino F M, Virzo R, Zarra G (eds) (2021) Provisional Measures Issued by International Courts and Tribunals. T.M.C Asser Press, The Hague.
Pasqualucci J M (1993) Provisional Measures in the Inter-American Human Rights System: An Innovative Development in International Law. Vanderbilt Journal of Transnational Law 26:803-863.
Pasqualucci J M (2012) The Practice and Procedure of the Inter-American Court of Human Rights. Cambridge University Press, Cambridge.
Pentassuglia G (2013) Protecting Minority Groups through Human Rights Courts: The Interpretive Role of the European and Inter-American Jurisprudence. In: Vrdoljak A F (ed) The Cultural Dimension of Human Rights. Collected Courses of the Academy of European Law, Vol. XXII/1. Oxford University Press, Oxford, pp. 73-116.
Piacentini de Andrade I (2012) Protective Measures in the Inter-American Human Rights System. Lawyers' Rights Watch Canada. https://www.lrwc.org/ws/wp-content/uploads/2012/03/Protective-measures-Inter-American-System.pdf. Accessed 27 February 2025.
Polymenopoulou E (2012) African Court on Human and Peoples' Rights, African Commission on Human and Peoples' Rights v Great Socialist People's Libyan Arab Jamahiriya, Order for Provisional Measures 25 March 2011. International and Comparative Law Quarterly 61:767-775.
Polymenopoulou E (2024) Sharia and Human Rights Law in the Constitutional Framework of Gulf States. Human Rights Quarterly 46:1-24.
Possi A (2017) 'It Is Better that Ten Guilty Persons Escape than that One Innocent Suffer': The African Court on Human and Peoples' Rights and Fair Trial Rights in Tanzania. African Human Rights Yearbook 1:311-336.
Rieter E (2010) Preventing Irreparable Harm: Provisional Measures in International Human Rights Adjudication. Human Rights Research Series Vol. 37. Intersentia, Antwerp.
Rieter E (2012) Provisional measures: binding and persuasive? Enabling human rights adjudicators to follow up on state disrespect. Netherlands International Law Review 59:165-198.
Rishmawi M (2005) The Revised Arab Charter on Human Rights: A Step Forward? Human Rights Law Review 5:361-376.
Rishmawi M (2015) The League of Arab States: Human Rights Standards and Mechanisms. Open Society Foundations and Cairo Institute for Human Rights Studies.
Rodríguez-Pinzón D (2013) Precautionary Measures of the Inter-American Commission on Human Rights: Legal Status and Importance. Human Rights Brief 20:13-18.

Rosenne S (2005) Provisional Measures in International Law. Oxford University Press, Oxford.
Saccucci A (2021) Interim Measures at the European Court of Human Rights: Current Practice and Future Challenges. In: Palombino F M, Virzo R, Zarra G (eds) Provisional Measures Issued by International Courts and Tribunals. T.M.C. Asser Press, The Hague, pp. 215-252.
Secretariat of the African Commission on Human and Peoples' Rights (2017) Recommendations and Resolutions Adopted by the African Commission on Human and Peoples' Rights 1988–2017.
Teferra Z M (2022) Provisional Measures in International Human Rights Law: The Practice of the African Court on Human and Peoples' Rights. African Human Rights Yearbook 6: 28-62.
UK Parliament (2024) House of Commons Library UK-Rwanda Migration and Economic Development Partnership. Research Briefing, 29 May 2024. https://commonslibrary.parliament.uk/research-briefings/cbp-9568/. Accessed 28 March 2025.
Viljoen F, Louw L (2004) The Status of the Findings of the African Commission: From Moral Persuasion to Legal Obligation. Journal of African Law 48:1-10.
Vitkauskaite-Meurice D (2010) The Arab Charter on Human Rights: the naissance of new regional human rights system or a challenge to the universality of human rights? Jurisprudencija 119:165-180.
Windridge O (2015) A watershed moment for African human rights: Mtikila and Others v Tanzania at the African Court on Human and Peoples' Rights. African Human Rights Law Journal 15:299-328.
Wolfrum R (2012) Interim (Provisional) Measures of Protection. In: Max Planck Encyclopedia of Public International Law. Oxford University Press, Oxford. https://hdl.handle.net/21.11116/0000-0004-FF67-A. Accessed 27 March 2025.
Zyberi G (2010). Provisional measures of the International Court of Justice in armed conflict situations. Leiden Journal of International Law 23:571-584.

Eleni Polymenopoulou, Associate Professor, Hamad Bin Khalifa University, College of Law, Qatar Foundation, Education City Doha, Qatar. https://www.hbku.edu.qa/en/cl/staff/eleni-polymenopoulou

Chapter 8
Advisory Opinions

Elena Abrusci

Contents

8.1 Introduction: The Role of Advisory Opinions Before Regional Human Rights Courts ... 172
8.2 The Powers of the Regional Human Rights Courts to Issue Advisory Opinions ... 174
8.2.1 The African Court on Human and Peoples' Rights ... 174
8.2.2 The Arab Court of Human Rights ... 175
8.2.3 The European Court of Human Rights ... 175
8.2.4 The Inter-American Court of Human Rights ... 176
8.3 Who May Request an Advisory Opinion? Standing Before the Regional Human Rights Courts ... 177
8.3.1 The African Court of Human and Peoples' Rights ... 178
8.3.2 The European Court of Human Rights ... 179
8.3.3 The Inter-American Court of Human Rights ... 180
8.4 The Subject Matter of Advisory Opinions ... 181
8.4.1 The African Court of Human and Peoples' Rights ... 181
8.4.2 The European Court of Human Rights ... 182
8.4.3 The Inter-American Court of Human Rights ... 184
8.5 The Interpretative Value of Advisory Opinions and the Question of Legal Precedent ... 185
8.6 The Impact of Advisory Opinions on Contentious Cases and State Practice ... 187
8.6.1 The African Court of Human and Peoples' Rights ... 187
8.6.2 The European Court of Human Rights ... 188
8.6.3 The Inter-American Court of Human Rights ... 189
8.7 Conclusions ... 191
References ... 192

Abstract This chapter provides a comparative analysis of how the regional human rights Courts address the question of advisory opinions, identifying similarities and differences. It considers their nature, the power of the Courts to issue (or reject) them and the relevant procedures. It includes a comparative analysis of the jurisdiction *ratione personae* and *ratione materiae* of the Courts *vis-à-vis* advisory opinions, exploring both the legal framework and the interpretation and implementation in judicial practice of the relevant provisions. Finally, the chapter discusses the legal

E. Abrusci (✉)
Brunel Law School, Brunel, University of London, Uxbridge, UK
e-mail: Elena.Abrusci@brunel.ac.uk

A. Almutawa and K. D. Magliveras (eds.), *A Comparison of the European, Inter-American, African and Arab Human Rights Courts: Institutional Aspects*,
https://doi.org/10.1007/978-94-6265-695-6_8

value of advisory opinions compared to contentious cases and provides an overview of the impact that they have had so far on subsequent case-law, on state practice and on the development of international human rights law.

Keywords Advisory opinions · Regional human rights systems · Jurisdiction · Admissibility · European Court of Human Rights · African Court of Human and Peoples' Rights · Inter-American Court of Human Rights · Arab Court of Human Rights

8.1 Introduction: The Role of Advisory Opinions Before Regional Human Rights Courts

Regional human rights courts are mostly known for their contentious jurisdiction and the adjudication of individual complaints brought against state parties. However, all the regional courts also have advisory jurisdiction and may issue opinions to guide and support state parties in their understanding, interpretation, and implementation of human rights.[1]

Generally, an advisory opinion is legal advice issued by an international court following a request (often by a state) to inform the resolution of a matter and provide support in the interpretation of specific rules. As Thomas Buergenthal observed, advisory opinions 'clarify or establish basic doctrines of international law and make important contributions to the conceptual evolution of the international law of human rights'.[2]

Compared to judgments in contentious cases, advisory opinions are not binding, which makes them often appear as the less relevant outputs of regional human rights courts. Given that human rights judgments are often not complied with by respondent states, the lack of binding force for advisory opinions could suggest that they have a minor role in shaping international human rights law practice. However, due to the reduced pressure that normally comes with non-contentious cases, regional courts may find themselves more at ease in exploring innovative interpretative paths and 'experiment' with human rights law. Indeed, advisory opinions have slowly become a powerful vehicle to express their views and positions on key issues and have impacted subsequent case-law and state practice.[3] Landmark opinions on the right to marry for

[1] The use of advisory opinions is not unique to regional human rights Courts. For instance, the ICJ has issued several opinions on very topical issues, e.g. ICJ, *The Legality of the Threat or Use of Nuclear Weapons*, Advisory Opinion, 9 July 1996, ICJ Reports 1996, p. 226 and ICJ, *Legal Consequences of the Construction of a Wall in the Occupied Palestinian Territory*, Advisory Opinion, 9 July 2004, ICJ Reports 2004, p. 136.

[2] Buergenthal 1985, p 25.

[3] Contesse 2021, p 369.

same-sex couples,[4] the rights of undocumented migrants,[5] environmental rights,[6] the right of parents-children following a gestational surrogacy[7] and on the prohibition of vagrancy laws[8] have shaped the development of international human rights law. The engagement of the regional courts with advisory opinions differs significantly: the Inter-American Court of Human Rights (IACtHR) has embraced them as a unique vehicle for 'sending messages' to state parties,[9] while the European Court of Human Rights (ECtHR) only rendered its first advisory opinion in 2018.[10] This different attitude reflects the specific history, development and features of the regional systems and provides further insights into their understanding of their own role as human rights adjudicators.[11] However, this could also raise issues of legitimacy and authority of the regional courts *vis à vis* the respective state parties.

The chapter explores the powers and procedures of the regional human rights courts in accepting (or rejecting) the request for advisory opinions and identifies commonalities and differences across the systems. Section 8.2 presents the power given by the constitutive documents to the Courts to issue advisory opinions, together with the matching power to exercise discretion and reject requests. Section 8.3 discusses how advisory opinion proceedings commence and, in particular, who can submit a request: state parties, the organs of the respective international organisations, NGOs or the Court itself (jurisdiction *ratione personae*). Section 8.4 addresses the question of the admissibility *ratione materiae*, exploring the subject matters that can be considered in an advisory opinion. Finally, Sect. 8.5 deals with the merit and practice of advisory opinions and comparatively analyses how they have influenced and impacted the subsequent case-law of the courts, the practice of state parties and the development and interpretation of international human rights law.

---

[4] IACtHR, *State Obligations Concerning Change of Name, Gender Identity, and Rights Derived from a Relationship Between Same-Sex Couples*, Advisory Opinion OC-24/17, 24 November 2017, Series A No. 24.

[5] IACtHR, *Rights and Guarantees of Children in the Context of Migration and/or in Need of International Protection*, Advisory Opinion OC-21/14, 19 August 2014, Series A No. 21.

[6] IACtHR, *The Environment and Human Rights*, Advisory Opinion OC-23/17, 15 November 2017, Series A No. 23.

[7] ECtHR, P16–2018-001, *Recognition in domestic law of a legal parent-child relationship between a child born through a gestational surrogacy arrangement abroad and the intended mother*, Advisory Opinion, 10 April 2019.

[8] ACtHPR, Request 001/2018, *Request for an Advisory Opinion by the Pan African Lawyers Union (PALU)* on *the Compatibility of Vagrancy Laws With the African Charter on Human and Peoples' Rights and Other Human Rights Instruments Applicable in Africa,* Advisory Opinion, 4 December 2020. See also Mwangi 2023.

[9] Baillet 2018, p 284.

[10] While the first advisory opinion under Article 47 ECHR was rendered in 2008, it was only in 2018 that the ECtHR rendered a substantial advisory opinion under Protocol 16 ECHR.

[11] For a broader discussion of the comparative features of the three systems, see Abrusci 2022.

8.2 The Powers of the Regional Human Rights Courts to Issue Advisory Opinions

All regional human rights courts have been endowed with the right to issue advisory opinions. Although there is a general homogeneity in terms of powers, slight differences in wording and formulations could allow different interpretation on admissibility as well as suggest a different role for, and impact of, the opinions.

8.2.1 The African Court on Human and Peoples' Rights

The ACtHPR was established by the Protocol adopted in 1998, which entered into force only in 2004 and rendered its first judgment in 2009. Yet, in its 20 years of functioning, it has delivered four advisory opinions and has struck out the requests for another ten, demonstrating full ownership and control over its power to issue opinions and reject requests when not admissible or not appropriate.

Article 4 of the Protocol establishing the ACtHPR provides that: '1. At the request of a Member State of the OAU [Organisation of African Union],[12] the OAU, any of its organs, or any African organization recognized by the OAU, the Court may provide an opinion on any legal matter relating to the Charter or any relevant human rights instruments, provided the subject matter of the opinion is not related to a matter being examined by the Commission.'

This is a very broad and generous provision, as it allows the ACtHPR to issue advisory opinions requested by a wide range of actors, well beyond the state parties, on a wide range of matters and without many requirements to be met. Advisory opinions are also regulated in the new Rules of the Court.[13] Rules 82–87 thereof provide more details on the requests, the procedures to be followed for written submissions and (potential) oral proceedings and for the delivery of opinions. Worth mentioning is that Rule 82 adds specific admissibility requirements for requesting advisory opinions, narrowing down the scope of the very broad Article 4(1).

In line with the other regional human rights courts, Article 4 of the Protocol does not require the ACtHPR to deliver an advisory opinion but only grants the power to do so. Such discretion in accepting and rejecting requests is crucial in understanding the interpretation of the ACtHPR's admissibility criteria. The ten requests the ACtHPR has stricken out were all considered to fall outside its jurisdiction *ratione materiae* or *ratione personae*, but the ACtHPR could have also rejected an admissible application. However, the Rules of Court do not mention anything in relation to its discretion to accept or reject an admissible request, thus leaving the matter currently unsettled. Only future cases may confirm what degree of discretion the ACtHPR has in this regard.

---

[12] In 2002, the OAU was succeeded by the African Union (AU) and, therefore, all references to the OAU are now to the AU.

[13] ACtHPR, Rules of Court, 1 September 2020, Section V (Rules 82–87).

8.2.2 *The Arab Court of Human Rights*

Even though the Arab Court is yet to become operational, the Statute establishing it provides it with the power to render advisory opinions. According to Article 21(1), it may issue an opinion regarding any legal issue relating to the Arab Human Rights Charter or to any other Arab convention on human rights based on a request made by the Council of the League of Arab States (LAS) or any of its subsidiary organisations or authorities. This is a somewhat broad provision, with the jurisdiction *ratione materiae* encompassing not just the Charter but also other Arab human rights instruments. However, it is very narrow in terms of jurisdiction *ratione personae*, as it only allows the LAS Council or subordinate agencies to present a request.[14] In line with the other regional systems, the ArabCtHR has only discretion to render opinions. Article 21(2) further requires the Court to give reasons for every opinion it renders and allows judges to issue separate opinions.

8.2.3 *The European Court of Human Rights*

Advisory opinions were not mentioned in the original text of ECHR. However, Protocol No. 2 ECHR, introduced the power for the ECtHR to deliver them.[15] In particular, Article 47 ECHR stipulates that '1. [t]he Court may, at the request of the Committee of Ministers, give advisory opinions on legal questions concerning the interpretation of the Convention and the Protocols thereto. 2. Such opinions shall not deal with any question relating to the content or scope of the rights or freedoms defined in Section I of the Convention and the Protocols thereto, or with any other question which the Court or the Committee of Ministers might have to consider in consequence of any such proceedings as could be instituted in accordance with the Convention.' This very restrictive formulation, especially if compared to the ACtHPR, could be rightly considered one of the main reasons why the ECtHR has rendered only a few advisory opinions to date.

The call for a wider advisory jurisdiction for the ECtHR increased over time, coming from both the state parties and the Court itself,[16] suggesting that the example of other international courts (such as the IACtHR or the ICJ) and the practice of

[14] Magliveras and Naldi 2016, p. 169.

[15] Protocol No. 2 to the Convention for the Protection of Human Rights and Fundamental Freedoms, Conferring upon the European Court of Human Rights Competence to Give Advisory Opinions, opened for signature 6 May 1993, ETS No. 44, entered into force on 21 September 1970. Note that all provisions amended or added by Protocol No. 2 were replaced by Protocol No. 11, opened for signature 11 May 1994, ETS No. 155, entered into force 1 November 1998.

[16] Council of Europe 2006, para 81; High Level Conference on the Future of the European Court of Human Rights, Brighton Declaration 19–20 April 2012, para 12(d); European Court of Human Rights 2012.

preliminary references in the European Union could strengthen its role and create an institutional dialogue between domestic courts and Strasbourg.[17]

This led to the adoption of Protocol No. 16 ECHR in October 2013, which expanded the ECtHR's powers to issue advisory opinions.[18] Article 1 reads as follows: '1. Highest courts and tribunals of a High Contracting Party, as specified in accordance with Article 10, may request the Court to give advisory opinions on questions of principle relating to the interpretation or application of the rights and freedoms defined in the Convention or the protocols thereto. 2. The requesting court or tribunal may seek an advisory opinion only in the context of a case pending before it.' Although not at the level of the ACtHPR or the IACtHR, Protocol No. 16 significantly expanded the advisory jurisdiction of the ECtHR, in particular by building a closer channel with domestic courts. Quite distinctively, this widening of the powers to render advisory opinions is specifically directed towards the national courts of contracting parties and not towards their governments or civil society actors. The entry into force of Protocol No. 16 has quickly increased the number of rendered advisory opinions, reaching seven by the end of 2023 compared to the mere three under Article 47.[19]

It is worth mentioning that both Article 48 ECHR and Article 2 of Protocol No. 16 explicitly allow the ECtHR to accept or reject the request for an advisory opinion, without specific constraints beyond the requirement to provide an explanation in case of rejection. This could counterbalance the worries about an already overburdened Court taking on an additional task with limited resources available.[20]

8.2.4 The Inter-American Court of Human Rights

The IACtHR is by far the most active in rending advisory opinions. Differently from the other regional Courts, its first output was an advisory opinion and it had issued eight opinions before ruling on its first contentious case.[21] Since its establishment, it has delivered thirty advisory opinions on extremely topical issues, exceptional in terms of content and impact on its own case-law and state practice.[22] A lot has been written on the IACtHR advisory jurisdiction's features and its distinctive approach,

[17] European Court of Human Rights 2012, paras 4–11 and 16. See also Dzehtsiarou and O'Meara 2014; Daka 2020; Dicosola et al. 2015; Moonen and Lavrysen 2021.

[18] Opened for signature 2 October 2013, CETS No. 214, entered into force 1 August 2018. Presently, twenty-four CoE Member States have ratified it.

[19] Information as provided by the ECtHR official database (https://hudoc.echr.coe.int), accessed 5 March 2025. The ECtHR has also refused requests for Advisory Opinion under Protocol 16, see P-16-2020-001 (requested by the Supreme Court of the Slovakia) and P-16-2023-002 (requested by the Supreme Court of the Estonia).

[20] Dzehtsiarou and O'Meara 2014.

[21] IACtHR, *Velasquez Rodriguez v Honduras*, Judgment (Merits), 29 July 1988, Series C No. 4.

[22] Contesse 2021.

highlighting its importance to advance human rights protection in the region.[23] As Contesse observes, there has been an historical evolution in the IACtHR's approach to advisory opinions, from a more cautious attitude to being more activist and interventionist, hinting to a new constitutional court role, which has challenged its authority and legitimacy.[24]

The legal basis is Article 64 ACHR, which reads '1. The member states of the Organization [of American States] may consult the Court regarding the interpretation of this Convention or of other treaties concerning the protection of human rights in the American states. Within their spheres of competence, the organs listed in Chapter VIII of the [OAS] Charter,[25] as amended by the Protocol of Buenos Aires, may in like manner consult the Court. 2. The Court, at the request of a member state of the Organization, may provide that state with opinions regarding the compatibility of any of its domestic laws with the aforesaid international instruments'.

The provision differs from the ECHR and the ArabCtHR Statute and resembles the ACHPR. The intent to have a broad scope for advisory opinions is confirmed by the *travaux preparatoires,* while the explicit power to advise on the 'compatibility of any [...] domestic law' is a *unicum* compared to the other regional systems.[26] Such a combination of broadness and specificity at the same time has encouraged the submission of requests and, as will be discussed in Sect. 8.5, had led to a proactive and activist attitude from the IACtHR.

In line with the other two systems, the IACtHR has full discretion to interpret the admissibility requirements and to reject any request even if otherwise admissible. As Judge Cançado Trindade commented, 'whenever the Court decides to respond or not to a request for an Advisory Opinion, it is exercising the power to determine its own competence, derived from a principle of general international law and not conditioned by the behaviour of the requesting state or organ.'[27]

8.3 Who May Request an Advisory Opinion? Standing Before the Regional Human Rights Courts

Advisory opinions can only be delivered if one of the actors having standing submits a formal request, as none of the four courts can issue opinions *motu proprio.* It follows that the decision on which specific actors to allow submitting requests defines the

[23] Ibid.; Buergenthal 1985; Baillet 2018.

[24] Contesse 2021, p. 382–388.

[25] These are: the General Assembly, the Meeting of Consultation of Ministers of Foreign Affairs, the Councils, the Inter-American Juridical Committee, the Inter-American Commission on Human Rights, the General Secretariat, the Specialised Conferences and the Specialised Organisations.

[26] Pasqualucci 2002, p. 249–251.

[27] IACtHR, *Reports of the Inter-American Commission of Human Rights (Art. 51 of the American Convention on Human Rights),* Advisory Opinion OC-15/97, 14 November 1997, Series A No. 15 (Judge Cançado Trindade concurring), para 6.

nature and role of advisory opinions. On the one hand, the African Court allows the broadest participation, also allowing NGOs to submit requests even if the restrictive interpretation has closed several doors to civil society interactions. On the other hand, the ECtHR and the IACtHR limit access to the organs of the international organisations that established them as well as to domestic courts and/or governments. Finally, the Statute of the ArabCtHR has adopted an even stricter approach, allowing only the LAS Council and subordinated agencies to bring a request.

8.3.1 The African Court of Human and Peoples' Rights

The ACtHPR Protocol has a very broad formulation in terms of what actors have standing before the Court. Still, six of the ten requests rejected were considered to be outside the ACtHPR's jurisdiction *ratione personae*. Five of these rejections were due to the lack of standing of NGOs before it. In addition to the AU and contracting parties, Article 4 ACtHPR Protocol enables 'any African organization recognized by the OAU' to bring a request for an advisory opinion. However, the interpretation given by the ACtHPR to this requirement significantly narrows down the possibility for African NGOs to lodge requests.

In the landmark *SERAP* case, the ACtHPR was for the first time called to decide whether it had jurisdiction *ratione personae* over NGOs, as provided by Article 4(1).[28] The Socio-Economic Rights and Accountability Project (SERAP) submitted a request claiming that it met the standing requirement being an African organisation (registered in Nigeria, an AU member) and recognised by African Commission on Human and Peoples' Rights as it was granted observer status before it. Despite the argument advanced by SERAP, by state parties, and by those who submitted *amicus curiae* briefs, the ACtHPR rejected the claims concluding that SERAP had no standing.[29] The Court agreed that it was an African NGO but considered that having observer status before the Commission was not the same as being recognised by the AU. From *SERAP* onwards, the Court has consistently interpreted the Article 4(1) requirement ('any African organisation recognised by the African Union') to apply only to those having observer status before the AU.[30] Ultimately, this stricter interpretation test leaves out most African NGOs willing and interested in bringing a

---

[28] ACtHPR, Request for Advisory Opinion No. 001/2012, *Socio-Economic Rights & Accountability Project (SERAP)*, Order, 15 March 2013.

[29] Chenwi 2020, p. 65.

[30] ACtHPR, Request 002/2014, *Rencontre Africain pour la Défense des Droits de l'Homme (RADDHO)*, Advisory Opinion, 28 September 2017; ACtHPR, Request 002/2015, *Centre for Human Rights of the University of Pretoria (CHR) and Coalition of African Lesbians (CAL)*, Advisory Opinion, 28 September 2017; ACtHPR, Request 002/2016, *Association Africaine de Défense des Droits de l'Homme*, Advisory Opinion, 28 September 2017; ACtHPR, Request 001/2016, *Centre for Human Rights of the University of Pretoria, Federation of Women Lawyers Kenya, Women's Legal Centre, Women Advocates Research and Documentation Centre and Zimbabwe Women Lawyers Association*, Advisory Opinion, 28 September 2018.

request for an advisory opinion, limiting in practice the broad scope and potential of the provision. As pointed out by Judge Rafâa Ben Achour in his Separate Opinion on four inadmissibility rulings, the standing requirement in question is more restrictive than that for contentious cases.[31] He acknowledged that the Court had 'its hands tied by the explicit terms of Article 4(1) of its Protocol and by the restrictive practice of the [African] Union in matters of granting observer status to NGOs'.[32] Therefore, he suggested an amendment to Article 4(1) or for the AU to change its policy to maximise the possibility for NGOs to have access to the advisory jurisdiction. Yet, echoing Chenwi,[33] the Court could have also opted for a more generous interpretation, if it was really interested in enabling more civil society actors to engage with its advisory jurisdiction.

As for all the other actors that can lodge a request for an opinion, there is little precedent or controversy. In the only other case rejected on standing, the individual submitting the request did not make it clear how and if it was authorised by the state of Libya.[34]

8.3.2 *The European Court of Human Rights*

The standing requirements for advisory opinions before the ECtHR change with the legal basis considered for the request. According to Article 47 ECHR, only the Council of Europe (CoE) Committee of Ministers may submit requests. This is a very strict and straightforward formulation, which was neither challenged nor discussed further in the three advisory opinions rendered so far. Such a close and strict standing also gives an idea of the focus and objectives of Article 47 advisory opinions, which are mainly administrative in nature and aim at supporting the Committee of Ministers in the exercise of its functions.

When Protocol No. 16 came into force, the procedure was expanded, allowing also the 'highest national courts and tribunals' to request advisory opinions on questions of principle relating to the interpretation or application of the rights and freedoms contained in the Convention or the Protocols.[35] This mechanism works in a similar way to, and it is explicitly inspired by the European Union's (EU) preliminary reference system.[36]

---

[31] ACtHPR, The four Advisory Opinions of 28 September 2017 - Individual Opinion of Judge Rafâa Ben Achour, 28 September 2017, para 6.

[32] Ibid., para 4.

[33] Chenwi 2020, p. 61–77.

[34] ACtHPR, Request 002/2011, *Request for advisory opinion by Advocate Marcel Ceccaldi on behalf of The Great Socialist People's Libyan Arab Jamahiriya*, Order, 30 March 2012.

[35] Protocol No. 16 ECHR, Article 1.

[36] Daka 2020. The preliminary reference procedure is established by Article 267 Treaty on the Functioning of the European Union (TFEU) of 13 December 2007 — consolidated version, O.J. C 202, 7.6.2016, p 47.

Standing is not granted generally to contracting parties but is limited to the most important judicial bodies within each state party. While administrative bodies and political authorities are clearly excluded, Protocol No. 16 does not clarify the exact meaning of the expression 'highest courts and tribunals'. Article 10 leaves this power of selection to each member state: 'Each High Contracting Party to the [ECHR] shall, at the time of signature or when depositing its instrument of ratification, or approval, by means of a declaration addressed to the Secretary General of the Council of Europe, indicate the courts or tribunals that it designates for the purposes of Article 1, paragraph 1 of this Protocol.' This allows each state party to identify the most appropriate and suitable judicial bodies within its jurisdiction, but this should not happen on a case-by-case basis to ensure consistency and coherence.

The decision to expand the advisory jurisdiction to domestic courts only, and not to the contracting states' governments or to NGOs, fits within the now established approach of the ECtHR to work closely with domestic legal institutions in a new 'age of subsidiarity'.[37] Therefore, advisory opinions could become an important instrument for cooperation between Strasbourg and national courts consolidating their relationship and strengthening ties, trust and legitimacy.

8.3.3 The Inter-American Court of Human Rights

As provided by Article 64 ACHR, all OAS member states and all listed organs are allowed to submit a request for an advisory opinion to the IACtHR.

All OAS members have standing, even those who are not party to the ACHR and have not accepted the IACtHR jurisdiction for contentious cases. The IACtHR has also been very clear in defining which entities within the member states have the authority to submit requests. In *Proposed Amendments to the Naturalization Provisions of the Constitutions of Costa Rica*, it did not consider the request of a Committee of Costa Rica's Legislative Assembly but waited for the request of the Minister for Foreign Affairs, recognising that it is the government or, in general, the executive branch that has the power to do so.[38] This decision was likely motivated by the intention to ensure consistency across state parties and not intervene in the domestic dynamics between the legislative and the executive.

Moreover, OAS organs, such as the Inter-American Commission on Human Rights (IACommHR) or the General Assembly may request opinions. However, their standing is limited to questions 'within their spheres of competence', namely matters in which they have 'legitimate institutional interest'.[39] In the case of the

[37] Spano 2014.

[38] IACtHR, *Proposed Amendments to the Naturalization Provisions of the Constitution of Costa Rica*, Advisory Opinion OC-4/84, 19 January 1984, Series A No. 4, para 11.

[39] IACtHR, *The Effect of Reservations on the Entry into Force of the American Convention on Human* Rights, Advisory Opinion OC-2/82, 24 September 1982, Series A No. 2, para 14, reported in (1983) *American Journal of International Law* 77: 640–642.

IACommHR, this applies to everything related to the ACHR as it concerns human rights. Calls for expanding standing to other entities, such as domestic courts, other OAS organs (e.g. the Inter-American Commission of Women or the Inter-American Agency for Cooperation and Development) or NGOs have all been rejected with concerns over the excessive burden on the Court's functioning.[40]

8.4 The Subject Matter of Advisory Opinions

The four regional Courts have different approaches towards their advisory jurisdiction *ratione materiae*. The ECtHR stands out as the most restrictive, yet respectful of the principle of subsidiarity, while the IACtHR emerges as the most generous in accepting a wide range of subject-matters. In the middle stands the ACtHPR, which has adopted a restrictive interpretation of a very broad jurisdiction provision. Likewise, the ArabCtHR could issue advisory opinions on matters related to the Arab Charter and to other Arab human rights instruments (they are not laid down in its Statute), thus potentially wider than the ECtHR.

8.4.1 The African Court of Human and Peoples' Rights

As observed above, the ACtHPR may provide an opinion on 'any legal matter relating to the [ACHPR] or any relevant human rights instruments'. This has allowed the Court to deal with a wide range of issues in the four opinions rendered so far. They include the right to participate in government and elections in times of health emergency (Covid-19 pandemic),[41] the compatibility of vagrancy law with the ACHPR,[42] and the standing of AU bodies before the Court in contentious cases.[43] The very broad scope, going beyond the ACHPR itself, mirrors the Court's jurisdiction in contentious cases.[44] Likewise, this wide-encompassing approach is similar to what has been observed for standing.

---

[40] Pasqualucci 2002, p 256–258.

[41] ACtHPR, Request 001/2020, *Request by the Pan African Lawyers Union (PALU) on the Right to Participate in the Government of One's Country in the Context of an Election Held During a Public Health Emergency or a Pandemic, Such as the Covid-19 Crisis,* Advisory Opinion, 16 July 2021.

[42] ACtHPR, *Request for an Advisory Opinion by the Pan African Lawyers Union (PALU) on the Compatibility of Vagrancy Laws,* above n. 8.

[43] ACtHPR, Request 002/2013, *The Standing of the African Committee of Experts on the Rights and Welfare of the Child before the African Court of Human and Peoples' Rights*, Advisory Opinion, 5 December 2014.

[44] Eno 2002; Rachovitsa 2019.

However, the formulation ‘relevant human rights instruments’ remains very vague[45] and the ACtHPR has rejected requests exactly on failure to meet this requirement. In the *LEADP, CIRDDOC and WARDC* cases, the ACtHPR rejected two requests from three African NGOs because the relevant provisions of the African Charter or other international human rights instruments were not specified and because ‘the issues raised by the Authors are of general public international law and not of human rights’. The requests concerned the interpretation of specific articles of the Rome Statute establishing the International Criminal Court and the hierarchy between international treaty obligations. Yet, the Court found that this was not within the definition of ‘relevant human rights instruments’.[46] In a powerful dissenting opinion, Judge Ouguergouz argued that the Rome Statute is a human rights instrument and that, as general public international law determines the application and interpretation of human rights, this ought to fall within the ACtHPR jurisdiction *ratione materiae*.[47] The Court’s restrictive approach is a missed opportunity for clarifying what constitutes a human rights treaty[48] and for joining the IACtHR in a broader understanding and progressive practice.

The ACtHPR might change its approach in the future, and in a subsequent contentious case it held that ‘in determining whether a Convention is a human rights instrument, it is necessary to refer in particular to the purposes of such Convention’.[49] Only future requests will tell whether the Court is ready to adopt this approach in its advisory jurisdiction as well.

8.4.2 The European Court of Human Rights

Advisory opinions under Article 47 ECHR have a very limited scope, allowing only procedural and administrative issues to be brought before the attention of the Court. Article 47(2) ECHR excludes ‘any question relating to the content or scope of the rights or freedoms defined in Section I of the Convention and the Protocols thereto, or […] any other question which the Court or the Committee of Ministers might have to consider in consequence of any such proceedings as could be instituted in accordance with the Convention.’ Applying these requirements in a very strict way, the ECtHR has rejected one of the three requests submitted so far by the Committee of Ministers

45 van der Mei 2005, p 38.

46 ACtHPR, Request 001/2014, *Coalition for the International Criminal Court, Legal Defence & Assistance Project (LEDAP), Civil Resource Development & Documentation Center (CIRDDOC) and Women Advocates Documentation Center (WARDC)*, Order, 5 June 2015; ACtHPR, Request 001/2015, *Coalition for the International Criminal Court, Legal Defence & Assistance Project (LEDAP), Civil Resource Development & Documentation Center (CIRDDOC) and Women Advocates Documentation Center (WARDC)*, Order, 29 November 2015.

47 Ibid., Dissenting Opinion of Judge Fatsah Ouguergouz in both cases, paras 16–20.

48 Chenwi 2020, p. 67.

49 ACtHPR, Application 001/2014, *Actions pour la Protection des Droits de l’Homme (APDH) v The Republic of Côte d’Ivoire*, Judgment, 18 November 2016, paras 54–65.

regarding the coexistence of the ECHR with the Convention on Human Rights and Fundamental Freedoms of the Commonwealth of Independent States because this was a matter that it might have to consider in a contentious case in the future.[50] As Dzehtsiarou and O'Meara argued, there is some concern that the advisory jurisdiction would overlap with its contentious one and lead to double adjudication of the same case.[51] The only two advisory opinions rendered so far dealt with the procedures concerning the election of judges to the ECtHR.[52]

Different requirements are in place for advisory opinions rendered under Protocol No. 16. As the aim of the Protocol was to 'strengthen the dialogue between the ECtHR and the national judicial authorities',[53] requests should concern current issues under discussion before national courts. In particular, they should not be abstract but closely linked to ongoing judicial proceedings and explain why the ECtHR's opinion is necessary for supporting the national court in deciding a pending case. For example, the ECtHR rejected the request by the Slovakian Supreme Court because 'the questions raised [...] do not concern an issue on which the requesting court would need the Court's guidance by way of an advisory opinion to be able to ensure respect for Convention rights when determining the case before it'.[54]

Requests by national courts should also be accompanied by further details on the domestic proceedings, the relevant factual and legal background of the case, the applicable domestic provisions and the relevant ECHR provisions.[55] It would still be within the ECtHR's discretion to accept the request on the basis that it 'raises a novel point of Convention law' or where 'the facts of the case do not seem to lend themselves to a straightforward application of the Court's case law, or [...] there appears to be an inconsistency in the case law'.[56]

The wording of the ECtHR jurisdiction *ratione materiae* together with the criteria for exercising its discretion confirm the Court's claimed objective to enhance its constitutional role.[57] Deeply rooted in the principle of subsidiarity, the ECtHR is keen to mirror the EU's preliminary reference mechanism and not to overstep the boundaries of national sovereignty. Therefore, its role is solely to support courts of last resort to ensure a consistent interpretation of the ECHR and avoid domestic precedents that could adversely affect subsequent interpretation and, inevitably, lead

---

[50] ECtHR, *Decision on the competence of the Court to give an advisory opinion,* A47–2004-001, Advisory Opinion, 2 June 2004.

[51] Dzehtsiarou and O'Meara 2014.

[52] ECtHR, *Advisory opinion on certain legal questions concerning the lists of candidates submitted with a view to the election of judges to the European Court of Human Rights*, A47–2008-01, Advisory Opinion, 12 February 2008; ECtHR, *Advisory opinion on certain legal questions concerning the lists of candidates submitted with a view to the election of judges to the European Court of Human Rights (no. 2),* A47–2010-001, Advisory Opinion, 22 January 2010.

[53] European Court of Human Rights 2012.

[54] ECtHR, *Decision on a request for an advisory opinion under Protocol no. 16 concerning the interpretation of Articles 2, 3 and 6 of the Convention,* P16–2020-001, 14 December 2020, para 23.

[55] European Court of Human Rights 2023, Article 92(2) and (12).

[56] Ibid.

[57] Council of Europe 2014, para 1.

to more applications for contentious proceedings.[58] Looking at the low number of requests and the already overburdened ECtHR, several scholars are sceptical on whether this ultimate goal can be achieved through advisory opinions.[59] Yet, the ECtHR jurisdiction *ratione materiae* clearly points in this direction.

8.4.3 The Inter-American Court of Human Rights

As previously explained, the IACtHR may deliver advisory opinions on: 1) questions concerning the interpretation of the ACHR; 2) questions relating to the interpretation of 'other treaties concerning the protection of human rights'; and 3) the compatibility of member states' domestic laws with their human rights obligations.

The first matter ensures that the ACHR receives uniform interpretation and application across the member states or by all OAS organs, also considering the language differences in the English, Spanish, Portuguese and French versions.[60] So far, most advisory opinions fall within this category. The Court has always interpreted the ACHR in an evolutionary way, 'within the framework of the entire legal system prevailing at the time of the interpretation'.[61] In the last four decades, the IACtHR has, among others, clarified the meaning of judicial guarantees from which no derogation is permitted[62] as well as the right to nationality,[63] and has expanded the boundaries of the right to marry and the right to a private life.[64]

Similarly to the ACtHPR, the IACtHR has jurisdiction over the interpretation of other international instruments, beyond the ACHR. However, differently from the ACtHPR, its interpretation is very broad. In one of its early advisory opinions, it clarified that 'other treaties' meant: 'any provision dealing with the protection of human rights set forth in any international treaty applicable in the American States, regardless of whether it be bilateral or multilateral, whatever be the principal purpose of such treaty, and whether or not non-member states of the inter-American system are or have the right to become parties thereto'.[65] This supports the IACtHR's view

[58] See also Gavrysh 2022, p 266–295.

[59] Daka 2020; Dzehtsiarou and O'Meara 2014.

[60] Pasqualucci 2002, p. 260.

[61] IACtHR, *The Right to Information on Consular Assistance in the Framework of the Guarantees of the Due Process of Law*, Advisory Opinion OC-16/99, 1 October 1999, Series A No. 16, para 113.

[62] IACtHR, *Habeas Corpus in Emergency Situations,* Advisory Opinion OC-8/87, 30 January 1987, Series A No. 87.

[63] IACtHR, *Proposed Amendments to the Naturalization Provision of the Constitution of Costa Rica,* above n. 38.

[64] IACtHR, *State Obligations Concerning Change of Name, Gender Identity, and Rights Derived from a Relationship Between Same-Sex Couples,* above n. 4.

[65] IACtHR, *Other Treaties subject to the Consultative Jurisdiction of the Court,* Advisory Opinion OC-1/82, 24 September 1982, Series A No. 1, para 52.

of advisory opinions as a tool to advance human rights protection and contrasts with the restrictive interpretation given by the ACtHPR.

The last category of the IACtHR's jurisdiction *ratione materiae* concerns the compatibility of state parties' domestic laws with the ACHR. This includes all national legislation and legal norms of any character and extends to draft legislation as well,[66] thus being potentially very useful in avoiding the approval of incompatible laws which will likely lead to future contentious cases. States may submit requests on the compatibility of their own domestic laws but not those of other states. However, in *International Responsibility for the Promulgation and Enforcement of Laws,* the IACtHR accepted a request from the IACommHR for an opinion on the compliance of the Peruvian constitutional proposals on the death penalty with the ACHR.[67] Peru accused the IACommHR of trying to achieve indirectly what it could not do directly, as Article 64(2) ACHR allows only OAS member states to request opinions on compatibility. However, the IACtHR concluded that the Commission had standing under Article 64(1) ACHR as regards its function to make recommendations to member states on compliance with the ACHR.[68] This exception has been criticised by some contracting parties as encroaching upon their own right to request an advisory opinion on their own domestic laws and considered it expedient to circumvent the sovereign decision of a state not to request an advisory opinion.

In conclusion, the wide jurisdiction *ratione materiae* provided by Article 64 ACHR has been amplified by the IACtHR's interpretation, to allow the broadest matters to be included in the requests for advisory opinions. This provides the basis for the expansive record of advisory opinions issued by the IACtHR so far.

8.5 The Interpretative Value of Advisory Opinions and the Question of Legal Precedent

Advisory opinions are non-binding and, as such, are often considered less influential and important than judgments in contentious litigation. As Baillet put it, advisory opinions should encourage rather than compel state compliance.[69]

In particular, it is not clear whether advisory opinions constitute legal precedents that could be used in subsequent advisory and contentious cases. While in the African system there is very little to no interaction between the advisory and the contentious jurisdiction (due to the low number of advisory opinions and the non-matching subject matters of contentious cases), the ECtHR and the IACtHR have developed

---

[66] IACtHR, *Proposed Amendments to the Naturalization Provision of the Constitution of Costa Rica,* above n. 38.

[67] IACtHR, *International Responsibility for the Promulgation and Enforcement of Laws,* Advisory Opinion OC-14/94, 9 December 1994, Series A No. 14.

[68] Ibid., paras 1 and 12.

[69] Baillet 2018, p. 256.

interesting practices that give non-binding advisory opinions a more authoritative role in human rights adjudication.

Article 5 of Protocol 16 ECHR makes advisory opinions explicitly non-binding. Consequently, the national judicial authorities that sought them have full discretion on whether to follow them. However, the Explanatory Report to the Protocol clarifies that the advisory opinions would form part of the case-law of the Court, alongside its judgments and decisions. It further explicitly confirms that the interpretation of the ECHR and the Protocols contained in advisory opinions has analogous effect to the interpretation given by the Court in judgments and decisions.[70] This suggests that they have a force of *res interpretata.*[71] In the practice of the ECtHR, it has become evident that advisory opinions are 'endowed with an authoritative interpretative value'[72] especially when they concern principles of law regarding primary rules, which the Court used in subsequent contentious cases, making them *res judicata.*[73] As Gavrysh comments, while advisory opinions are not binding for the contracting states or the Court itself, the ECtHR decided to 'bind itself, in order to ensure continuity of its jurisprudence'.[74]

In a similar fashion, the IACtHR's advisory opinions are considered non-binding.[75] However, since its first opinions, the Court has made it clear that they should be considered on the same level as contentious judgments. The IACtHR has always regarded them as 'the most effective means of demonstrating [its] usefulness and providing [it] with an opportunity to develop a consistent and influential body of human rights jurisprudence'.[76] As Judge Ferrer Mac-Gregor commented, advisory opinions 'serve as a legal source for all OAS Member States in order to contribute to human rights'.[77] Indeed, not only are they considered by the IACtHR equal to contentious judgments in their contribution to the development of international human rights law, but they have the additional advantage of potentially placing obligations on all OAS member states, even on those which have not ratified the ACHR, such as the United States.[78] This wider scope further amplifies the impact that advisory opinions could potentially have on state practice, even if the lack of enforcement mechanisms remains one of the biggest obstacles to actual change.

---

[70] Council of Europe 2014, para 27.

[71] Dicosola et al. 2015, p. 1409.

[72] Gavrysh 2022, p. 294.

[73] See ECtHR, Applications nos 1462/18 and 17,348/18, *C v France* and *E v France*, Judgment, 19 November 2019, ECHR 433 (2019), para 42; ECtHR, Application no. 11288/18, *D v France,* Judgment, 16 July 2020, para 67.

[74] Gavrysh 2022, p. 295.

[75] Baillet 2018; Contesse 2021.

[76] Lockwood 1984, p. 246.

[77] Ferrer Mac-Gregor 2015, p 96.

[78] IACtHR, *Restrictions to the Death Penalty*, Advisory Opinion OC-3/83, 8 September 1983, Series A No. 3, para 43.

IACtHR's advisory opinions also adopt the so-called 'conventionality control doctrine'. Created by the Court in a contentious case against Chile,[79] it soon found application in all advisory opinions, enhancing their value. This doctrine requires 'all state parties to the ACHR to interpret any national legal instruments in accordance with the ACHR and with the Inter-American *corpus juris* more generally. Wherever a domestic instrument is manifestly incompatible with the Inter-American *corpus juris*, state authorities must refrain from application of this law, in order to avoid any violation of internationally protected rights.'[80] The application of this doctrine to advisory opinions, imposing obligations on all member states and not just those requesting the opinion, has made the IACtHR act more and more like a constitutional court.[81] The doctrine has been praised by some scholars because it promotes unity and uniformity among Latin American judges and human rights law standards in the region.[82] However, other scholars strongly criticised it because it erodes the basic underpinning of subsidiarity and makes the IACtHR overstep its role as a human rights court by attempting to take on law-making functions, pushing the limits of its legitimacy.[83]

8.6 The Impact of Advisory Opinions on Contentious Cases and State Practice

8.6.1 The African Court of Human and Peoples' Rights

The four advisory opinions issued to date still have not found echoes in the Court's contentious cases, thus making it harder to establish any impact of the interpretative role. This is also due to the topics of the four opinions, as only two concerned substantive human rights issues (vagrancy laws and the right to political participation in times of pandemic) and are extremely narrow.

However, the impact of the ACtHPR advisory opinions is likely to increase in the future and become significant for two main reasons. First, the type of recommendations and language used by the ACtHPR in its advisory opinions suggest that it considers this tool as one for promoting human rights advancement in the region, aligning its practice to that of the IACtHR. For instance, in the 2020 Advisory Opinion on vagrancy laws, it concluded that all state parties have an obligation to review and amend, or completely repeal, all offences that target individuals because of their

---

[79] IACtHR, *Almonacid Arellano et al v Chile,* Judgment (Preliminary Objections, Merits, Reparations and Costs), 26 September 2006, Series C No. 154, para 124.

[80] Ferrer Mac-Gregor 2015, p 93.

[81] Contesse 2021.

[82] von Bogdandy and Uruena 2020, p 414–15; Ferrer Mac-Gregor 2017, p 89.

[83] Contesse 2017. See also Judge Eduardo Vio Grossi, Dissenting Opinion in *State obligations in relation to change of name, gender identity, and rights deriving from a relationship between same-sex couples,* above n. 4.

status rather than their action, considering them not compliant with the ACHPR and other key African instruments.[84] This was welcomed by NGOs and scholars as a very important decision, able to address one of the most widespread human rights threats in the continent.[85] Even though several African countries still have vagrancy laws in place (e.g. Zimbabwe arrested a man under vagrancy laws only in May 2023), it has become an important tool in the hands of the civil society to advocate for and request change in the legislation and the State's accountability.[86]

Second, while the ACtHPR has yet to reference its advisory opinions in contentious cases, the practice of referring to the IACtHR's advisory opinions as authoritative interpretation of human rights law standards is promising. In several cases, including *Niyonzima Augustine v. Tanzania*,[87] the ACtHPR used IACtHR advisory opinions to support important parts of its argument, considering them at the same level as contentious judgments. Once the ACtHPR has more diversified contentious cases to deal with and more advisory opinions under its belt, it is likely that it will start citing its own advisory opinions as well.

8.6.2 The European Court of Human Rights

The few advisory opinions issued so far by the ECtHR under Protocol No. 16 have proven to be extremely influential in both the ECtHR's case-law and domestic interpretation by national courts in a range of topical issues. The first such advisory opinion was requested by the French *Cour de Cassation* and concerned the recognition in domestic law of the legal relationship between a child born through a gestational surrogacy abroad and the intended mother. The Court held that Article 8 ECHR requires member states to ensure the parent-child relationship with the intended parent, provided that it leads to a prompt and effective outcome.[88] The ECtHR then used the same principle in a series of contentious cases on the same issues, finding France in breach of Article 8 ECHR, and making such an ECHR interpretation to be ultimately binding.[89]

In 2020, in two cases against Croatia, the ECtHR went further, adopting a principle established in a previous advisory opinion requested by Armenia.[90] Interestingly enough, Croatia has not ratified Protocol No. 16. Here the matter concerned the

[84] ACtHPR, *Request for an Advisory Opinion by the Pan African Lawyers Union (PALU) on the Compatibility of Vagrancy Laws,* above n. 8, para 154.

[85] Gavrysh 2022, p 292; Amnesty International 2023.

[86] Southern Africa Litigation Centre 2023.

[87] ACtHPR, Application 058/2016, *Niyonzima Augustine v United Republic of Tanzania*, Judgment, 13 June 2023, p 23, 36.

[88] ECtHR, *Recognition in domestic law of a legal parent-child relationship between a child born through a gestational surrogacy arrangement abroad and the intended mother*, above n 7, para 55.

[89] ECtHR, *C v France* and *E v France*, above n. 73, para 42; *D v France*, above n. 73, para 67.

[90] ECtHR, P16–2019-001, *The Use of the 'blanket reference' or 'legislation by reference' technique in the definition of an offence,* Advisory Opinion, 29 May 2020; ECtHR, Application no. 36908/

requirements set by Article 7 ECHR for a 'blanket reference' or 'legislation by reference' in the definition of a criminal offence. The ECtHR used the reasoning of its Opinion of May 2020 as precedent to rule against Croatia, considering advisory opinions to be as any other judgment.[91]

The importance of the ECtHR's advisory opinions beyond the countries that requested them is confirmed by the relevance they had in shaping domestic litigation, even for states that have not ratified Protocol No. 16. For instance, in 2021, the Italian Constitutional Court made extensive reference to the aforementioned advisory opinion on surrogacy to depart from the previous approach of the Italian case-law, notwithstanding that Italy has not ratified Protocol No. 16.[92] Arguably, it also confirmed that ECtHR advisory opinions constitute authoritative precedents that ought to be followed.[93]

8.6.3 The Inter-American Court of Human Rights

The IACtHR certainly aims to have an impact on states' practice and on the development of international human rights law with its opinions. This intent clearly emerges from the types of requests it has accepted, the way in which it has delivered and argued the opinions, the innovative and elaborated reasoning it provided, and the copious references to its opinions in contentious cases. As Contesse explains, the IACtHR 'rules through advice'.[94] Some of its advisory opinions have shaped the understanding of human rights beyond the Americas, promoting the advancement of human rights protection in a range of contexts.

To name but a few, the IACtHR has chosen to render opinions on issues relating to migrants, asylum seekers and undocumented workers, with clear underlying references to how these issues are poorly addressed in the United States of America and other countries of the region.[95] In the 2003 Opinion on *Undocumented Migrants,* the IACtHR found that contracting parties have a duty to respect migrant workers' equality and non-discrimination despite their undocumented status and, moreover,

---

13, *N.S. v Croatia,* Judgment, 10 September 2020; ECtHR, Application no. 2953/14, *Pantalon v Croatia,* Judgment, 19 November 2020.

91 ECtHR, *Pantalon v Croatia,* ibid., para 45 and *N.S. v Croatia,* ibid., para 83.

92 Corte Costituzionale, Judgment No. 32, 28 January 2021, English translation at: https://cortecostituzionale.it/documenti/download/doc/recent_judgments/Sentenza%20n.%2032%20del%202021%20red.%20Sciarra%20EN.pdf. Accessed 7 March 2025.

93 Gavrysh 2022, p 279.

94 Contesse 2021, p 369.

95 Baillet 2018; IACtHR, *Rights and Guarantees of Children in the Context of Migration and/or in Need of International Protection,* above n. 5; IACtHR, *The Institution of Asylum, and its Recognition as a Human Right under the Inter-American System of Protection,* Advisory Opinion OC-25/18, 30 May 2018, Series A No. 25; IACtHR, *Juridical Condition and Rights of the Undocumented Migrants,* Advisory Opinion OC-18/03, 17 September 2003, Series A No. 18.

held that the principle of non-discrimination has attained the status of *jus cogens.*[96] This was the first time an international court had said so. Even though it could have had a tremendous impact, in reality it has had 'little or no practical consequence',[97] having been mentioned only once by the UN Committee on the Elimination of Racial Discrimination (CERD) and accompanied by significant disagreement within the Committee.[98] In subsequent opinions on similar issues, such as the 2014 Opinion on the rights of children in the context of migration,[99] and the 2018 Opinion on the right to asylum,[100] the IACtHR transferred the conventionality control to advisory opinions, further binding member states to follow its rulings and, therefore, expanding their potential impact.

In 2017, the IACtHR rendered a landmark opinion on gender identity and same sex marriage at the request of Costa Rica. In the opinion, the Court recognised that failure to include same-sex couples in the definition of 'family' would defeat the purpose of the ACHR and concluded that 'the most simple and effective way to ensure the rights derived from the relationship between same-sex couples' is to extend existing institutions 'including marriage' to those couples.[101] Applying the conventionality control doctrine, the IACtHR then established that '[s]tates must ensure' the legalisation of same-sex marriage, addressing its conclusion to both Costa Rica and all other ACHR parties.[102] The Opinion has had a huge impact on the region and undoubtedly contributed to the legalisation process of same-sex marriage in the Americas.[103] Domestic courts have used the Opinion to issue seminal rulings extending the right to marry to same-sex couples, including the Supreme Court of Costa Rica[104] and the Constitutional Court of Ecuador.[105] The Opinion also received great praise by UN experts and NGOs, considering that it was the first ruling of an international court recognising a right to marry for same-sex couples.[106]

---

[96] IACtHR, *Juridical Condition and Rights of the Undocumented Migrants*, ibid., paras 102–110 and 161–172.

[97] Contesse 2021, p 386; Shelton 2016.

[98] CERD Committee, CERD/C/100/5, *Palestine v Israel*, Decision on Jurisdiction, 12 December 2019, para 3.24.

[99] IACtHR, *Rights and Guarantees of Children in the Context of Migration and/or in Need of International Protection*, above n. 5.

[100] IACtHR, *The Institution of Asylum, and its Recognition as a Human Right under the Inter-American System of Protection,* above n. 95.

[101] IACtHR, *State Obligations Concerning Change of Name, Gender Identity, and Rights Derived from a Relationship Between Same-Sex Couples*, above n. 4, para 218.

[102] Ibid., para 228.

[103] Contesse 2021, p 381.

[104] Constitutional Chamber of the Supreme Court of Costa Rica, Exp: 15–013971-0007-CO, Decision No. 12782–2018, 8 August 2018; Wolfson et al. 2022.

[105] Constitutional Court of Ecuador, Case No. 10–18-CN and No. 11–18-CN, *Same-Sex Marriage*, 12 June 2019; https://www.loc.gov/item/global-legal-monitor/2019-07-25/ecuador-constitutional-court-upholds-same-sex-marriage/. Accessed 7 March 2025.

[106] Abrusci 2018; OHCHR 2018.

In the same year, the IACtHR also issued a landmark advisory opinion on the environment, requested by Colombia.[107] It held that states have an obligation to prevent significant environmental damage within or outside their territory, as this could threaten the right to life and to physical integrity. It follows that states should regulate and supervise any activity taking place under their jurisdiction, including by performing environmental impact assessments, ensuring transparency, information and a right to participation for the affected population, and putting in place appropriate mitigation measures.

These groundbreaking and extremely progressive advisory opinions generated significant pushback from conservative groups and led to a wave of political and institutional backlash from five member states (Brazil, Chile, Argentina, Colombia and Paraguay).[108] In April 2019, they officially launched a diplomatic campaign against both the IACtHR and the IACommHR, requesting a more deferential approach closer to the model of the ECtHR's margin of appreciation doctrine.[109] These states were ultimately concerned about the expansion of the conventionality control doctrine and worried about the new activist role the IACtHR has taken for itself, exacerbated by the 'ruling by advice' of its advisory opinions.[110]

8.7 Conclusions

As this chapter has shown, the practice of advisory opinions differs across the regional human rights systems, mirroring the divergences the Courts have in other aspects of their structure, functioning and impact.[111] Advisory opinions, sometimes overlooked in academic discussion, are extremely important for understanding the judicial approach of any court and this is particularly true in the case of regional human rights courts. Moreover, both due to the value given to them by the courts in their contentious cases and to the impact they have on state practice and domestic courts' ruling, advisory opinions are becoming more and more relevant in shaping international human rights law. Furthermore, the different attitudes towards advisory opinions could be seen as further strategies to enhance the courts' legitimacy, with different understanding of what this entails.

The ACtHPR has a very broad and promising legal basis, allowing the widest range of actors to submit requests, potentially, on any kind of human rights issue. However, its restrictive and cautious approach in interpreting the admissibility requirements has

107 IACtHR, *The Environment and Human Rights*, above n. 6.

108 Soley and Steininger 2018.

109 Statement from the Governments of Argentina, Brazil, Chile, Colombia and Paraguay, submitted to the Inter-American Commission on Human Rights, 23 April 2019 (in Spanish) at: https://minrel.gob.cl/minrel/noticias-anteriores/comunicado-de-prensa-ministerio-de-relaciones-exteriores-ministerio-de. Accessed 7 March 2025.

110 Soley and Steininger 2018; Contesse 2021, p 401.

111 Abrusci 2022.

prevented the ACtHPR from fully engaging with the tool of advisory opinions. Yet, when it did so, it issued important rulings that have supported quests for substantial changes in the region, such as on vagrancy laws. One could see this cautious approach as an attempt to strengthen its legitimacy and not to overstep its boundaries, as the ACtHPR is still in the process of building its reputation and relationship with state parties. Only time will tell what strategy the Court will decide to adopt.

On the contrary, the ECtHR has a very clear idea of what its approach to advisory opinions should be and how to use them to promote its agenda of subsidiarity and a closer dialogue with national courts, to consolidate its legitimacy and role. Protocol 16 has offered the ECtHR another excellent tool in this respect, and it is using it to respectfully guide state parties in their harmonious interpretation of ECHR rights and freedoms.

Lastly, the IACtHR emerges as the 'expert' in rendering advisory opinions. Both in terms of number and groundbreaking arguments, the IACtHR has confirmed its nature as an activist Court and has managed to use advisory opinions to significantly advance the protection of human rights in the region and their interpretation globally. However, this proactive approach, sometimes pushing the limits of the interpretation of the admissibility requirements, has come at the price of a heightened backlash from its state parties, opposing a judicial organ that goes beyond its limits. While the IACtHR sees this activist approach as a way to gain legitimacy *vis-à-vis* its role as a human rights institution, this may lead to losing legitimacy from the perspective of the contracting parties.

References

Abrusci E (2018) The IACtHR Advisory Opinion: One Step Forward or Two Steps Back for LGBTI Rights in Costa Rica? EJIL Talk. 27 February 2018. https://www.ejiltalk.org/the-iacthr-advisory-opinion-on-gender-identity-equality-and-non-discrimination-for-same-sex-couples-one-step-forward-or-two-steps-back-for-lgbti-rights-in-costa-rica/. Accessed 5 March 2025.

Abrusci E (2022) Judicial Convergence and Fragmentation in International Human Rights Law. Cambridge University Press, Cambridge.

Amnesty International (2023) Advisory opinion of the Court requesting the abrogation of vagrancy laws. 25 June 2023. https://www.amnesty.org/en/latest/campaigns/2023/06/advisory-opinion-of-the-court-requesting-the-abrogation-of-vagrancy-laws/. Accessed 5 March 2025.

Baillet C M (2018) The strategic prudence of the Inter-American Court of Human Rights: rejection of requests for an advisory opinion. Revista de Direito Internacional [Brazilian Journal of International Law] 15:254-286.

Buergenthal T (1985) The Advisory Practice of the Inter-American Human Rights Court. American Journal of International Law 79:1-27.

Chenwi L (2020) The Advisory Proceedings of the African Court on Human and Peoples' Rights. Nordic Journal of Human Rights 38:61-77.

Contesse J (2017) The Last Word? Constitutional Dialogue and the Inter-American Court of Human Rights. International Journal of Constitutional Law 17:414-435.

Contesse J (2021) The Rule of Advice in International Human Rights Law. American Journal of International Law 115:367-408.

Council of Europe (2006) Report of the Group of Wise Persons to the Committee of Ministers. CM(2006)203. 15 November 2006. https://rm.coe.int/09000016805d7893. Accessed 5 March 2025.

Council of Europe (2014) Explanatory Report on Protocol No. 16 to the Convention for the Protection of Human Rights and Fundamental Freedoms. https://www.echr.coe.int/documents/d/echr/protocol_16_explanatory_report_eng. Accessed 5 March 2025.

Daka M (2020) Advisory Opinion and Preliminary Ruling Procedure - A Comparative and Contextual Note. Pravni vjesnik 36:289-307.

Dicosola M, Fasone C, Spigno I (2015) The Prospective Role of Constitutional Courts in the Advisory Opinion Mechanism Before the European Court of Human Rights: A Comparative Assessment with the European Union and the Inter-American System. German Law Journal 16:1387-1428.

Dzehtsiarou K, O'Meara K (2014) Advisory Jurisdiction and the European Court of Human Rights: A Magic Bullet for Dialogue and Docket-Control. Legal Studies 34:444-468.

Eno R W (2002) The Jurisdiction of the African Court on Human and Peoples' Rights. African Human Rights Law Journal 2:223-233.

European Court of Human Rights (2012) Reflection Paper on the Proposal to Extend the Court's Jurisdiction. https://www.echr.coe.int/documents/d/echr/Courts_advisory_jurisdiction_ENG. Accessed 5 March 2025.

European Court of Human Rights (2023) Updated Guidelines on the implementation of the advisory-opinion procedure introduced by Protocol No. 16 to the Convention (25 September 2023). https://www.echr.coe.int/documents/d/echr/guidelines_p16_eng. Accessed 5 March 2025.

Ferrer Mac-Gregor E (2015) Conventionality Control the New Doctrine of the Inter-American Court of Human Rights. American Journal of International Law Unbound 109:93-99.

Ferrer Mac-Gregor E (2017) What Do We Mean When We Talk About Judicial Dialogue: Reflections of a Judge of the Inter-American Court of Human Rights. Harvard Human Rights Journal 30:89-127.

Gavrysh K (2022) Establishing Judicial Precedents Through Advisory Opinions of the European Court of Human Rights. The Italian Review of International and Comparative Law 2:266-295.

Lockwood B B (1984) Advisory Opinions of the Inter-American Court of Human Rights. Denver Journal of International Law and Policy 13:245-267.

Magliveras K, Naldi G (2016) The Arab Court of Human Rights: A Study in Impotence. Revue Quebecoise de droit international 29:147-172.

Moonen T, Lavrysen L (2021) Abstract but Concrete, or Concrete but Abstract? A Guide to the Nature of Advisory Opinions under Protocol No. 16 to the ECHR. Human Rights Law Review 21:752-785.

Mwangi J W (2023) Request for Advisory Opinion by the Pan African Lawyers Union (PALU) on the Compatibility of Vagrancy Laws with the African Charter on Human and Peoples' Rights and Other Human Rights Instruments Applicable in Africa, No. 001/2018. American Journal of International Law 117:121-127.

OHCHR (2018) Independent Expert on Protection Against Violence and Discrimination Based on Sexual Orientation and Gender Identity, Sexual Orientation and Gender Identity: UN Expert Hails Historic Legal Opinion Issued in Americas (12 January 2018). https://www.ohchr.org/en/press-releases/2018/01/sexual-orientation-and-gender-identity-un-expert-hails-historic-legal. Accessed 5 March 2025.

Pasqualucci J M (2002) Advisory Practice of the Inter-American Court of Human Rights: Contributing to the Evolution of International Human Rights Law. Stanford Journal of International Law 38:241-288.

Rachovitsa A (2019) On New 'Judicial Animals': The Curious Case of an African Court with Material Jurisdiction of a Global Scope. Human Rights Law Review 19:255-289.

Shelton D (2016) Sherlock Holmes and the Mystery of Jus Cogens. Netherlands Yearbook of International Law 44:23-50.

Soley X, Steininger S (2018) Parting Ways or Lashing Back? Withdrawals, Backlash and the Inter-American Court of Human Rights. International Journal of Law in Context 14:237-257.

Southern Africa Litigation Centre (2023) Vagrancy laws: Discrimination based on poverty and status, 9 June 2023. https://www.southernafricalitigationcentre.org/vagrancy-laws-discrimination-based-on-poverty-and-status/. Accessed 7 March 2025.

Spano R (2014) Universality or Diversity of Human Rights? Strasbourg in the Age of Subsidiarity. Human Rights Law Review 14:487-502.

van der Mei A P (2005) The Advisory Jurisdiction of the African Court on Human and Peoples' Rights. African Human Rights Law Journal 5:27-46.

von Bogdandy A, Urueña R (2020) International Transformative Constitutionalism in Latin America. American Journal of International Law 114:403-442.

Wolfson E, Tueller J, Fromkin A (2022) The Freedom to Marry in Human Rights Law Worldwide: Ending the Exclusion of Same-Sex Couples from Marriage. Indiana International & Comparative Law Review 32:1-42.

Chapter 9
The Issuance of Judgments and Victims' Reparations

Konstantinos D. Magliveras and Ahmed Almutawa

Contents

9.1	The Different Purposes and Functions of Judgments	196
9.2	The Legal Validity of Judgments and the Question of Execution	197
9.3	The Temporal Element of Judgments	200
9.4	The Issuance of Judgments and Other Procedural Questions	202
9.5	Pilot Judgments	204
9.6	Errors, Reconsideration/Revision and Interpretation of Judgments	205
9.7	Reparation, Compensation and Just Satisfaction	207
9.8	Human Rights and Reparation	208
9.9	Provisions for Reparation	209
9.10	Prerequisites for Reparations	210
9.11	Reparation Awards	214
9.12	Conclusions	217
References		219

Abstract This chapter examines the role of the regional human rights Courts' judgments and the Courts' power to award reparation to the victims of human rights violations. It discusses the legal validity of judgments, and the respondent states' obligation to accept and implement them. It also analyses the temporal dimension: the time frame within which judgments should be delivered and the period within which respondent states must comply. Furthermore, it deals with procedural questions concerning the issuance of judgments (including dissenting opinions), the pilot judgments procedure, the reconsideration, revision and interpretation of judgments as well as the rectification of errors. The chapter then considers the issue of reparation. After explaining their justice-based purpose, it sets out the basic provisions

K. D. Magliveras (✉)
Department of Mediterranean Studies, University of the Aegean, GR - 85132 Rhodes, Greece
e-mail: kmagliveras@aegean.gr

A. Almutawa
Royal Academy of Police, Ministry of Interior, Jaw, Kingdom of Bahrain

Durham Law School, University of Durham, Durham, UK

A. Almutawa
e-mail: Ahmed.Almutawa84@gmail.com; Ao.almutawa@interior.gov.bh

A. Almutawa and K. D. Magliveras (eds.), *A Comparison of the European, Inter-American, African and Arab Human Rights Courts: Institutional Aspects*,
https://doi.org/10.1007/978-94-6265-695-6_9

that ground the Courts' power to award reparation. It then examines the prerequisites for reparation. Finally, it comparatively examines the awards made by IACtHR, the ACtHPR and the ECtHR, concluding that the victim-centred approach of the former two affords greater priority to individual justice than the more limited, corrective justice approach of the latter.

Keywords Binding force · Dissenting opinions · Implementation and compliance · Revision · Interpretation and errors · Pilot judgments · Reparation, restitution and compensation · Causation · Pecuniary and moral damage

9.1 The Different Purposes and Functions of Judgments

As discussed in Chap. 6, litigation before the regional human rights Courts commences when an application has been lodged complaining that the respondent (always a contracting party to the treaty establishing the relevant Court) has breached protected rights and freedoms. A typical application alleges facts and situations attributed to a respondent state The Court is asked, having applied the law (i.e. the relevant treaties) and having followed the rules of procedure, to determine whether there was a violation, and what are the consequences.

When a Court has not rejected an application on procedural or other grounds, it should deliver a judgment.[1] With the exception of the ACtHPR where it is strongly implied,[2] none of the other Courts' Statutes expressly states that there is an obligation to do so but equally none envisages the opposite, which effectively would constitute a denial of justice. Therefore, judgments will be rendered in all instances where a complaint meeting all relevant conditions and requirements has been lodged. However, the purpose of judgments goes beyond finding in favour of the applicant/s and recording a human rights violation or concluding that the facts do not prove an infraction. Thus, judgments, *inter alia*, analyse the relevant provisions in the applicable treaty/ies; comment on the respondent state's behaviour, actions or inaction; point out deficiencies in domestic legislation; confirm whether the existing legal position still holds or, due, e.g., to recent developments, a different stance should be taken. Moreover, the judgments' text and operative provisions enable domestic courts and legislators, human rights NGOs and other interested parties (e.g. practitioners) to follow new directions in case law.

In essence, judgments from each of the three operating Courts function cumulatively. Over time, they lead to a given jurisprudence, which strengthens each regional human rights system, advances its legitimacy and authority,[3] and promotes a uniform

[1] Cf. Article 42(6) IACtHR Rules of Procedure: the Court may decide upon preliminary objections, merits, reparations and costs in a single judgment.

[2] Article 28(1) ACtHPR Protocol, repeated in Rule 69(1) ACtHPR Rules, discussed *infra*.

[3] Keller and Marti 2015, p 830.

application by contracting states.[4] As has been argued, 'it is necessary to rely on [ECtHR] case law before national courts ... and to refer to precedent decisions of the [ECtHR] regarding violations of the [ECHR articles] at issue'.[5] This submission holds true for all Courts and so does the following ECtHR *obiter dictum*:

> [R]ulings serve not only to decide those cases brought before it but, more generally, to elucidate, safeguard and develop the rules instituted by the [ECHR] ... contributing to the observance by the States of the[ir] engagements ... Although the primary purpose of the [ECHR] system is to provide individual relief, its mission is also to determine issues on public-policy grounds in the common interest, thereby raising the general standards of protection of human rights and extending human rights jurisprudence throughout the community of the [ECHR] States.[6]

But judgments may serve another very important goal, namely, become an indicator for the level of human rights protection in contracting states. In its entirety it applies only to the ECHR system given that all parties have accepted the ECtHR's right to receive, without restrictions, individual applications. For the IACtHR, it applies to the twenty states that have accepted its contentious jurisdiction. And in the comparatively restrictive African system, to the eight states that have presently filed declarations under Article 34 ACtHPR Protocol (see Chap. 3). Notwithstanding this submission, it should be emphasized that the Courts' work is strictly judicial, and they may not pronounce upon the general human rights situation in any contracting state.

Finally, judgments record the data of each litigation, including the names of the presiding and other judges; the date of adoption and delivery; the names of litigant parties and their representatives; a summary of submissions / arguments (including *amicus curiae*); the facts of the case and the procedure followed; the legal reasoning; and the operative provisions, namely the ruling, the decision on compensation / reparations (if any),[7] and the decision on the award of costs (if any).[8] As such, each judgment is a written testament of particular human rights litigation in perpetuity.

9.2 The Legal Validity of Judgments and the Question of Execution

Judgments are (legally) binding and this extends to all litigant parties. If they find in favour of the applicant, their operating part compels the respondent state to do something (obligatory action) or abstain from continuing doing something (obligatory omission). That judgments are compulsory is commonplace in transnational

---

[4] To that extent, the ECtHR Registry publishes 'Case-Law Guides' informing legal practitioners about important judgments delivered, see European Court of Human Rights 2023.

[5] Council of Bars and Law Societies of Europe 2020, p 5

[6] ECtHR, *Jeronovičs v Latvia*, Judgment, 5 July 2016, Application No. 44898/10, para 109.

[7] African Court on Human and People's Rights 2019a.

[8] Rule 74(1) ECtHR Rules of Court, Article 65(1) IACtHR Rules of Procedure, and Rule 71(1) ACtHPR Rules of Court. As is to be expected, the ArabCtHR Statute does not contain any relevant provisions.

courts, whether the ICJ,[9] ITLOS,[10] or the CJEU.[11] Since the respondents before the human rights Courts are by definition Member States of the respective international organisation (CoE, OAS, AU and LAS),[12] arguably accepting and implementing all judgments is a membership duty for those states that have accepted the respective Court's jurisdiction. However, in the case of inter-state applications, the human rights Courts' Statutes do not have a clause akin to Article 94(2) UN Charter, which allows, if the respondent state fails to perform the judgment's obligations, the other party to have recourse to the Security Council and request measures to be taken.

As regards the ECtHR, the binding force is regulated in Articles 44 and 46(1) ECHR; for the IACtHR in Article 67 ACHR; for the ACtHPR in Article 28(2) ACtHPR Protocol; and for the ArabCtHR in Article 35(3) ArabCtHR Statute. Overall, these provisions stipulate that judgments shall be final, irrevocable and not subject to appeal. While the ECHR does not proscribe the review of judgments in the form of an appeal by either applicants or respondent states, a request for review is not available.[13]

Respondent states that lost the litigation are obliged to execute the operating provisions. While this topic is analysed in Chap. 10, a few general comments will be made here. According to Article 46(1) ECHR, 'The High Contracting Parties undertake to abide by the final judgment of the Court in any case to which they are parties'.[14] Article 68(1) ACHR reads virtually the same and so does Article 30 ACtHPR Protocol, but with two very important additions: (a) it allows the ACtHPR to stipulate the time period for compliance with judgments, and (b) it requires contracting parties to guarantee their execution.[15] This allows the ACtHPR to monitor compliance,[16] and to hold 'Compliance Hearings'; the very first took place in November 2024.[17]

Article 26 ArabCtHR Statute takes a rather different path to judgments' execution: by equating them to final judgments rendered by domestic courts, it makes them immediately enforceable against states parties to the dispute.[18] Arguably, the Statute

---

[9] Article 94(1) UN Charter and Articles 58 and 59 ICJ Statute.

[10] Article 33 ITLOS Statute.

[11] Articles 260(1) and 280 TFEU and Article 121 CJEU Rules of Procedure, lastly amended on 30 November 2022.

[12] While the constitutive instruments of these organisations do not refer to the human rights treaties and/or to the Courts' founding instruments adopted under their auspices, arguably these treaties are part of the respective organisation's legal system, which Member States must respect *in toto*.

[13] See Article 31(3) IACtHR Rules of Procedure stipulating that judgments may not be contested in any way.

[14] The word 'parties' means those that acted as applicants, respondents or exercised third-party intervention pursuant to Article 36 ECHR; European Court of Human Rights Registry 2024, p 86.

[15] See further, Rule 80 ACtHPR Rules of Court.

[16] *Ibid.*, Rule 81.

[17] Concerning, ACtHPR, *African Commission on Human and Peoples' Rights v Republic of Kenya*, Judgment (Merits), 26 May 2017, and Judgment (Reparations), 23 June 2022, Application No. 006/2012.

[18] Cf. Article 3 United Nations (New York) Convention on the Recognition and Enforcement of Foreign Arbitral Awards, signed on 10 June 1958, entered into force on 7 June 1959, 330 *UNTS* 3.

transforms ArabCtHR judgments into judgments issued by the highest court in the State concerned (in the sense that there is no right for further appeal against it). While this formulation has the obvious advantage that judgments are, with automaticity one could say, domesticated, its effectiveness will depend on the severity of the domestic legislation in enforcing judgments against the State. The same is true as regards Article 68(2) ACHR: it provides that the operating provisions ordering compensatory damages may be executed pursuant to the domestic procedure governing judgments' execution against the state.

Notwithstanding how each regional human rights system envisages the execution of judgments, they all converge in that the contracting parties' legal obligation to implement judgments is binding on all branches of State authority. Importantly, they may not be avoided by the lack of political will or by invoking technical problems or by any other difficulties (e.g. inadequate resources, conflicting constitutional provisions, opposing domestic laws, etc.).[19]

For example, Peru wrote to the IACtHR that its judgment in *Castillo Petruzzi*[20] 'lacks impartiality and infringes on the Political Constitution of the State, being, therefore, impossible to execute'.[21] Additionally, Peru submitted a written communication to the OAS Secretary General, where it reiterated that the Court 'can not order Peru to modify its norms', and claimed that the judgment was inconsistent with the Court's earlier jurisprudence and did not observe due process.[22] In a brief rebuttal based on the law of treaties, the IACtHR said that the obligation enshrined in the aforementioned Article 68(1) ACHR corresponded to the basic principle of the law of international state responsibility *pacta sunt servanda* and that it had already stated that respondent states may not, for reasons of domestic law, fail to assume already established international responsibility.[23] Finally, it interpreted the 'definite and unappealable nature of [its] judgments' as compelling respondent states to fulfil them in an integral manner.[24]

While this is the law, how each contracting state actually perceives and applies it does differ, sometimes widely. For example, in the United Kingdom, if a court of justice is satisfied that a legislative instrument is incompatible with ECHR protected rights, it may make a declaration of incompatibility.[25] However, the declaration

---

[19] Council of Europe Parliamentary Assembly 2023, para 5 at p 3, which led to the adoption of Resolution 2494 on 26 April 2023.

[20] IACtHR, *Castillo Petruzzi* et al. *v Peru*, Judgment (Merits, Reparations and Costs), 30 May 1999, Series C No. 52.

[21] IACtHR, *Castillo Petruzzi* et al. *v Peru*, Order (Compliance with Judgment), 17 November 1999, Series C No. 59, para 2.

[22] *Ibid.*, para 3.

[23] IACtHR, *International Responsibility for the Promulgation and Enforcement of Laws in Violation of the Convention (Arts. 1 and 2 of the American Convention on Human Rights)*, Advisory Opinion, OC-14/94, 9 December 1994, Series A No. 14, para 35. Cf. Article 27 VCLT.

[24] IACtHR, *Petruzzi v Peru*, Order (Compliance), para 6.

[25] Human Rights Act 1998, s 4.

will not affect the instrument's continuing operation or enforcement,[26] because the supremacy of Parliament in adopting that law must be respected.[27]

9.3 The Temporal Element of Judgments

The temporal element has two manifestations: the time frame within which judgments should be delivered and the period of time that respondent states have to execute, implement and comply with the operative provisions. The former depends on several factors, including the volume of applications received, the degree of difficulty that the cases present and whether there are new legal questions to be addressed, the need to collect adequate evidence and clarify events, and the fact that respondent states may not co-operate. In turn, this temporal element has to do with the Courts' efficiency and effectiveness in delivering 'human rights justice'. According to Article 25(1) ArabCtHR Statute, the deadline for delivering judgments is rather strict: sixty days from completion of deliberations, for the ACtHPR somewhat more lenient (ninety days).[28] However, the treaties creating the other two Courts as well as the respective Rules of Court are silent. Realistically speaking, having laid down a deadline for ECtHR judgments would be unwise given the very large number of applications. On the other hand, the ECtHR should be overseen for possible delays in issuing judgments. To put it into context, reference will be made to the CoE Commissioner for Human Rights, who in the past castigated excessive delays in the domestic administration of justice and warned of associated risks for the rule of law because 'justice delayed is justice denied'.[29] While this is of course correct, arguably, as a legal principle, the rule of law also transcends international organisations, especially those with human rights Courts.[30]

From a legal point of view, when a deadline exists but is not observed, the legality of the judgment delivered may be impaired. Additionally, the excessive delay in issuing a judgment that cannot be objectively justified could, theoretically speaking, result in the Court's (collective) liability, if damage can be shown.[31] The Courts'

[26] The British government regularly issues reports setting out its position on the implementation of adverse ECtHR judgments as well as on declarations of incompatibility; for the Report covering the period August 2023 to July 2024, see UK Ministry of Justice 2024.

[27] See UK Ministry of Justice 2023, p 5. In *A (FC) and others (FC) (Appellants) v Secretary of State for the Home Department (Respondent)*, Judgment, 16 December 2004, [2004] UKHL 56, the House of Lords made a declaration of incompatibility, which later led the British Parliament to replace Part 4 of the Anti-terrorism, Crime and Security Act 2001 with the Prevention of Terrorism Act 2005.

[28] Article 28(1) ACtHPR Protocol and Rule 69(1) ACtHPR Rules.

[29] Council of Europe Commissioner for Human Rights 2007.

[30] For the rule of law forming part of the CoE's legal order, see Magliveras 2023, p 115.

[31] Cf. Article 340(2) TFEU (in the case of non-contractual liability, the EU shall 'make good any damage caused by its institutions in the performance of their duties') in conjunction with Article 41(3) Charter of Fundamental Rights. See further, Court of Justice of the European Union, *FIAMM*

statutes do not deal with such matters, while ACtHPR practice shows that there are no consequences if the ninety days rule is not observed. Presumably, a judgment issued after four months is acceptable,[32] not so, however, when the judgment does not indicate when deliberation ended and was delivered several years after the closure of pleadings.[33]

As regards the second manifestation of the temporal element, only Article 30 ACtHPR Protocol provides that the Court will stipulate the deadline for respondent states to comply. Generally, the ACtHPR 'orders' respondent states to fulfil / execute pecuniary and non-pecuniary reparations within six months, to be extended to one year if warranted. For example, in a series of judgments against Tanzania, the ACtHPR ordered it to take within six months all necessary constitutional and legislative measure to remove from the Penal Code the death penalty's mandatory imposition, to vacate the applicants' death sentence and to repeat the sentencing aspects of the proceedings within one year.[34]

However, even if there is no provision to regulate the period of judgment implementation, arguably, there is an (unwritten) obligation that respondent states ought to do so promptly, without resorting to techniques delaying execution. Moreover, respondent states must submit reports detailing the measures taken at domestic level usually between six months[35] and one year[36] following the judgment's notification.[37] Even though this is connected to monitoring execution (see Chap. 10), it could be treated as an indication of the time period that the respective Court regards as adequate for compliance. Finally, it is important to note that these obligations continue to attach to respondent states even if they later repudiated the treaty establishing the relevant

and Others v Council and Commission, Judgment (GC), 9 September 2008, Joined Cases C-120 & 121/06 P, ECLI:EU:C:2008:476, para 184 (referring to the possibility of damages when a lawful act impinged upon a fundamental right's essence, here, the right to property).

32 ACtHPR, *Baedan Dogbo Paul & Another v Republic of Côte d'Ivoire*, Judgment (Merits and reparations), 5 September 2023, Application No. 019/2020 (found violation of Article 7(1) ACHPR (right to an appeal)).

33 ACtHPR, *Crospery Gabriel & Another v United Republic of Tanzania*, Judgment (Merits and reparations), 13 February 2024, Application No. 050/2016, p 4 (found that the mandatory imposition of the death penalty by hanging in Tanzania violated Article 4 ACHPR (right to life) and Article 5 ACHPR (right to dignity)).

34 ACtHPR, *Dominick Damian v United Republic of Tanzania*, Judgment, 4 June 2024, Application No. 048/2016, p 51; ACtHPR, *Nzigiyimana Zabron v United Republic of Tanzania*, Judgment, 4 June 2024, Application No. 051/2016, p 61.

35 E.g. *ibid.*

36 E.g. IACtHR, *Cuéllar Sandoval* et al. *v El Salvador*, Judgment (Merits, Reparations and Costs), 18 March 2024, Series C No. 521, p 58.

37 There appears to be no specific deadline in the CoE system, see Rules of the Committee of Ministers for the supervision of the execution of judgments and of the terms of friendly settlements (2006, lastly amended on 6 July 2022), https://www.coe.int/en/web/execution/rules-and-working-methods. Accessed 31 March 2025.

Court or their membership in the respective international organisation was terminated voluntarily (withdrawal)[38] or involuntarily (expulsion).[39]

9.4 The Issuance of Judgments and Other Procedural Questions

All regional human rights Courts' judgments, including any previous decisions and orders adopted in the same case, must be fully and compellingly reasoned,[40] an obligation founded on the rule of law. Among others, it has to do with the Courts' legitimacy: if judgments are issued, whose conclusions are poorly substantiated or not supported by the facts or if there are hints of politicisation, Courts might lose the trust of contracting states and/or of potential applicants.[41] A similar effect could be brought about if there is excessive judicialization of the process or if Courts reject requests for advisory opinions.[42] On the other hand, respondent states may invoke what they perceive to be as 'problematic' judgments to launch an attack against a Court.[43] To decide whether opposition to 'problematic' judgments is justified or not is a fairly difficult exercise. However, when the ECHR contracting states feel that they must collectively proclaim that the ECtHR's independence must be respected and the binding nature of its judgments reinforced,[44] one should look deeper into the often-fragile relationship between states and Courts. In this regard, suffice to mention the recent ECtHR Judgment in *Verein KlimaSeniorinnen Schweiz*,[45] which the Swiss federal government politely but resolutely criticized,[46] while a non-binding resolution of the Swiss Parliament's lower chamber was far more vocal concluding that there was no reason to follow the Judgment because Switzerland met the human rights requirements set out in it.[47]

According to Article 45(1) ECHR, judgments as well as decisions that declare applications admissible or inadmissible must provide reasons, while both Article

[38] Naldi and Magliveras 2014.

[39] E.g. Russia's expulsion from the CoE, Magliveras 2023; Council of Europe 2023, p 17; European Court of Human Rights 2024, paras 10–11.

[40] Cf. Rule 68 ACtHPR Rules using the generic term 'decisions' to include judgments, rulings, orders, opinions, instructions, directions or 'any other form of pronouncement as the Court deems necessary'.

[41] Cf. Jennings 1998, pp. 473–474.

[42] Baillie 2018.

[43] Generally, Oquendo 2018.

[44] See High Level Conference meeting in Copenhagen, Copenhagen Declaration, 13 April 2018, para 6 https://www.echr.coe.int/documents/d/echr/Copenhagen_Declaration_ENG. Accessed 29 March 2025.

[45] ECtHR, *Verein KlimaSeniorinnen Schweiz and Others v Switzerland*, Judgment [GC], 9 April 2024, Application No. 53600/20.

[46] Bundesrat 2024.

[47] Nationalrat 2024.

66(1) ACHR and Article 28(6) ACtHPR Protocol stipulate that 'reasons shall be given for the judgment of the Court'. The duty to state reasons is repeated in the respective Rules of Court. Thus, judgments must contain 'the reasons in point of law',[48] the 'legal reasoning'[49] or the 'legal arguments'.[50] Finally, Article 25(4) ArabCtHR Statute provides that 'The Court shall have the authority to justify its decision', which could be interpreted not as an obligation but as discretion. That judgments must be adequately reasoned also bears on the dialectic between the Courts, the applicants and the respondents, which are by definition sovereign states. The latter are bound to respect more a Court that explains in detail and with sound legal argumentation why and how protected human rights were breached. For the same reasons, possibly the execution of that Court's judgments might be more forthcoming. Equally, applicants will continue to have faith in that Court's impartiality and independence. All in all, its legitimacy would only augment.

For a judgment to be adopted, participating judges must take a vote. Effectively, judges have to decide if protected rights and freedoms were violated or not and, if confirmed, to rule on how it will be rectified by ordering remedial measures, by awarding the victims reparation, compensation, just satisfaction, etc.[51] It follows that when judgments find in favour of the applicant, the situation prevailing at the time must be reversed and the injured party / victim must be guaranteed the continued enjoyment of the rights and freedoms breached by the respondent state. As violations have negative consequences for victims, judgments, which to an extent make good the violation, have negative consequences for respondent states (obligatory corrective measures, compensation, etc.).

No Court Statute demands or expects judgments to be unanimous, as it would have been excessive and counterproductive leading to long delays until unanimity was achieved. Therefore, it is sufficient that a majority of judges are willing to reach the same conclusions. The democratic rule that the majority binds the minority is applied here as well. However, judges objecting to the Court's majority findings, or to the measures ordered to rectify the violation, etc., are not deprived of the opportunity to record their views. Therefore, separate and dissenting (or partly dissenting) opinions as well as declarations are expressly allowed.[52]

[48] Rule 74(1)(h) ECtHR Rules.

[49] Rule 71(1)(h) ACtHPR Rules

[50] Article 65(1)(f) IACHR Rules.

[51] Article 41 ECHR and Rule 75 ECHR Rules, Article 63(1) ACHR and Article IACHR Rules, Article 27(1) ACtHPR Protocol and Rule 69(3) ACtHPR Rules.

[52] Article 45(2) ECHR and Rule 74(2) ECHR Rules; Article 66(2) ACHR and Article 65(2) IACtHR Rules; Article 28(7) ACtHPR Protocol and Rule 65(2) ACtHPR Rules; Article 25(2) ArabCtHR Statute.

9.5 Pilot Judgments

Pilot judgments are procedural devices to address situations where courts of justice receive or expect to receive very high volumes of lawsuits concerning the same or closely connected legal questions. They are rather different from *actio popularis* or, in European Union parlance, collective redress mechanisms.[53] Here, the court is faced with far too many applicants, who act in their own name and have the same grievance, and if the court were to deal with each lawsuit separately, it would have examined and ruled on other lawsuits only after an unacceptably long period of time. Presently the ECtHR and the ACtHPR have in place pilot judgments procedures, the former having inspired the latter.[54]

The accession of a very large number of states from Central and Eastern Europe as well as from the former Soviet Union into the CoE during the 1990s, and their automatic recognition of the ECtHR's jurisdiction, was obviously going to lead to a dramatic increase in complaints and it was rather likely that they would concern similar alleged violations against the same respondent states. By 2004, almost sixty per cent of the caseload concerned these countries.[55] But it was also established that much older members were not remedying their domestic legislation even though they had been time and time again found in breach of the same ECHR provisions. These are the so-called 'repetitive cases'.[56] Thus, in *Athanasiou v. Greece*, which concerned the excessive length of judicial proceedings, the ECtHR noticed that between June 2007[57] and December 2010 it had delivered *circa* fifty judgments recording a violation of Article 6(1) ECHR and fifteen judgments recording Article 13 ECHR breaches, while another two hundred similar cases were pending at the time against Greece.[58]

To deal with this matter, the text of ECHR was not changed through an amendment protocol. On the contrary, contracting parties adopted a resolution inviting the Court to identify in its judgments 'what it considers to be an underlying systemic problem and the source of this problem, in particular when it is likely to give rise to numerous applications'. The purpose was to assist contracting parties in finding appropriate solutions but also the Committee of Ministers in supervising judgments' execution.[59] The first judgment responding to the Resolution was delivered only one month later.[60] Even though it was not termed as a 'pilot-judgment', by delivering

[53] European Commission 2013.

[54] Sánchez 2021, p 828; African Court on Human and Peoples' Rights 2019a/2019b, pp. 107–108.

[55] European Court of Human Rights 2005, pp. 118–119.

[56] Wildhaber 2009, pp. 69–75.

[57] Council of Europe Committee of Ministers 2007.

[58] ECtHR, *Vassilios Athanasiou et autres c. Grèce*, Judgment, 21 December 2010, Application No. 50973/08, paras 45 *et seq.*

[59] Resolution Res(2004)3 on judgments revealing an underlying systemic problem adopted by the Committee of Ministers on 12 May 2004, accompanied by Recommendation REC(2004)6 to member states on the improvement of domestic remedies (12 May 2004).

[60] ECtHR, *Broniowski v Poland*, Judgment (Merits), 22 June 2004, Application No. 31443/96, ECHR 2004-V.

a single judgment the ECtHR effectively settled over 160 pending cases (the 'Bug River claims'), while offering a solution to tens of thousands of potential applicants.[61] Later on, the ECtHR started expressly referring to 'the pilot-judgment' and the relevant procedure was inserted as Rule 61 to the Court Rules in February 2011.[62] Thus, the Court applied it in *Athanasiou v. Greece* because 'of the long-standing and persistent nature of the problem, the considerable numbers of persons in Greece who were affected and the urgent need to provide them with prompt and appropriate redress at national level'.[63] Several aspects of the ECtHR pilot-judgment procedure have been criticised,[64] including that it might not be appropriate for all categories of cases.[65]

As was the approach taken by the ECHR system, in the African system the ACtHPR Protocol was not amended to introduce pilot-judgments but, in the (new) Rules of Court of 2020, the relevant procedure was inserted in Rule 66. More specifically, a pilot-judgment procedure may be requested by the parties or the Court could initiate it, if a number of applications filed against the same respondent state reveal a structural or systemic problem. The application selected for this procedure shall be processed as a matter of priority, while the Court reserves the right to commence a friendly-settlement agreement to resolve the disputes between the parties.[66] Pursuant to Rule 66(3), the pilot judgment's operative provisions shall identify the nature of the structural or systemic problem, the type of remedial measures that respondent state must take domestically and the time period of the implementation. Should the respondent state fail to comply therewith, the ACtHPR shall resume examination of any adjourned applications. So far, the ACtHPR has not produced any pilot judgments and the target to have at least five pilot judgments delivered by 2025 appears undoable.[67]

9.6 Errors, Reconsideration/Revision and Interpretation of Judgments

Regarding the rectification of errors, as well as requests for revision or interpretation of judgments, the ECHR contains no relevant provisions (they are laid down in the Rules of Court), while the ACHR and the ACtHPR Protocol have very general

[61] Caflisch 2006, p 411. Finally, a friendly settlement was reached: ECtHR, *Broniowski v Poland*, Judgment (Friendly settlement), 28 September 2005, Application No. 31443/96, paras 38 *et seq.* Generally, see Keller et al. 2010.

[62] Haider 2013; Glas 2016.

[63] ECtHR, *Athanasiou v Greece*, paras 45 *et seq.* For an analysis of the twenty-eight procedures set in motion between 2004 and mid-2019, see Glas 2019.

[64] Sainati 2015, pp. 159–160, 165–171.

[65] Kurban 2016.

[66] Friendly settlement is also available in the European system, see Article 39 ECHR; Fikfak 2022.

[67] African Court on Human and Peoples' Rights 2021, p 20.

provisions, which are detailed in the IACHR Rules and ACtHPR Rules, respectively. However, surprisingly the ArabCtHR Statute has elaborate provisions given its overall brevity. Article 25(3) thereof stipulates that the Court 'shall be able to reconsider judgments in exceptional cases, determined in Article 27'. Pursuant to the latter provision, the parties to a dispute have six months from the day the judgment was serviced to lodge a petition for reconsideration, which shall be accepted in the six instances set out in Article 27(2) ArabCtHR Statute. These include cases which can be objectively verified (e.g. the judgment breached an essential procedural rule, new facts have emerged, lack of clarified reasoning), instances where the Court itself must admit that it erred (e.g. flagrantly exceeding its jurisdiction) and cases that require considerable proof (e.g. the judgment was likely influenced by deceit, fraud or falsification, a judge was influenced and this led him/her to change his/her opinion). Finally, Article 25(4) provides that the ArabCtHR shall have the authority to decide claims of omission, which, if broadly interpreted, could also include petitions for errors' correction.

Article 28(4) ACtHPR Protocol provides that 'the Court may interpret its own decision', by which it means 'judgment', because Rule 77(1) Rules of Court stipulates that any party may, for the purpose of executing a *judgment,* apply for an interpretation of the *judgment* within twelve months from the date of its notification (emphasis added). The application must concern only the judgment's operative provisions. It is at the Court's discretion whether there will be a hearing of the application, in which case the other party shall be invited to submit written comments. Pursuant to Rule 77(4), the Court may decide that the application will suspend the judgment's execution.

The ACtHPR may also review its judgments in light of new facts or evidence of decisive influence, this not being considered as an appeal against a judgment.[68] Rule 78(1) Rules of Court envisages two cumulative deadlines: the application must be lodged within six months of the new evidence and not later than five years of the judgment's delivery. As with interpretation, the other party/ies shall be invited to submit written observations, and the Court may suspend the judgment's execution. However, acceptance of the application is not automatic: under Rule 78(3), the Court shall first rule on admissibility and then on substance. Finally, according to Rule 79, 'clerical errors' may be rectified at the Court's own motion or when a party requested no later than one month after the judgment's delivery.

Pursuant to Article 67 ACHR and Article 68(1) IACtHR Rules of Court, the IACtHR shall interpret disagreements as to the meaning or scope of judgments on preliminary objections, merits, reparations or costs at the request of a party within ninety days from notification thereof. As with the ACtHPR, the participation of the other parties is guaranteed, but, under Article 68(4) IACtHR Rules of Court, the request shall not suspend the judgment's effect. Moreover, whenever possible, the IACtHR shall be composed of the same judges who delivered the original judgment. Finally, pursuant to Article 76 Rules of IACtHR Court, the IACtHR may rectify on its own motion 'obvious mistakes, clerical errors, or errors in calculation', or

[68] Article 28(3) in conjunction with the aforementioned Article 28(2) ACtHPR Protocol.

if so requested within one month by a party. It is possible to combine requests for interpretation and of errors' rectification.[69] Revision of judgments is not envisaged in the Inter-American system.

Finally, the ECtHR Rules of Court provide for interpretation (Rule 79),[70] revision (Rule 80) and rectification of errors (Rule 81). The deadline for requesting interpretation is one year. The request will be declined if the original Chamber finds that there is no reason to warrant considering it. Otherwise, as is the case with the other Courts, written comments will be invited by the other parties and the interpretation will take the form of a judgment. Revision may be requested if a new fact is discovered having a 'decisive influence' on an already delivered judgment. Again, the request, to be lodged at the latest six months after knowledge of the fact was acquired, may be declined if the original Chamber believes that it does not merit consideration. If the request is not refused, the procedure to be followed is analogous to that of interpretation. Finally, the provision on correcting errors is very similar to Article 76 IACtHR Rules of Court.

9.7 Reparation, Compensation and Just Satisfaction

Reparation for human rights violations is generally accepted as an obligation imposed on states by the demands of justice.[71] For the UN, recognition of a victim's right to reparation is grounded in 'the international legal principles of accountability, justice and the rule of law'.[72] The right to a remedy, which incorporates a right to reparation, is recognised, *inter alia*, by the UDHR,[73] as well as the regional human rights charters and conventions.[74] The primary obligation to ensure an appropriate remedy, which entails 'Adequate, effective and prompt reparation for harm suffered', falls on the state.[75] However, since the right to a remedy is fundamental to 'justice and the rule of law', it is unsurprising that regional human rights Courts have an independent power to award reparation. The following discussion considers the scope and use of that power.

---

69 IACtHR, *Flores Bedregal* et al. *v Bolivia*, Judgment (Interpretation of the Judgment on Preliminary Objections, Merits, Reparations and Costs and Rectification of errors in the Judgment), 14 March 2024, Series C No. 520.

70 Generally, Björgvinsson 2023.

71 Shelton 2005, pp. 8–9.

72 UN General Assembly 2005, preamble.

73 Article 8. For an account of reparations under the international legal framework, see Shelton 2022.

74 ACHPR, article 7; ACHR, article 25; ECHR, article 13; ArabCHR, article 12.

75 UN General Assembly 2005, principle 11.

9.8 Human Rights and Reparation

Without a right to appropriate reparation, human rights are 'an empty promise'.[76] The violation of a legally protected right is, by definition, a legal wrong and justice demands that any such wrongs are adequately and effectively redressed.[77] Grounded in the concept of corrective justice,[78] states have a duty to restore the victim's losses caused by a violation of the victim's human rights for which the state is responsible.[79] Ideally, reparation for a violation of human rights would correct any injustice by restoring victims to the position they were in prior to the violation.[80] This goal of 'restitution rather than compensation'[81] is embodied in the Latin maxim of *restitutio in integrum*.[82]

While full restitution is 'an ideal target' it is not 'truly attainable'.[83] The pragmatic goal must be to 'establish a new situation that is as similar as possible to the preceding one'.[84] Nevertheless, because it embodies 'the idea that a right is more than a commodity' capable of being 'traded' for financial compensation,[85] the ideal of full restitution remains the lodestar for reparation. Despite this, financial compensation, which should be 'appropriate and proportional',[86] remains the main form of victim-centred reparation.[87]

Beyond corrective justice, reparation for human rights violations serves three other purposes: deterrence; condemnation; and restorative justice (reconciliation).[88] The aim of deterrence pervades all forms of reparation,[89] but requires a sufficiently severe sanction to be effective.[90] Similarly, all forms of reparation require states to take responsibility for human rights violations, acknowledge the wrong done to victims and reinforce the condemnation of wrongdoing inherent to an adverse judgment.[91] Restorative justice aims to re-establish a good or 'right' relationship between the state and the victim.[92] Thus, reparation measures should recognise individuals as

---

[76] Nowak 2014, p 10.

[77] Cançado Trindade 2011, pp. 63–75. See also Buyse 2008, p 135.

[78] Shelton 2005, p 291.

[79] Coleman 1997, p 56.

[80] UN General Assembly 2005, principle 19.

[81] Shelton 2005, p 21.

[82] Buyse 2008, p 129.

[83] IACtHR, *Bámaca-Velásquez v Guatemala*, Judgment (Reparation and Costs), 22 February 2002, Series C No. 91, Concurring opinion of Judge Garcia Ramirez.

[84] *Ibid.*

[85] Buyse 2008, p 133.

[86] UN General Assembly 2005, principle 20.

[87] Chavez 2017, p 374.

[88] *Ibid.*, p 373.

[89] *Ibid.*, p 374.

[90] Shelton 2005, p 14.

[91] *Ibid.*, p 12.

[92] Boyes-Watson 2018, p 16.

socially-situated, dignified agents by facilitating participation 'in their own justice processes'.[93]

9.9 Provisions for Reparation

Beyond the right to 'appeal to competent national organs' for the violation of human rights under Article 7, there is no general provision for any remedy, reparation, or compensation in the ACHPR.[94] However, Article 27 ACtHPR Protocol provides that, where the ACtHPR finds a violation of a protected right then 'it shall make appropriate orders to remedy the violation, including the payment of fair compensation or reparation'. This affords the ACtHPR a wide discretion, limited only by the need to ensure any order for compensation or reparation is appropriate.[95] However, applicants seeking reparation must make an explicit and evidence-based request.[96]

Article 12 of the ArabCHR provides for a 'right to seek a legal remedy' before the national courts. This is supplemented by explicit rights to compensation for victims of torture, unlawful arrest or detention and miscarriages of justice.[97] Furthermore, Article 23 of the ArabCHR requires each State Party to ensure that victims of violations of Charter rights have an effective remedy. However, unlike the ACtHPR Protocol, the ArabCtHR Statute makes no provision for 'remedy or reparation or compensatory damages', which is a significant weakness.[98] This may, however, be remedied by future amendments to the Statute, or by the Rules of Court.

Under Article 41 of the ECHR, the ECtHR may 'afford just satisfaction to the injured party' where there has been a violation of a protected right. This power, which supplements the Court's power to order individual measures 'for the specific benefit of the applicant' under Article 46,[99] only applies 'if necessary' and where 'the internal law of the High Contracting Party concerned allows only partial reparation to be made'. Applicants 'must make a specific claim',[100] and any award will be limited to the sum claimed.[101] Article 41 also provides 'discretion' to award compensation for harm caused by a violation. The award may cover pecuniary and non-pecuniary damage alongside costs and expenses, but there is no power to award punitive damages or 'make symbolic awards'.[102] Awards must be equitable, which

---

[93] Skelton 2018, p 40.

[94] For a specific provision, see Article 21(2).

[95] Mutangi 2023, p 14.

[96] ACtHPR Rules of Court, Rule 40.

[97] ArabCHR Statute, Articles 8, 14, and 19 respectively. See Almutawa 2023, para 7.

[98] Magliveras and Naldi 2016, p 167.

[99] Donald et al. 2012, p 44.

[100] ECtHR Rules of Court, Rule 60.

[101] ECtHR (2024) Practice Directions, annexed to the Rules of Court, p 75.

[102] *Ibid.*, p 74.

allows for reduced or no compensation where the 'public vindication' inherent to the judgment is considered by the ECtHR to be sufficient redress.[103]

Under Article 63 of the ACHR, which was intentionally strengthened by the drafters to afford the IACtHR 'expansive formal powers to order reparations',[104] the Court 'shall rule that the injured party be ensured the enjoyment' of a violated right. Furthermore, the IACtHR has the power to remedy, where 'appropriate', the consequences of the 'measure or situation that constituted the breach' and to award 'fair compensation' to the injured party. Like the ACtHPR and the ECtHR, claims for reparations and costs must be included in the application, and the alleged victim's brief to the Court.[105]

9.10 Prerequisites for Reparations

Grounded in the principle of *restitutio in integrum* and the international legal obligation on states to make reparation for 'any breach of an engagement',[106] all three of the operative human rights Courts have acknowledged their power to award reparation.[107] This power acknowledges the importance of individual justice. To secure that justice, applicants must satisfy three conditions, common to all three courts. First is the procedural requirement that the applicant has explicitly claimed reparation. Second, the applicant must show that the claims for reparation relate to victims of human rights violations. Third, the applicant must prove a sufficient causal connection between the violation and the claim for reparation.

Regarding the first condition, the ECtHR will usually only award reparation, including costs, where they are reasonable, necessary, related to the violation,[108] and specifically claimed, with the award limited to the amount claimed by the applicants.[109] Exceptions have been made where justified by the circumstances, such as where the applicant lacked legal capacity,[110] or where equity required a higher

---

[103] *Ibid.*

[104] Pasqualucci 2012, p 190.

[105] IACtHR Rules of Procedure, Articles 35, 40.

[106] PCIJ, *Germany v Poland (Factory at Chorzów)*, Judgment, 13 September 1928, Series A No. 17, p 29.

[107] ACtHPR, *Tanganyika Law Society and The Legal and Human Rights Centre v The United Republic of Tanzania*; *Reverend Christopher R. Mtikila v The United Republic of Tanzania*, Judgment, 14 June 2013, Application Nos. 009/2011 and 011/2011, para 124; ECtHR, *De Wilde, Ooms and Versyp ('Vagrancy') v Belgium (Article 50)*, Judgment, 10 March 1972, Application Nos. 2832/66; 2835/66; 2899/66; IACtHR, *Blake v Guatemala*, Judgment (Reparation and Costs), 22 January 1999, Series C No. 48, paras 30–31.

[108] ECtHR, *Sidabras and others v Lithuania*, Judgment, 23 June 2015, Application Nos. 50,421/08 and 56,213/08, para 123.

[109] ECtHR, *Abdi Ibrahim v Norway*, Judgment, 10 December 2021, Application No. 15379/16, paras 164–177.

[110] ECtHR, *X v Croatia*, Judgment, 17 July 2008, Application No. 11223/04, paras 61–63.

payment than was claimed for moral damages.[111] The IACtHR also requires an explicit claim for reparation and costs.[112] In *Mtikila*, the ACtHPR was prepared to rely on its own initiative to order the State, as a measure of satisfaction, to publish the merits judgment in the official gazette and a national newspaper.[113] In *Zongo*, however, the Court refused to consider any reparation not explicitly requested.[114] Similarly, in *Konaté*, the Court held that it 'cannot rule *ultra petita*' and must 'limit itself to the amount claimed'.[115] This decision was regarded as having regrettably 'abandoned the progressive and courageous' approach the Court took in *Mtikila*.[116] However, the cases can be distinguished since the award in *Mtikila* was non-pecuniary. Nevertheless, while the ACtHPR will limit an order for material compensation strictly to the amount claimed,[117] it is willing to quantify and order compensation for moral damage in response to requests for any measures considered 'appropriate' by the Court to provide 'adequate reparation'.[118]

Regarding victimhood, this is unproblematic for those immediately affected by a violation of a protected right. However, victim status may also apply to those affected by the violation because of their relationship to the immediate victims. This is context-dependent, but for the ACtHPR it extends to 'close relatives ... who can reasonably be considered as having suffered moral prejudice' and includes the spouses, children and parents of the immediate victim.[119] The ECtHR also allows that victims include those directly affected by the violation,[120] as well those indirectly affected, such as spouses and other dependent relatives.[121] For the IACtHR, reparations may be claimed by injured parties, namely those harmed by the immediate and

[111] ECtHR, *Stradovnik v Slovenia*, Judgment, 13 April 2006, Application No. 24784/02, para 25.

[112] IACtHR, *Velásquez-Rodriguez v Honduras*, Judgment (Reparation and Costs), 21 July 1989, Series C No. 7, para 42.

[113] ACtHPR, *Mtikila v Tanzania*, Ruling (Reparations), 13 June 2014, Application No. 011/2011, paras 45–46.

[114] ACtHPR, *Beneficiaries of late Norbert Zongo and others v Burkina Faso*, Judgment, 28 March 2014, Application No. 013/2011, para 2.

[115] ACtHPR, *Lohé Issa Konaté v Burkina Faso*, Judgment (Reparations), 3 June 2016, Application No. 004/2013, para 50.

[116] Mutangi 2023, p 22. See also Sánchez 2021, pp. 819–820.

[117] ACtHPR, *John Mitwa v United Republic of Tanzania*, Judgment. 13 February 2024, Application No. 044/2016, paras 126–128.

[118] ACtHPR, *Anaclet Paulo v United Republic of Tanzania*, Judgment, 21 September 2018, Application No. 020/2016, paras 100–107; ACtHPR, *Dominick Damian v United Republic of Tanzania*, Judgment, 4 June 2024, Application No. 048/2016, paras 148–151.

[119] ACtHPR, *Zongo v Burkina Faso*, paras 45–50.

[120] ECtHR, *Brumarescu v Romania*, Judgment, 28 October 1999, Application No. 28342/95, para 50.

[121] See ECtHR, *Velikova v Bulgaria*, Judgment, 18 May 2000, Application No. 41488/98; ECtHR (2024) Practice Directions, annexed to the Rules of Court, p 77.

proximate effects of a violation.[122] As with the other Courts, this may include dependent family members of the more immediate victim,[123] with the notion of 'family' being understood 'in a broad and flexible manner'.[124] For the IACtHR, only human beings may be victims,[125] but for the other two Courts victims can also include legal entities.[126] For the ACtHPR, the concept of victim also applies to 'communities, peoples or groups with a common identity' that benefit from collective rights to 'culture, development, self-determination, a language and property'.[127] Thus, the Ogiek people were collectively considered to be victims in a case concerning their eviction from ancestral lands.[128] Similarly, the IACtHR held that indigenous peoples may collectively fall within the concept of an injured party, or victim.[129]

Regarding causation, corrective justice demands that the party responsible for a violation should correct the consequential losses suffered by the victims. This requires a sufficient causal connection between the violation and any losses claimed in reparation.[130] Thus, the ACtHPR will only consider claims for 'damages resulting from identified wrongful acts'.[131] The ECtHR similarly requires a violation of a protected right with a 'clear causal link' between the violation and the damages claimed.[132] The IACtHR also requires a proven causal connection between the violation and the damages claimed in reparation.[133]

The proof required to satisfy the demands for a causal connection depends on the type of damage. For material damage, the burden lies on the applicant to prove the requisite causal link. For the ACtHPR, proof requires a 'preponderance of evidence', that the human rights violation caused the losses claimed,[134] and claims will be

---

[122] IACtHR, *Aloeboetoe et al v Suriname*, Judgment (Reparation and Costs), 10 September 1993, Series C No. 15, paras 48–49.

[123] IACtHR, *Bámaca-Velásquez v Guatemala*, para 33.

[124] IACtHR, *Blake v Guatemala*, paras 36, 38.

[125] By virtue of ACHR, Article 1(2). See IACtHR, *Members of the 'José Alvear Restrepo' Lawyers Collective v Colombia,* Judgment, 18 October 2023, Series C No. 506, paras 6–7.

[126] ECtHR (2024) Practice Directions, annexed to the Rules of Court, p 77; ACtHPR, *Zongo v Burkina Faso*, paras 63–67.

[127] African Court on Human and Peoples' Rights 2019b.

[128] ACtHPR, *African Commission on Human and Peoples' Rights v Republic of Kenya*, Judgment (Reparations), 23 June 2022, Application No. 006/2012, para 44.

[129] IACtHR, *Kaliña and Lokono Peoples v Suriname*, Judgment, 25 November 2015, Series C No. 309, para 273.

[130] ACtHPR, *Amir Ramadhani v United Republic of Tanzania*, Judgment (Reparations), 25 June 2021, Application No. 010/2015, para 19.

[131] ACtHPR, *Zongo v Burkina Faso*, para 25.

[132] ECtHR, *Hode and Abdi v United Kingdom*, Judgment, 6 November 2012, Application No. 22341/09, paras 61–63; ECtHR, *Öneryildiz v Turkey*, Judgment, 30 November 2004, Application No. 48939/99, para 166.

[133] IACtHR, *Bámaca-Velásquez v Guatemala*, para 43; IACtHR, *Cuéllar Sandoval v El Salvador*, para 116.

[134] ACtHPR, *African Commission on Human and Peoples' Rights v Kenya*, para 40.

dismissed where applicants fail to prove a loss or the necessary causal link.[135] However, the burden of proof may shift to the respondent State where it has 'exclusive access' to the 'relevant information'.[136] The IACtHR has discretionary flexibility when determining whether a claim is sufficiently well proven by the submitted evidence.[137] In this regard it will bear in mind the procedural imbalance between the parties and has the power to obtain 'on its own motion, any evidence it considers helpful'.[138] The IACtHR may also reverse the burden of proof where the necessary evidence is under the control of the state.[139] The ECtHR requires the causal link to be proven through supporting documents for pecuniary damage.[140] The standard of proof required by the ECtHR is comparatively high and has been criticised as 'unduly stringent'.[141] All three courts, however, will use their discretion to equitably determine the quantum where applicants have been unable to precisely quantify their losses.[142]

For moral damages, the IACtHR considers that the violation itself may be sufficient proof of moral damage.[143] Following the IACtHR, the ACtHPR held that the casual connection could be satisfied as 'an automatic consequence' of human rights violation, with no further proof required.[144] This allows for 'a presumption of moral prejudice' in the event of a violation,[145] but the Court may still assess whether the violation 'has caused or is likely to have caused' the moral damage claimed.[146] In contrast, the ECtHR maintains that a causal nexus is essential and will not automatically accept the connection between a violation and moral damage.[147] However, it also accepts that the nature of the violation may make the claim for

[135] ACtHPR, *Crospery Gabriel and another v United Republic of Tanzania*, Judgment (Merits and Reparations), 13 February 2024, Application No. 050/2016, paras 127–128.

[136] African Court on Human and Peoples' Rights 2019b.

[137] IACtHR, *Velásquez Rodríguez v Honduras*, Judgment (Merits), 29 July 1988, Series C No. 4, para 127.

[138] IACtHR, *Bámaca-Velásquez v Guatemala*, paras 13–15. The Court relied on Article 44 (now Article 58) of the Rules of Procedure.

[139] IACtHR, *Velásquez Rodríguez v Honduras*, para 135.

[140] ECtHR, *Hode and Abdi v United Kingdom*, paras 61–63; ECtHR, *Öneryildiz v Turkey*, para 166.

[141] Shelton 2005, pp. 323, 326.

[142] ACtHPR, *African Commission on Human and Peoples' Rights v Kenya*, paras 66–67, 70; ECtHR, *Öneryildiz v Turkey*, para 166; IACtHR, *Cuéllar Sandoval v El Salvador*, paras 167–171.

[143] IACtHR, *Bámaca-Velásquez v Guatemala*, para 63.

[144] ACtHPR, *Zongo and others v Burkina Faso*, para 55; ACtHPR, *African Commission on Human and Peoples' Rights v Kenya*, para 87.

[145] ACtHPR, *Baedan Dogbo Paul and Baedan M'Bouke Faustin v Republic of Côte d'Ivoire*, Judgment, 5 September 2023, Application No. 019/2020, para 165.

[146] ACtHPR, *Ramadhani v Tanzania*, para 29.

[147] ECtHR, *Woods v United Kingdom*, Judgment, 20 November 2007, Application No. 60274/00, para 23.

moral damage 'incontestable'.[148] For all three courts, the quantum of compensation for moral damage is determined equitably,[149] which may lead to criticisms of inconsistency and a lack of transparency.[150]

9.11 Reparation Awards

Given the grounding principle of *restitutio in integrum*, it is unsurprising that all three courts deny that reparations have a punitive role.[151] Nevertheless, it has been argued that the courts, particularly the IACtHR and the ACtHPR, have developed an expansive approach that carries with it punitive elements. It may, however, be countered that the courts' creative approach to reparations is more concerned with condemnation and non-repetition or deterrence.[152] Despite expanding its approach through individual measures to secure restitution, the ECtHR retains the most 'restrictive approach' of the three courts to reparations.[153]

Under the ECHR, the concept of 'just satisfaction' should be distinguished from the international law concept of satisfaction as applied by the IACtHR and the ACtHPR. Rather than being a type of non-pecuniary reparation, just satisfaction refers to 'reparation in general', which is normally monetary compensation for material damage, for moral damage, (pain, suffering, anxiety, a sense of injustice and 'harm to moral well-being),[154] and for costs.[155] In an approach that appears to prioritise constitutional over individual justice,[156] the power to award just satisfaction is considered 'incidental' to the Court's main task of ensuring that states observe their obligations under the ECHR.[157] Under the principle of subsidiarity the primary responsibility to secure *restitutio in integrum* lies with the state.[158] Article 41 ECHR empowers the Court with a discretion to award appropriate just satisfaction only

[148] ECtHR, *Kadiķis v Latvia*, Judgment, 4 August 2006, Application No. 62393/00, para 67.

[149] ACtHPR, *Ramadhani v Tanzania*, para 12; ECtHR, *Halford v United Kingdom*, Judgment, 25 June 1997, Application No. 20605/92, para 76; IACtHR, *Velásquez-Rodriguez v Honduras*, Judgment (Reparation and Costs), para 27.

[150] Gonzalez-Salzberg 2021, p 89.

[151] IACtHR, *Velásquez Rodríguez v Honduras*, Judgment (Merits), para 134; ECtHR (2024) Practice Directions, annexed to the Rules of Court, p 74.

[152] Chavez 2017.

[153] Burgorgue-Larsen 2024, pp. 419–21.

[154] ECtHR, *Molla Sali v Greece*, Judgment (Just Satisfaction), 18 June 2020, Application No. 20452/14, para 33.

[155] Bernhardt 2005, p 246.

[156] See Wildhaber 2003.

[157] ECtHR (2024) Practice Directions, annexed to the Rules of Court, p 74.

[158] ECtHR, *Proceedings Under Article 46 § 4 in the Case of Ilgar Mammadov v Azerbaijan*, Judgment, 29 May 2019, Application No. 15172/13, paras 151, 193–194.

where the national law fails to provide for full reparation.[159] While, *restitutio in integrum* is the ideal, the more pragmatic goal is for 'just, fair compensation'.[160] In applying this standard, all of the circumstances of the case are relevant, including the gravity of the violation, public policy and the parties' conduct.[161] Relying on the symbolic value of an adverse judgment as just satisfaction, the ECtHR, with rare exceptions,[162] will not award nominal or symbolic damages.[163]

Beyond financial compensation, individual measures to secure restitution may also be ordered under Article 46 ECHR. The choice of measures employed to achieve restitution is generally for the state.[164] However, the 'Court can in certain situations indicate the specific remedy or other measure'.[165] This applies to a 'narrow field of cases',[166] such as the restitution of property[167] or the release of an applicant arbitrarily imprisoned in breach of the rule of law, where the ECtHR has held that violation leaves 'no real choice' as to the remedy.[168] Where there is a systemic or structural issue, the ECtHR may utilise the pilot judgment procedure to order more general measures.[169] For such measures, the Court will specify their aim but leave the 'practical steps' of implementation to the respondent state.[170] Nevertheless, just satisfaction under Article 41 ECHR is the 'go-to remedy' and the imposition of non-monetary remedies is far less common.[171]

In contrast to the ECtHR's 'parsimonious',[172] 'cost-centred' approach, the IACtHR, with the ACtHPR following its lead,[173] has taken a restorative justice, 'victim-centred' approach that consistently orders 'remedies that respond to victims'

---

159 ECtHR, *Brumarescu v Romania*, Judgment (Just Satisfaction), 23 January 2001, Application No. 28342/95, para 20.

160 Ichim 2015, p 16.

161 ECtHR, *Keenan v United Kingdom*, Judgment, 3 April 2001, Application No. 27229/95, paras 123–130, 138; ECtHR, *McCann and others v United Kingdom*, Judgment, 27 September 1995, Application No. 18984/91, para 219; ECtHR, *Tomasi v France*, Judgment, 27 August 1992, Application No. 12850/87; Shelton 2005, p 295; Wildhaber 2003, pp. 12–13.

162 ECtHR, *Engel and Others v The Netherlands (Article 50)*, Judgment, 23 November 1976, Application Nos. 5100/71; 5101/71; 5102/71; 5354/72; 5370/72, para 10.

163 ECtHR, *Lehideux and Isorni v France*, Judgment, 23 September 1998, Application No. 24662/94, para 63.

164 ECtHR, *Brumarescu v Romania*, Judgment (Just Satisfaction), para 20.

165 ECtHR, *Mammadov v Azerbaijan*, paras 154–155.

166 Leach 2005, p 163.

167 ECtHR, *Papamichalopoulos v Greece,* Judgment, 31 October 1995, Application No. 14556/89, para 38.

168 ECtHR, *Assanidze v Georgia*, Judgment, 8 April 2004, Application No. 71503/01, paras 202–203. See Mowbray 2017.

169 ECtHR, *Broniowski v Poland*, Judgment, 28 September 2005, Application No. 31443/96.

170 ECtHR, *Pârvu v Romania*, Judgment, 30 August 2022, Application No. 13326/18, paras 107–113.

171 Fikfak 2019, pp. 1093, 1095.

172 Roach 2019, p 40.

173 Plagis 2020, p 51.

demands for recognition, restoration, and accountability'.[174] This approach relies on five types of reparation: compensation; restitution; rehabilitation; satisfaction; and non-recurrence.[175] Like the ECtHR, both the IACtHR and the ACtHPR award compensation for material and moral damages, which encompasses loss of opportunity, 'suffering and affliction', harm to the significant values of the victims and their families, and non-financial changes in their 'conditions of existence'.[176] Both the ACtHPR and the IACtHR have been willing, somewhat creatively, to order respondent states to establish compensation funds or 'services of collective interest', which may require consultation with the community and may benefit all members of the community affected by the violations,[177] including those victims that were not party to the proceedings.[178] Pecuniary reparations are primarily concerned with the corrective justice goal of restitution, but the ACtHPR has been willing to award token damages for moral prejudice if requested by the applicants.[179] The IACtHR has also been prepared to award nominal damages where appropriate.[180]

Non-monetary reparations include measures aimed at restitution, such as returning ancestral lands,[181] returning property,[182] reinstatement of employment,[183] or releasing an unlawfully detained person.[184] Reparation as satisfaction appears to focus on restorative justice. Measures include those grounded in the recognition of a right to truth and the prevention of impunity such as[185]: public investigation and the punishment of wrongdoers; the location and return of the victims remains;

[174] Antkowiak 2011, p 281, 289.

[175] IACtHR, *Asociación Civil Memoria Activa v Argentina*, Judgment, 26 January 2024, Series C No. 516, para 285; Mutangi 2023, p 1; ACtHPR, *Mtikila v Tanzania*, Ruling (Reparations), 13 June 2014, Application No. 011/2011, paras 34–37.

[176] IACtHR, *Asociación Civil Memoria Activa, ibid.*, para 334.

[177] IACtHR, *Mayagna (Sumo) Awas Tigni Community v Nicaragua*, Judgment, 31 August 2001, Series C No. 79, para 167; IACtHR, *Kaliña and Lokono People v Suriname*, Judgment, 25 November 2015, Series C No. 309, paras 295 297.

[178] ACtHPR, *African Commission on Human and Peoples' Rights v Kenya*, paras 66–77; ACtHPR, *La LIDHO, le MIDH, la FIDH and others v Republic of Côte d'Ivoire*, Judgment (Merits and Reparations), 5 September 2023, Application No. 041/2016, paras 209–215.

[179] ACtHPR, *La LIDHO, ibid.*, para 221.

[180] IACtHR, *Gangram-Panday v Suriname*, Judgment, 21 January 1994, Series C No. 16, para 70.

[181] ACtHPR, *African Commission on Human and Peoples' Rights v Kenya*, paras 110–117.

[182] IACtHR, *Palamar Iribarne v Chile*, Judgment, 22 November 2005, Series C No. 135, para 250.

[183] IACtHR, *Apitz Barbera et al v Venezuela*, Judgment, 5 August 2008, Series C No. 182, para 246.

[184] ACtHPR, *Zabron v Tanzania*, paras 200–207; ACtHPR, *Kabalabala Kadumbagula and another v United Republic of Tanzania*, Judgment, 4 June 2024, Application No. 031/2017, paras 133–135.

[185] IACtHR, *Asociación Civil Memoria Activa v Argentina*, paras 293–296.

and the publication of a summary of the judgment to publicly acknowledge responsibility.[186] Like the ECtHR, the merits judgment is considered 'a type of reparation and moral satisfaction'[187] but, with notable exceptions,[188] is more likely to be awarded in conjunction with, rather than as an alternative to, financial compensation for moral damage. Other measures of satisfaction include: ensuring the recognition and protection of the property rights of indigenous peoples;[189] memorialisation of the victims and a widely disseminated 'public act of recognition of international responsibility', the details of which should be agreed with the victims.[190] The IACtHR has also ordered the State to create and broadcast an audiovisual documentary and establish a publicly accessible historical archive to ensure historical memory as an element of satisfaction.[191] Reparations may also include measures for rehabilitation, including psychological and psychiatric treatment.[192] Finally, respondent States may be required to implement legislative and administrative changes and training to avoid repetition.[193]

9.12 Conclusions

The issuance of judgments is the most important stage of human rights litigation. Since it usually takes several years for a judgment to be issued, any protection to be offered to applicants in the meantime is afforded by means of interim measures orders (see Chap. 6). The operating provisions of judgments are not only about confirming or not a human rights treaty's violation. When a breach is recorded, what is of significance for both applicants and respondent states are the measures that the Court dictates, and, at a minimum, that the violation be promptly terminated and not repeated. The measures' content will depend on several factors, including the nature of the case, the violation's severity and the need to terminate impunity. For purposes of illustration, in a case that had affected a very large number of people, the IACtHR ordered the respondent state to undertake all of the following: investigate, prosecute

---

186 IACtHR, *Bámaca-Velásquez v Guatemala*, paras 73–86; ACtHPR, *La LIDHO v Côte d'Ivoire*, paras 228–232.

187 IACtHR, *Velásquez-Rodriguez v Honduras*, Judgment (Reparation), para 36.

188 IACtHR, *Petruzzil v Peru*, Judgment (Merits), paras 223–225.

189 IACtHR, *Saramaka People v Suriname*, Judgment, 28 November 2007, Series C No. 172, para 194.

190 IACtHR, *Cuéllar Sandoval v El Salvador*, paras 141–144. The ACtHPR has not rejected memorialisation as an option but prefers to rely on publication of a summary of the judgment as sufficient satisfaction in this regard: ACtHPR, *La LIDHO v Côte d'Ivoire*, paras 228, 258; ACtHPR, *African Commission on Human and Peoples' Rights v Kenya*, paras 129–133.

191 IACtHR, *Asociación Civil Memoria Activa v Argentina*, paras 309, 312.

192 IACtHR, *Cuéllar Sandoval v El Salvador*, para 133; ACtHPR, *La LIDHO v Côte d'Ivoire*, paras 236–239.

193 IACtHR, *Cuéllar Sandoval v El Salvador*, paras 153–160; ACtHPR, *La LIDHO v Côte d'Ivoire*, paras 244–249.

and punish those responsible for the events that led to the violation; publish the judgment, create an audiovisual documentary about the case and establish a historical archive; take specific measures to guarantee non-repetition of the violation; and pay compensation to the victims for pecuniary and immaterial damage.[194]

Another aspect of the human rights Courts' judgments that goes well beyond applicants and respondent States is the possibility that, through their constant and consistent jurisprudence, they form general principles of law applicable to the international legal system. While the formation of general principles is presently before the UN International Law Commission,[195] the argument here is that, instead of resorting to the general principles of law,[196] primarily by referring to and citing each other's judgments,[197] the Courts themselves create legal principles that the community of nations could then apply domestically or in inter-state transactions.

Contingent on an adverse judgment, the provision of reparations is essential to the delivery of justice to the victims of human rights violations. While the ECtHR has been criticised for an 'inconsistent and parsimonious' approach lacking coherence,[198] and insufficiently focused on the victims,[199] the IACtHR 'has been largely praised for its innovative role in the award of reparations'.[200] Although the ECtHR has expanded its approach through the use of individual and general measures, awarding reparations remains incidental to its main task of ensuring state compliance with the ECHR.

For the IACtHR and the ACtHPR, which has relied heavily on the former's jurisprudence, awarding reparations is a core tool for enhancing the protection of human rights. However, the IACtHR's approach, and by implication that of the ACtHPR, may be characterised as 'highly intrusive',[201] raising questions of legitimacy and exacerbating problems of compliance.[202] Some of the differences between the approaches may be explained by different social and historical contexts. However, the more victim-centred approach of IACtHR and ACtHPR goes beyond the essentially corrective justice approach of the ECtHR to engage with restorative justice and affords greater priority to individual justice, albeit that some of the more creative measures might be criticised for exceeding the demands of individual justice.

---

[194] IACtHR, *Active Memory Civil Association v. Argentina*, Judgment (Merits, Reparations and Costs), 26 January 2024, Series C No. 516.

[195] International Law Commission 2023, pp. 22 *et seq.*

[196] Cf. Article 38(1)(c) ICJ Statute.

[197] See e.g. ECtHR, *Yelena Ivanovna Pivkina against Russia and 6 other applications*, Decision, 29 June 2023, Application No. 2134/23, citing both an IACtHR Judgment (*Ivcher-Bronstein v. Peru*) and an IACtHR Advisory Opinion (*Denunciation of the American Convention on Human Rights and the Charter of the Organization of American States and the consequences for State human rights obligations*).

[198] Roach 2019, p 40; Ichim 2015, p 24.

[199] Antkowiak 2011, p 319.

[200] Gonzalez-Salzberg 2021, p 87.

[201] Çalı 2018, pp. 217–218.

[202] Attanasio 2016, p 851.

References

African Court on Human and Peoples' Rights (ACtHPR) (2019a) Comparative Study on the Law and Practice of Reparations for Human Rights Violations. September 2019. https://www.african-court.org/wpafc/wp-content/uploads/2020/11/Comparative-Study-on-the-Law-and-Practice-of-Reparations-for-Human-Rights-Violations.pdf. Accessed 31 March 2025.

African Court on Human and Peoples' Rights (ACtHPR) (2019b) African Court of Justice and Human Rights) Fact Sheet on Filing Reparation Claims. Adopted during the Fifty-Third Ordinary Session of the African Court on Human and Peoples' Rights, Arusha, Tanzania, 10 June - 5 July 2019 (Revised October 2020). https://www.african-court.org/wpafc/wp-content/uploads/2020/10/FACT-SHEET-ON-FILING-REPARATION-CLAIMS-Revised-October-2020.pdf. Accessed 31 March 2025.

African Court on Human and Peoples' Rights (ACtHPR) (2021) Strategic Plan 2021-2025 'Deepening trust in the African Court by enhancing its efficiency and effectiveness'. https://www.african-court.org/wpafc/african-court-on-human-and-peoples-rights-strategic-plan-2021-2025/. Accessed 31 March 2025.

Almutawa A (2023) Arab Court of Human Rights. In: Fabri H (ed) Max Planck Encyclopedia of International Procedural Law. Oxford University Press, Oxford.

Antkowiak T (2011) An Emerging Mandate for International Courts: Victim-Centred Remedies and Restorative Justice. Stanford Journal of International Law 47:279-332.

Attanasio D (2016) Extraordinary Reparations, Legitimacy, and the Inter-American Court. University of Pennsylvania Journal of International Law 37:814-871.

Baillie CM (2018) The Strategic Prudence of the Inter-American Court of Human Rights: Rejection of Requests for an Advisory Opinion. Revista de Direito Internacional [Brazilian Journal of International Law] 15:255-277.

Bernhardt R (2005) Just Satisfaction under the European Convention on Human Rights. In: Ragazzi M (ed) International Responsibility Today: Essays in Memory of Oscar Schachter. Martinus Nijhoff, Leiden, pp. 243-252.

Björgvinsson DT (2023) Interpretation of Judgments: European Court of Human Rights. Max Planck Encyclopedia of International Procedural Law. Oxford University Press, Oxford.

Boyes-Watson C (2018) Looking at the past of restorative justice: Normative reflections on its future. In: Gavrielides T (ed) Routledge International Handbook of Restorative Justice. Routledge, London, pp. 7-20.

Bundesrat (2024) Bundesrat klärt seine Haltung zum EGMR-Urteil über den Klimaschutz. Medienmitteilung. 28 August 2024. https://www.admin.ch/gov/de/start/dokumentation/medienmitteilungen.msg-id-102244.html. Accessed 31 March 2025.

Burgorgue-Larsen L (2024) The 3 Regional Human Rights Courts in Context: Justice That Cannot Be Taken for Granted. Oxford University Press, Oxford.

Buyse A (2008) Lost and Regained? Restitution as a Remedy for Human Rights Violations in the Context of International Law. ZaöRV/Heidelberg Journal of International Law 68:129-53.

Caflisch L (2006) The Reform of the ECtHR: Protocol No. 14 and Beyond. Human Rights Law Review 6:403–415.

Çalı B (2018) Explaining variation in the intrusiveness of regional human rights remedies in domestic orders. International Journal of Constitutional Law 16:214-34.

Cançado Trindade A A (2011) The Access of Individuals to International Justice. Oxford University Press, Oxford.

Chavez L (2017) New remedial responses in the practice of regional human rights courts: Purposes beyond compensation. International Journal of Constitutional Law 15:372-92.

Coleman J (1997) The Practice of Corrective Justice. In: Owen D (ed) Philosophical Foundations of Tort Law. Oxford University Press, Oxford, pp. 53-72.

Council of Bars and Law Societies of Europe (2020) The European Court of Human Rights - Questions & Answers for Lawyers. Update 2021.

Council of Europe (2023) Reykjavík Declaration - Reykjavík Summit. 4th Summit of Heads of State and Government of the Council of Europe, 16-17 May 2023. https://edoc.coe.int/en/the-council-of-europe-in-brief/11619-united-around-our-values-reykjavik-declaration.html. Accessed 31 March 2025.

Council of Europe Commissioner for Human Rights (2007) Long delays in court proceedings threaten the rule of law. Comment. Strasbourg, 15 October 2007. https://www.coe.int/en/web/commissioner/blog/2007. Accessed 31 March 2025.

Council of Europe Committee of Ministers (2006) Rules for the supervision of the execution of judgments and of the terms of friendly settlements. Amended on 6 July 2022 at the 1439th meeting of the Ministers' Deputies. https://www.coe.int/en/web/execution/rules-and-working-methods. Accessed 31 March 2025.

Council of Europe Committee of Ministers (2007) Interim Resolution CM/ResDH(2007)74 on excessively lengthy proceedings in Greek administrative courts and the lack of an effective domestic remedy. 6 June 2007.

Council of Europe Parliamentary Assembly (2023) Implementation of judgments of the European Court of Human Rights. Report. Doc. 15742. 11 April 2023. https://rm.coe.int/implementation-of-the-judgments-of-the-european-court-of-human-rights-/1680aaaa60. Accessed 31 March 2025.

Donald A, Gordon J, Leach P (2012) The UK and the European Court of Human rights. Equality and Human Rights Commission Research Report 83. https://www.equalityhumanrights.com/sites/default/files/83._european_court_of_human_rights.pdf. Accessed 31 March 2025.

European Commission (2013) Recommendation of 11 June 2013 on common principles for injunctive and compensatory collective redress mechanisms in the Member States concerning violations of rights granted under Union Law, O.J. L 201, 26.7.2013, p 60.

European Court of Human Rights (2005) Annual Report 2004. https://www.echr.coe.int/documents/d/echr/annual_report_2004_eng. Accessed 31 March 2025.

European Court of Human Rights (2023) Guide on Article 3 of the European Convention on Human Rights - Prohibition of torture. Updated on 31 August 2024. https://ks.echr.coe.int/documents/d/echr-ks/guide_art_3_eng. Accessed 31 March 2025.

European Court of Human Rights (2024) Guide on Article 46 of the European Convention on Human Rights - Binding force and execution of judgments. Updated on 31 August 2024. https://ks.echr.coe.int/documents/d/echr-ks/guide_art_46_eng. Accessed 31 March 2025.

European Court of Human Rights Registry (2024) Rules of Court: Third-party intervention under Article 36§2 of the Convention or under Article 3, second sentence, of Protocol No. 16. Practice direction issued by the President of the Court in accordance with Rule 32 of the Rules of Court on 13 March 2023. https://www.echr.coe.int/documents/d/echr/Rules_Court_ENG. Accessed 31 March 2025.

Fikfak V (2019) Changing State Behaviour: Damages before the European Court of Human Rights. European Journal of International Law 29:1091-125.

Fikfak V (2022) Against Settlement before the European Court of Human Rights. International Journal of Constitutional Law 20:942–975.

Glas LR (2016) The Functioning of the Pilot-Judgment Procedure of the European Court of Human Rights in Practice. Netherlands Quarterly of Human Rights 34:41-70.

Glas LR (2019) The Execution Process of Pilot Judgments Before the Committee of Ministers. Human Rights & International Legal Discourse 13:73-97.

Gonzalez-Salzberg D (2021) Non-Pecuniary Damage under the American Convention on Human Rights: An Empirical Analysis of 30 Years of Case Law. Harvard Human Rights Journal 34:81-116.

Haider D (2013) The Pilot-Judgment Procedure of the European Court of Human Rights. Martinus Nijhoff Publishers, Leiden.

High Level Conference (2018) High Level Conference meeting in Copenhagen 12 - 13 April 2018, Copenhagen Declaration. https://www.echr.coe.int/documents/d/echr/Copenhagen_Declaration_ENG. Accessed 4 August 2024. Accessed 31 March 2025.

Ichim O (2015) Just Satisfaction Under the European Convention on Human Rights. Cambridge University Press, Cambridge.

International Law Commission (2023) Seventy-fourth session (24 April–2 June and 3 July–4 August 2023). UN Doc. A/78/10. https://legal.un.org/ilc/reports/2023/english/a_78_10_advance.pdf. Accessed 31 March 2025.

Jennings RY (1998) Collected Writings of Sir Robert Jennings, Vol. 1. Kluwer Law International, The Hague.

Keller H, Marti C (2015) Reconceptualizing Implementation: The Judicialization of the Execution of the European Court of Human Rights' Judgments. European Journal of International Law 26:829–850.

Keller H, Forowicz M, Engi L (2010) Friendly Settlements before the European Court of Human Rights: Theory and Practice. Oxford University Press, Oxford.

Kurban D (2016) Forsaking Individual Justice: The Implications of the European Court of Human Rights' Pilot Judgment Procedure for Victims of Gross and Systematic Violations. Human Rights Law Review 16:731–769.

Leach P (2005) Beyond Bug River—A New Dawn for Redress Before the European Court of Human Rights? European Human Rights Law Review 2:148-164.

Magliveras K (2023) Legal and Procedural Issues Arising from the Expulsion of The Russian Federation from the Council of Europe. International and Comparative Law Review 23:95-116.

Magliveras K, Naldi G (2016) The Arab Court of Human Rights: A Study in Impotence. Revue Québécoise de Droit International 29:147-172.

Mowbray A (2017) An Examination of the European Court of Human Rights' Indication of Remedial Measures. Human Rights Law Review 17:451-478.

Mutangi T (2023) Tracing the developing reparations jurisprudence of African Court on Human and Peoples' Rights as reflected in its first cases of *Mtikila, Zongo* and *Konate*. In: Fuentes A, Rudman A (eds) Human Rights Adjudication in Africa. Pretoria University Law Press, Pretoria, pp. 1-28.

Naldi G, Magliveras K (2014) The Law and Practice Regarding Denunciation of Treaties and Withdrawal from International Organisations with Specific Reference to Human Rights. Polish Yearbook of International Law Vol. XXXIII, pp. 95-127.

Nationalrat (2024) Erklärung des Nationalrates. Urteil des EGMR 'Verein KlimaSeniorinnen Schweiz u.a. vs Schweiz'. 24.054. Adopted 12 June 2024. https://www.parlament.ch/centers/eparl/curia/2024/20240054/RK-N%20Text%20Erkl%C3%A4rung%20DF.pdf. Accessed 31 March 2025.

Nowak M (2014) The Right of Victims of Human Rights Violations to a Remedy: The Need for a World Court of Human Rights. Nordic Journal of Human Rights 32:3-17.

Oquendo AR (2018) The Politicization of Human Rights: Within the Inter-American System and Beyond. New York University Journal of International Law and Politics 50:1-73.

Pasqualucci J (2012) The Practice and Procedure of the Inter-American Court of Human Rights, 2nd edn. Cambridge University Press, Cambridge.

Plagis M (2020) The Making of Remedies: The (R)evolution of the African Court on Human and Peoples' Rights' Remedies Regime in Fair Trial Cases. African Journal of International and Comparative Law 28:45-71.

Roach K (2019) The Disappointing Remedy? Damages as a Remedy for Violations of Human Rights. University of Toronto Law Journal 69:33-63.

Sánchez K (2021) The Right to Reparations in the Contentious Process Before the African Court on Human and Peoples' Rights: A Comparative Analysis on Account of the Revised Rules of Court. African Human Rights Law Journal 21:812-835.

Sainati T (2015) Human Rights Class Actions: Rethinking the Pilot-Judgment Procedure at the European Court of Human Rights. Harvard International Law Journal 56:147-205.

Shelton D (2005) Remedies in International Human Rights Law, 2nd edn. Oxford University Press, Oxford.

Shelton D (2022) Reparations in Human Rights Law. In: Murray R, Long D (eds) Research Handbook on Implementation of Human Rights in Practice. Edward Elgar, Cheltenham, pp. 36-57.

Skelton A (2018) Human rights and Restorative Justice. In: Gavrielides T (ed) Routledge International Handbook of Restorative Justice. Routledge, London, pp. 32-42.

UK Ministry of Justice (2023) Responding to human rights judgments. Report to the Joint Committee on Human Rights on the Government's response to human rights judgments 2022 - 2023. Presented to Parliament by the Lord Chancellor and Secretary of State for Justice by Command of His Majesty, CP 958. November 2023.

UK Ministry of Justice (2024) Responding to human rights judgments. Report to the Joint Committee on Human Rights on the Government's response to human rights judgments 2023 - 2024. Presented to Parliament by the Lord Chancellor and Secretary of State for Justice by Command of His Majesty, CP 1192. November 2024.

UN General Assembly (2005) Resolution 60/147: Basic Principles and Guidelines on the Right to a Remedy and Reparation for Victims of Gross Violations of International Human Rights Law and Serious Violations of International Humanitarian Law. 16 December 2005.

Wildhaber L (2003) Article 41 of the European Convention on Human rights: Just Satisfaction under the European Convention on Human Rights. Baltic Yearbook of International Law Online, 3:1-18.

Wildhaber L (2009) Pilot Judgments in Cases of Structural or Systemic Problems on the National Level. In: Wolfrum R, Deutsch UR (eds) The European Court of Human Rights Overwhelmed by Applications: Problems and Possible Solutions. Springer, Berlin, pp. 69-75.

Chapter 10
Execution of Judgments and Supervisory Mechanisms

Magnus Killander and Brian Kibirango

Contents

10.1 Introduction 224
10.2 Obligations Imposed on State Parties 226
10.2.1 Obligations: African Court on Human and Peoples' Rights 226
10.2.2 Obligations: European Court of Human Rights 227
10.2.3 Obligations: Inter-American Court of Human Rights 227
10.2.4 Obligations: Arab Court of Human Rights 228
10.3 Compliance Trends 228
10.3.1 Introduction 228
10.3.2 Compliance Trends: African Court on Human and Peoples' Rights 229
10.3.3 Compliance Trends: European Court of Human Rights 230
10.3.4 Compliance Trends: Inter-American Court of Human Rights 231
10.4 Mechanisms for Monitoring the Execution of Judgments 232
10.4.1 Introduction 232
10.4.2 Mechanisms: African Court on Human and Peoples' Rights 232
10.4.3 Mechanisms: European Court of Human Rights 234
10.4.4 Mechanisms: Inter-American Court of Human Rights 236
10.4.5 Mechanism: Arab Court of Human Rights 239
10.5 Efforts at Reform 240
10.5.1 Introduction 240
10.5.2 Reform: African Court on Human and Peoples' Rights 241
10.5.3 Reform: European Court of Human Rights 242
10.5.4 Reform: Inter-American Court of Human Rights 243
10.6 Conclusion 243
References 244

Abstract This chapter provides a comparative analysis of how regional human rights systems address the question of execution of judgments issued by the respective Courts, and the supervisory mechanisms utilised for that purpose. It considers the obligations imposed on the contracting parties to the treaties that establish the regional

M. Killander · B. Kibirango (✉)
Faculty of Law, Centre for Human Rights, University of Pretoria, Pretoria, South Africa
e-mail: brian.kibirango@up.ac.za

M. Killander
e-mail: magnus.killander@up.ac.za

A. Almutawa and K. D. Magliveras (eds.), *A Comparison of the European, Inter-American, African and Arab Human Rights Courts: Institutional Aspects*,
https://doi.org/10.1007/978-94-6265-695-6_10

human rights Courts in respect of the execution of judgments, the effectiveness of the supervisory mechanisms available to oversee their execution, as well as how the process could be improved. The chapter considers both specific State compliance through the implementation of remedies in individual cases and general State compliance through the implementation of domestic measures to prevent future violations. Through this comparative analysis of the execution of judgments, and their supervision, the chapter examines the issue of partial or non-compliance and discusses the effectiveness of the respective regimes in remedying human rights violations.

Keywords Compliance · Effectiveness · Execution · Implementation · Judgments · Supervision · Remedying violations

10.1 Introduction

Regional human rights courts are currently "at the centre of the debate on the scope and effectiveness" of international human rights law.[1] This is on account of their increasing contribution to the adjudication of cases challenging human rights violations, as well as in addressing "general and systemic problems in the area of human rights protection, ranging from more technical matters like deficiencies in the effective implementation of the right to a fair and speedy trial to politically highly sensitive human rights issues".[2] When a regional human rights court hands down a judgment finding a violation of human rights, the respondent State is required to take the measures necessary to comply with the orders and related recommendations issued by the court. This applies to remedies awarded to the victims in the specific case, such as payment of compensation, the release of an arbitrarily detained person or the prosecution of those responsible for the violation. It also applies to general measures, such as amending national legislation to comply with a human rights treaty. Generally, compliance with the judgments of the regional human rights courts leaves a lot to be desired. This is hardly surprising given that many States fail to implement judgments delivered against them by their own national courts.[3]

This chapter discusses the legal framework and practice in relation to the enforcement of the judgments of the ACtHPR, the ECtHR and the IACtHR. Although the ArabCtHR has not yet been established, as it is still short of the seven ratifications required under Article 33 of the Statute,[4] a few reflections can be made regarding the prospects of that Court ensuring effective execution of its judgments based on the enabling Statute.

Engaging with the issue of the enforcement of regional human rights courts' judgments is crucial considering the belief among many actors that their establishment

[1] Grote et al. 2021, p. 2.

[2] Ibid.

[3] See e.g. Council of Europe 2023a, pp. 28–29.

[4] Almutawa 2021.

would resolve the difficulties associated with the enforcement of human rights. For instance, it has been noted, in respect to the African human rights system, that "the push…for the creation of the African Court on Human and Peoples' Rights" was informed by "the lack of enforcement of the decisions of the African Commission and the voluntary nature of compliance with its decisions".[5] However, it must also be recognised that the impact of regional human rights courts goes beyond compliance with their judgments, to influencing national law and policy.[6]

By and large, the regional courts have exhibited a modest level of strength in asserting their position as enforcers of human rights. The ECtHR has by far delivered the most judgments; according to its 2023 Annual Report, it delivered judgments relating to 6931 applications.[7] In comparison, the IACtHR delivered 33 judgments in 2023, of which seven were judgments interpreting previous judgments, becoming the year in which the largest number of judgments on merits was issued.[8] On its part, the ACtHPR has disposed of a total of 220 cases since it became operative in 2006. These are disaggregated as follows: 205 out of 355 applications in contentious matters and all of the 15 requests for advisory opinions it received.[9] However, it should be noted that some of the States that had the highest number of cases filed against them before the ACtHPR have since withdrawn their consent allowing individuals and civil society organisations to directly access the Court, as discussed later.

Accordingly, this chapter explores how the three operational regional human rights courts, and the regional international organisations under which they are established, have approached the execution and enforcement of judgments. While these courts rely on persuasion to achieve compliance with judgments, there is an important distinction between the ECtHR on the one side, and the IACtHR and the ACtHPR on the other side. The latter two courts oversee enforcement themselves, while in the case of the ECtHR, this role is largely undertaken by the Committee of Ministers (CoM), the principal decision-making organ of the Council of Europe (CoE). While the Inter-American legal framework is not clear on the issue of enforcement, under the African human rights system, the Protocol establishing the ACtHPR foresees a role for the Executive Council of the African Union (AU), established under Article 5 of the AU Constitutive Act as one of its principle organs[10]: "(t)he Council of Ministers [now, Executive Council] shall be notified of the judgment and shall monitor its execution on behalf of the Assembly."[11] However, in practice the ACtHPR has been left to fend for itself, short of the support from the Executive Council anticipated by the Court Protocol.

[5] Nmehielle 2013, p. 318.

[6] Von Bogdandy et al. 2024.

[7] Council of Europe 2024, p. 14.

[8] Inter-American Court of Human Rights 2024, pp. 7, 57 et seq.

[9] African Court on Human and Peoples' Rights 2024, p. 4.

[10] The Executive Council is constituted by "Ministers of Foreign Affairs or such other Ministers or Authorities as are designated by the Governments of Member States"; AU Constitutive Act, Article 10.

[11] Article 29(2) ACtHPR Protocol.

The chapter starts with a discussion of the obligations imposed on contracting parties with respect to execution of judgments. This is followed by an overview of the trends of compliance with the judgments issued by the three Courts in operation, while offering a basis for a subsequent discussion of the supervisory mechanisms' effectiveness, including a discussion of the relevant aspects of the ArabCtHR in anticipation of its operationalisation. The chapter concludes by highlighting some of the areas that may need to be improved or reformed to make the execution and supervision more effective.

10.2 Obligations Imposed on State Parties

For each of the Courts discussed in this chapter, the founding treaty provides that their judgments are binding. Where a violation of the respective human rights treaty has been found, respondent States are required to comply with the orders issued by the Court. This section discusses the relevant provisions of the treaties establishing the regional human rights courts and the relevant rules adopted by the Courts themselves.

10.2.1 Obligations: African Court on Human and Peoples' Rights

Judgments issued by the ACtHPR are final and binding on litigant parties.[12] State parties are required to comply with any judgment in any case to which they are a party, and to guarantee execution of the judgment within the time stipulated by the Court.[13] This obligation also applies to a default judgment.[14]

Under Rule 81 of the Rules of Court, respondent States are enjoined to report to the Court on their progress with implementing the judgments issued against them.[15] The Court may validate the information provided by States in these reports through information secured from other credible sources, including at an implementation hearing.[16] It is noted, however, that Rule 81 is crafted in a way that does not suggest that the ACtHPR must at all times seek such supplementary information or hold implementation hearings. In contrast to the African Commission on Human and Peoples' Rights and to the African Committee of Experts on the Rights and Welfare

[12] Protocol to the African Charter on Human and Peoples' Rights on the Establishment of an African Court on Human and Peoples' Rights [African Court Protocol], Article 28(2); ACtHPR Rules of Court [African Rules of Court], adopted 1 September 2020, Rule 72.

[13] African Court Protocol, Article 30.

[14] African Rules of Court, Rule 63(1).

[15] Ibid., Rule 81.

[16] Ibid.

of the Child,[17] the Court has, as of August 2024, yet to hold implementation hearings and relies on media reports and feedback it receives from States. Such feedback is principally provided through email correspondences, which do not allow for rebuttal by other affected parties.[18] This means that the Court often chooses to rely solely on the information provided by the State, if any, which may be inaccurate.

10.2.2 Obligations: European Court of Human Rights

Article 46(1) ECHR provides that a respondent State must comply with a final judgment issued against it. Final judgments are those delivered by the Grand Chamber as well as Chamber judgments where none of the parties have requested referral to the Grand Chamber or no request for referral to the Grand Chamber has been filed within three months of the Chamber judgment, or where a Grand Chamber panel has rejected the request for referral.[19] According to the CoE Parliamentary Assembly (PACE), "the legal obligation for the States Parties to the [ECHR] to implement the Court's judgments is binding on all branches of State authority and cannot be avoided through the invocation of technical problems or obstacles which are due, in particular, to the lack of political will, lack of resources or national legislation, including the constitution".[20] It also called on State parties to "ensure that effective national co-ordination mechanisms are in place and have sufficient hierarchy and resources to be able to implement judgments and to co-ordinate responses in an efficient and informative manner".[21]

Respondent States are required to report to the CoM, within six months, on the measures they have taken to implement, execute and/or comply with a judgment. This obligation is based on Article 46(2) ECHR, which mandates the CoM to supervise the execution of final judgments.

10.2.3 Obligations: Inter-American Court of Human Rights

The obligation of States to implement the decisions issued by the IACtHR is provided for in Article 68 ACHR. This provision requires that States implement the judgments promptly and in good faith. Moreover, the IACtHR considers the implementation of

[17] See Murray et al. 2017; Fokala 2021, p. 488.

[18] See e.g. '2023 Report on Implementation of Decisions Delivered by the Court—Status as at 30 November 2023' in African Court on Human and Peoples Rights 2024, Annex II.

[19] ECHR, Article 44(2).

[20] Council of Europe Parliamentary Assembly 2023a, para 5..

[21] Ibid., para 7.5.

its judgments to be a crucial component of the right to access international justice.[22] Under Article 69(1) of the Rules of Procedure, a State party subject to the Court's jurisdiction is required to submit to the IACtHR a report of the progress it has made with regards to implementing the judgment in question. From the wording of most of its judgments, the IACtHR expects States to have made substantial progress with implementing judgment orders within a period of one year, after which it requires them to report back on developments regarding execution.[23]

10.2.4 Obligations: Arab Court of Human Rights

Article 26 ArabCtHR Statute provides that "the Court's rulings are enforceable against States Parties to the dispute. They shall be enforced immediately against a State Party, as if they were final judgments rendered by its national judiciary". This is a bold and determinate provision unique to the ArabCtHR as the issue of enforceability of judgments of the other regional human rights Courts is not clearly delineated.

10.3 Compliance Trends

10.3.1 Introduction

It has been observed that the "(e)ffective implementation of decisions of international human rights bodies remains a significant challenge, across the regional mechanisms and for UN treaty bodies".[24] As will be discussed below, the implementation information provided by the ACtHPR, the IACtHR and the CoE CoM confirm this challenge in relation both to individual remedies and to measures that are considered to be necessary to prevent future violations, such as the amendment of domestic legislation.

[22] IACtHR, 'Learn about the Monitoring Compliance with Judgment', https://www.corteidh.or.cr/conozca_la_supervision.cfm?lang=en. Accessed 14 March 2025.

[23] See, e.g., IACtHR, *Guzmán Albarracín et al v Ecuador*, Judgment (Merits, reparations and costs), 24 June 2020, Series C no. 405, para 276(13).

[24] Sandoval et al. 2020, p. 71, citing Open Society Justice Initiative 2013. Also see Heyns et al. 2024; Principi 2017, p. 9.

10.3.2 Compliance Trends: African Court on Human and Peoples' Rights

Generally, respondent States have not complied with the requirement to execute, let alone report to the ACtHPR, on the progress with implementing the judgments issued against them.[25] The non-implementation of judgments was cited as one of the early warning signs of resistance to the Court in its nascent stages,[26] and remains a serious concern. This concern is supported by recent manifestations of the predicted resistance to the ACtHPR. For example, Rwanda is reported to have "informed the Court that it will no longer cooperate with it".[27] Rwanda's position threatens the future of States' cooperation with the ACtHPR, considering that it has previously played a historical frontline role in withdrawing the Declaration under Article 34(6) of the Court Protocol allowing for direct access by individuals and NGOs.[28]

After Rwanda, three more contracting States have withdrawn their Article 34(6) Declarations. These are Tanzania, Benin and Côte d'Ivoire. Tanzania's withdrawal, effected in November 2019, was justified on the ground that its Declaration was implemented contrary to the reservations it had submitted.[29] Benin followed in March 2020, because of the Court's ruling of 14 February 2020 which had suspended the execution of a judgment rendered by its domestic courts which Benin considered an interference and "unnecessary intrusion in its economic environment".[30] Finally, Côte d'Ivoire withdrew their Declaration in April 2020 without giving any specific

[25] Daly and Wiebusch 2018, p. 306; Adjolohoun 2020.

[26] Daly and Wiebusch 2018, pp. 294–295.

[27] African Court on Human and Peoples' Rights 2023, Annex 2, p. 21.

[28] Rwanda attributed its withdrawal of the Declaration to a development that it claims was 'never envisaged' at the time it made the Declaration, namely that the ACtHPR would, on the basis of said Declaration, later admit a case filed by 'a Genocide convict who is a fugitive from justice' thereby providing them 'a platform for re-invention and sanitization, in the guise of defending the human rights of the Rwandan citizens', see Republic of Rwanda, Ministry of Foreign Affairs and Cooperation, 'Withdrawal for review by the Republic of Rwanda from the Declaration made under Article 34(6) of the Protocol to the African Charter on Human and Peoples' Rights on the establishment of an African Court on Human and Peoples' Rights', 24 February 2016. https://www.african-court.org/wpafc/wp-content/uploads/2020/10/Withdrawal-Rwanda.pdf. Accessed 15 March 2025.

[29] The United Republic of Tanzania, Ministry of Foreign Affairs, Notice of withdrawal of the Declaration made under Article 34(6) of the Protocol to the African Charter on Human and Peoples' Rights on the Establishment of an African Court on Human and Peoples' Rights, 14 November 2019. https://www.african-court.org/wpafc/wp-content/uploads/2020/10/Withdrawal-Tanzania_E.pdf. Accessed 15 March 2025.

[30] Republic of Benin, Ministry of Foreign Affairs and Cooperation, 'Withdrawal Notice', 15 March 2020. https://www.african-court.org/wpafc/wp-content/uploads/2020/10/Withdrawal-Benin.pdf. Accessed 15 March 2024.

reasons.[31] For context, at the time the four States withdrew their Declarations, they shared the largest percentage (85 percent) of the litigation before the ACtHPR.[32]

A key challenge identified by the ACtHPR is the "non-reporting by Respondent States of the measures taken to implement its judgments".[33] A major culprit in this regard is Tanzania, the very State where the Court sits. Tanzania's pattern of non-implementation and non-reporting to the Court on execution has been described as one "of stubborn refusal by the government to abide by the ACtHPR's judgments or engage with its orders".[34] Other contracting parties that have not complied with this requirement include Rwanda, Benin, Mali and Libya.[35]

The refusal or failure of States to report to the ACtHPR on the steps taken to implement the judgments issued deprives it of access to timely and first-hand information on whether the situations that had infringed protected human rights and fundamental freedoms persist or whether the necessary measures have been taken domestically. Importantly, the ACtHPR is deprived of the opportunity to supervise and guide States on how to overcome challenges, if any, as well as how to ensure that the measures taken best serve the interests of justice.

10.3.3 Compliance Trends: European Court of Human Rights

CoE Member States have taken various general measures to comply with ECtHR judgments. These measures usually include constitutional and legal reforms, clarification of administrative procedures, domestic courts changing their procedures and approach in case law, retrial of cases irregularly handled, as well as reforms carried out in the police force, in public prosecutions and in prisons.[36] Notably, in the case of measures requiring legal reforms, before the CoM concludes that the State has complied with the judgment, it additionally examines the application of such reforms in practice.[37]

Regarding individual remedies, the just satisfaction ordered by the ECtHR is usually paid by respondent States, albeit sometimes not within the stipulated time frame of six-months. Overall, the number of cases in which just satisfaction is not paid by States within the six-month period is lower than those in which it is fully

[31] Republic of Côte d'Ivoire, Ministry of Foreign Affairs 'Withdrawal Notice', 29 April 2020. https://www.african-court.org/wpafc/wp-content/uploads/2020/10/withdrawal-Cote-divoire.pdf. Accessed 15 March 2024.

[32] Adjolohoun 2020, p. 2.

[33] African Court on Human and Peoples' Rights 2021, para 15.

[34] Daly and Wiebusch 2018, p. 307.

[35] African Court on Human and Peoples' Rights 2024, Annex 2.

[36] See e.g. Council of Europe 2023a, pp. 16–20.

[37] Ibid.

paid.[38] However, many respondent States are reluctant to implement the reforms needed to fully comply with the judgments and cases may, therefore, remain open on the agenda of the CoM for a long time. Indeed, the 2023 PACE Resolution on the implementation of ECtHR judgments followed concerns over retrogression in respondent States implementing them. Particularly in issue was the increase in the backlog of judgments pending at the CoM from 5231 as at year-end of 2019 to 6256 as of 1 March 2023.[39]

10.3.4 Compliance Trends: Inter-American Court of Human Rights

The IACtHR issues orders on monitoring compliance with the execution of judgments. According to the Court's website, it has issued more than 800 such orders.[40] Similar to the other regional human rights courts, the enforcement of IACtHR judgments is challenging and takes time.[41]

A recent study on compliance found that in the first three decades of its existence (1989–2019), the IACtHR issued a total of 1872 reparation orders in some 257 cases where the respondent State was found to have breached protected rights and freedoms.[42] This translates into an average of slightly over seven orders per case. Orders issued have included: restitution, rehabilitation, satisfaction, guarantees of no repetition, the obligation to investigate and to sanction perpetrators, monetary indemnification, and reimbursement of legal costs.[43] The study reveals a pattern of some orders being more likely to be complied with compared to others. More specifically, those orders which required respondent States to prosecute alleged perpetrators and to ensure non-repetition of violations registered the least compliance (respectively, 14 and 23 percent) while compliance with orders for indemnification, satisfaction and legal costs registered rates of compliance between 55 and 58 percent).[44]

---

[38] Ibid. In the case of Ukraine, the CoE has acknowledged its 'decreased capacity to execute judgments' due to the raging war context in its territory. In particular, "the war of aggression has not only caused extraordinary suffering but has also had very severe consequences on Ukraine's national capacity to promptly execute the Court's judgments both in terms of individual measures (the ability to locate applicants and pay just satisfaction) and the adoption of general measures required to resolve long standing structural problems." Council of Europe 2024, p. 11.

[39] Council of Europe Parliamentary Assembly 2023a, para 3.

[40] See IACtHR, 'Orders on the Monitoring Compliance with Judgment', at: https://www.corteidh.or.cr/supervision_de_cumplimiento.cfm?lang=en. Accessed 16 March 2025.

[41] See, e.g., Pérez-Liñán et al. 2022; Cruz Marin 2020.

[42] Pérez-Liñán et al. 2022.

[43] Ibid.

[44] Ibid.

10.4 Mechanisms for Monitoring the Execution of Judgments

10.4.1 Introduction

This section discusses the frameworks put in place by the treaties under which the courts operate, the courts themselves, or the political organs of the international organisations to which they belong.

10.4.2 Mechanisms: African Court on Human and Peoples' Rights

Monitoring the execution of ACtHPR judgments is assigned to the AU Executive Council, which acts on behalf of the Assembly of Heads of State and Government (Assembly).[45] The same applies to default judgments.[46] To that end, the ACtHPR is obliged to notify the Executive Council of all judgments when issued.[47] It is further required to include in its annual reports, which are submitted to the AU Assembly's regular sessions, information regarding those cases where respondents State have not complied with judgments.[48] The ACtHPR Protocol does not elaborate on why the Court should notify the Assembly of both the judgments issued and the incidents of non-compliance. It is also not clear what the mandate of the Assembly is when reports on respondent States' non-compliance are filed.[49]

Regarding the role of the Assembly and the Executive Council, it has been argued that it is expected "at the minimum…to keep 'a mere record of implementation of judgments' in the internal legal orders of recalcitrant States".[50] It will be submitted that the obligations of the Executive Council extend to "inscribe the issue of implementation by a particular State on its agenda until the State complies", failing which the Assembly could impose sanctions under Article 23(2) of the AU Constitutive Act.[51]

For its part, the ACtHPR has submitted Activity Reports since 2006; and with a specific sub-section on 'Non-compliance with Order of the Court' since 2014. Despite signposting that States have not complied with its judgments, there is still considerable non-compliance. It appears that the AU political organs (Assembly,

[45] African Court Protocol, Article 9(2). The Protocol refers to the Council of Ministers of the Organisation of African Unity as this was the competent organ at the time of its adoption..

[46] African Court Protocol, Article 29(2).

[47] African Court Protocol, Article 9(2) and African Rules of Court, Rule 73(2).

[48] African Court Protocol, Article 31.

[49] Viljoen 2012, p. 445.

[50] Ibid., p. 446.

[51] Ibid.

Executive Council, the AU Commission), have not been eager to support the work of the ACtHPR. The Executive Council has been rebuked for having "to date contributed little" to monitoring the execution of judgments.[52] It has been reported, in this regard, that the Assembly openly instructed the ACtHPR not to include in its Activity Reports the names of those Member States that had not complied with judgments.[53]

This has not been helped by "the minimalist monitoring mechanism established under Article 29 of the African Court Protocol, whereby a mere call to comply stands as sanction for non-compliance".[54] For instance, in its Decision on the 2017 Activity Report of the Court, the Executive Council welcomed: "the steps taken by Burkina Faso to comply with the judgments of the Court and encourage[d] all Member States and other relevant stakeholders to emulate the example of Burkina Faso".[55] Furthermore, in all of its resolutions on the Court's Activity Reports, the Executive Council has implored States that have not yet done so, to ratify the Court Protocol and to deposit the declaration under the aforementioned Article 34(6) of the Court Protocol.

However, these calls have largely gone unanswered as evidenced by the Executive Council's Resolution on the 2023 Activity Report of the Court, which noted "with concern the low level of compliance with the decisions of the Court."[56] The ACtHPR has notably highlighted to the Executive Council the failure of its "calls" to cause a difference in the attitude of States towards its judgments. In this regard, the 2017 Activity Report of the Court noted the following in the case of judgment orders issued against Libya:

> [i]n spite of repeated reminders from the Court, its undertaking during the 31st Ordinary Session of the [Committee of Permanent Representatives (PRC)] and over four Executive Council Decisions, Libya has failed and continues to refuse to comply with the Court Orders for Provisional Measures and Judgment issued in respect of a matter brought against her.[57]

In light of this, it has been recommended that the Executive Council should be empowered to do more than "mere monitoring of the Court's report … under article 29(2) of the African Court Protocol".[58] Latest developments indicate the Executive Council's willingness to support the Court in addressing non-compliance. For example, its decision on the Court's Activity Report of 2023

> calls on the [AU] Commission, in collaboration with the African Court and other relevant AU Organs and Institutions, to undertake a study on the state of compliance with decisions of AU human rights bodies, including in particular, the reasons for the low level of compliance,

---

[52] Sandoval et al. 2020, p. 74.

[53] Adjolohoun 2020, p. 21.

[54] Ibid.

[55] African Union Executive Council 2018, para 9.

[56] African Union Executive Council 2024, para. 9.

[57] African Court on Human and Peoples' Rights 2018, para 52.

[58] Adjolohoun 2020, p. 33, citing African Court on Human and Peoples' Rights 2020, paras 19, 60–61.

> and make concrete recommendations to the Executive Council, on how to enhance Member States' compliance with such decisions.[59]

This reflects the Council's determination to understand the complexities surrounding the implementation of ACtHPR's decisions, which should inform the designing of appropriate responses. The recommended study needs to engage and gather proposals from stakeholders outside the AU, such as national human rights institutions, academia and NGOs working around execution and implementation.

10.4.3 Mechanisms: European Court of Human Rights

Article 46(2) ECHR, as amended by Protocols No. 11 and No. 14, mandates the CoM to supervise the implementation of judgments. The Department for the Execution of Judgments of the ECtHR assists both the CoM in its oversight mandate and the States in their efforts to comply with them.[60] The CoE attaches a lot of importance to the implementation of judgments as seen in the budgetary allocations. In 2022, for instance, the CoE budget for the "effective implementation" of judgments was more than 36 million euro, nearly half the ECtHR budget.[61]

The first step in the execution of judgments is that the CoM invites the State against which a violation has been found by the ECtHR to "inform it of the measures" it "has taken or intends to take".[62] Effectively, the CoM expects to receive an action plan to be provided within six months of the judgment. A State should submit an action report as soon as it considers that it has completed the execution of the judgment.[63]

The deputies of the Ministers participating in the CoM meet four times a year for three-day meetings. The Department for the Execution of Judgments prepares detailed notes on cases to be considered at the meeting with draft decisions for the CoM to consider. Apart from the action plans and action reports of States, other States as well as injured parties, NGOs, and national human rights institutions can submit relevant information. All information is publicly available on the website of the Department. If the CoM is convinced that some of the measures have been implemented, it adopts an interim resolution, and if all (i.e. individual and general) measures have been dealt with, it adopts a resolution, and the case is considered closed.

ECtHR judgments are classified by the CoM as leading or repetitive. The Committee uses a standard supervision system for most judgments but can decide to use 'enhanced supervision' for specific cases. Standard supervision refers to the

---

[59] African Union Executive Council 2024, para 11.

[60] For further details, see the Department's website at https://www.coe.int/en/web/execution. Accessed 15 March 2025.

[61] Council of Europe 2022.

[62] Council of Europe 2017, para 6.

[63] Council of Europe Committee of Ministers 2008, ch III, section 19.

procedure used where enhanced supervision is unwarranted. It "relies on the fundamental principle that it is for respondent States to ensure the effective execution of the Court's judgments and decisions" with the CoM's role in such cases limited to "ensuring that adequate action plans/reports have been presented and verif[ying] the adequacy of the measures announced and/or taken at the appropriate time".[64]

Enhanced supervision applies to "cases requiring urgent individual measures, pilot judgments, judgments disclosing major structural and/or complex problems as identified by the Court and/or the CoM, and interstate cases".[65] It allows the Committee of Ministers to "closely follow progress of the execution of a case, and to facilitate exchanges with the national authorities supporting execution".[66] Only cases under, or considered for, enhanced supervision, are discussed at the Committee meetings. At the initiative of a State or the Secretariat, the CoM can move a judgment from standard to enhanced supervision or vice versa. This is done in exceptional cases, because of the specific nature of the case.

The CoM can refer a case back to the ECtHR in two situations, both requiring a two-thirds majority of its members. First, where execution was hindered by a lack of clarity in the judgment the case may be referred back to the Court for interpretation. Second, where the CoM determines that a respondent State has refused to comply with a judgment, it may request the Court to confirm it. If the Court agrees, the Committee will decide on the measures to be taken. The legal basis is Article 46(4) ECHR:

> If the Committee of Ministers considers that a High Contracting Party refuses to abide by a final judgment in a case to which it is a party, it may, after serving formal notice on that Party and by decision adopted by a majority vote of two-thirds of the representatives entitled to sit on the committee, refer to the Court the question whether that Party has failed to fulfil its obligation under paragraph 1 [of Article 46].

Read in conjunction with Article 46(5):

> If the Court finds a violation of paragraph 1 [of Article 46], it shall refer the case to the Committee of Ministers for consideration of the measures to be taken.

The ECtHR has only heard two cases under this procedure, both dealing with arbitrary detention. The first case was *Ilgar Mammadov v Azerbaijan*, where the Court had found that the applicant's rights under the ECHR had been violated in relation to criminal charges brought against him and his subsequent pre-trial detention.[67] In December 2017, the CoM referred the case back to the ECtHR under Article 46(4) ECHR. The Grand Chamber delivered its judgment in May 2019, holding that Azerbaijan had failed to fulfil its obligation under Article 46(1) ECHR because it had not implemented the 2014 judgment in full.[68] The second case was *Kavala v*

---

[64] Department for the Execution of Judgments of the European Court of Human Rights, 'Glossary'. https://www.coe.int/en/web/execution/glossary. Accessed 15 March 2025.

[65] Ibid.

[66] Ibid.

[67] ECtHR, Application no. 15172/13, *Ilgar Mammadov v Azerbaijan*, Judgment, 22 May 2014.

[68] ECtHR, Proceedings under Article 46§4 in the case of *Ilgar Mammadov v Azerbaijan*, Judgment (infringement proceedings), 29 May 2019, Application no. 15172/13.

Türkiye,[69] which the CoM referred to the Court on 2 February 2022.[70] Five months later, the Grand Chamber held that Türkiye had violated the ECHR by not releasing the applicant. After this judgment, the CoM took further action by, among others, establishing a Liaison Group of Ambassadors to assist the Chair in engaging with the Turkish authorities.[71]

Of note in the European system is the political will exhibited by the CoE Member States to ensure that ECtHR judgments are promptly and fully implemented because "the fundamental importance of the execution of the Court's judgments and the effective supervision of that process ... ensure the long-term sustainability, integrity and credibility of the Convention system".[72] To this end, PACE advocates for projects that support national parliaments and parliamentarians in the process of effecting "reforms necessary to implement the Court's judgments – and holding governments to account for taking timely action to implement such judgments".[73] This is in keeping with PACE's earlier recommendation to national parliaments to implement the "Basic principles for parliamentary supervision of international human rights standards".[74] Evidently, PACE considers national parliaments to be critical players in the implementation of ECtHR judgments and in a recent document it put forward strategies for them to execute this role.[75]

Finally, the Parliamentary Assembly has recommended the introduction of other strategies for enhancing implementation of ECtHR judgments, including "the procedure of enhanced political dialogue in cases of noncompliance with judgments of the Court".[76]

10.4.4 *Mechanisms: Inter-American Court of Human Rights*

Under the Inter-American system, the IACtHR is itself the main body responsible for assessing compliance with its judgments. As has been submitted, the IACtHR.

> has proved to be the most innovative in responding to implementation challenges despite its limited resources…compliance hearings have proven to be particularly important given their ability to promote dialogue with stakeholders and to build better understanding of the barriers that need to be addressed to move implementation forward.[77]

---

[69] ECtHR, Application no. 28749/18, *Kavala v Turkey*, Judgment, 10 December 2019.

[70] ECtHR, Application no. 28749/18, Proceedings under Article 46§4 in the case of *Kavala v Türkiye*, Judgment (infringement proceedings), 11 July 2022.

[71] See Ministers' Deputies, 1451st meeting, 6–8 December 2022 (DH), H46–40, *Kavala v Türkiye* (Application No. 28749/18), CM/Notes/1451/H46-40, https://rm.coe.int/0900001680a91b86. Accessed 14 March 2025.

[72] Council of Europe 2023b, Appendix IV, para. 8.

[73] CoE Parliamentary Assembly 2023b, p. 1.

[74] CoE Parliamentary Assembly 2023a, paragraph 8.

[75] Council of Europe Parliamentary Assembly 2023d.

[76] Council of Europe Parliamentary Assembly 2023c.

[77] Sandoval 2021, p. 2.

The Court has been praised for having taken affirmative steps for the execution of judgments,[78] including the adoption of the revised Rules of Procedure in November 2009, which set out, among others, the procedure for monitoring compliance with judgments and other Court decisions.[79] In particular, respondent States are required to submit to the Court a report on the steps taken in implementing judgments rendered against them as well as other decisions, including order for provisional measures.[80] The Court is required to collect observations on States' reports by the victims or their legal representatives.[81] Thereafter, State reports and victims' observations must be subjected to further scrutiny, which is done through presentation of observations by the Inter-American Commission on Human Rights.[82] The Court may also validate the information on compliance reports through other sources, such as expert opinions or opinions that it considers appropriate.[83]

The Court furthermore has the discretion, when it deems it appropriate, to hold a hearing between the State and the victims' representatives to monitor compliance with its decisions in which case the opinions of the Commission are also required to be heard.[84] It has been calculated that the IACtHR has held implementation hearings in relation to almost all States that have accepted its jurisdiction.[85]

Relatedly, the Court introduced the practice of conducting on-site hearings. The first such hearings were held in Honduras and in Panama in 2015.[86] Experience shows that the Court's implementation hearings tend to be more effective when conducted on-site. On-site hearings facilitate participation of critical actors, such as government officials, because of the proximity to their ordinary workstations, as well as other stakeholders especially victims who would have been excluded by the cost implications of travel and associated expenses had they been held at the seat of the Court.[87] At the end of the hearing, when all relevant information has been obtained, the "Tribunal" determines "the state of compliance with its decisions and issue the relevant orders".[88]

The IACtHR commendably publishes information on the status of cases which are at the stage of monitoring respondent States' compliance.[89] The Court's website contains information relating to the cases, which are disaggregated according to

[78] Sandoval et al. 2020, p. 74.

[79] IACtHR, Rules of Procedure, Article 9.

[80] Ibid., Article 69(1).

[81] Ibid.

[82] Ibid.

[83] Ibid., Article 69(2).

[84] Ibid., Article 69(3).

[85] Sandoval 2021.

[86] Inter-American Court of Human Rights 2016, p. 7.

[87] See, generally, Sandoval 2021.

[88] IACtHR, Rules of Procedure, Article 69(4).

[89] See IACtHR, 'Cases at the Monitoring Compliance with Judgment Stage' (only in Spanish), at https://www.corteidh.or.cr/casos_en_supervision_por_pais.cfm?lang=en. Accessed 15 March 2025.

the respondent States, the reparations ordered by the Court, as well as a report on the nature of compliance. It should, however, be noted that this information is only provided in Spanish but some details in English are given in the Court's annual reports.

So far, the response rate from States in relation to requests from the IACtHR has been quite good. For example, in the course of 2022,

> the Court received 426 reports and attachments from the States in 183 cases at the stage of monitoring compliance with Judgment. Additionally, over the course of the year, the Court receive 483 briefs with observations from either the victims or their legal representatives, or from the Inter-American Commission in 180 cases at the stage of monitoring compliance with Judgment. All these briefs were promptly forwarded to the parties.[90]

During 2022, the IACtHR held six virtual hearings and 11 hearings in person relating to measures that had been adopted to execute judgments. Fourteen hearings were in private and three in public. In 2023, the number of hearings increased to twenty-six. on implementation.[91]

Since 2015, except for the Covid-years 2020 and 2021, the IACtHR has undertaken on-site visits and has held hearings in twelve OAS Member States.[92] For example, in March 2022, a high level IACtHR delegation that included the President, Vice-President, Registrar and Deputy Registrar visited Panama to conduct on-site verification and hold a private hearing in relation to the implementation of provisional measures ordered in July 2020. To offer another example, in October 2022 implementation hearings were held in Uruguay (in connection with the IACtHR's ordinary session which took place in that country) as well as compliance hearings in Argentina in the presence of a Court judge, the Registrar and the head of the Unit that is responsible for monitoring compliance with judgments. The latter delegation further had a meeting with senators from the Argentinean National Congress to discuss "seven guarantees of non-repetition that involve the adoption of domestic laws or their amendment ordered in the Judgments" against Argentina. Finally, the delegation met with the Public Prosecution Service in relation to the identification and prosecution of those responsible for human rights violations in cases that had been brought against Argentina.[93]

It is evident that the IACtHR is still overburdened by the monitoring exercise. This is revealed in its Annual Report of 2022, which notes that:

> Monitoring compliance with the Court's Judgments has become one of the most demanding activities of the Court, because each year there is a considerable increase in the number of cases at this stage. Numerous measures of reparation are ordered in each Judgment, and the Court monitors their implementation, rigorously and continually, until every reparation ordered has been fully complied with. When assessing compliance with each reparation, the Court makes a thorough examination of the way in which the different components are executed, and how they are implemented with regard to each victim who benefits from the

[90] Inter-American Court of Human Rights 2023, p. 75.

[91] Inter-American Court of Human Rights 2024, p. 82.

[92] Ibid., p. 85.

[93] Inter-American Court of Human Rights 2023, pp. 84 et seq.

> measures, because there are numerous victims in most cases. Currently, 280 cases are at the stage of monitoring compliance, and this entails monitoring 1492 measures of reparation.[94]

In the 2023 Annual Report, the IACtHR reported that 295 cases with 1577 measures of reparation were being monitored for compliance.[95] The number of cases under monitoring will continue to increase given that the number of new cases added each year far exceeds the number of cases closed due to full compliance.

10.4.5 Mechanism: Arab Court of Human Rights

The Statute provides that all judgments to be rendered by the ArabCtHR are final,[96] unless reconsidered by the Court under Article 27 of the Court Statute. As already noted, the ArabCtHR is also unique in the sense that its judgments are enforced in the same way as those delivered by national courts.[97] Arguably, this implies that execution of judgments rendered by the Arab Court cannot be avoided, which means that, compared to the other regional human rights courts, it may have greater prospects of its judgments being enforced by States. However, enforceability is dependent on political will, as suggested by comparison with the experience of the Economic Community of West African States (ECOWAS) Community Court of Justice. Article 24(2) of the Protocol Relating to the Community Court of Justice provides[98]:

> Execution of any decision of the Court shall be in form of a writ of execution, which shall be submitted by the Registrar of the Court to the relevant Member State for execution according to the rules of civil procedure of that Member State.

Like Article 26 ArabCtHR Statute, this provision makes the judgments of the ECOWAS Court enforceable as if they were national court judgments.[99] Despite a dearth of data on compliance with the ECOWAS Court judgments, its experience makes it questionable whether such provisions indeed assist with enforcement in the absence of political will, particularly in the context of a lack of adherence to the rule of law in many member States.[100] It remains to be seen whether ArabCtHR judgments would similarly be ignored when politically expedient.

---

[94] Ibid., p. 71.

[95] Inter-American Court of Human Rights 2024, p. 80.

[96] ArabCtHR Statute, Article 25(3).

[97] Ibid., Article 26.

[98] Supplementary Protocol A/SP.1/01/05 amending the preamble and Articles 1, 2, 9 and 30 of Protocol A/P.1/7/91 relating to the Community Court of Justice and Article 4(1) of the English version of the said Protocol, done on 19 January 2005.

[99] If a treaty is not directly applicable in the national legal order this would require incorporation into national law of such a provision. See the judgment of the High Court of Accra, Ghana in the *Mba* case (*Matter of Chude Mba v The Republic of Ghana*, Suit No. HRCM/376/15 (2016)), where the applicant sought unsuccessfully to enforce in Ghana a judgment of the Economic Community of West African States Community Court of Justice; Frimpong Oppong 2017.

[100] Adjolohoun 2013, p. 370.

Notably, under Article 4 ArabCtHR Statute, the Assembly of States Parties is required to provide “a mechanism for execution of judgments” issued by the ArabCtHR. The Court is also required to annually report to the Assembly “a list of cases in which judgments were issued and a list of judgments that the parties did not comply with in their execution”.[101] The Statute does not clearly indicate what is expected of the Assembly in respect of the judgments, but seems to suggest that the Court’s report is submitted simply “for approval”.[102] Such ambiguities could be attributed to the limited level of consultation and generally the secrecy with which the process leading to the adoption of the Arab Human Rights Court Statute has been associated.[103]

The arrangement requiring the Court to report to the Assembly has been criticised.[104] However, this is not new as it aligns with the practice that has been developed in other regional international organisations such as the AU. Nevertheless, there is a need to strongly consider recommendations such as calls made by the International Commission of Jurists for a review of the Statute to “provide for an independent and effective monitoring mechanism that supervises the execution of the Court’s judgments”.[105] Notably, under Article 4 of the Court Statute, the Assembly is required to provide a mechanism for execution of judgments. Finally, this is a matter to be addressed in the Rules of Court, if and when it is operationalized.

10.5 Efforts at Reform

10.5.1 Introduction

The procedures regarding the execution of judgments are constantly evolving. As illustrated below, the courts have taken varied approaches, but all still struggle with implementation of their judgments. Various reforms to further improve the enforcement system have been suggested and are discussed in this section.

[101] Statute of the Arab Court of Human Rights, Article 29(1).

[102] Ibid., Article 29(2).

[103] See, for instance, International Commission of Jurists 2015, p. 10 reporting on its several unsuccessful attempts at accessing the draft Statute as well as seeking an opportunity to input into it.

[104] Almutawa 2021, p. 511.

[105] This recommendation was reportedly inspired by the practice in the other regional human rights systems such as Article 46 ECHR, which expressly mandates the CoM to supervise the execution of ECtHR judgments considering, among others, the extent to which the remedies prescribed for victims of human rights violations have been fulfilled, as well as the adoption of measures to prevent reoccurrence.

10.5.2 Reform: African Court on Human and Peoples' Rights

The ACtHPR recognises the enduring need to instrumentalise its judicial processes in order to "continue to create a positive impact on the lives of African citizens".[106] Noting non-compliance with its judgments as one of the major impediments to the Court's work,[107] its Strategic Plan sets out, as one of the key steps to be taken in the five-year period 2021–2025, to "attain at least 30% compliance with its decisions".[108] One of the outputs envisioned in the Strategic Plan is investing in improving levels of cooperation with its stakeholders to foster greater synergies (Output 2.2) by, among others, ensuring that the Court "possesses adequate human, technical and financial resources".[109] Furthermore, the Court, together with the African Commission on Human and Peoples' Rights, developed a Complementarity Roadmap for 2023–2025 in which the two bodies committed, among others, to use their respective mechanisms to urge States to comply with the outcomes of the Court (Judgments) and of the Commission (recommendations and resolutions).[110] At the request of the Court, the AU Executive Council called on States to establish National Focal Points "to ensure effective follow up on all matters relating to the Court, including on compliance with the Court's decisions".[111] By the end of 2023, focal points had been appointed in fifteen States, namely: Algeria, Botswana, Burkina Faso, Burundi, Cameroon, Cape Verde, Central African Republic, Democratic Republic of Congo, Malawi, Mauritania, Mozambique, Senegal, South Africa, Uganda and Zimbabwe.[112]

Furthermore, the ACtHPR introduced the position of Senior Legal Officer in charge of compliance and monitoring implementation of judgments, whose mandate is to support the Court and to liaise with the AU Assembly, the Executive Council, the Member States and other stakeholders on how best to implement and execute judgments. The establishment of this office was also highlighted by the first joint meeting of the legal officers of the Court, the African Commission on Human and Peoples' Rights and the African Committee on the Rights and Welfare of the Child

---

[106] African Court on Human and Peoples' Rights 2021, paras 13, 15.

[107] As of 2020, only 7 percent of the Court's judgments had attained full compliance, 18 percent partial compliance while 75 percent had not been complied with at all, ibid., para 15.

[108] Ibid., para 13.

[109] Ibid., para 17.

[110] See African Court on Human and Peoples' Rights 2023, Annex 3: 'Complementary roadmap of the African Commission on Human and Peoples' Rights and the African Court on Human and Peoples' Rights', para 14.

[111] African Union Executive Council 2023, para 13; ACtHPR Activity Report 2022, Draft Decision on the 2022 Activity Report of the African Court on Human and Peoples' Rights, para 11.

[112] African Union Executive Council 2024, para 4.

(ACERWC) held in January 2022.[113] The meeting recommended, among others, for the Court:

> to ensure that effective complementarity is fully realised through the operationalisation of their Rules of Procedure in relation to utilising the contentious jurisdiction of the Court generally, and on compliance with its decisions more specifically.[114]

There are several strategies that could contribute to the gradual fulfilment of an effective ACtHPR. To begin with, during the aforesaid joint retreat, legal officers of the ACtHPR, the Commission and the ACERWC made a proposal to include the issue of compliance with the ACtHPR judgments "in their treaty monitoring function through the State reporting procedures".[115] The periodic review by the Commission and ACERWC often benefits from the physical presence of, and direct dialogue with, State delegates, including those from agencies with potential influence in the implementation of judgments. A direct dialogue with State officials at these review cycles is thus likely to be more effective than the Court's current mode of monitoring implementation, which relies on asynchronous correspondences mostly done through email.

10.5.3 Reform: European Court of Human Rights

The Brighton Declaration adopted at the end of the 2012 High Level Conference on the Future of the European Court of Human Rights noted that the increasing number of judgments would lead to an increasing workload for the CoM in supervising implementation.[116] The Declaration called on State parties to improve "domestic capacities and mechanism" for the execution of judgments, to publicise their action plans regarding the execution of judgments, and to facilitate a role for national parliaments to play. It further highlighted the importance of the principle of subsidiarity and called upon the CoM to focus on "strategic and systemic issues" and to ensure stronger publicity about its work.[117] The 2015 Brussels Declaration included an Action Plan on supervision of the execution of judgments in which the CoM was encouraged to use interim resolutions, to make referrals to the Court, to provide technical support to States, to promote synergies among the CoE organs, to exchange

---

[113] See para 2 of 'Annex V: Report of this Joint Retreat' in African Court on Human and Peoples' Rights 2023. The retreat sought to provide a forum for the legal officers of the three bodies 'to exchange ideas on substantive and operational issues that they face in relation to their work and the best practices to enhance their productivity and ultimately that of their respective Organs through enhanced complementarity and synergy', para 3.

[114] 'First joint retreat of legal officers of the African Commission, the African Court and the ACERWC held from 26–28 January 2022 in Maputo, Mozambique' in African Court on Human and Peoples' Rights 2023, Annex V, para 37.

[115] Ibid., para 48.

[116] High Level Conference on the Future of the European Court of Human Rights, Brighton Declaration, 2012, paras 26–28. See also Council of Europe Committee of Ministers 2008.

[117] Brighton Declaration, para 29 (supra n. 116).

good practices, to ensure transparency and to increase the resources available to the Department for the Execution of Judgments.[118]

The 2018 Copenhagen Declaration noted the positive impact of the pilot judgment procedure to improve national implementation.[119] However, "[i]neffective national implementation of the [ECHR], in particular in relation to serious systemic and structural human rights problems, remains the principal challenge confronting the Convention system".[120] The Declaration called on CoE Member States to take preventive measures so as not to violate the ECHR, including systematically checking draft legislation for compatibility with it.[121]

10.5.4 Reform: Inter-American Court of Human Rights

The IACtHR has generally tried to innovate ways of dealing with some of the issues. For instance, in 2015, it established a unit within the Court to monitor compliance with judgments, and in 2022 it decided to designate judges as judge rapporteurs for specific respondent States.[122] The main challenge remains the lack of financial resources and the lack of interest from the political bodies of the OAS.

10.6 Conclusion

The execution system of the CoE is built on the notion that issues needing to be dealt with will be identified through the individual complaint system set up under the ECHR. The CoM and the well-resourced Secretariat established to assist it are meticulous in identifying both individual and general measures States may need to adopt in order to comply with judgments. The Committee can involve the ECtHR in the process, but so far this has been very rare to the point of wondering what the underlying reasons are. Despite the resources available to the system, there are still extensive delays, particularly in relation to respondent States initiating or implementing general measures.

The bigger role of the respective Courts in the supervision of judgments in the Inter-American and African human rights system can be seen from the perspective of States lacking the political will to contribute to an effective supervisory system. It is

---

[118] High-level conference on the implementation of the European Convention on Human Rights, our shared responsibility, Brussels, 26–27 March 2015, Brussels Declaration, Action Plan, Part C 'Supervision of the execution of judgments'.

[119] Copenhagen Declaration of the High-Level Conference meeting in Copenhagen on 12 and 13 April 2018, para 17.

[120] Ibid., para 12.

[121] Ibid., para 16.

[122] Inter-American Court of Human Rights 2023.

very likely that the League of Arab States system will also suffer from lack of political will. This is already evidenced, on the one hand, by the fact that the Statute does not provide for individuals access to the ArabCtHR and, on the other hand, because the Statute lingers unratified. In the absence of the political will of member States as a collective, the courts need to build pressure on individual States to act promptly and efficiently for what is at stake are the rights and freedoms of people, which are not negotiable. The tools developed by the IACtHR, such as compliance hearings and on-site visits, are useful in this regard. Suggested initiatives, for example to systematically consider compliance with ACtHPR judgments in the State reporting procedure, may also play a role but would again depend on how seriously States are willing to engage with this process.

References

Adjolohoun HS (2013) The ECOWAS Court as a human rights promoter? Assessing five years impact of the Koraou slavery judgment. Netherlands Quarterly of Human Rights 31:342-371.

Adjolohoun HS (2020) A Crisis of Design and Judicial Practice? Curbing State Disengagement from the African Court on Human and Peoples' Rights. African Human Rights Law Journal 20:1-40.

African Court on Human and Peoples' Rights (2018) Activity Report of the African Court on Human and Peoples' Rights 1 January 2017–31 December 2017, EX.CL/1057(XXXII). https://www.african-court.org/wpafc/activity-report-of-the-african-court-on-human-and-peoples-rights-1-january-31-december-2017/. Accessed 15 March 2025.

African Court on Human and Peoples' Rights (2020) Activity Report of the African Court on Human and Peoples' Rights 1 January 2019—31 December 2019, EX.CL/1204(XXXVI). https://www.african-court.org/wpafc/activity-report-of-the-african-court-on-human-and-peoples-rights-1-january-31-december-2019/. Accessed 15 March 2025.

African Court on Human and Peoples' Rights (2021) Strategic Plan 2021-2025 'Deepening trust in the African Court by enhancing its efficiency and Effectiveness'. https://www.african-court.org/wpafc/african-court-on-human-and-peoples-rights-strategic-plan-2021-2025/. Accessed 15 March 2025.

African Court on Human and Peoples' Rights (2023) Activity Report of the African Court on Human and Peoples' Rights 1 January 2022—31 December 2022, EX.CL/1409(XLII). https://www.african-court.org/wpafc/report-of-the-african-court-on-human-and-peoples-rights-afchpr-2022/. Accessed 15 March 2025.

African Court on Human and Peoples' Rights (2024) Activity Report of the African Court on Human and Peoples' Rights 1 January 2023—31 December 2023, EX.CL/1492(XLIV). https://www.african-court.org/wpafc/activity-report-of-the-african-court-on-human-and-peoples-rights-afchpr-1-january-31-december-2023/. Accessed 15 March 2025.

African Union Executive Council (2018) 'Decision on the 2017 Activity Report of the African Court on Human and Peoples' Rights', EX.CL/Dec.994(XXXII) Rev.1, 26 January 2018.

African Union Executive Council (2023) 'Decision on the Activity Report of the African Court on Human and Peoples' Rights (AfCHPR) including outcome of the PRC-AFCHPR retreat held in Arusha, Tanzania, March 2022', EX.CL/Dec.1197(XLII), 16 February 2023.

African Union Executive Council (2024) 'Decision on the 2023 Activity Report of the African Court on Human and Peoples' Rights (AfCHPR)', EX.CL/Dec.1245(XLIV), 15 February 2024.

Almutawa A (2021) The Arab Court of Human Rights and the Enforcement of the Arab Charter on Human Rights. Human Rights Law Review 21:506-532.

Council of Europe (2017) Rules of the Committee of Ministers for the supervision of the execution of judgments and of the terms of friendly settlements. https://rm.coe.int/16806eebf0. Accessed 15 March 2025.
Council of Europe (2022) Council of Europe Programme and Budget 2022-2025 (2023 adjusted) CM(2023) 1, 15 December 2022.
Council of Europe (2023a) Supervision of the Execution of Judgments and Decisions of the European Court of Human Rights - 16th Annual Report of the Committee of Ministers 2022. https://rm.coe.int/annual-report-2022/1680aad12f. Accessed 15 March 2025.
Council of Europe (2023b) Reykjavík Summit of the Council of Europe: United around our values (Reykjavík Declaration). CM(2023)57-final, 16-17 May 2023. https://www.coe.int/en/web/execution/political-declarations. Accessed 15 March 2025.
Council of Europe (2024) Supervision of the Execution of Judgments and Decisions of the European Court of Human Rights 2023 - 17th Annual Report of the Committee of Ministers. https://rm.coe.int/annual-report-2023/1680af6e81. Accessed 15 March 2025.
Council of Europe Committee of Ministers (2008) Recommendation CM/Rec(2008)2 to Member States on efficient domestic capacity for rapid execution of judgments of the European Court of Human Rights, 6 February 2008. https://www.coe.int/en/web/human-rights-intergovernmental-cooperation/echr-system/recommendation-on-execution-judgments. Accessed 15 March 2025.
Council of Europe Parliamentary Assembly (2023a) Implementation of judgments of the European Court of Human Rights. Resolution 2494, 26 April 2023, https://pace.coe.int/en/files/31772. Accessed 15 March 2025.
Council of Europe Parliamentary Assembly (2023b) Implementation of judgments of the European Court of Human Rights (Report), Document 15742, 11 March 2023. https://rm.coe.int/implementation-of-the-judgments-of-the-european-court-of-human-rights-/1680aaaa60. Accessed 15 March 2025.
Council of Europe Parliamentary Assembly (2023c) The Reykjavik Summit of the Council of Europe: United around values in the face of extraordinary challenges, Recommendation 2245, 24 January 2023. https://pace.coe.int/en/files/31592. Accessed 15 March 2025.
Council of Europe Parliamentary Assembly (2023d) Reykjavik Follow-up: The Role of PACE and National Parliamentarians in Improving the Timely and Effective Implementation of Judgments of the European Court of Human Rights: Revised information note, AS/Jur (2023) 37, 23 November 2023. https://rm.coe.int/implementation-of-judgments-of-the-european-court-of-human-rights-12th/1680ad9a89. Accessed 15 March 2025.
Cruz Marin P (2020) Compliance of Judgments of the Inter-American Court of Human Rights. https://ssrn.com/abstract=3647326. Accessed 15 March 2025.
Daly TG, Wiebusch M (2018) The African Court on Human and Peoples' Rights: Mapping Resistance against a Young Court. International Journal of Law in Context 14:294–313.
Fokala E (2021) Do not forget the Nubians: Kenya's compliance with the decisions of African regional treaty bodies on the plight and rights of Nubians. De Jure Law Journal 54: 476-492.
Frimpong Oppong R (2017) Recent Developments—The High Court of Ghana declines to enforce an ECOWAS judgment. African Journal of International and Comparative Law 25:127-132.
Grote R, Morales Antoniazzi M, Paris D (eds) (2021) Research Handbook on Compliance in International Human Rights Law. Edward Elgar, Cheltenham.
Heyns C, Viljoen F, Murray R (eds) (2024) The Impact of the United Nations Human Rights Treaties on the Domestic Level: Twenty Years On, 2nd rev. edn. Brill, Leiden.
Inter-American Court of Human Rights (2016) Annual Report 2015. https://www.corteidh.or.cr/sitios/informes/docs/ENG/eng_2015.pdf. Accessed 15 March 2025.
Inter-American Court of Human Rights (2023) Annual Report 2022. https://www.corteidh.or.cr/docs/informe2022/ingles.pdf. Accessed 15 March 2025.
Inter-American Court of Human Rights (2024) Annual Report 2023. https://www.corteidh.or.cr/informes_anuales.cfm?lang=en. Accessed 15 March 2025.

International Commission of Jurists (2015) The Arab Court of Human Rights: A Flawed Statute for an Ineffective Court.https://www.icj.org/wp-content/uploads/2015/04/MENA-Arab-Court-of-Human-Rights-Publications-Report-2015-ENG.pdf. Accessed 15 March 2025.

Murray R, Long D, Ayeni V, Somé A (eds) (2017) Monitoring implementation of the decisions and judgments of the African Commission and Court on Human and Peoples' Rights. African Human Rights Yearbook 1:150-166.

Nmehielle VO (2013) Seven years in business: Evaluating developments at the African Court on Human and Peoples' Rights. Law, Democracy and Development 17:317-341.

Open Society Justice Initiative (2013) From Rights to Remedies: Structures and Strategies for Implementing International Human Rights Decisions. https://www.justiceinitiative.org/uploads/7d34546e-dfe6-450b-82ec-77da3323d4bd/from-rights-to-remedies-20130708.pdf. Accessed 15 March 2025.

Pérez-Liñán A, Schenoni L, Morrison K (2022) Compliance in Time: Lessons from the Inter-American Court of Human Rights. International Studies Review 25:1-23.

Principi F (2017) Implementation of Decisions under Treaty Body Complaints Procedures: Do States Comply? How Do They Do It? Sabbatical Report, Treaty Bodies Branch, UN Office of the High Commissioner for Human Rights (OHCHR).

Sandoval C (2021) The Power of Hearings: Unleashing Compliance with Judgments of the Inter-American Court. University of Bristol Law School Capstone Series on Implementing Human Rights Decisions: Reflections, Successes, and New Directions. https://www.bristol.ac.uk/media-library/sites/law/hric/2021-documents/2.%20The%20power%20of%20hearings_Sandoval%20ENG.pdf. Accessed 15 March 2025.

Sandoval C, Leach P, Murray R (2020) Monitoring, Cajoling and Promoting Dialogue: What Role for Supranational Human Rights Bodies in the Implementation of Individual Decisions? Journal of Human Rights Practice 12:71-100.

Viljoen F (2012) International Human Rights Law in Africa. Oxford University Press, Oxford.

Von Bogdandy A et al (eds) (2024) The Impact of the Inter-American Human Rights System—Transformations on the Ground. Oxford University Press, Oxford.

Magnus Killander, Professor of Human Rights Law, Centre for Human Rights, Faculty of Law, University of Pretoria.

Brian Kibirango, Doctoral candidate, Centre for Human Rights, Faculty of Law, University of Pretoria.

Chapter 11
Regional Human Rights Justice: Past, Present and the Future

Konstantinos D. Magliveras

Contents

11.1 How It All Started and How It Developed 248
11.2 The Four Regional Human Rights Courts and Other Judicial Bodies of Regional Organisations, Which, Directly or Indirectly, Adjudicate Human Rights Issues 251
11.3 The Value of the Regional Human Rights Courts' Judgments as Evidence of Violation of Membership Obligations in the Respective International Organisation 256
11.4 The Regional Human Rights Courts, Criminal Jurisdiction, the International Criminal Court and the African Experiment in Combining Human Rights and International Crimes.. 258
11.5 Interactions: The Exchanges and Influences Between the Regional Human Rights Courts 259
11.6 The Case for a Global Human Rights Court of Justice 262
References 265

Abstract Following an overview of the beginnings and the development of human rights protection since the end of World War II and the role of the regional human rights Courts, the chapter discusses the relationship and possible overlap between these Courts and the judicial organs of regional international organisations which, directly or indirectly, are in a position to rule in cases that involve or raise human rights issues and concerns. Thereafter, the chapter discusses the value that the regional human rights Courts' judgments might have as objective and independent evidence of the violation of obligations by the Member States of the respective regional organisations. The relationship between the regional human rights Courts, the exercise of criminal jurisdiction, the International Criminal Court as well as the establishment in Africa of a continental court with the jurisdiction to adjudicate alleged human rights violations and try alleged perpetrators of international crimes are considered next. Furthermore, the chapter investigates the various forms of communication that have shaped interactions between the human rights Courts. Finally, it offers some thoughts on the possibility of creating a global human rights court of justice.

K. D. Magliveras (✉)
Department of Mediterranean Studies, University of the Aegean, GR - 85132, Rhodes, Greece
e-mail: kmagliveras@aegean.gr

A. Almutawa and K. D. Magliveras (eds.), *A Comparison of the European, Inter-American, African and Arab Human Rights Courts: Institutional Aspects*,
https://doi.org/10.1007/978-94-6265-695-6_11

Keywords Development of human rights protection · Regional human rights courts and criminal jurisdiction · African Court of Justice and Human Rights · Communication between courts · Global human rights court

11.1 How It All Started and How It Developed

The aim behind establishing a regional human rights court of justice is no other but to create a specialised international court endowed with the jurisdiction to rule on allegations that one or more states have breached one or more rights from a list of protected fundamental freedoms. Presently, the creation of a regional human rights court appears to be a rather straightforward affair, provided that a group of states is willing to be subjected to the scrutiny of an independent and impartial bench;[1] whether it will actually be operationalised is a different matter, as vividly shown by the ArabCtHR whose Statute lingers largely unratified. However, in the aftermath of World War II, it was much more than a novel idea; it was a revolution in the process of consolidating the international justice system that had been broken in the preceding years. And so was also the drafting of a catalogue of rights and freedoms, which would be protected by the legal force of a ratified treaty and not simply by the declaratory power of the UN Bill of Rights.[2] This was the twin task upon which the newly established Council of Europe embarked as a matter of the utmost importance: the negotiation of a human rights treaty featuring, among others, a court of justice competent to rule authoritatively and with finality on whether contracting parties safeguard its provisions, protect the envisaged rights and freedoms and abstain from a list of prohibited acts.

The following abstract from one of the very first proposals to set up what eventually became the ECtHR reveals how revolutionary the whole endeavour was:

> That, pending the drawing up of subsequent agreements of the European Charter on Rights and Freedoms, an international agreement for the establishment of a *European Court of Justice* should be approved; this Court will consider violations of the fundamental rights of freedom, which are now guaranteed by the constitutional, legislative and political customs of each of the States (emphasis added).[3]

[1] *Contra*, Burgorgue-Larsen 2024, p. 11 ('The myth of the easy, almost instantaneous creation of control mechanisms by states, on the basis of a process they promoted and supported, must be debunked once and for all'). It could be counter-argued that the proliferation of regional international organisations - starting no less with the establishment of LAS in March 1945—has allowed States to agree more readily to limitations in their sovereign rights and powers.

[2] UN General Assembly, Resolution 217 (III), 'International Bill of Human Rights—A Universal Declaration of Human Rights', 10 December 1948.

[3] Council of Europe 1977, p. 6.

Four years after the ECHR came into force, a namesake 'European Court of Justice' became the judicial body ensuring respect of the law in a separate international organisation, the European Economic Community,[4] while the 'European Court of Human Rights' became the international enforcement machinery of the ECHR; it rendered its first judgment on merits in 1961[5] and found the first violation seven years later.[6] While this was an extremely important development for the prevalence of institutional multilateral judicial mechanisms ensuring that the obligations emanating from human rights treaties are observed, it should also be viewed from another perspective. As is well known, the ECHR's conclusion was one of 'the first steps for the collective enforcement of certain of the Rights stated in the Universal Declaration [of Human Rights]'.[7] The ECHR could have stopped there, i.e. turning specific UDHR rights and freedoms from political pronouncements to binding legal obligations. As regards questions relating to the ECHR's interpretation and application, including inter-state disputes alleging violations thereof, jurisdiction by means of a compromissory clause could have been given to the International Court of Justice to determine them.[8]

This might have been a cost effective disputes settlement method in the early 1950s. But Member States were resolved to set up the ECtHR and to endow it with the power to rule on decisions, measures and actions undertaken by a contracting party's authorities 'completely or partially in conflict with the obligations arising from the [ECHR]'.[9] Originally, acceptance of ECtHR jurisdiction was considerably narrower compared to the present time. Arguably, this was a reflection of the status of international justice at the time: states had the right (and were under no obligation) to declare that they recognised as *ipso facto* compulsory and without special agreement the jurisdiction of an international court.[10] It took a considerable change in attitude towards the duties that could derive from international law as well as the acceptance that the ECHR creates obligations *erga omnes partes* for states and direct rights for individuals, so that all ECHR parties recognize the ECtHR's jurisdiction as compulsory and without exceptions.

These developments should be contrasted with events in the Americas in the closing years of the 1940s. The adoption of the American Declaration of the Rights and Duties of Man as Resolution XXX by the Ninth International Conference of American States in Bogotá on 2 May 1948, more than seven months before the UDHR, was the culmination of that continent's long standing practice on regionalism and wide held beliefs on the inalienable nature of the rights of man and the need to be protected. Like in the case of the UN and the UDHR, American States rejected the idea

[4] See Article 164 Treaty establishing the European Economic Community, signed on 25 March 1957, 294 *UNTS* 3.

[5] ECtHR, Application No. 332/57, *Lawless v. Ireland (No. 3)*, Judgment (Merits), 1 July 1961.

[6] ECtHR, Application No. 1936/63, *Neumeister v. Austria*, Judgment, 27 June 1968.

[7] See the Preamble of the original (1950) ECHR text, 213 *UNTS* 221.

[8] See Article 36(1) ICJ Statute; Tomuschat 2019, p. 742.

[9] Article 50 in conjunction with Article 45 of the 1950 ECHR text.

[10] *Ibid.*, Article 46. Cf. Article 36(2) ICJ Statute, 1 *UNTS* XVI, which substantially reproduces the content of Article 36(2) PCIJ Statute, 6 *LNTS* 391.

of adopting a binding treaty (it was considered to be too progressive) and opted instead for a declaration.[11] What is, however, noteworthy is that the Ninth International Conference had asked the Inter-American Juridical Committee to prepare a draft statute for an inter-American human rights court, a proposal that the Committee itself rejected as premature.[12] The rest is history: the founding instrument of the Organisation of American States, which was also concluded at the Conference,[13] had only a few references to human rights.[14] Later on, the Protocol of Buenos Aires added Article 106 to the OAS Charter envisaging '[a]n inter-American convention on human rights determin[ing] the structure, competence, and procedure of [an Inter-American Commission on Human Rights], as well as those of other organs responsible for these matters'.[15] It took twenty-one years after the revolutionary American Declaration for the continent to have its regional human rights treaty, complete with a Commission and a Court.

For an international or regional human rights system to operate at its optimum, any changes require not only a considerable period of time to mature but also must meet with the approval of all States concerned.[16] For example, at the time of writing, half of the ECHR parties have still not signed and/or ratified Protocol No. 16 ECHR, which was concluded in October 2013, and came into effect five years later. It allows the highest courts of justice of contracting parties to request advisory opinions from the ECtHR.[17] As far as the other three regional human rights Courts are concerned, they have still to make compulsory jurisdiction into an obligation. In particular, under Article 62(1) ACHR, Article 34(6) ACtHPR Protocol as well as under Articles 19 and 20 ArabCtHR Statute, parties still have the very wide discretion to recognise the respective Court's jurisdiction.[18] There is no indication that this state of affairs will change at any time soon.[19]

Thus, in the American, African and Arab human rights systems participating States continue to have the option of not being subject to the respective Court's compulsory jurisdiction.[20] This reality cannot but raise difficult questions on the level of the protection offered in these systems and on their effectiveness. On the other hand, it is an undisputed fact that the restricted or unrestricted access of alleged victims to a human rights Court is a matter to be decided by the Member States of the

---

[11] Paúl 2017.

[12] Quintana 2024.

[13] Charter of the Organization of American States, signed on 30 April 1948, entered into force on 13 December 1951, OAS Treaty Series Nos. 1-C and 61; 119 *UNTS* 48.

[14] See *e.g.* Article 5(f) OAS Charter: 'The American States proclaim the fundamental rights of the individual without distinction as to race, nationality, creed or sex'.

[15] Signed in Buenos Aires on 27 February 1967, entered into force on 12 March 1970, OAS Treaty Series No. A 41; [1967] 6 *ILM* 310.

[16] Generally, see Huneeus and Madsen 2018.

[17] See Chap. 8.

[18] See Chap. 3.

[19] For a contemporary overview of the regional human rights systems, see Bantekas and Oette 2024, p. 245.

[20] Generally, see Hampson et al. 2018.

international organisations in question. Arguably, the current state of international human rights law has still not been advanced to the stage of expecting that regional systems will feature a court of justice (or comparable judicial mechanism) to which all participating States will be answerable. However, as will now be discussed, the existence of judicial organs in several regional international organisations having a broad mandate extending to ruling on human rights matters could, to an extent, compensate for this state of affairs.

11.2 The Four Regional Human Rights Courts and Other Judicial Bodies of Regional Organisations, Which, Directly or Indirectly, Adjudicate Human Rights Issues

Over time, the Council of Europe has shaped a model for the promotion and protection of fundamental freedoms. The relevant basic parameters are as follows: a regional international organisation concludes a multilateral treaty to protect human rights, which is open to its own Member States, and makes provision for a supervisory judicial mechanism, which invariably takes the form of a specialised international court of justice.[21] In the 1950s, it would have been very difficult to foretell that this model's basic principles would actually be followed in other regions of the world in the next decades. Presently, it is equally hard to predict whether this model will be applied in the remaining parts and regions of the world as well, effectively having the global population covered by at least one and in many instances by two or more regional human rights systems.

To that effect one should be reminded that the human rights Courts have been established solely in the context of regional international organisations (Council of Europe, OAS, OAU, LAS). This is because the promotion and protection of fundamental freedoms has been pursued almost exclusively by international organisations. At a global level, this is also true with the United Nations, whose universal membership has accepted most of the nine so-called 'core international human rights treaties' in very large numbers and, for many decades now, has been subject to the scrutiny that is exercised by the corresponding 'treaty bodies'.[22]

At the same time, there exist many other international organisations of a regional remit that pursue a human rights agenda with different levels of intensity. Their contribution should not be underestimated, even if, from an institutional perspective, the level of human rights protection might appear to be rather basic. They could conveniently be divided into two categories. The first category comprises those organisations under the auspices of which human rights instruments have been

[21] Generally, see Stapel 2022.

[22] While UN treaty bodies are outside the scope of the present book, their linkage to the regional human rights Courts and vice versa should be acknowledged; see, generally, Galand 2023; McGregor 2013.

adopted. Here one is not concerned with whether these instruments are binding upon Member States or are of a declaratory character. What is of concern is that they have not been endowed with a (legal) mechanism having the original and compulsory authority to rule authoritatively on Member States' alleged violations of the respective instrument, even though there might exist (statutory) organs with the broad mandate to supervise the situation of human rights domestically. There are five regional organisations broadly falling into this category: three of them have created relevant organs (the Association of Southeast Asian Nations (ASEAN),[23] the Organisation of Islamic Cooperation (OIC),[24] and the Commonwealth of Independent States (CIS)[25]), the fourth (the Andean Community) has no such organ,[26] while the binding nature of its human rights instrument shall be decided 'in due time',[27] while the fifth (MERCOSUR) refers to 'established institutional mechanisms' without specifying which these are.[28]

The second category comprises those regional organisations having an institutional architecture comprising a court of justice, which could directly, indirectly or incidentally entertain legal actions with human rights content, hear complaints involving the non-observance of fundamental freedoms by the respondent contracting parties, and so on. The judicial bodies[29] broadly falling into this category include the Court of Justice of the European Union (CJEU),[30] the European Free Trade Area (EFTA) Court,[31] the Court of Justice of the Economic Community of West African

---

[23] The ASEAN Human Rights Declaration adopted on 19 November 2012, and the ASEAN Intergovernmental Commission on Human Rights; Naldi and Magliveras 2014.

[24] Cairo Declaration of the Organization of Islamic Cooperation on Human Rights adopted on 28 November 2020, and the OIC Independent Permanent Commission of Human Rights.

[25] CIS Convention on Human Rights and Fundamental Freedoms, adopted on 26 May 1995, entered into force 11 August 1998, and the CIS Commission on Human Rights, which was the subject of a Council of Europe Committee of Ministers' request for an ECtHR advisory opinion under Article 47 ECHR: ECtHR (Grand Chamber), *Decision on the Competence of the Court to Give an Advisory Opinion*, 2 June 2004.

[26] The Court of Justice of the Andean Community, originally established in 1979 as the Court of Justice of the Cartagena Agreement and subsequently modified by the Protocol of Trujillo (1996), has no authority to entertain human rights related questions, see the Protocol of Cochabamba Amending the Treaty Creating the Court of Justice of the Andean Community, signed on 28 May 1996, entered into force on 21 August 1999. Kingah and Molano-Cruz 2014.

[27] See Article 96(2) Andean Charter for the Promotion and Protection of Human Rights, signed on 26 July 2002. Apparently it still remains a legally non-binding instrument.

[28] See Article 2 Asunción Protocol to the Treaty Establishing a Common Market on the Commitment to the Promotion and Protection of Human Rights of MERCOSUR, signed on 20 June 2005, entered into force on 3 April 2010, 2897 *UNTS* 105.

[29] See also International Law Commission 2024, p. 34 note 85.

[30] The CJEU controls compliance with the EU Charter of Fundamental Freedoms, which was solemnly proclaimed in 2000 and, after being amended, it was proclaimed again in 2007; see *e.g.*, CJEU, Cases C-8/15 P to C-10/15 P, *Ledra Advertising Ltd and Others v European Commission and European Central Bank (ECB)*, Judgment, 20 September 2016, EU:C:2016:701.

[31] The EFTA Court has on several occasions cited both ECHR provisions and ECtHR case law: EFTA Court 2024; Helmersen 2021.

States (ECOWAS),[32] the Tribunal of the Southern Africa Development Community (SADC),[33] the Court of Justice of the East African Community (EAC),[34] the Court of Justice of the Common Market for Eastern and Southern Africa (COMESA),[35] and the Caribbean Court of Justice.[36]

Two observations should be made. The first concerns the changing type of the international organisations featuring courts of justice having a human rights jurisdiction and/or dimension. Originally, they were of a primarily political—diplomatic remit but, later on, it was the so-called 'regional integration organisations' (RIOs) and, specifically, the 'regional economic integration organisations' (REIOs). Indeed, all international organisations mentioned in the previous paragraph are RIOs, and most of them are REIOs (which in the African parlance are known as 'Regional Economic Communities' (RECs)).

The second observation is that the establishment of new international courts of justice has led to a situation where, in the same region, there might be more than one judicial organ / court of justice with the authority or the capacity to rule on alleged human rights violations. In theory, the more courts are able to rule on human rights violations, the more protection is afforded to the population of the respective region,

---

32 Established under Article 15 ECOWAS Revised Treaty, adopted on 24 July 1993, entered into force on 23 August 1995, 2373 *UNTS* 233, and Protocol A/P.l/7/91 on the Community Court of Justice, adopted on 6 July 1991. See, *e.g.*, Application No. ECW/CCJ/APP/47/23, *Oluwatimilehin Adebayo v. Federal Republic of Nigeria*, Judgment, 3 December 2024 (Court affirmed its jurisdiction to hear human rights cases); Application No. ECW/CCJ/APP/03/24, *Shalimar Abbiusi v. The Republic of Ghana*, Judgment, 22 November 2024 (applicant's right to liberty under Article 6 ACharterHPR was violated, Court awarded USD 10,000 compensation as reparation); Nyinevi and Nketiah 2023.

33 Established under Articles 9 and 16 SADC Treaty, signed on 17 August 1992, entered into force on 30 September 1993, and Protocol on the Tribunal and Rules thereof, signed on 7 August 2000. Following its decision in the celebrated human rights case *Mike Campbell and Others v. Republic of Zimbabwe*, SADC (T) No. 2/2007, Judgment, 28 November 2008, the Tribunal's operation has effectively been suspended; Magliveras and Naldi 2021.

34 Established under Article 23 Treaty for the establishment of the East African Community, concluded on 30 November 1999, entered into force on 7 July 2000, 2144 UNTS 255. See, *e.g.*, EACJ First Instance Division, Reference No. 8 of 2011, *Professor Nyamoya Francois v. Attorney General of the Republic of Burundi & Secretary General of the EAC*, Judgment, 28 February 2014 (the 'mere inclusion of allegations of human rights violations' in an application will not prevent the Court from exercising its authority to interpret the EAC Treaty). Note that the rule of law, natural justice and transparency are firmly embedded in the Court's jurisprudence, EACJ First Instance Division, Application No. 25 of 2022, *Mike Sonko Gideon Kioko Mbuvi v. The Attorney General of the Republic of Kenya*, Judgment, 28 November 2024.

35 Established under Article 7 COMESA Treaty, adopted on 5 November 1993, entered into force on 8 December 1994, 2314 *UNTS* 265. So far, there has been no case involving the alleged violation of human rights.

36 See Agreement Establishing the Caribbean Court of Justice, adopted on 14 February 2001, entered into force on 23 July 2003, 2255 *UNTS* 319. It is a hybrid judicial institution: a municipal court of last resort for Caribbean States and an international court with compulsory and exclusive jurisdiction to rule on the interpretation and application of the Revised Treaty of Chaguaramas Establishing the Caribbean Community, adopted on 5 July 2001, entered into force on 4 February 2002, 2259 *UNTS* 293. Anderson 2011.

assuming of course that all relevant states have accepted the compulsory jurisdiction of the respective courts. To put this observation into context, if the ArabCtHR were ratified by all LAS Member States, those ten members, which are located in Africa, will be under the jurisdiction of both the ArabCtHR and the ACtHPR. And there is also the possibility that specific African LAS members could come under the jurisdiction of other regional courts as well; for example Egypt, Comoros and Djibouti under the COMESA Court of Justice, and Somalia under the EAC Court of Justice. Such potential overlapping jurisdiction arguably raises several questions, including the primacy among the various regional and sub-regional courts, the delivery of conflicting judgments and whether respondent States are obliged to follow them, and *forum shopping*.[37] As regards the ArabCtHR, its Statute has envisaged this possibility: Article 18 disallows the Court to hear a case that has the same subject matter as another case which has been filed before another regional human rights Court. This formulation, however, leaves open the question whether the ArabCtHR could entertain a case having the same subject matter as an application submitted to and examined by one of the UN treaty bodies.

There is also the prospect that, in the foreseeable future, the EU will accede to the ECHR,[38] even though the EU will not participate as a member of the Council of Europe (as all other contracting parties do).[39] However, it should be noted that the CJEU has interpreted EU law not to allow conferring exclusive jurisdiction for the judicial review of EU acts, including in the light of fundamental rights, to an international court, which is not part of the EU's institutional and judicial framework.[40] While this interpretation is not conducive to the EU's accession to the ECHR, there is nothing extraordinary about it. After all, Article 62 of the original ECHR (now Article 55) compels parties, except by special agreement, not to avail themselves of treaties for the purpose of submitting disputes concerning the ECHR's interpretation or application to a means of settlement other than those provided for in the ECHR.

As regards the Americas, the potential co-existence of jurisdiction between the IACtHR and a subsequently created regional court of justice has been addressed. The case in point is the Central American Court of Justice (CACJ), which was established in the early 1990s in the context of the Central American Integration System (SICA);[41] it should not be confused with the namesake Court that functioned in the beginning of the twentieth century.[42] Article 25 of the Convention on the CACJ Statute provides that 'The Court's competence does not include jurisdiction over human rights matters, which belongs exclusively to the Inter-American Court of

[37] Generally, see Akhavan 2019; Lixinski 2008.

[38] See Article 59(2) ECHR; Article 6(2) TEU. See further Council of Europe Steering Committee for Human Rights 2023.

[39] Article 59(1) ECHR.

[40] CJEU, *Opinion 2/13*, 18 December 2014, ECLI:EU:C:2014:2454, para. 256, confirming CJEU, *Opinion 1/09*, 8 March 2011, EU:C:2011:123, paras 78, 80 and 89.

[41] See Article 12 of the Protocol of Tegucigalpa to the Charter of the Organization of Central American States (ODECA), signed on 13 December 1991, entered into force on 1 February 1993, 1695 *UNTS* 382.

[42] Caserta and Madsen 2022.

Human Rights'.[43] It follows that the CACJ will not entertain applications involving human rights violations allegedly committed by SICA Member States, if the latter are contracting parties to the ACHR and have also accepted the IACtHR's contentious jurisdiction.[44]

But reference should also be made to the Caribbean Court of Justice (CCJ), because litigation before it could involve important human rights issues. Thus, in *Attorney General and Others v Joseph and Boyce*, the Court of Appeal of Barbados confirmed the mandatory sentence of death by hanging imposed on the defendants,[45] who later petitioned for commutation of the death sentences and, in 2004, applied to the IACommHR seeking declarations that their rights under the ACHR had been violated. A particular problem was that, while Barbados, a common law jurisdiction, had ratified the ACHR in 1982, it had not promulgated the legislation necessary to incorporate it into domestic law. The CCJ held that, although citizens of Barbados derived no rights under treaties concluded between States, the promotion of universal standards of human rights showed a tendency towards a confluence of domestic and international rules, which could give rise to certain legitimate expectations. Thus, the CCJ clarified that the intersection of international treaties with national law could result in according human rights to citizens.[46] In the present case, the application of the principle of legitimate expectations effectively meant that Barbados could not have proceeded with the execution of the two men without the proceedings before the IACommHR having been completed.

The aftermath of the case is also of significance because it shows how a regional human rights system endowed with a court of justice could rectify problematic situations and bring about changes in domestic legislation. In particular, on 17 September 2004, the IACommHR submitted to the IACtHR a request for the adoption of provisional measures[47] so that Barbados take all necessary actions to preserve the lives of the two sentenced men (it referred to them as 'alleged victims') because otherwise the processing of their cases before the Inter-American system would be hindered. On the same day, the IACtHR President issued an Order requiring Barbados to adopt the same; Barbados never informed the Court on the measures adopted. On 28 February 2006, the IACommHR issued Report No. 03/06 on the admissibility and merits of the applications, and addressed certain recommendations to Barbados. As these were not adopted, in June 2006 the Commission submitted the case to the IACtHR.[48] In

---

[43] Concluded on 10 December 1992, entered into force on 2 February 1994, 1821 *UNTS* 292.

[44] CACJ, *Ricardo Duarte Moncada v. Gobierno de Nicaragua, Alcaldía de Managua y Banco Centroamericano de Integración Económica*, resolución N° 1–1–1-95, 13 January 1995, Gaceta Oficial Corte Centroamericana de Justicia, N° 1, 1 June 1995, p. 27. But see Nyman Metcalf and Papageorgiou 2005, p. 63 (suggesting that the Court may interpret relevant treaties on a case-by-case basis and, consequently, these could include the ACHR as well).

[45] See Section 2 of Barbados' Offences Against the Person Act of 1994.

[46] CCJ, Appeal No CV 2 of 2005; BB Civil appeal No 29 of 2004, *Attorney General and Superintendent of Prisons and Chief Marshal v. Jeffrey Joseph and Lennox Ricardo Boyce*, Judgment, 8 November 2006.

[47] See Chap. 7.

[48] Inter-American Commission on Human Rights 2007.

November 2007, the Court unanimously concluded that Barbados was in breach of Articles 4(1) and 4(2) ACHR (right to life) in conjunction with Article 1(1) thereof (contracting parties' obligation to respect the rights and freedoms recognised herein) and ordered Barbados, within a reasonable time, to ensure that its Constitution and laws are brought into compliance with the ACHR.[49] According to the Court, the mandatory death sentence imposed on those convicted of murder in Barbados violates the ACHR protected right to life as it is arbitrary and disregards the obligation to restrict the death penalty's application to the most serious crimes.

A year later, the IACommHR brought another case before the IACtHR, which also concerned the imposition of mandatory death sentence in Barbados. The case is noteworthy because Barbados complied with the aforementioned CCJ judgment on the principle of legitimate expectations and its consequences. In particular, Barbados informed the Commission that warrants of execution had not been issued because, according to *Attorney General v. Joseph and Boyce*, 'no warrant of execution can be issued while either the [Commission or the Court] is processing the petition .... the doctrine of legitimate expectations provide an individual the right to conclude his petition before the [Commission]'.[50] In the present case, the IACtHR found Barbados to be again in breach of its obligations under the ACHR.[51]

11.3 The Value of the Regional Human Rights Courts' Judgments as Evidence of Violation of Membership Obligations in the Respective International Organisation

As mentioned, the four regional human rights Courts should be regarded as international courts of justice, albeit with a specialised jurisdiction. Even though they were established in the context of international organizations, they are not the legal organs / judicial dispute settlement mechanisms of the corresponding four international organisations. Moreover, the fact that their operation is financed by these organisations[52] does not necessarily make them their organs and they may very well remain

[49] IACtHR, *Boyce* et al. *v. Barbados*, Judgment (Preliminary Objection, Merits, Reparations and Costs), 30 November 2007, Series C No. 169; Coveney 2014.

[50] Application of the Inter-American Commission on Human Rights Before the Inter-American Court of Human Rights, Case 12,645, *Tyrone Dacosta Cadogan v. Barbados*, 31 October 2008, para. 19.

[51] IACtHR, *Dacosta-Cadogan v. Barbados*, Judgment (Preliminary Objections, Merits, Reparations, and Costs), 24 September 2009, Series C No. 204.

[52] See Article 50 ECHR, Article 26 IACtHR Statute. For the approval of the ACtHPR's budget for the year 2025, see AU Executive Council 'Decision on the Reports of the Sub-committees of the Permanent Representatives Committee (PRC)', AU Doc. EX.CL/Dec.1265(XLV), 19 July 2024, paras 4–5.

outside the formal institutional architecture.[53] Notwithstanding these considerations, it should not escape one's attention that these courts are effectively authorised to rule on the acts, omissions and the behaviour of Member States, to record their violations of human rights and demand that measures are taken to rectify the breaches of fundamental freedoms committed by them, to award compensation to the victims, etc. The protected rights and freedoms are either those laid down in the multilateral treaty that established the respective Court (the case of the ECtHR[54]) or those set out in said treaty as well as in other relevant agreements ratified by litigant parties, the latter being principally those concluded under the aegis of the international organisation in question and the UN (the case of the ACtHPR[55]).[56]

It is also interesting to note that of these four organisations only the AU has a judicial organ (the African Court of Justice), which, however, has never been operationalised.[57] Seen from another perspective, the judgments of the three human rights Courts in operation are effectively determinations on whether Member States observe or violate their duties and obligations flowing from the constitutive instruments of the respective IOs pertaining to fundamental freedoms. More specifically, these flow from Article 3 CoE Statute, Articles 3(l), 17 and 45 OAS Charter, and Articles 3(i), 4(m) and 4(o) AU Constitutive Act. It follows that the corpus of the judgments given by a human rights court against State A or State B could also serve as evidence of violation of membership obligations. However, to the best of one's knowledge, this connection has not yet been made by the highest ranking organs of the respective organisations. This might change in the future, if the four organisations at play were to consider that the continued participation of a Member State with an abysmal human rights record, as shown by the number of convictions issued by the Court in question, is untenable.

[53] Cf. IACtHR Statute Article 1 ('...an autonomous judicial institution') and Article 27(2) ('... relations ...with the OAS shall be governed through special agreements').

[54] Articles 19 and 32(1) ECHR.

[55] Article 3(1) ACtHPR Protocol. See also, Article 64(1) ACHR: '1. The member states of the [OAS] may consult [the IACtHR] regarding the interpretation of ... other treaties concerning the protection of human rights in the American states'.

[56] See Chap. 4.

[57] Magliveras and Naldi 2024, p. 190.

11.4 The Regional Human Rights Courts, Criminal Jurisdiction, the International Criminal Court and the African Experiment in Combining Human Rights and International Crimes

The regional human rights Courts should not be regarded as courts of criminal jurisdiction, even though on many occasions the breach of the human rights treaties over which each Court exercises jurisdiction would constitute the commission of a criminal offence under domestic law.[58] For example, to subject someone to torture or to cruel treatment, etc.[59] would be treated as the perpetration of the criminal offence of grievous bodily harm, including psychiatric injury. Moreover, if such a breach were to constitute a violation of peremptory norms of international law as well (e.g. through the alleged commission of war crimes or crimes against humanity), there would be an obvious rapport between the regional Courts and the International Criminal Court (ICC). Even though the ICC is not a human rights court and was not devised as one, it does share with the regional Courts a very significant task, namely to fight impunity at an international level.[60]

Notwithstanding this proximity in their roles, it should not go unnoticed that, unlike the ICC, the complaints before the regional Courts may not be brought against natural persons, even if the individual who is alleged to have perpetrated the human rights violations happens to be a head of State, in other words the person who is the personification of that State's sovereignty in the global community. This is explained by the fact that a respondent State is not only responsible to secure to everyone within its jurisdiction all protected rights and freedoms[61] but is also accountable and answerable for all human rights breaches committed by anyone (whether natural persons or legal persons) within its territory.[62] On the contrary, the defendants before the ICC cannot be States but only individuals.[63] Moreover, the ICC cannot 'punish' States even when the defendant head of State is found to have deliberately perpetrated war crimes, crimes against humanity, etc.[64] by employing the State apparatus to pursue State interests and goals.

Of course, any regional international organisation may decide to establish its own criminal justice tribunal to try the most serious crimes of concern to the global community, irrespective of whether a human rights court is already in operation. And while the ICC was created 'for the sake of present and future generations' as the independent permanent judicial organ to put an end to impunity and to act when States

[58] Generally, see Huneeus 2013; Grover 2010.

[59] See Article 3 ECHR, Article 5(2) ACHR, Article 5 AfricanCHPR, Article 8(1) ArabCHR.

[60] Kaul 2011.

[61] See Article 1 ECHR, Article 1 ACHR, Article 1 AfricanCHPR, Article 3 ArabCHR.

[62] Meron 1991, pp. 136 *et seq.*

[63] See Article 1 Rome Statute of the International Criminal Court, adopted on 17 July 1998, entered into force on 1 July 2002, 2187 *UNTS* 3; presently there are 125 contracting parties.

[64] *Ibid.*, Article 5.

do not exercise their criminal jurisdiction over those responsible for international crimes,[65] a regional international organisation might still want to supplement its human rights court with a judicial organ that would be competent to try the alleged perpetration of international crimes. Indeed, the parallel existence of these two organs was decided by the AU Member States in 2014, when they approved a protocol on amendments (the so-called 'Malabo Protocol') to the Protocol on the Statute of the African Court of Justice and Human Rights.[66] The Malabo Protocol attached to the African Court of Justice and Human Rights (the judicial organ, which was established in 2008 by the merger of the African Court of Justice and the ACtHPR, but has yet to operate)[67] a so-called 'International Criminal Law (ICL) Section'. The latter has been endowed with the jurisdiction to prosecute and try individuals (but not states) for allegedly perpetrating the fourteen international crimes mentioned in the Malabo Protocol, in other words akin to a regional ICC with expanded jurisdiction *ratione materiae*.[68]

The creation of the ICL Section was mostly a reaction to the AU' disillusion with the work of the ICC.[69] It is, however, regrettable that the project of having a human rights court and a court of criminal jurisdiction operating in the context of the same regional organisation has been largely abandoned, not least on account of the following two reasons. First, it would have transformed the model of the regional human rights court. Second, and more importantly, it would have developed the model of a regional organisation's judicial organ with expansive competence to rule on alleged infractions relating to the organisation's internal legal order,[70] to human rights as well as to transnational crimes. Angola was the first Member State to submit an instrument of ratification of the Malabo Protocol;[71] fourteen more are required to enter into force.

11.5 Interactions: The Exchanges and Influences Between the Regional Human Rights Courts

Until now, the regional human rights systems have broadly followed the Council of Europe model, as was originally conceived, namely a multilateral treaty having a substantive law section (listing all protected rights and freedoms as well as all prohibited acts) and a procedural / institutional section (establishing a human rights

---

[65] *Ibid.*, Preamble.

[66] See Assembly of Heads of State and Government, 'Decision on the Draft Legal Instruments', AU Doc. Assembly/AU/Dec. 529 (XXIII), 27 June 2014.

[67] Due to the lack of the required number of ratifications of the Protocol on the Statute of the African Court of Justice and Human Rights, adopted on 1 July 2008; Naldi and Magliveras 2012.

[68] Generally, see Magliveras 2017.

[69] Naldi and Magliveras 2015.

[70] Generally, see Amao et al. 2021.

[71] On 31 May 2024; De Silva and Amadi 2024.

commission and a human rights court of justice).[72] To that extent, these systems and, in particular, the regional Courts they have created are bound to have more aspects in common than not. One does not expect that they will be identical: each region has its own origins, history, priorities and preoccupations, and has developed differently. Therefore, these factors cannot but be reflected and taken into consideration in the respective treaties. As regards the substantive law, one is familiar with the *fiat* from the 1993 Vienna Declaration that while 'all human rights are universal, indivisible and interdependent and interrelated' and must be treated 'in a fair and equal manner, on the same footing', there are 'national and regional particularities and various historical, cultural and religious backgrounds [which] must be borne in mind' but the latter may not affect the promotion and protection of human rights, even if the 'political, economic and cultural systems' of States are taken into account.[73]

It follows that the regional Courts rule on basically the same rights, freedoms and prohibited acts. Therefore, they are bound to be interested in developments taking place in the other Courts or they may cite their judgments to give more authority or credence to their own decisions or, when confronted with complicated issues, to look into how the bench of another Court addressed it and dealt with it, etc.[74] Thus, over the years, a kind of dialogue has been formed between the three Courts, primarily though their judgments. The term 'transjudicial communication' has been used in the literature.[75] However, it has been argued that, in the case of the IACtHR, the adaptation of precedents from outside the Americas might have been done at the expense of insufficiently considering the views and opinions of contracting parties.[76]

The following two examples from ACtHPR case law show the tendency to cite and take into consideration the jurisprudence of other Courts.[77] More specifically, in *Rashidi v Tanzania*,[78] with respect to body searches that bear on the intimacy of the individual, it cited an ECtHR decision[79] and, when argued that restitution is a remedy applicable where other measures such as compensation are not relevant or sufficient, it cited decisions by three regional Courts: the IACtHR,[80] the ECtHR,[81] and the ECOWAS Community Court of Justice.[82] And in *Nganyi v. Tanzania*, during

72 Generally, see Gros Espiell 1989.

73 World Conference on Human Rights, Vienna Declaration and Programme of Action, A/CONF.157/23, 12 July 1993, para. 5.

74 Generally, see Bertoni 2009.

75 Voeten 2009.

76 Neuman 2008. See also Chap. 8.

77 For the ECtHR, see Nußberger 2017.

78 ACtHPR, Application No. 009/2015, *Lucien Ikili Rashidi v United Republic of Tanzania*, Judgment, 28 March 2019.

79 ECtHR, Application No. 51246/08, *El Shennawy v. France*, Judgment (Merits), 20 January 2011.

80 IACtHR, *María Elena Loayza-Tamayo v. Peru*, Judgment (Reparations and Costs), 27 November 1998, Series C No 53.

81 ECtHR, Application No. 14556/89, *Papamichalopoulos and Others v Greece*, Judgment (Article 50), 31 October 1995.

82 ECOWAS Community Court of Justice, Application No. ECW/CCJ/APP/20/13, *Mohammed El Tayyib Bah v. Republic of Sierra Leone*, Judgment No. ECW/CCJ/JUD/11/15, 4 May 2015.

proceedings on reparation, the ACtHPR justified its conclusion that claimants could substitute the deceased applicants as the legal representatives of their beneficiaries on the ground that this was the 'accepted practice in international human rights proceedings'; as proof it referred to the relevant ECtHR practice.[83] And, later on, it cited an IACtHR case as example of systemic violations of human rights.[84] Finally, an interesting case of cross-citations between the ECtHR and the IACtHR has been recorded. More specifically, in 2010, the ECtHR cited an IACtHR judgment delivered in 2003, which had concluded that 'a threat to torture can amount to torture', while IACtHR judgments given in 2000 and in 2004 had cited an ECtHR judgment on the threat of torture delivered in 1982.[85]

Over and above these rather indirect forms of communication,[86] for several years now, the three regional human rights Courts have been meeting at regular intervals. More specifically, in 2018 they adopted the San José Declaration and established a so-called 'Permanent Forum of Institutional Dialogue'. The occasion was the fortieth anniversary of the ACHR's entry into force and the creation of the IACtHR.[87] The stated aims of the Permanent Forum are to carry out common work towards strengthening the protection of human rights, increasing the access of the people under the Courts' jurisdiction to international justice, contributing to State efforts to strengthen democratic institutions and human rights protective mechanisms, and overcoming the common challenges and threats that affect the validity of human rights.[88]

The Permanent Forum was operationalised the following year when the three Courts signed a Memorandum of Understanding (MoU) to that effect.[89] It was further agreed that it should meet biennially in private and public sessions on a rotational basis and, where necessary, it should involve other regional and global human rights stakeholders. Moreover, that knowledge-sharing should be undertaken on 'topical human rights issues'; the following were mentioned: migration, violence against women, environmental hazards, climate change, bioethics, terrorism, and mass data surveillance. It was also resolved to enhance the dialogue with national courts of justice and to share jurisprudence with them. To that extent, it is interesting that they decided to publish annually an electronic report to cover their leading judgments and

---

[83] ACtHPR, Application No. 006/2013, *Wilfred Onyango Nganyi and 9 Others v. United Republic of Tanzania*, Judgment (Reparations), 4 July 2019, para. 18.

[84] *Ibid.*, para. 81 citing IACtHR, Case of the 'Street Children' *Villagrán-Morales* et al. *v. Guatemala*, Judgment (Reparations and Costs), 26 May 2001, Series C No. 77.

[85] Nilsson 2023, pp. 270–271.

[86] Šipulová 2025 (claiming the existence of a 'judicial alliance' that runs within the regional (human rights) Courts as a form of resistance and deference to political actors (the IACtHR, the ECtHR and the CJEU are mentioned), but giving no further details).

[87] Inter-American Court of Human Rights 2020.

[88] Declaration of San José, 18 July 2018, at: https://www.echr.coe.int/documents/d/echr/San_Jose_Declaration_2018_ENG. Accessed 7 April 2025.

[89] See Kampala Declaration, The African Court on Human and Peoples' Rights, the European Court of Human Rights and the Inter-American Court of Human Rights, at the First International Human Rights Forum, 28 to 29 October 2019, at: https://www.echr.coe.int/documents/d/echr/Kampala_Declaration_ENG. Accessed 7 April 2025.

to offer commentaries. It has been called the 'Joint Law Report' and, so far, there have been three volumes published.[90]

The third meeting of the Permanent Forum took place in San José on 25–26 May 2023. It culminated in the signing of the (second) San José Declaration, which extended the Kampala MoU for a period of six years and resolved that the ACtHPR will host the fourth meeting in the course of 2025.[91] The following extract from the Declaration's Preamble not only reveals the close links developed between the three Courts but also confirms their (indirect) discourse through their judgments:

> [t]aking into account the historical context of institutional and jurisprudential dialogue, the prior collaborative work and joint efforts among the African Court on Human and Peoples' Rights, the European Court of Human Rights, and the Inter-American Court of Human Rights, which have facilitated the exchange of conceptual and jurisprudential standards from each court for the mutual benefit of their respective systems [...].

11.6 The Case for a Global Human Rights Court of Justice

All three regional Courts have made it clear that they are not and should not be regarded as appellate bodies for the judgments given by the respondent States' domestic courts of justice, including constitutional courts. On the contrary, their jurisdiction and mandate in applications lodged by individuals is principally to ascertain whether domestic courts have complied with the applicable human rights standards,[92] and to draw the consequences for respondent States in cases of non-compliance. As is expressly stated in Article 18 ArabCtHR Statute, 'The jurisdiction of the Court is complementary to the national judiciary and does not supplant it'. But a very fine balance must be maintained: if a regional Court were to find that the domestic court of final resort has erred in the terms of the human rights treaty/ies binding upon the respondent State, the domestic court's judgment is effectively nullified (to the extent that it violated protected rights and freedoms). The strict requirement of the exhaustion of all domestic judicial remedies that is laid down in the constitutive instruments of the four regional Courts[93] means that, in the ordinary course of things, the 'offending' instrument and the reason for the complaint to the human rights Court is a domestic judgment, which was issued by a domestic court and which, inadvertently, on purpose, or out of ignorance, has failed to give effect to the complainant's protected rights.

This rapport between the legal orders of contracting parties and the role and powers of the regional human rights Courts might be quite different in the case of the

---

[90] The third volume was published in November 2023 and concerns the year 2021, at: https://www.african-court.org/wpafc/joint-law-report-african-court-european-court-inter-american-court-volume-3-2021/. Accessed 7 April 2025.

[91] At: https://prd-echr.coe.int/documents/d/echr/san_jose_declaration_2023_eng. Accessed 7 April 2025.

[92] See, *e.g.*, ACtHPR, Application No. 012/2018, *Glory Cyriaque Hossou v. Republic of Benin*, Judgment, 13 November 2024, para. 23.

[93] See Chap. 5.

judicial organs of regional international organisations, especially those belonging to the category of REIOs, reference to which was made *supra,* when adjudicating cases with a human rights dimension. Notwithstanding that it is beyond the scope of the present volume to discuss the dynamics and the consequences of this type of human rights litigation, the fact remains that there is presently a large number of universal, regional and sub-regional courts, judicial organs and bodies as well as *quasi*-judicial mechanisms, which are able to make pronouncements on whether states follow or not their human rights obligations.

This reality raises the possibility of having a global human rights court established at some future point. The idea is certainly not a novel one; it was already put forward at the time the UDHR was being negotiated, while the contemporaneous the Genocide Convention referred to an (hypothetical) 'international penal tribunal' which could have jurisdiction over those parties willing to accept its jurisdiction as an alternative to alleged perpetrators being tried by a competent domestic court.[94] In the 2000s and 2010s it was revived,[95] even the text of a court statute has been proposed.[96] Arguably, the premise of these proposals has been to attach such a world human rights court to the UN. Moreover, the proposals have also been sometimes associated with overhauling the UN treaty body system[97] and consolidating the UN core human rights treaties.[98]

One could understand why the project of a global human rights court has been associated so closely with the UN: having succeeded in remaining until the present day the only global political international organisation, with no competition from any other multilateral organisation and with vast experience and knowledge on multiparty negotiations and treaty drafting, the UN appears to be the only logical forum to initiate such a project. Moreover, as explained *supra*, all aspects of human rights have always been advanced in the context of international organisations. It is submitted that, if the project of a universal human rights court ever attracts the necessary momentum in the international community to be regarded as viable and not only as an academic exercise, it should be disassociated from the UN, not least for the following reason. The UN has for very long been politicized. Often, deliberations follow the pattern of solely supporting friendly nations and opposing every other nation, without examining or caring for the proposal's merits. The UN Assembly, the organ that would take under its wings a global human rights court's project, is dominated by all sorts of Member States' groups and blocs.[99] As was observed already in the mid-1980s, 'the blocs have been the happy hunting grounds, as it were, of the most radical factions in the United Nations'.[100] To put it otherwise, a group

[94] Article VI Convention on the Prevention and Punishment of the Crime of Genocide, approved on 9 December 1948, entered into force on 12 January 1951, 78 *UNTS* 277.

[95] *E.g.* Trechsel 2003; Kirkpatrick 2014.

[96] Kozma et al. 2010; elaborated in Nowak 2018.

[97] Generally, see Gaer 2018.

[98] Generally, see Magliveras 2020.

[99] Generally, see Smith 2006; Mingst et al. 2022, p. 81.

[100] Kirkpatrick 1984, p. 367.

of countries would be prepared to go for or against a proposal only because another group has asked it, regardless of the proposal's qualities.

Therefore, provided there is consensus that this project is of value, it might stand a much better chance of success if it were disassociated from the work of an(y) international organisation. It might be better if like-minded countries, able and willing to deliver a judicial organ, pursued a project pertaining to the institutional aspects of human rights protection, which, in time, would achieve repute and be trusted by an increasing number of States, and hopefully by those not under the jurisdiction of a regional human rights Court. Or it could be perceived as an alternative human rights judicial forum and become direct competitors with the existing Courts, attracting (or not) contracting parties from the treaties establishing the regional human rights Courts. Gradually, it could become a highly regarded trustworthy organ, which should open the way to reach the level of universality.

Moreover, if for the sake of argument, future treaties and conventions on fundamental freedoms, irrespective of whether they were sub-regional or regional or trans-regional, were concluded outside the confines of international organisations, they could very well contain a compromissory clause giving to the judicial organ in question the power and the jurisdiction to adjudicate human rights cases. The example of the ever increasing number of cases before the ICJ, which are based on compromissory clauses in its favour,[101] is a development of significance that should be evaluated in securing an even better protection of rights and freedoms. The emphasis here is to abandon the present understanding that all aspects of promoting, protecting and safeguarding fundamental rights must emanate from the UN and/or from some regional international organisation and to propose a different model that could accommodate inter-regional human rights treaties entrusting the supervision of the obligations to a 'world human rights court'.

On the other hand, why should States, which already accept the jurisdiction of a regional court, be prepared to join another, if not identical, essentially very similar, human rights court? Could one argue that the more courts (even with overlapping jurisdiction) exist, the better? Moreover, how expansive will such a world court's substantive law be (e.g. will it include a right to a healthy environment and/or a right to (drinkable) water?); which will be its powers of having judgments enforced, and how will instances of non-compliance be addressed? Will the respondent parties be only States? Or States and individuals? Possibly, legal persons and companies as well? And there are of course many other crucial points to be addressed. Even though there are no questions to which skilled jurists cannot give a satisfactory reply,[102] only

[101] See *e.g.* from pending cases, ICJ, *Application of the Convention against Torture and Other Cruel, Inhuman or Degrading Treatment or Punishment* (*Canada and the Netherlands v. Syrian Arab Republic*) instituted on 8 June 2023; *Application of the Convention on the Prevention and Punishment of the Crime of Genocide in the Gaza Strip* (*South Africa v. Israel*), instituted on 29 December 2023; *Alleged Breaches of Certain International Obligations in respect of the Occupied Palestinian Territory* (*Nicaragua v. Germany*) instituted on 1 March 2024.

[102] Cf. ICJ, *Armed Activities on the Territory of the Congo* (New Application: 2002) *(Democratic Republic of the Congo v. Rwanda*), Judgment (Jurisdiction and Admissibility) I.C.J. Reports 2006, p. 6, Joint Separate Opinion of Judges Higgins, Kooijmans, Elaraby, Owada and Simma, paras

States can deal with grand schemes that involve crucial matters of policy. Given the current state of affairs in the international community, it is unlikely that States will embark on such a world court any time soon or at all. However, the discussion should be kept alive and not be abandoned.

References

Akhavan P (2019) Forum Shopping and Human Rights: Staring at the Empty Shelves. In: Scheinin M (ed) Human Rights Norms in 'Other' International Courts. Cambridge University Press, Cambridge, pp. 412-437.

Amao O, Olivier M, Magliveras K (eds) (2021) The Emergent African Union Law - Conceptualization, Delimitation, and Application. Oxford University Press, Oxford.

Anderson W (2011) The Role of the Caribbean Court of Justice in Human Rights Adjudication: International Treaty Law Dimensions. Annual Lillich Memorial Lecture at Florida State University, 14 March 2011. Available at: https://ccj.org/wp-content/uploads/2021/03/Remarks-by-the-Honourable-Mr-Justice-Winston-Anderson-at-the-Annual-Lillich-Memorial-Lecture-at-Florida-State-University_20110314.pdf. Accessed 31 January 2025.

Bantekas I, Oette L (2024) International Human Rights Law and Practice. Cambridge University Press, Cambridge.

Bertoni EA (2009) The Inter-American Court of Human Rights and the European Court of Human Rights: A Dialogue on Freedom of Expression Standards. European Human Rights Law Review 332-352.

Burgorgue-Larsen L (2024) The 3 Regional Human Rights Courts in Context: Justice That Cannot Be Taken for Granted. Oxford University Press, Oxford.

Caserta S, Madsen MR (2022) The World's Most Powerful International Court? The Central American Court of Justice and the Quest for De Facto Authority (1907-2020). American University International Law Review 37:483-549.

Council of Europe (1977) First Session of the Constitutional Assembly of the Council of Europe (August–September 1949), Plenary Setting of 17 August 1949, Motion (proposed by Mr Ruini and other representatives) in Council of Europe, Preparatory work on Article 1 of the European Convention on Hyman Rights, Strasbourg le 31 mars 1977, Cour (77) 9.

Council of Europe Steering Committee for Human Rights (2023) Interim Report to the Committee of Ministers, for information, on the negotiations on the accession of the European Union to the European Convention on Human Rights, including the revised draft accession instruments in appendix. CDDH(2023)R_EXTRA ADDENDUM, 4 April 2023.

Coveney C (2014) Boyce et al. v. Barbados. Loyola of Los Angeles International and Comparative Law Review 36:1029-1047.

De Silva N, Amadi M (2024) The Malabo Protocol's 10th Anniversary Revives Advocacy for an African Criminal Court. EJIL:Talk!, December 25, 2024. Available at: https://www.ejiltalk.org/the-malabo-protocols-10th-anniversary-revives-advocacy-for-an-african-criminal-court/. Accessed 31 January 2025.

EFTA Court (ed) (2024) The EFTA Court: Developing the EEA over Three Decades. Hart Publishing, Oxford.

Gaer FD (2018) The Institutional Future of the Covenants: A World Court for Human Rights? In: Moeckli D, Keller H (eds) The Human Rights Covenants at 50: Their Past, Present, and Future. Oxford University Press, Oxford, pp. 334-356.

22–23: the development of the law by the human rights courts does not create a 'schism' between general international law but should be seen as the way that they develop the law so as to meet contemporary realities.

Galand AS (2023) Defer or Revise? Horizontal Dialogue Between UN Treaty Bodies and Regional Human Rights Courts in Duplicative Legal Proceedings. Human Rights Law Review 23(2), https://doi.org/10.1093/hrlr/ngad009. Accessed 31 January 2025.

Gros Espiell H (1989) La Convention Américaine et la Convention Européenne des Droits de l'Homme. Analyse Comparative. Recueil des Cours de l'Académie de Droit International, The Hague Vol. 218, p. 220.

Grover SC (2010) The European Court of Human Rights as a Pathway To Impunity for International Crimes. Springer, Cham.

Hampson F et al (2018) Inaccessible apexes: Comparing access to regional human rights courts and commissions in Europe, the Americas, and Africa. International Journal of Constitutional Law 16:161–186.

Helmersen ST (2021) The EFTA Court and International Law. Oslo Law Review 8(1): 30–46.

Huneeus A (2013) International Criminal Law by Other Means: The Quasi-criminal Jurisdiction of the Human Rights Courts. American Journal of International Law 107:1-44.

Huneeus A, Madsen MR (2018) Between universalism and regional law and politics: A comparative history of the American, European, and African human rights systems. International Journal of Constitutional Law 16:136–160.

Inter-American Commission on Human Rights (2007) Annual Report 2006. OEA/Ser.L/V/II.127, Doc. 4 rev. 1, 3 March 2007. Available at: https://cidh.oas.org/annualrep/2006eng/TOC.htm. Accessed 31 January 2025.

Inter-American Court of Human Rights (2020) Dialogue between Regional Human Rights Courts. Available at: https://www.corteidh.or.cr/sitios/libros/todos/docs/dialogo-en.pdf. Accessed 31 January 2025.

International Law Commission (2024) Report of the International Law Commission Seventy-fifth session (29 April–31 May and 1 July–2 August 2024). UN Doc. A/79/10.

Kaul P (2011) Human Rights and the International Criminal Court. Address at the international conference 'The Protection of Human Rights through the International Criminal Court as a Contribution to Constitutionalization and Nation—Building', 21 January 2011. Available at: https://www.icc-cpi.int/news/address-second-vice-president-judge-hans-peter-kaul-international-conference-protection-human. Accessed 31 January 2025.

Kingah S, Molano-Cruz G (2014) Addressing Human Rights in the Court of Justice of the Andean Community and the Tribunal of the Southern African Development Community. Colombia Internacional 81:99-127.

Kirkpatrick J (2014) A Modest Proposal: A Global Court of Human Rights. Journal of Human Rights 13:230–248.

Kirkpatrick JJ (1984) The United Nations as a Political System: A Practicing Political Scientist's Insights into U.N. Politics. World Affairs 146:358-368.

Kozma J, Nowak M, Scheinin M (2010) A World Court of Human Rights - Consolidated Draft Statute and Commentary, May 2010. Available at: https://www.eui.eu/documents/departmentscentres/law/professors/scheinin/consolidatedworldcourtstatute.pdf. Accessed 31 January 2025.

Lixinski L (2008) Choice of Forum in International Human Rights Adjudication and the Unity / Fragmentation Debate: Is Plurality the Way Ahead? 18 Italian Yearbook of International Law 18:183-200.

Magliveras K (2017) Substituting the International Criminal Justice for an African Criminal Justice? International Organizations Law Review 14:291-320.

Magliveras K (2020) The Case for a Comprehensive Global Human Rights Treaty under UN Auspices. In: Wouters J, Lemmens K, Van Poecke T, Bourguignon M (eds) Can We Still Afford Human Rights? - Critical Reflections on Universality, Costs and Proliferation. Edward Elgar Publishing, Cheltenham, pp. 47-68.

Magliveras K, Naldi G (2021) When Politics Prevail Over the Rule of Law: The Demise of the SADC Tribunal. International Human Rights Law Review 10:124-154.

Magliveras K, Naldi G (2024) The African Union (AU), 3rd edn. Wolters Kluwer, Alphen aan den Rijn.

McGregor L (2013) The Relationship of the UN Treaty Bodies and Regional Systems. In: Sheeran S, Rodley N (eds) Routledge Handbook of International Human Rights Law. Routledge, Abingdon, pp. 505-520.
Meron T (1991) Human Rights and Humanitarian Norms as Customary Law. Oxford University Press, Oxford.
Mingst KA, Karns MP, Lyon AJ (2022) The United Nations in the 21st Century, 6th edn. Routledge, Abingdon.
Naldi G, Magliveras K (2012) The African Court of Justice and Human Rights: A Judicial Curate's Egg. International Organizations Law Review 9:387-453.
Naldi G, Magliveras K (2014) The ASEAN Human Rights Declaration. International Human Rights Law Review 3:183-208.
Naldi G, Magliveras K (2015) The African Union's International Criminal Court: An Appraisal. African Yearbook of International Law 21:299-343.
Neuman GL (2008) Import, Export, and Regional Consent in the Inter-American Court of Human Rights. The European Journal of International Law 19:101-123.
Nilsson I (2023) On the Path to Universalism? The Role of External Instruments in the European Court of Human Rights Jurisprudence. Nordic Journal of International Law 92:248-282.
Nowak M (2018) A World Court of Human Rights. In: Oberleitner G (ed) International Human Rights Institutions, Tribunals, and Courts. Springer, Singapore. https://doi.org/10.1007/978-981-10-4516-5_10-1. Accessed 31 January 2025.
Nußberger A (2017) The ECtHR's Use of Decisions of International Courts and Quasi-Judicial Bodies. In: Müller A (ed) Judicial Dialogue and Human Rights. Studies on International Courts and Tribunals. Cambridge University Press, Cambridge, pp. 419-432.
Nyinevi C Nketiah A (2023) The Law and Politics of Access to the ECOWAS Court in Human Rights Cases. In: Fuentes A, Rudman A (eds) Human Rights Adjudication in Africa: Challenges and Opportunities within the African Union and Sub-Regional Human Rights Systems. Pretoria University Law Press, Pretoria, pp. 62-68.
Nyman Metcalf K, Papageorgiou I (2005) Regional Integration and Courts of Justice. Intersentia, Antwerp.
Paúl Á (2017) Los trabajos preparatorios de la Declaración Americana de los Derechos y Deberes del Hombre y el origen remoto de la Corte Interamericana, Universidad Nacional Autónoma de México. Available at: https://archivos.juridicas.unam.mx/www/bjv/libros/10/4660/17.pdf. Accessed 31 January 2025.
Quintana F-J (2024) The (Latin) American Dream? Human Rights and the Construction of Inter-American Regional Organisation (1945–1948). Journal of the History of International Law / Revue d'histoire du droit international 25:560–591.
Šipulová K (2025) The Light and the Dark Side of Judicial Resistance. Law & Policy 47(1). https://doi.org/10.1111/lapo.12247. Accessed 31 January 2025.
Smith CB (2006) Politics and Process at the United Nations: The Global Dance. Lynne Rienner Publishers, Boulder, CO.
Stapel S (2022) Regional Organizations and Democracy, Human Rights, and the Rule of Law: The African Union, Organization of American States, and the Diffusion of Institutions. Palgrave Macmillan, Cham.
Tomuschat C (2019) Article 36. In: Zimmermann A et al (eds) The Statute of the International Court of Justice: A Commentary, 3rd edn. Oxford University Press, Oxford, pp. 712–798.
Trechsel S (2003) World Court for Human Rights. Northwestern Journal of International Human Rights 1:1–19.
Voeten E (2009) Borrowing and Nonborrowing among International Courts. The Journal of Legal Studies 39:547-547.

Konstantinos D. Magliveras is professor of the law of international organisations and an attorney at law.

Table of Cases and Advisory Opinions

I. Regional Human Rights Courts

A. African Court of Human and Peoples' Rights

Actions pour la Protection des Droit de l'Homme (APDH) v Republic of *Côte* d'Ivoire, Judgment, 18 November 2016, Application No. 001/2014.

African Commission on Human and Peoples' Rights v. Great Socialist People's Libyan Arab Jamahiriya, Order (Provisional Measures), 25 March 2011, Application No. 004/2011.

African Commission on Human and Peoples' Rights v Republic of Kenya, Judgment (Merits), 26 May 2017, Application No. 006/2012.

African Commission on Human and Peoples' Rights v Republic of Kenya, Judgment (Reparations), 23 June 2022, Application No. 006/2012.

Akwasi Boateng & 351 Others v Republic of Ghana, Ruling (Jurisdiction), 27 November 2020, Application No. 059/2016.

Alex Thomas v United Republic of Tanzania, Judgment (Merits), 20 November 2015, Application No. 005/2013.

Ally Rajabu and Others v United Republic of Tanzania, Judgment (Merits and Reparations), 28 November 2019, Application No. 007/2015.

Amir Ramadhani v United Republic of Tanzania, Judgment (Reparations), 25 June 2021, Application No. 010/2015.

Anaclet Paulo v United Republic of Tanzania, Judgment (Merits and Reparations), 21 September 2018, Application No. 020/2016.

Andrew Ambrose Cheusi v United Republic of Tanzania, Judgment (Merits and Reparations), 26 June 2020, Application No. 004/2015.

Anudo Ochieng Anudo v United Republic of Tanzania, Judgment, 22 March 2018, Application No. 012/2015.

Association Juriste d'Afrique pour la Bonne Gouvernance v Republic of *Côte* d'Ivoire, Decision, 16 June 2011, Application No. 006/2011.

A. Almutawa and K. D. Magliveras (eds.), *A Comparison of the European, Inter-American, African and Arab Human Rights Courts: Institutional Aspects*, https://doi.org/10.1007/978-94-6265-695-6

Ataborg Denis Atemnkeng v The African Union, Judgment, 15 March 2013, Application No. 014/2011.

Ayadhi Fathi and Others v Republic of Tunisia, Ruling (Provisional Measures), 17 March 2023, Application No. 001/202.

Baedan Dogbo Paul & Another v Republic of *Côte* d'Ivoire, Judgment (Merits and Reparations), 5 September 2023, Application No. 019/2020.

Baghdadi Ali Mahmoudi v Republic of Tunisia, Judgment (Jurisdiction), 26 June 2012, Application No. 007/2012.

Benedicto Daniel Mallya v United Republic of Tanzania, Judgment, 26 September 2019, Application No. 018/2015.

Beneficiaries of late Norbert Zongo, Abdoulaye Nikiema alias Ablasse, Ernest Zongo and Blaise Ilboudo & the Burkinabe Human and Peoples' Rights Movement v Burkina Faso, Ruling (Preliminary Objections), 21 June 2013, Application No. 013/2011.

Beneficiaries of late Norbert Zongo, Abdoulaye Nikiema alias Ablasse, Ernest Zongo and Blaise Ilboudo & the Burkinabe Human and Peoples' Rights Movement v Burkina Faso, Judgment (Merits), 28 March 2014, Application No. 013/2011.

Collectif des Anciens Travailleurs du Laboratoire (ALS) v Republic of Mali, Ruling (Jurisdiction and Admissibility), 28 March 2019, Application No. 042/2016.

Crospery Gabriel & Another v United Republic of Tanzania, Judgment (Merits and Reparations), 13 February 2024, Application No. 050/2016.

Daniel Amare and Mulugeta Amare v Republic of Mozambique and Mozambique Airlines, Decision, 16 June 2011, Application No. 005/2011.

Delta International Investments SA, Mr. AGL de Lange and Mrs. M. de Lange v Republic of South Africa, Decision, 30 March 2012, Application No. 002/2012.

Dexter Eddie Johnson v Republic of Ghana, Ruling, 28 March 2019, Application No. 016/2017.

Dominick Damian v United Republic of Tanzania, Judgment (Merits and Reparations), 4 June 2024, Application No. 048/2016.

Ekollo Moundi Alexandre v Republic of Cameroon and Federal Republic of Nigeria, Decision, 23 September 2011, Application No. 008/2011.

Femi Falana v African Union, Ruling (Jurisdiction), 26 June 2012, Application No. 001/2011.

Frank David Omary and Others v United Republic of Tanzania, Judgment (Merits and Reparations), 28 March 2014, Application No. 001/2012.

Godfred Anthony and Ifunda Kisite v United Republic of Tanzania, Ruling (Jurisdiction and Admissibility), 26 September 2019, Application No. 015/2015.

Glory Cyriaque Hossou and another v Republic of Benin, Ruling (Jurisdiction), 2 December 2021, Application No. 016/2020.

Glory Cyriaque Hossou v Republic of Benin, Judgment (Merits and Reparations), 13 November 2024, Application No. 012/2018.

Houngue Éric Noudehouenou v Republic of Benin and Others, Ruling (Provisional Measures), 20 December 2022, Application No. 010/2021.

Ibrahim Ben Mohamed Ben Ibrahim Belguith v Republic of Tunisia, Judgment (Merits and Reparations), 22 September 2022, Application No. 017/2021.

Ingabire Victoire Umuhoza v Republic of Rwanda, Ruling (Jurisdiction), 3 June 2016, Application No. 003/2014.

Ingabire Victoire Umuhoza v Republic of Rwanda, Judgment (Merits), 24 November 2017, Application No. 003/2014.

Jebra Kambole v United Republic of Tanzania, Judgment, 15 July 2020, Application No. 018/2018.

John Mitwa v United Republic of Tanzania, Judgment. 13 February 2024, Application No. 044/2016.

Juma Haruna v United Republic of Tanzania, Ruling (Jurisdiction and Admissibility), 7 November 2023, Application No. 034/2016.

Kabalabala Kadumbagula and another v United Republic of Tanzania, Judgment, 4 June 2024, Application No. 031/2017.

Kijiji Isiaga v United Republic of Tanzania, Judgment (Merits), 21 March 2018, Application No. 032/2015.

Komi Koutché v Republic of Benin, Ruling (Provisional Measures), 2 April 2020, Application No. 020/2019.

Komi Koutché v Republic of Benin, Ruling (Jurisdiction and Admissibility), 22 September 2022, Application No. 013/2020.

La LIDHO, Le MIDH, La FIDH and Others v Republic of *Côte* d'Ivoire, Judgment, 5 September 2023, Application No. 041/2016.

Laurent Munyandilikirwa v Republic of Rwanda, Ruling, 2 December 2021, Application No. 023/2015.

Legal & Human Rights Centre and Tanzanian Human Rights Defenders Coalition v United Republic of Tanzania, Judgment, 13 June 2023, Application No. 039/2020.

Lohe Issa Konaté v Burkina Faso, Judgment (Merits), 5 December 2014, Application No. 004/2013.

Lohé Issa Konaté v Burkina Faso, Judgment (Reparations), 3 June 2016, Application No. 004/2013.

Lucien Ikili Rashidi v United Republic of Tanzania, Judgment (Merits and Reparations), 28 March 2019, Application No. 009/2015.

Mamadou Diakité and Another v Republic of Mali, Ruling (Admissibility), 28 September 2017, Application No. 009/2016.

Mama Seidou Samiratou v Republic of Benin, Ruling (Jurisdiction and Admissibility), 5 September 2023, Application No. 054/2019.

Mauridi Swedi alias Mswezi Kalijo v United Republic of Tanzania, Ruling (Jurisdiction and Admissibility), 7 November 2023, Application No. 026/2017.

Michelot Yogogombaye v Republic of Senegal, **Judgment**, 15 December 2009, Application No. 001/2008.

Mohamed Abubakri v United Republic of Tanzania, Judgment, 3 June 2016, Application No. 007/2013.

Reverend Christopher R. Mtikila v United Republic of Tanzania, Ruling (Reparations), 13 June 2014, Application No. 011/2011.

National Convention of Teachers Trade Union v Republic of Gabon, Decision, 15 December 2011, Application No. 012/2011.

Nguza Viking (Baba Seya) and Jonson Nguza (Papi Kocha) v United Republic of Tanzania, Judgment (Reparations), 8 May 2020, Application No. 006/2015.

Niyonzima Augustine v United Republic of Tanzania, Judgment (Merits and Reparations), 13 June 2023, Application No. 058/2016.

Nzigiyimana Zabron v United Republic of Tanzania, Judgment (Merits and Reparations), 4 June 2024, Application No. 051/2016.

Request for advisory opinion by Advocate Marcel Ceccaldi on behalf of the Great Socialist People's Libyan Arab Jamahiriya, Order, 30 March 2012, Request No. 002/2011.

Request for Advisory Opinion by the African Committee of Experts on the Rights and Welfare of the Child on the Standing of the African Committee of Experts on the Rights and Welfare of the Child before the African Court of Human and Peoples' Rights, Advisory Opinion, 5 December 2014, Request No. 002/2013.

Request for Advisory Opinion by Association Africaine de Défense des Droits de l'Homme on the consistency with the African Charter on Human and Peoples' Rights of the Draft Model Law on Mining on Community Land in Africa, Advisory Opinion, 28 September 2017, Request No. 002/2016.

Request for Advisory Opinion by Centre for Human Rights of the University of Pretoria (CHR) and Coalition of African Lesbians (CAL) on Interpretation of the term 'considered' in Article 59 (3) of the African Charter on Human and Peoples' Rights regarding the Activity Report of the African Commission on Human and Peoples' Rights, Advisory Opinion, 28 September 2017, Request No. 002/2015.

Request for Advisory Opinion by Centre for Human Rights of the University of Pretoria, Federation of Women Lawyers Kenya, Women's Legal Centre, Women Advocates Research and Documentation Centre and Zimbabwe Women Lawyers Association On State Obligations under Article 6(d) of the Protocol to the African Charter on Human and Peoples' Rights on the Rights of Women in Africa, Advisory Opinion, 28 September 2018, Request No. 001/2016.

Request for Advisory Opinion by the Coalition for the International Criminal Court, the Legal Defence & Assistance Project (LEDAP), the Civil Resource Development & Documentation Center (CIRDDOC) and the Women Advocates Documentation Center (WARDC), Order (Strike out), 5 June 2015, Request No. 001/2014.

Request for Advisory Opinion by the Coalition for the International Criminal Court, the Legal Defence & Assistance Project (LEDAP), the Civil Resource Development & Documentation Center (CIRDDOC) and the Women Advocates Documentation Center (WARDC), Order (Strike out), 29 November 2015, Request No. 001/2015.

Request for an Advisory Opinion by the Pan African Lawyers Union (PALU) on the Compatibility of Vagrancy Laws with the African Charter on Human and Peoples' Rights and Other Human Rights Instruments Applicable in Africa, Advisory Opinion, 4 December 2020, Request No. 001/2018.

Request for an Advisory Opinion by the Pan African Lawyers Union (PALU) on the Right to Participate in the Government of One's Country in the Context of an Election Held During a Public Health Emergency or a Pandemic, such as the Covid-19 Crisis, Advisory Opinion, 16 July 2021, Request No. 001/2020.

Request for an Advisory Opinion by Rencontre Africain pour la Défense des Droits de l'Homme (RADDHO) on institution of legal action before the African Commission on Human and Peoples' Rights or the African Court on Human and Peoples' Rights following an unconstitutional change of government, Advisory Opinion, 28 September 2017, Request No. 002/2014.

Request for Advisory Opinion by Socio-Economic Rights & Accountability Project (SERAP) on the decision of the Southern Africa Development Community (SADC) to suspend the SADC Tribunal, Order, 15 March 2013, Request No. 001/2012.

Rutabingwa Chrysanthe v Republic of Rwanda, Judgment (Jurisdiction and Admissibility), 11 May 2018, Application No. 022/2015.

Sébastien Germain Marie Aikoué Ajavon v Republic of Benin, Ruling (Provisional Measures), 17 April 2020, Application No. 062/2019.

Sébastien Germain Marie Aikoué Ajavon v Republic of Benin, Judgment, 4 December 2020, Application No. 062/2019.

Soufiane Ababou v People's Democratic Republic of Algeria, Decision, 16 June 2011, Application No. 002/2011.

Tanganyika Law Society and the Legal and Human Rights Centre v United Republic of Tanzania and Reverend Christopher Mtikila v United Republic of Tanzania, Judgment, 14 June 2013, Application Nos 009/2011 & 011/2011.

Tike Mwambipile & Equality Now v United Republic of Tanzania, Ruling ((Jurisdiction and Admissibility), 1 December 2022, Application No. 042/2020.

Urban Mkandawire v Republic of Malawi, Judgment, 21 June 2013, Application No. 003/2011.

Wilfred Onyango Nganyi & 9 Others v United Republic of Tanzania, Judgment (Merits), 18 March 2016, Application No. 006/2013.

Wilfred Onyango Nganyi & 9 Others v United Republic of Tanzania, Judgment (Reparations), 4 July 2019, Application No. 006/2013.

Youseff Ababou v Kingdom of Morocco, Decision, 2 September 2011, Application No. 007/2011.

B. European Court of Human Rights

A and Others v United Kingdom, Judgment, 19 February 2009, Application No. 3455/05.

Abdi Ibrahim v Norway, Judgment, 10 December 2021, Application No. 15379/16.

Abdollahi v Turkey, Decision (Strike out), 3 November 2009, Application No. 23980/08.

A.D. v Greece, Judgment, 4 April 2023, Application No. 55363/19.

Advisory opinion on certain legal questions concerning the lists of candidates submitted with a view to the election of judges to the European Court of Human Rights, Advisory Opinion, 12 February 2008, A47-2008-01.

Advisory opinion on certain legal questions concerning the lists of candidates submitted with a view to the election of judges to the European Court of Human Rights (no. 2), Advisory Opinion, 22 January 2010, A47-2010-001.

Recognition in domestic law of a legal parent-child relationship between a child born through a gestational surrogacy arrangement abroad and the intended mother, Advisory Opinion, 10 April 2019, Request no. P16-2018-001.

Advisory opinion concerning the use of the 'blanket reference' or 'legislation by reference' technique in the definition of an offence and the standards of comparison between the criminal law in force at the time of the commission of the offence and the amended criminal law, Advisory Opinion, 29 May 2020, Request No. P16-2019-001.

Al-Dulimi and Montana Management Inc. v Switzerland, Judgment, 21 June 2016, Application No. 5809/08.

Alekseyev and Others v Russia, Judgment, 27 November 2018, Applications Nos. 14988/09 and 50 others.

Alekseyev and Others v Russia, Judgment, 16 January 2020, Application Nos. 26624/15 and 76 others.

Aoulmi v France, Judgment (extracts), 17 January 2006, Application No. 50278/99.

Al-Saadoon and Mufdhi v United Kingdom, Judgment, 2 March 2010, Application No. 61498/08.

Al-Skeini and Others v United Kingdom, Judgment, 7 July 2011, Application No. 55721/07.

Animal Defenders International v United Kingdom, Judgment, 22 April 2013, Application No. 48876/08.

A.S.B. v the Netherlands, Decision (Strike out), 10 July 2012, Application No. 4854/12.

Assanidze v Georgia, Judgment, 8 April 2004, Application No. 71503/01.

Ayuntamiento de Mula v Spain, Decision, 1 February 2001, Application No. 55346/00.

Babar Ahmad and Others v United Kingdom, Judgment, 10 April 2012, Applications Nos. 24027/07; 11949/08; 36742/08; 66911/09; 67354/09.

Banković and Others v Belgium and Others, Decision (Admissibility), 12 December 2001, Application No. 52207/99.

Bayatyan v Armenia, Judgment, 7 July 2011, Application No. 23459/03.

Beg S.P.A. v Italy, Judgment, 20 May 2021, Application No. 5312/11.

Big Brother Watch and Others v United Kingdom, Judgment, 25 May 2021, Application Nos. 58170/13; 62322/14; and 24960/15.

Blečić v Croatia, Judgment, 8 March 2006, Application No. 59532/00.

'Blondje' v the Netherlands, Decision, 15 September 2009, Application No. 7245/09.

Borg and Vella v Malta, Decision, 3 February 2015, Application No. 14501/12.

Brogan and Others v United Kingdom, Judgment, 29 November 1988, Application Nos. 11209/84; 11234/84; 11266/84; and 11386/85.

Broniowski v Poland, Judgment (Merits), 22 June 2004, Application No. 31443/96.

Broniowski v Poland, Judgment (Friendly settlement), 28 September 2005, Application No. 31443/96.

Brumarescu v Romania, Judgment (Merits), 28 October 1999, Application No. 28342/95.

Brumarescu v Romania, Judgment (Just Satisfaction), 23 January 2001, Application No. 28342/95.

C v France and E v France, Judgment, 19 November 2019, Applications Nos. 1462/18 & 17348/18.

Case 'Relating to Certain Aspects of the Laws on the Use of Languages in Education in Belgium' v Belgium, Judgment (Merits), 23 July 1968, Application Nos. 1474/62; 1677/62; 1691/62; 1769/63; 1994/63; 2126/64.

Centre for Legal Resources on behalf of Valentin Câmpeanu v Romania, Judgment, 17 July 2014, Application No. 47838/08.

Centrum för rättvisa v Sweden, Judgment, 25 May 2021, Application No. 35252/08.

Chassagnou and Others v France, Judgment, 29 April 1999, Application No. 25088/94.

Chahal v United Kingdom, Judgment, 15 November 1996, Application No. 22414/93.

Cossey v the United Kingdom, Judgment, 29 August 1990, Application No. 10843/84.

C.P. v United Kingdom, Decision, 21 December 2010, Application No. 300/11.

Cruz Varas and Others v Sweden, Judgment, 20 March 1991, Application No. 15576/89.

D v France, Judgment, 16 July 2020, Application No. 11288/18.

Decision on a request for an advisory opinion under Protocol no. 16 concerning the interpretation of Articles 2, 3 and 6 of the Convention, 14 December 2020, Request No. P16-2020-001.

Decision on the competence of the Court to give an advisory opinion, Advisory Opinion, 2 June 2004, A47-2004-001.

Demir and Baykara v Turkey, Judgment, 12 November 2008, Application No. 34503/97.

De Saedeleer v Belgium, Judgment, 24 July 2007, Application No. 27535/04.

De Wilde, Ooms and Versyp ('Vagrancy') v Belgium (Article 50), Judgment, 10 March 1972, Application Nos. 2832/66& 2835/66.

El Shennawy v France, Judgment (Merits), 20 January 2011, Application No. 51246/08.

Engel and Others v The Netherlands,, Judgment, 8 June 1976, Application No. 5100/71; 5101/71; 5102/71; 5354/72; 5370/72.

Engel and Others v The Netherlands (Article 50), Judgment, 23 November 1976, Application Nos. 5100/71; 5101/71; 5102/71; 5354/72; 5370/72.

Fedotova and Others v Russia, Judgment, 17 January 2023, Application Nos. 40792/10, 30538/14 & 43439/14.

Fernie v United Kingdom, Decision (Admissibility), 5 January 2006, Application No. 14881/04.

F.G. v Sweden, Judgment, 23 March 2016, Application No. 43611/11.

F.H. v Sweden, Judgment, 20 January 2009, Application No. 32621/06.

F.N. v United Kingdom, Judgment (Merits), 27 May 2008, Application No. 26565/05.

Findlay v United Kingdom, Judgment, 25 February 1997, Application No. 22107/93.

Folgerø and Others v Norway, Judgment, 29 June 2007, Application No. 15472/02.

Fox, Campbell and Hartley v United Kingdom, Judgment, 30 August 1990, Application Nos. 12244/86, 12245/86; 12383/86.

Georgia v Russia (I), Decision (Admissibility), 30 June 2009, Application No. 13255/07.

Georgia v Russia (I), Judgment (Merits), 3 July 2014, Application No. 13255/07.

Georgia v Russia (II), Judgment (Merits), 21 January 2021 (rectified on 29 January 2021), Application No. 38263/08.

Glukhin v Russia, Judgment, 4 July 2023, Application No. 11519/20.

Golder v United Kingdom, Judgment, 21 February 1975, Application No. 4451/70.

Halford v United Kingdom, Judgment, 25 June 1997, Application No. 20605/92.

Handyside v United Kingdom, Judgment, 7 December 1976, Application No. 5493/72.

Hasanali Aliyev and Others v Azerbaijan, Judgment, 9 June 2022, Application No. 42858/11.

Hassan v United Kingdom, Judgment, 16 September 2014, Application No. 29750/09.

Hilal Mammadov v Azerbaijan, Judgment, 4 February 2016, Application No. 81553/12.

Hode and Abdi v United Kingdom, Judgment, 6 November 2012, Application No. 22341/09.

Husayn (Abu Zubaydah) v Poland, Judgment, 24 July 2014, Application No. 7511/13.

Ilaşcu and Others v Moldova and Russia, Judgment, 8 July 2004, Application No. 48787/99.

Incal v Turkey, Judgment, 9 June 1998, Application No. 22678/93.

Ireland v United Kingdom, Judgment, 18 January 1978, Application No. 5310/71.

Ivanova and Cherkezov v Bulgaria, Judgment, 21 April 2016, Application No. 46577/15.

Jeronovičs v Latvia, Judgment, 5 July 2016, Application No. 44898/10.

Johnston and Others v Ireland, Judgment, 18 December 1986, Application No. 9697/82.

Kadiķis v Latvia, Judgment, 4 August 2006, Application No. 62393/00.
Karoussiotis v Portugal, Judgment, 1 February 2011, Application No. 23205/08.
Kavala v Turkey, Judgment, 10 December 2019, Application No. 28749/18.
Kavala v Türkiye, Judgment (Infringement proceedings), 11 July 2022, Application No. 28749/18.
Keenan v United Kingdom, Judgment, 3 April 2001, Application No. 27229/95.
Kemmache v France (No. 3), Judgment, 24 November 1994, Application No. 17621/91.
Kılıç v Turkey, Judgment, 28 March 2000, Application No. 22492/93.
Lawless v Ireland (No. 3), Judgment (Merits), 1 July 1961, Application No. 332/57.
Lehideux and Isorni v France, Judgment, 23 September 1998, Application No. 24662/94.
Loizidou v Turkey, Judgment (Preliminary Objections), 23 March 1995, Application No. 15318/89.
Loizidou v Turkey, Judgment, 18 December 1996, Application No. 15318/89.
M. v United Kingdom, Decision (Strike out), 1 December 2009, Application No. 16081/08.
M.A. v Switzerland, Judgment, 18 November 2014, Application No. 52589/13.
Malone v United Kingdom, Judgment, 2 August 1984, Application No. 8691/79.
Mamatkulov and Askarov v Turkey, Judgment, 4 February 2005, Application Nos. 46827/99 & 46951/99.
Mammadov v Azerbaijan, Judgment (Merits and Just Satisfaction), 22 May 2014, Application no. 15172/13.
Mammadov v Azerbaijan, Judgment (Infringement proceedings), 29 May 2019, Application No. 15172/13.
Marckx v Belgium, Judgment, 13 June 1979, Application No. 6833/74.
McCann and Others v United Kingdom, Judgment, 27 September 1995, Application No. 18984/91.
McFarlane v Ireland, Judgment, 10 September 2010, Application No. 31333/06.
M.E. v Sweden, Decision (Strike out), 8 April 2015, Application No. 71398/12.
M.K. and Others v Poland, Judgment, 23 July 2020, Application Nos. 40503/17; 42902/17; 43643/17.
Molla Sali v Greece, Judgment (Just Satisfaction), 18 June 2020, Application no. 20452/14.
N v United Kingdom, Judgment, 27 May 2008, Application No. 26565/05.
Neumeister v Austria, Judgment, 27 June 1968, Application No. 1936/63.
N.S. v Croatia, Judgment, 10 September 2020, Application No. 36908/13.
N.S.K. v United Kingdom, Communicated Case, 5 April 2023, Application No. 28774/22.
Öcalan v Turkey, Judgment, 12 May 2005, Application No. 46221/99.
Olaechea Cahuas v Spain, Judgment (extracts), 10 August 2006, Application No. 24668/03.
Öneryildiz v Turkey, Judgment, 30 November 2004, Application No. 48939/99.
Opuz v Turkey, Judgment, 9 June 2009, Application No. 33401/02.

Osman v United Kingdom, Judgment, 28 October 1998, Application No. 23452/94.

Othman (Abu Qatada) v United Kingdom, Judgment, 17 January 2012, Application No. 8139/09.

Pantalon v Croatia, Judgment, 19 November 2020, Application No. 2953/14.

Papamichalopoulos and Others v Greece (Article 50), Judgment, 31 October 1995, Application No. 14556/89.

Pârvu v Romania, Judgment, 30 August 2022, Application No. 13326/18.

Patera v The Czech Republic, Judgment (Merits and Just Satisfaction), 26 April 2007, Application No. 25326/03.

Peacock v United Kingdom, Decision, 5 January 2016, Application No. 52335/12.

Privacy International and Others v United Kingdom, Decision, 7 July 2020, Application No. 46259/16.

Radio France and Others v France, Judgment, 30 March 2004, Application No. 53984/00.

Rantsev v Cyprus and Russia, Judgment, 7 January 2010, Application No. 25965/04.

Ringeisen v Austria, Judgment, 16 July 1971, Application No. 2614/65.

Roman Zakharov v Russia, Judgment, 4 December 2015, Application No. 47143/06.

Rowe and Davis v United Kingdom, Judgment, 16 February 2000, Application No. 28901/95.

Saadi v United Kingdom, Judgment, 29 January 2008, Application No. 13229/03.

Salduz v Turkey, Judgment, 27 November 2008, Application No. 36391/02.

Sallam v The Netherlands, Decision, 11 December 2012, Application No. 20328/08.

Sandu and Others v The Republic of Moldova and Russia, Judgment, 17 July 2018, Application Nos. 21,034/05 and 7 others.

Scoppola v Italy (No. 2), Judgment, 17 September 2009, Application No. 10249/03.

Sejdić and Finci v Bosnia and Herzegovina, Judgment, 22 December 2009, Application Nos. 27996/06 & 34836/06.

Selmouni v France, Judgment, 28 July 1999, Application No. 25803/94.

Shamayev and Others v Georgia and Russia, Judgment, 12 April 2005, Application No. 36378/02.

Sidabras and Others v Lithuania, Judgment, 23 June 2015, Application Nos. 50421/08 & 56213/08.

Soering v United Kingdom, Judgment, 7 July 1989, Application No. 14038/88.

Stoll v Switzerland, Judgment, 10 December 2007, Application No. 69698/01.

Stradovnik v Slovenia, Judgment, 13 April 2006, Application No. 24784/02.

Sunday Times v United Kingdom (No. 2), Judgment, 26 November 1991, Application No. 13166/87.

Svetova and Others v Russia, Judgment, 24 January 2023, Application No. 54714/17.
Taxquet v Belgium, Judgment, 16 November 2010, Application No. 926/05.
Tomasi v France, Judgment, 27 August 1992, Application No. 12850/87.
Vallianatos and Others v Greece, Judgment, 7 November 2013, Application Nos. 29,381/09 & 32,684/09.
Vassilios Athanasiou et autres c. Grèce, Judgment, 21 December 2010, Application No. 50973/08.
Vavřička and Others v The Czech Republic, Judgment, 8 April 2021, Application No. 47621/13.
Velikova v Bulgaria, Judgment, 18 May 2000, Application No. 41488/98.
Verein gegen Tierfabriken Schweiz (VgT) v Switzerland (no. 2), Judgment, 30 June 2009, Application No. 32772/02.
Verein Klimaseniorinnen Schweiz and Others v Switzerland, Judgment, 9 April 2024, Application No. 53600/20.
Woods v United Kingdom, Judgment, 20 November 2007, Application No. 60274/00.
X v Croatia, Judgment, 17 July 2008, Application No. 11223/04.
X. and Y. v The Netherlands, Judgment, 26 March 1985, Application No. 8978/80.
Yağmurdereli v Turkey, Judgment, 4 June 2002, Application No. 29590/96.
Yelena Ivanovna Pivkina against Russia and 6 other applications, Decision, 29 June 2023, Application No. 2134/23.

C. Inter-American Court of Human Rights

Active Memory Civil Association v. Argentina, Judgment (Merits, Reparations and Costs), 26 January 2024, Series C No. 516.
Almonacid-Arellano et al. v Chile, Judgment (Preliminary Objections, Merits, Reparations and Costs), 26 September 2006, Series C No. 154.
Aloeboetoe v Suriname, Judgment (Reparation and Costs), 10 September 1993, Series C No. 15.
Apitz Barbera et al. v Venezuela, Judgment, 5 August 2008, Series C No. 182.
Atala Riffo and Daughters v Chile, 24 February 2012, *Series* C No. 239.
Baena-Ricardo et al. v Panama, Judgment (Merits, Reparations and Costs), 2 February 2001, Series C No. 72.
Bámaca-Velásquez v Guatemala, Judgment (Reparation and Costs), 22 February 2002, Series C No. 91.
Bámaca-Velásquez v *Guatemala,* Order (Provisional Measures and Monitoring Compliance with Judgment), *27 January 2009, Series E No. 10.*
Barrios Altos v Peru, Judgment (Merits), 14 March 2001, Series C No. 87.
Bedoya Lima et al. v Colombia, Judgment (Merits, Reparations and Costs), 26 August 2021, Series C No. 431.

Blake v Guatemala, Judgment (Preliminary Objections), 2 July 1996, Series C No. 27.

Blake v Guatemala, Judgment (Reparation and Costs), 22 January 1999, Series C No. 48.

Boyce et al. v Barbados, Judgment (Preliminary Objection, Merits, Reparations and Costs), 30 November 2007, Series C No. 169.

Cabrera-García and Montiel-Flores v Mexico, Judgment (Preliminary Objections, Merits, Costs), 26 November 2010, Series C No. 220.

Caesar v Trinidad and Tobago, Judgment (Merits), 11 March 2005, Series C No. 123.

Castillo Petruzzi et al. v Peru, Judgment (Merits, Reparations and Costs), 30 May 1999, Series C No. 52.

Castillo-Petruzzi et al. v Peru, Order (Compliance with Judgment), 17 November 1999, Series C No. 59.

Communities of Jiguamiandó and Curbaradó regarding Colombia, Order (Provisional Measures), 22 May 2013, Series E No. 13.

Constitutional Court v Peru, Judgment (Competence), 24 September 1999, Series A No. 55.

Cuéllar Sandoval et al. v El Salvador, Judgment (Merits, Reparations and Costs), 18 March 2024, Series C No. 521.

Dacosta-Cadogan v Barbados, Judgment (Preliminary Objections, Merits, Reparations, and Costs), 24 September 2009, Series C No. 204.

Denunciation of the American Convention on Human Rights and the Charter of the Organization of American States and the consequences for State human rights obligations, Advisory Opinion OC-26/20, 9 November 2020, Series A No. 26.

Entitlement of Legal Entities to Hold Rights under the Inter-American Human Rights System, Advisory Opinion OC-22/16, 26 February 2016, Series A No. 22.

Flores Bedregal et al. v Bolivia, Judgment (Interpretation of the Judgment on Preliminary Objections, Merits, Reparations and Costs and Rectification of errors in the Judgment), 14 March 2024, Series C No. 520 Haitians and Haitian-Origin Dominicans v Dominican Republic, Order (Provisional Measures), 14 September 2000, Series E No 3.

Gangaram-Panday v Suriname, Judgment (Merits, Reparation and Costs), 21 January 1994, Series C No. 16.

Gomes Lund et al. ("Guerrilha do Araguaia") v Brazil, Judgment (Preliminary Objections, Merits, Reparations and Costs), 24 November 2010, Series C No. 219.

González et al. ('Cotton Field') v Mexico, Judgment (Preliminary Objection, Merits, Reparations and Costs), 16 November 2009, Series C No. 205.

González Medina and Family v Dominican Republic, Judgment (Preliminary Objections, Merits, Reparations and Costs), 27 February 2012, Series C No. 240.

Guzmán Albarracín et al. v Ecuador, Judgment (Merits, Reparations and Costs), 24 June 2020, Series C No. 405.

Habeas Corpus in Emergency Situations (Arts. 27(2), 25(1) and 7(6) American Convention on Human Rights), Advisory Opinion OC-8/87, 30 January 1987, Series A No. 8.

Heliodoro Portugal v Panama, Judgment (Preliminary Objections, Merits, Reparations and Costs), 12 August 2008, Series C No. 186.

Hilaire, Constantine and Benjamin et al. v Trinidad and Tobago, Judgment (Merits, Reparations and Costs), 21 June 2002, Series C No. 94.

Indigenous Communities of the Lkaka Honat Association v Argentina, Judgment, 6 February 2020, Series C No. 420.

International Responsibility for the Promulgation and Enforcement of Laws in Violation of the Convention (Arts. 1 and 2 of the American Convention of Human Rights), Advisory Opinion OC-14/94, 9 December 1994, Series A No. 14.

Interpretation of the American Declaration of the Rights and Duties of Man within the Framework of Article 64 of the American Convention on Human Rights, Advisory Opinion OC-10/89, 14 July 1989, Series A No. 10.

I.V. v Bolivia, Judgment (Preliminary Objections, Merits, Reparations and Costs), 30 November 2016, Series C No. 329.

Ivcher-Bronstein v Peru, Judgment (Competence), 24 September 1999, Series C No. 54.

James et al. v Trinidad and Tobago, Order (Provisional Measures), 7 May 1999, Series E No. 11.

James et al. v Trinidad and Tobago, Order (Provisional Measures), 2 December 2003, Series E No. 16.

Juridical Condition and Rights of Undocumented Migrants, Advisory Opinion OC-18/03, 17 September 2003, Series A No. 18.

Kaliña and Lokono Peoples v Suriname, Judgment (Merits, Reparations and Costs), 25 November 2015, Series C No. 309

Kankuamo Indigenous People regarding Colombia, Order (Provisional Measures), 3 April 2009, Series E No. 4.

Kichwa Indigenous People of Sarayaku regarding the Republic of Ecuador, Order (Provisional Measures), 4 February 2010, Series E No.4.

La Cantuta v Peru, Judgment (Merits, Reparations and Costs), 29 November 2006, Series C No. 162.

'La Nación' Newspaper Case regarding Costa Rica, Order (Provisional Measures) 7 September 2001, Series E No. 4.

Loayza-Tamayo v Peru, Judgment (Reparations and Costs), 27 November 1998, Series C No 53.

B v El Salvador, Order (Provisional Measures), 19 August 2013, Series E No. 2.

'Mapiripán Massacre' v Colombia, Order (Provisional Measures), 27 June 2005, Series E No. 1.

'Mapiripán Massacre' v Colombia, Judgment (Merits, Reparations and Costs), 15 September 2005, Series C No. 134.

'Mapiripán Massacre' v Colombia, Order (Provisional Measures), 1 March 2011, Series E No. 4.

Mayagna Awas Tingni Community v Nicaragua, Judgment (Merits, Reparations and Costs), 31 August 2001, Series C No. 79.

Mayagna (Sumo) Awas Tingni Community v Nicaragua, Order (Provisional Measures), Order, 26 November 2007, Series E No. 2.

Mendoza Prisons v. Argentina, Order (Provisional Measures), 30 March 2006, Series E No. 3.

Members of the 'José Alvear Restrepo' Lawyers Collective v Colombia, Judgment, 18 October 2023, Series C No. 506.

Mery Naranjo et al. v Colombia, Order (Provisional Measures), 5 July 2006, Series E No. 1.

Miguel Castro-Castro Prison v Peru, Judgment (Merits, Reparations and Costs), 25 November 2006, Series C No. 160.

Moiwana Community v Suriname, Judgment (Preliminary Objections, Merits, Reparations and Costs) 15 June 2005, Series C No. 124.

Murillo et al. v Costa Rica, Judgment, 28 November 2012, Series C No. 257.

'Other Treaties' subject to the Consultative Jurisdiction of the Court (Art. 64 American Convention on Human Rights), Advisory Opinion OC-1/82, 24 September 1982, Series A No. 1.

Palamara Iribarne v Chile, Judgment (Merits, Reparations and Costs), 22 November 2005, Series C No. 135.

Palma Mendoza et al. v Ecuador, Judgment (Preliminary Objection and Merits), 3 September 2012, Series C No. 247.

Peace Community of San José de Apartadó v Colombia, Order (Provisional Measures), 18 June 2002, Series E No. 3.

Perozo et al. v Venezuela, Judgment (Preliminary Objections, Merits, Reparations, and Costs), 28 January 2009, Series C No. 195.

Plan de Sánchez Massacre v Guatemala, Judgment (Merits), 29 April 2004, Series C No. 105.

Proposed Amendments to the Naturalization Provisions of the Constitution of Costa Rica, Advisory Opinion OC-4/84, 19 January 1984, Series A No. 4.

Pueblos Rama y Kriol, Comunidad Negra Creole Indígena de Bluefields and others v Nicaragua, Judgment (Merits, Reparations and Costs), 1 April 2024, Series C No. 522.

Reports of the Inter-American Commission of Human Rights (Art. 51 of the American Convention on Human Rights), Advisory Opinion OC-15/97, 14 November 1997, Series A No. 15.

Restrictions to the Death Penalty (Articles 4(2) and 4(4) American Convention on Human Rights), Advisory Opinion OC-3/83, 8 September 1983, Series A No. 3.

Rights and Guarantees of Children in the Context of Migration and/or in Need of International Protection, Advisory Opinion OC-21/14, 19 August 2014, Series A No. 21.

Ríos et al. v Venezuela, Judgment (Preliminary Objections, Merits, Reparations, and Costs), 28 January 2009, Series C No. 194.

Santo Domingo Massacre v Colombia, Judgment (Preliminary Objections, Merits and Reparations), 30 November 2012, Series C No. 259.

Saramaka People v Suriname, Judgment (Preliminary Objections, Merits, Reparations, and Costs), 28 November 2007, Series C No. 172.

State Obligations Concerning Change of Name, Gender Identity, and Rights Derived from a Relationship Between Same-Sex Couples, Advisory Opinion OC-24/17, 24 November 2017, Series A No. 24.

The Effect of Reservations on the Entry into Force of the American Convention on Human Rights (Arts. 74 And 75), Advisory Opinion OC-2/82, 24 September 1982, Series A No. 2.

The Environment and Human Rights (States Obligations in Relation to the Environment in the Context of the Protection and Guarantee of the Rights to Life and to Personal Integrity: Interpretation and Scope of Articles 4(1) and 5(1) in Relation to Articles 1(1) and 2 of the American Convention on Human Rights), Advisory Opinion OC-23/17, 15 November 2017, Series A No. 23.

The Institution of Asylum and its Recognition as a Human Right under the Inter-American System of Protection (Interpretation and Scope of Articles 5, 22(7) and 22(8), in relation to Article 1(1) of the American Convention on Human Rights), Advisory Opinion OC-25/18, 30 May 2018, Series A No. 25.

The Right to Information on Consular Assistance in the Framework of the Guarantees of the Due Process of Law, Advisory Opinion OC-16/99, 1 October 1999, Series A No. 16.

The Word 'Laws' in Article 30 of the American Convention on Human Rights, Advisory Opinion OC-6/86, 9 May 1986, Series A No. 6.

Ticona Estrada et al. v Bolivia, Judgment (Merits, Reparations and Costs), 27 November 2008, Series C No. 191.

Trujillo-Oroza v Bolivia, Judgment (Reparations and Costs), 27 February 2002, Series C No. 92.

Velásquez -Rodriguez v Honduras, Judgment (Preliminary Objections), 26 June 1987, Series C No. 1.

Velásquez -Rodriguez v Honduras, Judgment (Merits), 29 July 1988, Series C No. 4.

Velásquez-Rodriguz v Honduras, Judgment (Reparation and Costs), 21 July 1989, Series C No. 7.

Villagrán-Morales et al. v Guatemala, Judgment (Reparations and Costs), 26 May 2001, Series C No. 77.

Viviana Gallardo et al., Advisory Opinion (Order), 13 November 1981, No. G 101/81, Series A (1984).

Yakye Axa Indigenous Community v Paraguay, Judgment, 17 June 2005, Series C No. 125.

II. Regional Human Rights Commissions

A. African Commission on Human and Peoples' Rights

Amnesty International v Zambia, Decision, 5 May 1999, Communication No. 212/98.

Article 19 v Eritrea, Decision, 30 May 2007, Communication No. 275/2003.

Civil Liberties Organization v Nigeria, Decision, 22 March 1995, Communication No. 129/94.

Democratic Republic of Congo v Burundi, Rwanda, Uganda, Decision, 29 May 2003, Communication No. 227/99.

Hossam Ezzat & Rania Enayet (represented by Egyptian Initiative for Personal Rights & INTERIGHTS) v The Arab Republic of Egypt, Decision, 25 February 2016, Communication No. 355/07.

International Pen, Constitutional Rights Project, Interights on behalf of Ken Saro-Wiwa Jr. and Civil Liberties Organisation v Nigeria, Decision, 31 October 1998, Communication Nos. 137/94, 139/94, 154/96 and 161/97.

Liesbeth Zegveld and Messie Ephrem v Eritrea, Decision, 20 November 2003, Communication No. 250/2002.

Obert Chinhamo v Zimbabwe, Decision, 28 November 2007, Communication No. 307/05.

Sir Dawda K Jawara v Gambia, Ruling, 11 May 2000, Communication Nos. 147/95-149/96.

The Social and Economic Rights Action Center and the Center for Economic and Social Rights v Nigeria, Decision, 27 October 2001, Communication No. 155/96.

Zimbabwe Lawyers for Human Rights and IHRDA (on behalf of Andrew Barclay Meldrum) v Zimbabwe, Decision, 3 April 2009, Communication No. 294/2004.

B. European Commission on Human Rights

Cruz Varas and Others v Sweden, Report of the Commission, 7 June 1990, Application No. 15576/89.

Denmark, Norway, Sweden and Netherlands v Greece (I), Report of the Commission, 4 October 1969, **Application** Nos. 3321–3/67 **to 3323/67 and** 3344/67.

Denmark, France, Norway, Sweden & Netherlands v Turkey, Report of the Commission, 7 December 1985, Application **Nos. 9940/82 to 9944/82**.

Government of the Kingdom of Greece v Government of the United Kingdom of Great Britain and Northern Ireland (First Cyprus Case), Report of the Commission, 26 September 1958, Application No. 176/56.

C. Inter-American Commission on Human Rights

Ana Teresa Yarce et al. (Comuna 13) v Colombia, Merits, Report No. 86/13, 4 November 2013, Case Nos. 12.595, 12.596 and 12.621.

Application of the Inter-American Commission on Human Rights Before the Inter-American Court of Human Rights in the case of Tyrone Dacosta Cadogan v Barbados, 31 October 2008, Case No. 12,645.

Baby Boy v United States, Annual Report of the Inter-American Commission on Human Rights 1980–1981, Resolution 23/81OEA/Ser.L/V/II.54, Doc. 9 rev. 1, 6 March 1981, Case No. 2141.

John Doe et al. v Canada, Report no. 78/11, Merits, 21 July 2011, Case No. 12.586.

Carlos García Saccone v Argentina, Report No. 8/98, Admissibility, 2 March 1998, Application No. 11.671.

Cecilia Rosana Nuñez Chipana v Venezuela, Report No. 89/05, Admissibility, 24 October 2005, Application No. 12.103.

Guillermo Patricio Lynn v Argentina, Report No. 69/08, Admissibility, 16 October 2008, Application No. 681-00.

José Francisco Cid v Argentina, Report No. 83/17, Admissibility, 7 July 2017, Application No. 151-08.

José Tomás Tenorio Morales and Others (Ervin Abarca Jimenez Union for Higher Education Professionals of the National Engineering University) v Nicaragua, Report No. 41/16, 11 September 2016, Application no. 142-04.

Leaders of the 19 de Abril Carazo Movement and Others regarding Nicaragua, Resolution 52/2018, 17 September 2018, PM Nos. 840/18; 841/18; 779/18.

Mery Naranjo et al. v Colombia, Report No. 46/07, Admissibility, 23 July 2007, Application No. 231-05.

Migueliuth Sandoval Cruz and the family of journalist Ángel Eduardo Gahona regarding Nicaragua, Resolution 41/2018, 12 June 2018, PM No. 669-18.

Mustafa Adam Al-Hawsawi regarding the United States of America, Resolution 25/2015, 7 July 2015, PM No. 422-14.

Néstor Rolando López and Others v Argentina, Report No. 3/11, Inadmissibility, 5 January 2011, Application No. 491-98.

Pedro Velásquez Ibarra v Argentina, Report No. 40/06, Admissibility, 15 March 2006, Application No. 11.214.

Peter Blaine v Jamaica, Report No. 96/98, Inadmissibility, 17 December 1998, Application No. 11.827.

Thelmo Reyes Palacios v Mexico, Report No. 14/18, Admissibility, 24 February 2018, Application No. 1057-07.

Victoria Piedad Palacios Tejada de Saavedra v Peru, Admissibility, Report No. 16/18, 24 February 2018, Application No. 884-07.

Workers dismissed from Ecopetrol v Colombia, Report No. 49/17, Admissibility, 25 May 2017, Application No. 384–08.

Yerling Marina Aguilera Espinoza and 17 other human rights defenders regarding Nicaragua, Resolution No. 70/18, 17 September 2018, PM Nos. 939/18, 1067/18.

Zaheer Seepersad regarding Trinidad and Tobago, Resolution No. 28/2017, 4 August 2017, PM No. 440-16.

Zaheer Seepersad regarding Trinidad and Tobago, Resolution to lift precautionary measures No. 65/2023, 15 October 2023, PM No. 440-16.

III. Other International and Domestic Courts, Tribunals and Committees

A. Caribbean Court of Justice

Attorney General and Superintendent of Prisons and Chief Marshal v Jeffrey Joseph and Lennox Ricardo Boyce, Judgment, 8 November 2006, Appeal No CV 2 of 2005; BB Civil Appeal No 29 of 2004.

B. Central American Court of Justice

Ricardo Duarte Moncada v Gobierno de Nicaragua, Alcaldía de Managua y Banco Centroamericano de Integración Económica, resolución N° 1-1-1-95, 13 January 1995, Gaceta Oficial Corte Centroamericana de Justicia, N° 1, 1 June 1995.

C. Committee on the Elimination of Racial Discrimination (CERD)

Palestine v Israel, Decision (Jurisdiction), 12 December 2019, CERD/C/100/5.

D. Constitutional Court of Ecuador

Regarding the consultation of constitutionality Articles 81 of the Civil Code and 52 of the Organic Law on Identity and Civil Data Management (Same-sex marriage), 12 June 2019, Case No. 10-18-CN/19.

Regarding the consultation issued by the Court of the Criminal Chamber of the Higher Court of Justice of Pichincha About compatibility between Article 67 of the Constitution and Advisory Opinion OC-24 of the Inter-American Court of Human Rights (Same-sex marriage), 12 June 2019, Case No. 11-18-CN/19.

E. Court of Justice of the East African Community

Mike Sonko Gideon Kioko Mbuvi v The Attorney General of the Republic of Kenya, Judgment, 28 November 2024, Application No. 25 of 2022 (Arising from Reference no. 35 of 2022).

Professor Nyamoya Francois v Attorney General of the Republic of Burundi & Secretary General of the East African Community, Judgment, 28 February 2014, Reference No. 8 of 2011.

F. Court of Justice of the Economic Community of West African States

Mohammed El Tayyib Bah v Republic of Sierra Leone, Judgment No. ECW/CCJ/JUD/11/15, 4 May 2015, Application No. ECW/CCJ/APP/20/13.

Oluwatimilehin Adebayo v Federal Republic of Nigeria, Judgment No. ECW/CCJ/JUD/44/24, 3 December 2024, Application No. ECW/CCJ/APP/47/23.

Shalimar Abbiusi v The Republic of Ghana, Judgment No. ECW/CCJ/JUD/41/24, 22 November 2024, Application No. ECW/CCJ/APP/03/24.

G. Court of Justice of the European Union

FIAMM and Others v Council and Commission, Judgment (GC), 9 September 2008, Joined Cases C-120 & 121/06 P, ECLI:EU:C:2008:476.

Ledra Advertising Ltd. and Others v European Commission and European Central Bank (ECB), Judgment, 20 September 2016, Cases C-8/15 P to C-10/15 P, EU:C:2016:701.

Opinion 1/09, 8 March 2011, EU:C:2011:123.

Opinion 2/13, 18 December 2014, ECLI:EU:C:2014:2454.

H. Federal Constitutional Court of Germany

Judgment of the Second Senate of 30 June 2009-2 BvE 2/08 -, paras. 1-421, BVerfGE 123, 167-437.

I. High Court of Accra, Ghana

Matter of Chude Mba v The Republic of Ghana, Suit No. HRCM/376/15 (2016).

J. International Court of Justice

Allegations of Genocide under the Convention on the Prevention and Punishment of the Crime of Genocide (Ukraine v Russian Federation: 32 States Intervening), Judgment (Preliminary Objections), 2 February 2024.

Alleged Breaches of Certain International Obligations in respect of the Occupied Palestinian Territory (Nicaragua v Germany), Provisional measures, 30 April 2024.

Application of the Convention on the Prevention and Punishment of the Crime of Genocide in the Gaza Strip (South Africa v Israel), Order (Provisional measures), 26 January 2024, I.C.J. Reports 2024, p. 3.

Application of the Convention on the Prevention and Punishment of the Crime of Genocide in the Gaza Strip (South Africa v Israel), Order (Provisional measures), 28 March 2024.

Application of the Convention on the Prevention and Punishment of the Crime of Genocide (The Gambia v. Myanmar), Order (Provisional measures), 23 January 2020, ICJ Reports 2020, p. 3.

Armed Activities on the Territory of the Congo (New Application: 2002) (Democratic Republic of the Congo v Rwanda), Judgment (Jurisdiction and Admissibility), ICJ Reports 2006, p. 6.

Certain Phosphate Lands in Nauru (Nauru v Australia), Judgment (Preliminary Objections), 26 June 1992, ICJ Reports 1992, p. 240.

Certain Questions of Mutual Assistance in Criminal Matters (Djibouti v France), Judgment, 4 June 2008, ICJ Reports 2008, p. 177.

Elettronica Sicula S.P.A. (USA v Italy), Judgment, 20 July 1989, ICJ Reports 1989, p 15.

Immunities and Criminal Proceedings (Equatorial Guinea v France), Judgment (Preliminary Objections), 6 June 2018, ICJ Reports 2018, p 336.

Interpretation of Peace Treaties with Bulgaria, Hungary and Romania (Second Phase), Advisory Opinion, 18 July 1950, ICJ Reports 1950, p 231.

Legal Consequences of the Construction of a Wall in the Occupied Palestinian Territory, Advisory Opinion, 9 July 2004, ICJ Reports 2004, p. 136.

Military and Paramilitary Activities in and against Nicaragua (Nicaragua v United States of America), Judgment (Jurisdiction and Admissibility), 26 November 1984, ICJ Reports 1984, p 392.

Oil Platforms (Iran v USA), Judgment (Merits), 6 November 2003, ICJ Reports 2003, p 161.

The Legality of the Threat or Use of Nuclear Weapons, Advisory Opinion, 9 July 1996, ICJ Reports 1996, p. 226.

K. Permanent Court of International Justice

Germany v Poland (Factory at Chorzów), Judgment, 13 September 1928, Series A No. 17.

L. Supreme Court of Costa Rica

Acción de Inconstitucionalidad, 8 August 2018, Decision No. 12782-2018, Exp. 15-013971-0007-CO.

M. Tribunal of the Southern African Development Community

Mike Campbell and Others v Republic of Zimbabwe, Judgment, 28 November 2008, SADC (T) No. 2/2007.

N. United Kingdom House of Lords / Supreme Court

A (FC) and Others (FC) (Appellants) v Secretary of State for the Home Department (Respondent), Judgment, 16 December 2004, [2004] UKHL 56.

O. United States Supreme Court

Dobbs, State Health Officer of the Mississippi Department of Health et al. v Jackson Women's Health Organization, Decision, 24 June 2022, 597 U.S. 215 (2022).

Donald J. Trump, President of the United States, et al. v JGG, et al., Decision, 7 April 2025, 604 US _ (2025).

P. World Trade Organization Appellate Body

European Communities v Korea - Definitive Safeguard Measure on Imports of Certain Dairy Products, Report, 14 December 1999, WT/DS98/AB/R.

MIX
Papier aus verantwortungsvollen Quellen
Paper from responsible sources
FSC® C105338
FSC
www.fsc.org

If you have any concerns about our products,
you can contact us on
ProductSafety@springernature.com

In case Publisher is established outside the EU,
the EU authorized representative is:
Springer Nature Customer Service Center GmbH
Europaplatz 3, 69115 Heidelberg, Germany

Printed by Libri Plureos GmbH
in Hamburg, Germany